WILLY LEY'S

EXOTIC ZOOLOGY

WILLY LEY'S
EXOTIC
ZOOLOGY

Illustrated by Olga Ley

BONANZA BOOKS · NEW YORK

This 1987 edition is published by Bonanza Books, distributed
by Crown Publishers, Inc., 225 Park Avenue South, New York,
New York 10003, by arrangement with Viking Penguin, Inc.

Portions of the text are derived from the author's earlier books:
*The Lungfish, the Dodo, and the Unicorn; Dragons in Amber;
Salamanders and Other Wonders.*

Printed and Bound in the United States of America

Library of Congress Cataloging in Publication Data

Ley, Willy, 1906-1969.
Willy Ley's exotic zoology.

Reprint. Originally published: Exotic zoology. New York :
Viking Press, 1959.
1. Living fossils.   2. Animals, Mythical.   3. Paleontology.
I. Title.   II. Title: Exotic zoology.
QL88.5.L49   1987   591   86-29879
ISBN 0-517-62545-8

h g f e d c b a

CONTENTS

v

Foreword

I DO NOT know how many readers will be surprised by the intelligence that the foreword of a book is usually the last thing to be written. But that's how it is done, and if a reason has to be given it is that the foreword contains the afterthoughts. The customary afterthought is that the reader may wish an explanation on why the book was written.

This, in my case, and in the case of this book, requires a fairly lengthy explanation. The public associates my name with *rockets, missiles, and space travel*—and these, of course, also form the title of one of my books. So what is a man who is known as an advocate of space travel, as a historian of rocketry and so forth, doing writing a book on animals, extinct, rare, or unknown?

The answer is that I thought my scientific career would lie in this field. I grew up, so to speak, in the shadow of the Museum of Natural History in Berlin. I spent most of my youthful Sundays there. I once got a bad mark in composition in high school, writing on the subject "What Do I Want to Be When I Am Grown and Why?" Most of my classmates wrote very "safe" papers. One wanted to be a doctor because his father was one—and he wanted to help humanity too, of course. Others had the Civil Service in mind, which was something that was likely to find approval. Some said they had to keep up the family tradition, meaning they would take over their fathers' businesses. I wrote that I wanted to be an explorer. I forget what reasons I gave. I do remember that my teacher made a little speech, saying that I deserved a good mark for my style and that the reasoning, "such as it was," was logical too. Except that the whole thing was, of course, nonsense. A boy with a family background of business on one side and church on the other just doesn't want to be an explorer, or, if he does, he certainly won't become one.

The speech left me unconvinced. I was never quite sure whether my studies would earn me the title of "zoologist" or "geologist," but I kept exploring, in a manner of speaking, looking especially into such corners as others had neglected. And then, when I was nineteen, Professor Hermann Oberth's work "The Rocket into Interplanetary Space" came along. But in spite of this, and all that has happened since, I still like to take a day, or several, off from rockets and look at dodos, man-eating trees, or just a plain old mammoth skeleton.

I have already, if only by implication, answered a question which is often asked of a writer: "How long did it take you to write this book?" There is only one answer (which is never believed, incidentally): "All my life." A book like the present one cannot be written because somebody said to himself that he would do it and began doing research. You might be able to do this with one chapter, but the book as a whole is the outcome of a lifetime of interest, a lifetime of collecting material, a lifetime of "exploring."

In this particular case something else must be added. I have written three such books before. They were entitled: *The Lungfish, the Dodo, and the Unicorn* (1941, revised 1948), *Dragons in Amber* (1951), and *Salamanders and Other Wonders* (1955). While these three books revolved around related themes, they had to be independent, which means that overlapping and repetition could not be avoided. Now it so happened that all three books fell due for reprinting at about the same time. It also happened that each one was due for some revisions; a lot can be (and has been) learned in a number of years. Also there were new things to be added.

Doing all this—new themes, additions, revisions, and eliminations —in one full sweep, resulted in this book. It may surprise many who know me only as a rocket man. But I hope it will not disappoint them.

Willy Ley

Introduction: The Fathers of Zoology

In the story of every science there are certain names which recur again and again—usually the names of men who did much to advance their science, but sometimes of the men who did something first, or of those who succeeded in combining a "first" with doing much. The science of zoology is no exception.

But before considering its "fathers," we should see how the science itself came into being. Of course man always knew the animals which lived around him, but that did not by itself create anything like a science of zoology. There was at best a hunter's classification. Horses were good to eat and not very dangerous to hunt. Wild cattle was still better to eat but they were even more dangerous than wild pigs, with which the savor of the flesh and the danger of the hunt neatly counterbalanced each other. Wolves, on the other hand, were very dangerous and also unsavory. Knowledge of this kind always existed, but it was a kind of self-contained knowledge that did not progress because it couldn't. Something had to be added, the *new* animal, the strange beast, the one that was not commonplace.

Only travel could furnish this addition.

Only travelers could come across animals they had never seen before. Only returned travelers could spread the tale about such unheard-of animals. The newness aroused curiosity, and in time men would actually set out "in quest of new lands and strange beasts," as they still do. And even if the travel had a specific goal—the geographer Sophus Ruge once said that "the Spaniards went as far as there was gold, the Portuguese as far as there were spices, and the Russians as far as there were furs"—no traveler or explorer would fail to record the strange new beasts which he encountered or about which he was told.

1

Aristotle, the teacher of Alexander the Great, realized the facts quite clearly when he said that all science begins with marveling, that is, with curiosity. And since Aristotle himself had an infinite capacity for curiosity, his is the first of the names which are oft-mentioned when stories with zoological themes are told. He was one of those who did something "first"; he observed, he dissected, but mainly he wrote down the facts. He produced one of the cornerstones of every science, the first list of what is known to exist.

But the first major landmark in this early stage of the science of zoology came when Rome had replaced Athens as the center of political and cultural activity. It was the famous *Natural History* of about half a hundred books written by Caius Plinius Secundus (A.D. 23–79), known as Pliny the Elder. This work shows a tremendous increase in the number of known facts; it also marks, incidentally, the sunset of Mediterranean culture. Soon afterward the Roman Empire began to decline, and after its collapse, and the most valiant efforts of the Byzantines on the one hand and of the Arabs on the other could hardly preserve the knowledge gained, much less increase it and improve it.

As far as the science of zoology is concerned, that long arctic night from Rome to Renaissance was at last dispersed by the voluminous *Historia Animalium* of Konrad Gesner of Zürich in Switzerland. The name of the diligent, learned, honest Konrad Gesner, poor City Physician of Zürich, has come down to us adorned with two highly laudatory epithets. His contemporaries called him *Plinius Germanicus.* Though he wrote in Latin, even in his own time the German translation of his natural history was evidently more popular than the original; indeed, the German edition remained *the* natural history of expert and layman alike for two full centuries. The other appellation was posthumous; later generations spoke of him as "the Father of Zoology."

Gesner's *Historia Animalium,* the first volume of which appeared in 1555, ten years before his death, was an extension of Pliny's *Natural History*. From the point of view of scientific method it was not, strictly speaking, an improvement, though of course there were enormous improvements in detail. The Roman Pliny had been a cavalry colonel and had wielded his stylus accordingly; the German Pliny was a scholar.

The amount of knowledge had increased tremendously. Pliny had told all he knew about animals in one volume of encyclopedic proportions; Gesner needed five such tomes. But fundamentally the Swiss natural history, like the Roman one, was a "list" of all the known animals and a "treasure" of all the known facts about them.

The next stage in the development of zoology was not to follow until, two hundred years later, the Swedish savant Karl von Linné (Carolus Linnaeus) finally undertook the task which, according to the Book of Genesis, had been Adam's: to name all the animals and plants. Linnaeus realized that Adam had not made a very scientific job of it. True, the animals did have names, but these names not only differed from language to language (and often enough within the territory of one language, from province to province), they also lacked scientific accuracy and scientific usefulness all around. One particularly important thing could not be done with those "common" names: they were of no use for classification. Gesner had been forced to arrange his animals in alphabetical order, no other order being possible. But Gesner had—with apologies to his readers—made a number of exceptions to his alphabetical rule. Domestic cattle, the wisent (European bison), the aurochs (urus), and some "other cattle from strange lands" obviously belonged together, and to treat them under the letters C (cow), B (bison), and A (aurochs), respectively, would be to lose sight of their relationship.

Linnaeus saw here a solution, which consisted in the introduction of two-part names, based exclusively on Latin and Greek roots. Linnaeus was not actually the first to use such two-part names (the Dutchman Rumphius, of whom more is said elsewhere in the book, had done so before him), but he was the first to use them systematically. By basing them on classical languages, he achieved internationality, and by having them in two parts, he could show relationships.

For example: cattle in general received the name *Bos,* and each kind received a second name which determined its variety. The urus, already extinct in Linnaeus's time, became *Bos primigenius;* domestic cattle became *Bos domesticus;* the wisent or European bison became *Bos bison,* the Indian water buffalo *Bos indicus.* Horses became the *Equines,* the ordinary horse *Equus caballus* (the horse of the rider, the cavalier, the *caballero*), and the donkey *Equus asinus.* Then Linnaeus proceeded a step further and established families, classes, and orders.

This task represented a tremendous amount of work. And while the result might look somewhat overwhelming at first glance, on account of the large number of forbidding Latin and Greek words, it was really an achievement of simplification.

Then out of this achievement another thought—as we know now, the most important thought of all—began to grow and to take form. Was it possible that the "families" of Linnaeus's system were actual families? That the relationships indicated by the first parts of the Latin double names not only expressed anatomic similarities but also might express genetic relationships? That these animals had not been created according to slightly changed blueprints but had evolved from one prototype, one original blueprint? That, for example, all the various kinds of *Bos* were diverging descendants of *one* original *Bos?* That, generally speaking, animals living now had evolved from others?

Linnaeus himself, however, was attempting to bring rigidity and order out of chaos, not to suggest evidence of fluidity and change. Consequently he stated categorically that "the existing species of animals are now as they were created in the beginning."

If Linnaeus's system had been less useful than it was and if Linnaeus had been less of an authority than he was, that one sentence would hardly have caused much trouble. As it was, that sentence, termed later somewhat ponderously "the dogma of the stability of the species," blocked the road ahead for a number of years. The combined efforts of the Frenchmen Geoffroy Saint-Hilaire (father and son) and Lamarck, the Englishmen Darwin, Wallace, and Huxley, and the Germans Haeckel, Vogt, and Gegenbaur were required to overcome its immobilizing effects.

The early evolutionists, who had to fight Linnaeus's dogma, said many unkind words about it. And because of this, a great many of the followers of Darwin and Haeckel received the impression that Linnaeus had never done anything useful, that his name was known only because he had successfully opposed progress. It is, of course, difficult to contradict in a spirit of admiration. Actually Linnaeus's life work contributed more to the evolutionists than his dogma of the stability of species hindered them. After all, it is easier to step over tabooed boundaries in a well-mapped territory than to find a path through a complete wilderness.

Linnaeus had slammed one door, and between him and Darwin there came another important door-slammer. This was Cuvier, a very brilliant French scientist and founder of a science that is as fascinating in its subject matter as it is important: the science of paleontology.

Fossils had been known since classic times. Greek authors had described several petrified fish, suggesting that they might have developed from normal fish eggs that hatched in wet sand instead of water. Later on learned people somehow managed to evade fossils and the questions raised by them. If the fossils were large and impressive, mythological explanations were found; if they were small, they were taken to be mineral "freaks of nature" or experimental models made by God before the creation of actual living beings. Probably the first scientist who recognized all fossils as remains of creatures that had once been alive was a Swiss, Johann Jakob Scheuchzer.

Baron Georges Léopold Chrétien Frédéric Dagobert Cuvier agreed with Scheuchzer wholeheartedly. But while Scheuchzer had spoken about his fossil fish as once living animals that had died individually, Cuvier began to speak of whole species and even larger groups that no longer existed. Furthermore, once Cuvier and his followers began taking an interest in "extinct species," they could not help noticing that there were "new" species too. Those in existence seemed not simply to have survived the extinct varieties but to have come later, after the others had died out.

With such conceptions Cuvier crossed another and very important boundary line. Since the dim days of the first tribal migrations, exploration had progressed steadily, if somewhat spasmodically, until it finally had embraced practically the entire earth. But it had been strictly confined in time to the present or to the past of written human history. This was not by reason of any logic or prejudice, but simply because of the ignorance that there could be any other past. Cuvier crossed this boundary "in quest of new lands and strange beasts," and his report was of overwhelming interest.

Carried away by his own enthusiasm, he even made the sweeping statement that this new line of zoological research which he had opened was the only one left that was still promising. In the past of the planet there were innumerable discoveries waiting to be made, whereas it seemed at least very unlikely, if not impossible, that there remained any living animals still to be discovered. While the first part of that statement was perfectly correct, as any fossil-hunter since Cuvier knows, the second part was not merely an exaggeration; it was seriously wrong. The pages of this book teem with names of animals that have been discovered since Cuvier (early in the nineteenth century) made this statement and even of some that are still being sought. Nonetheless, we have Cuvier to thank for crossing the borderline between the animal world of today and that of the past, and for bringing to light the new worlds beyond it. It is not to his discredit that Cuvier himself did not dream that this boundary is full of holes through which countless "living fossils" have slipped. It is merely amusing that the man who boldly crossed the border did his very best to strengthen it, to plug the numerous gaps, and to deny its flimsiness in general.

Naturally Cuvier's discoveries and conceptions led him straight into a dilemma of a very special kind. The more he worked in his chosen field, the more extinct varieties he brought to light, the more he was forced to see that some of these strange types, while apparently unconnected with anything living, bore a haunting resemblance to one another. It was almost like having a collection of creatures of another planet, different from those of earth, differing widely also among themselves, but still belonging to the same creation. That was it, he thought: they *were* of another creation.

The great question was where to put this other and different creation in time. The Church allowed for about six thousand years since the creation of the earth itself, a figure derived by the learned Rabbi Shemayah Hillel by careful—though occasionally contradictory—adding up of the genealogical tables of the Old Testament. Cuvier had to look for another and more convenient estimate of the age of the earth. There did exist another one on the physical experiments and mathematical calculations of Cuvier's compatriot, the Comte de Buffon, which led to the conclusion that life began about 40,000 years ago.

With the help of Buffon's expanded time-scale Cuvier arrived at his famous Theory of Cataclysms. This satisfied Cuvier's personal taste; it did not contradict Linnaeus's dogma; and—just as important if not more so—it did not offend the ideas harbored at that time by the various Christian churches. Executed in a brilliant style, with all the superb rhetoric at the author's disposal, Baron Cuvier's book on this theory became a best-seller. This, briefly, is the theory:

In the beginning God created the world in general and our earth in particular and the plants on the face of the earth and the animals on the land and in the water. This, however, was not the Creation of the Bible. After a certain and probably lengthy time there occurred a cataclysm. Every known and unknown volcano shook the earth with violent eruptions; hot lava and ashes fell all over the planet and killed all life on the continents. The seas boiled for weeks, killing and cooking every living creature. The very air became glowing hot; there was no refuge, no survival. When the catclysm finally abated, only the planet itself was left. Naturally it was dead and sterile; and if it were not to remain thus for all time to come, it needed a new creation.

A new creation took place. While fish and amphibians had been predominant in the first creation, another type of animal, reptiles, was characteristic of the second. The reptiles remained in power until the next cataclysm came. The third creation consisted mainly of mammals. The cataclysm that ended their rule differed in method though not in effectiveness. It was caused, not by heat and fire, but by cold and ice. When the planet grew warm again, the fourth creation followed, the one described in the first book of the Bible.

It follows, of course, that we are living in the interval between two cataclysms. There is a slender chance that God regards the present creation as perfect and final and that He will not destroy it, but if another cataclysm were to come, it would certainly be as thorough as all the others.

This theory of cataclysms established the idea of a succession of geological periods. The next step, as every schoolboy now knows, was to clear away Cuvier's artificial obstacles to an orderly and uninterrupted flow of geologic history. These obstacles were the cataclysms. After the first surprise effect wore off, nobody believed in them very seriously. Goethe called them a *vermaledeite Polterkammer der Weltgeschichte* ("accursed pelting chamber of world history"), the existence of which he refused to acknowledge.

The man who succeeded in disproving the existence of cataclysms and in wrecking the whole theory beyond repair was an Englishman, Sir Charles Lyell. Lyell quietly discarded the slightly hysterical outbursts from the Continent and replaced them with *time*. He showed that all the geological changes of the past could be explained by the continuous action of those natural forces we know from everyday life. Wind and rain, the grinding surf, flowing rivers, melting ice, can change the faces and even the outlines of continents, he declared, if only they are granted enough time in which to work. Lyell was not satisfied with Buffon's figure. He wanted *more* time, and *still more* time. The term "a million years" was employed, somewhat jokingly at first, then seriously, and finally merely as a unit of measurement.

The question of geologic time underwent a rather amusing development. More than one scientist set out to investigate the duration of earth's geologic history in order to prove to Lyell and to his followers that there simply was no past long enough to satisfy their demands, only to end by granting even more time than his former antagonists had been discussing. At first this was a family matter among geologists, but soon astronomers and physicists joined in, and when finally radium and radioactivity were discovered, time was again considerably extended—in fact multiplied—until at present a grand total of about five billion years is generally accepted.

Because he also slammed a door shut, Cuvier has received more contemptuous treatment even than Linnaeus. It is forgotten that his cataclysmic theory was in a sense forced upon him not only by the religious bias of his age but also by the shortness of the period granted him by the science of his time. In the end it was the necessary thoroughness of Cuvier's cataclysms that destroyed the validity of his theory. Since by his definition a cataclysm was a catastrophe embracing the whole earth and wiping out every form of life, it followed that it was impossible for any kind of creature to exist in more than one period. Cuvier did not merely imply this, he said it. *L'homme fossile n'existe pas,* he wrote: fossil man does not exist. So if an animal were discovered that was undeniably a "living fossil" —that is, an animal that still existed even though it had lived during a preceding period—or if genuine fossilized human bones were found in undisturbed layers from another period the idea of cataclysms was bound to perish in a cataclysm itself. As a matter of fact, some living fossils—for example, the sharks—were already well known during Cuvier's time, though not then recognized as such. Actually, however, Cuvier's hypothesis was discarded not as a result of one such discovery but on general grounds, as demonstrated by Lyell.

The first volume of Lyell's *Principles of Geology* had just appeared when a young British naturalist embarked for a leisurely trip around the world. The young man, whose name was Charles Darwin, took a copy of this book with him when he stepped aboard the *Beagle.* When during his trip he found evidence forcing the idea of evolution upon him, the main obstacle that would have prevented such a conception—Cuvier's cataclysms—had been cleared away by Lyell's work. Only forces that existed here and now had shaped the face of the earth from period to period. What if Linnaeus was wrong and the species had not remained the same? What if those species had been shaped and reshaped slowly, almost imperceptibly, by forces that are also operating at present? If so, it must be possible to find these forces. While they might be too slow to be watched at work, the evidence offered by Cuvier himself and by his followers might permit us to see what they had done in the past.

When Darwin returned from his trip, the theory of evolution had been conceived. That he needed several decades to develop it to a point where he thought it ripe for publication is a historical fact, but unimportant. What he did with his wondering thoughts during his visit to the Western Hemisphere represented the third stage in the development of zoology. Gesner's lists had been the first stage and Linnaeus's system the second. The scientific double names now advanced from their lowly status as convenient handles of classification to become an expression of natural relationships.

The theory of evolution marked the dawn of a new and very busy day in zoology and in general in all the sciences that deal with living things. Although it caused—naturally—a lot of controversy and although both sides in those controversies can be accused of having made senselessly sweeping statements and even wrong assertions, the general feeling that emerged was that this, at long last, brought some sense to all these sciences.

Since then, zoology has continued, in a reasonably orderly manner, to make vast progress. But this book is not concerned with the main stream of its discoveries and classifications. They are interesting and good textbook material, but such textbooks exist by the carload. Here I am investigating some bypaths—unexpected turns of events, cases which interrupted routine, facts which made learned men sit back and say, "Now I remember that somebody once told me . . ." For convenience, these investigations have been grouped into five divisions. As might be expected of living—or formerly living—things, some don't fit too neatly into these divisions, and some could equally well have been put into one as another. But this is not very important, because after all the whole book is about things which did not fit, with some explorations into the reasons. As is suitable in a science which began with the beginning of travel, these explorations take in some remote parts of the world, and, inevitably, they cover a great deal of geologic as well as historic time.

PART ONE

MYTH?

Konrad Gesner's unicorn (*Historia Animalium*, vol. I, 1551)

CHAPTER 1

The Legend of the Unicorn

Of ALL the mythical animals that have ever inhabited the pages of old books or decorated the walls of castles, the most charming and impressive—I am tempted to write, the most mythical—is indubitably the unicorn. Presumably part of its impressiveness lies in its aloofness: it does not voluntarily deal with people. The other fairy-tale fauna which gradually developed during the latter part of the Middle Ages always had some connection with humanity. Dragons guarded treasures and stole fair maidens. Basilisks killed anybody who happened to come near. Giants usually behaved like the overgrown louts they were. But the unicorn stood aloof. And the unicorn was the only one that was beautiful.

Under these circumstances it is almost sad to have to report that the story of the unicorn begins with a classical error, or at least what looks like an error several handfuls of centuries later.

The books of the Old Testament were of course originally written in Hebrew. In the third century B.C. it was felt that they should be translated into the universal language of educated people of the time, namely Greek. A group of scholars, later simply called the Seventy, went to work and in due time produced the version of the Bible which is now called the Septuagint. Of course there were the usual difficulties which accompany any translation. Idiomatic terms do not match in the two languages between which the transfer of ideas is to take place. Or else a word may have several meanings in one of the two languages and just one specific meaning in the other one. And so forth. In addition to these purely linguistic difficulties, which usually can be overcome with knowledge and persistence, one often runs into the problem of local facts of Nature. A plant which is

13

common in one country and has a common name may not exist at all
in the other country. The same goes for animals.

The Seventy ran into one of these cases.

The Hebrew writers had spoken with some awe about an animal
which they called *Re'em*. They knew it well; hence they had not
bothered to describe it. They had not even stated its size. All one
could gather from their statements was that the animal was exceedingly intractable in every respect. By implication it was also large,
for the fiercest and most intractable small animal still fails to inspire
awe. The Seventy needed a Greek word to substitute for *Re'em*. It
is not reported how long they hesitated, but finally, possibly under
the influence of dim recollections of more or less vague rumors, they
used the Greek word *monokeros*. In English this means unicorn.

By so doing the Seventy established a precedent which later Bible
translators had to follow. The Latin version, the Vulgate, said
unicornus, the French Bible said *licorne,* and Dr. Martinus Luther
in Germany wrote *Einhorn;* all meaning the same—one- or single-
horned. And that is why Job 39:9–12, in the King James version
of the English Bible, reads:

Will the unicorn be willing to serve thee, or abide by thy crib?

Canst thou bind the unicorn with his band in the furrow? or will he
harrow the valleys after thee?

Wilt thou trust him, because his strength is great? or wilt thou leave thy
labour to him?

Wilt thou believe him, that he will bring home thy seed, and gather it
into thy barn?

This passage, incidentally, is not the only one in the Bible that
mentions the re'em; there are seven altogether, three of them in the
Psalms.

The translation of re'em into monokeros had one main result:
for many centuries to come the existence of the unicorn could not be
doubted; it was mentioned in the Bible.

Before we go on with the story of the unicorn legend it might be
well to find out just what the re'em really was. For some time
scholars of antiquity in general and of the Bible in particular thought
that the writers of the original had meant the oryx antelope, of which
the Arab name is *rim*. In fact, the oryx did have the reputation of
being a formidable enemy, one that could by no means be trusted.
The logic was sound but it collapsed just the same when an animal

called *rîmu* showed up in Assyrian texts. This time there were pictures to go with the texts and the pictures showed that the animal in question was *not* an antelope. It was a wild ox. Zoologists had little trouble identifying it; it was the *Bos primigenius* of zoological works, the wild and large ancestor of our domestic cattle: the urus.

None of the Seventy had presumably ever seen an urus, since it no longer existed where they lived at the time they lived. But it would have been possible for them to have seen one, because at the time they were making their translation the urus, now extinct, was still alive in the forests north of the Alps, in the immense and frightening Hercynian Forest which the Romans, Julius Caesar among them, later described with all the rhetorical flourishes of which they were capable.

Now that the identity of the re'em is established it remains to trace the reverse of the linguistic decision of the Seventy. If the re'em was not the monokeros, what was the monokeros?

And here the story of the unicorn begins in earnest.

The unicorn made its first appearance in the writings of Ctesias, Greek historian and one-time body physician of the Persian King Artaxerxes II. Ctesias returned from Persia around the year 398 B.C., and while residing at Cnidus wrote two works. One of these was a history of Persia in twenty-three books, of which all but fragments have been lost. The other was a book on India, which is still known to us in the form of a condensed abstract made some thirteen hundred years later by one Photius, then Patriarch of Constantinople. Part of this abstract runs as follows:

There are in India certain wild asses which are as large as horses, and larger. Their bodies are white, their heads dark red, and their eyes dark blue. They have a horn on the forehead which is about a foot and a half in length. The dust filed from this horn is administered in a potion as a protection against deadly drugs. The base of this horn, for some two hands'-breadth above the brow, is pure white, the upper part is sharp and of a vivid crimson; and the remainder, or middle portion, is black. Those who drink out of these horns, made into drinking vessels, are not subject, they say, to convulsions or to the holy disease [epilepsy]. Indeed, they are immune even to poisons if, either before or after swallowing such, they drink wine, water, or anything else from these beakers. . . .

This report, a few lines that grew into a library of hundreds of volumes, needs a little explanation. Ctesias, in writing about India, wrote about a country he had never seen for himself. If the parts

Re'em of the Ishtar Gate: so-called "unicorn of Babylon," actually the urus

preserved by Photius are a fair sample of the original, his book was a compilation of hearsay, a description based on the tales of travelers, and probably bore no stronger resemblance to its subject than an American movie does to American everyday life.

It is fairly easy to see that the "wild ass of India" in Ctesias's book is based on the Indian rhinoceros, with admixtures of features of some other animal. That there "is much rhinoceros in it" can be asserted without lengthy discussion. Not only is the rhinoceros the only naturally one-horned animal, but also it has other features that agree with Ctesias's story. He mentioned somewhere else, for example, that this animal is swift of foot and that its speed increases while running. This applies to the rhinoceros. It also corresponds with facts of rhinoceros lore that the horn was said to be of pharmaceutical value. Rhinoceros horn was and still is considered a powerful drug in the Far East, and wealthy and elderly Chinese literally pay its weight in gold because they hope to regain their manhood by taking pulverized rhinoceros horn internally. Beakers of rhinoceros horn were frequent even in ancient times. And some of them were adorned with the three colors Ctesias described as the natural colors of the horn. It is probable that there was some mystic value attached to this color scheme, although we do not know now what or why. Those features of Ctesias's "wild ass" that are not traceable to the rhinoceros probably came from an antelope of some sort. The black buck of India suggests itself, and

Urus (*Bos primigenius*); redrawn from a Polish painting of about 1600 A.D. The original, probably from life, is the only known picture, but the artist is unknown

it is an odd coincidence that the natives of the countries where these antelopes abound still claim that there are many one-horned freaks among them.

Another school of thought, led by a German, Professor Schrader, cited Ctesias as evidence that the origin of the unicorn legend is the re'em. The Assyrian and Babylonian bas-reliefs had been copied by the Persians on the walls of the Royal Palace in Persepolis, where Ctesias no doubt saw them. Professor Schrader pointed out that these bas-reliefs show the urus in very strict profile, so strict, in fact, that only one horn is visible. Dr. Othenio Abel and Professor C. Antonius strengthened Professor Schrader's arguments by calling attention to the fact that these famous bas-reliefs—aside from being somewhat heraldic in design—are not absolutely accurate in detail. Although there is no mistaking the general appearance of the urus, small details are either missing or wrong, because the artists no longer had live models at their disposal. The Babylonian bas-reliefs date from the time of King Nebuchadnezzar (around 600 B.C.), when the urus had already been extinct in Mesopotamia for about a century. By the time the Persians copied them on the walls of the Royal Palace, the urus was already something of a fabulous monster. Its size, strength, and fierceness made it particularly suited to attracting myths within a short time. When Ctesias the Greek came to Persia, in all probability there was a sufficient supply of fables on hand to be related to travel-

ing foreigners. Also, it can be safely assumed that Ctesias was only
superficially acquainted with the languages he heard spoken around
him in Persepolis.

In spite of all this I do not think that Ctesias was noticeably influenced by the Persian reliefs. The next important sources of the unicorn
legend after Ctesias point another way. These sources are Roman:
Aelian, who wrote in Greek although he lived in Italy; Pliny the Elder;
and Julius Solinus.

Aelian spoke of inaccessible mountains in the interior of India and
of the strange beasts that could be found there. Among them, he said,
"is the unicorn, which they call *cartázonos*. This animal is as large
as a full-grown horse, it has a mane, tawny hair, feet like an elephant,
and a tail like a goat. It is exceedingly swift." At first glance descriptions of this kind seem to be merely *caprices zoologiques,* with the
unicorn growing more and more fantastic. Actually Aelian was only
trying to describe the rhinoceros, its heavy feet, its small tail, and
its other characteristics. The name *cartázonos* is probably a Greek
corruption of the Sanskrit word *kartajan,* Lord of the Desert, or,
better, Lord of the Wilderness.

Pliny, with his habit of military precision, came still closer to the
original when he wrote:

> The Orsaean Indians hunt an exceedingly wild beast called monoceros,
> which has a stag's head, an elephant's feet, and a boar's tail. The rest of
> the body is like that of a horse. It makes a deep lowing noise, and one
> black horn two cubits long projects from the middle of the forehead. This
> animal, they say, cannot be taken alive.

We are apt to smile when we read this description nowadays. But
if compared word for word with a good photograph of an Indian
rhinoceros it is not so bad at all. It is the words chosen that make
us smile; the facts are not so wrong.

The climax of all unicorn descriptions was reached by Julius Solinus
in his *Polyhistoria*. This Roman found a worthy translator in Arthur
Golding (1587), who rendered the original as:

> But the cruellest is the Unicorne, a monster that belloweth horrible,
> bodyed like a horse, footed like an elephant, tayled like a Swyne, and
> headed like a Stagge. His horn sticketh out of the midds of hys forehead, of
> a wonderful brightness about foure foote long, so sharp, that whatsoever he
> pusheth at, he striketh it through easily. He is never caught alive; kylled
> he may be, but taken he cannot bee.

Dr. Odell Shepard, who has traced the literary history of the unicorn in his delightful book *The Lore of the Unicorn* (Boston: Houghton Mifflin, 1930), remarks of this passage: "Whatever rhetoric can do to make the unicorn impressive Solinus has done." And Golding did everything to preserve the flavor of the original Latin.

Soon after Solinus the history of the unicorn "goes wild." The Semitic literature delighted in exaggerating its size to impossible dimensions. The Arabs said that the unicorn loved to pierce elephants with its horn (later, in medieval Europe, similar stories made their appearance, sometimes about the unicorn, sometimes about the rhinoceros), but that it never succeeded in shaking the carcass from its horn. Thus, after three or four dead elephants had accumulated on its horn, the unicorn lost its mobility and fell prey to the roc. The Jews competed with the Arabs in unicorn tales worthy of Baron von Münchhausen or Paul Bunyan and quoted the Talmud about its size, which was so incredible that Noah could not find room for it in the Ark, so that it had to swim for the entire duration of the Flood and could only occasionally rest the tip of its horn on the Ark.

Travelers to those magic countries in the East did not forget to look for the unicorn. And if they really found it—that is, the real "unicorn," the rhinoceros—they were often bitterly disappointed. Instead of a glorious and colorful wonder animal, they saw a rather ugly monster. Marco Polo could not conceal his disappointment when he wrote:

They have wild elephants, and great numbers of unicorns, hardly smaller than elephants in size. Their hair is like that of a buffalo, and their feet like those of an elephant. In the middle of the forehead they have a very large black horn. You must know that they do not wound with their horn but only with their tongue and their knees. For on the tongue they have very long sharp spines, so that when they become furious against someone, they throw him down, and crush him under their knees, wounding him with their tongue. Their head is like that of a wild boar, and is always carried bent to the ground. They delight in living in mire and mud. It is a hideous beast to look at, and in no way like what we think and say in our countries, namely a beast that lets itself be taken in the lap of a virgin. Indeed, I assure you that it is quite the opposite of what we say it is.

Small wonder that such a disappointing sight usually caused disbelief that the rhinoceros was the unicorn. This elephantine and ugly creature could not be the same as that glamorous one! They had to be different animals—both with one horn, it was true, but otherwise as different as night and day. The rhinoceros had to be overcome by brute strength while the unicorn yielded to much more subtle measures.

This was the strangest and most curious development in unicorn lore. It was Christian mythology that had slowly but surely made the unicorn a slave to virgins. According to ancient tradition it could not be captured, but the new Christian legend found an exception. Yes, it could be captured, but not by a man. A virgin must go into the forest where the unicorn roams and wait there patiently. Then, after a little while, the unicorn would come and put its horn into the lap of the virgin, lose its power and fierceness, and fall asleep. Then the hunters who had hidden themselves in trees would come and take the royal beast prisoner. The medieval myth has, strange to say, baffled learned commentators for a substantial number of decades. They wrote in endless circles around it, not one of them having the courage to look in the right direction. After all, what is white, dark at the base and tipped with red, and loses its power in the lap of a virgin? Maybe a symbolism can be so obvious that it is not recognized, but I harbor considerable doubts about it.

But while the legend of the unicorn went off into erotic fantasies in one direction, it simultaneously veered into very practical matters in another. From the days of Ctesias the horn of the unicorn— called "alicorn" to avoid the cacaphonous term "unicorn horn"— had been taken to be an antidote against any kind of poison an assassin might concoct. It worked "unfailingly" in several ways. If the poison had already been swallowed, scrapings of alicorn had to be taken internally. It was safer to form the alicorn into a beaker so that any poison mixed into liquids would be eliminated in advance. Or if the alicorn were used to touch food it would reveal the presence of poison in some manner, thus guarding the feasting king or nobleman. Naturally many people, from the merchant prince who was merely rich to the real prince who wielded power, wanted to possess an alicorn, or parts of one, since they were most frequently the ones whom a rival or an enemy might want to poison. Naturally the price of alicorn climbed accordingly, and quite soon it reached a simple mark: "weight for weight, alicorn for gold."

It was inevitable under these circumstances that alicorn was falsified.

Some traders were unscrupulous enough to try to pass the horn of a rhinoceros as alicorn; superstition doubled back on itself in this case. There were also horns of black bucks and other antelopes on the market. In Northern Europe *unicornum verum* and *unicornum falsum* were strictly distinguished. The former, "true alicorn," was usually found in the earth—actually mammoth tusks—while the false alicorn came in quantities from the North—actually the tusk of the narwhal, a marine mammal. In fact, practically all the unicorn pictures in ancient books show a horn evidently based on the tusk

Gesner's "unicorn of the seas," actually the narwhal (*Historia Animalium*, vol. III, 1555). The "horn" is mistakenly drawn on top of the head, instead of as a tusk protruding from the mouth.

of the male narwhal. That the female does not possess this tusk makes its function seem very mysterious. If it were a weapon or useful as a tool, both sexes would show it. It seems really to be as much an ornament in nature as it became on the king's table or in the apothecary's shop.

A few skeptical Italians during the Renaissance were the first to attack the supposed medical virtue of alicorn. They fought against every pharmacist who had one chained to the counter in his store. The apothecary was very proud of his alicorn, but not too proud, of course, to refuse a sale if the heap of gold coins on his counter grew large enough.

Popular belief in alicorn remained strong for a long time and it put some learned men into difficult situations from time to time. The very learned Konrad Gesner of Zürich, who lived during the sixteenth century, was the municipal physician of his town, salaried to care for those who could not pay. But he also had private patients who, if they were wealthy enough, insisted on having alicorn prescribed for them if nothing else helped.

Gesner fully agreed with his Italian colleagues that alicorn was worthless. But a patient who is sick, and possibly in pain, is hard to convince. So Gesner, from time to time, did prescribe alicorn, but in writing about this he made the sly remark that in such a case he "neither forgot nor neglected" to prescribe other medicines simultaneously. It took a very long time for alicorn finally to disappear from the stock lists of pharmacies; the last of the "must" lists issued for London pharmacies to contain alicorn was printed in 1741.

All this time the belief in the animal had slowly faded. Even those who defended alicorn for its medical value (and for their profit) conceded that the animal from which the horns came might be almost or even completely extinct. One can almost see the apothecary foretelling the extinction of mankind very soon as a consequence. Fortunately he himself still had an alicorn but, of course, he was now more reluctant than ever to part with it.

The death blow to the unicorn—as far as the scientific world was concerned—fell in 1827 when Baron Cuvier declared that a single-horned animal with a cloven hoof was impossible, for such an animal would have a divided frontal bone and no horn could possibly grow upon the division. The existence of the rhinoceros does not contradict Cuvier, because the horn of the rhinoceros is not—as I should have stated earlier—a true horn. A true horn, like that of a cow, consists of a horny sheath covering a bony core which is connected with the bones of the skull. Now the "horn" of the rhinoceros does not show such a division into sheath and core; it consists, so to speak, of a bundle of immensely tough bristles glued together. Such a pseudo-horn need not follow Cuvier's rule.

It is true that Cuvier's later disciples, the paleontologists of around the year 1900, began to believe that they had found the original unicorn. In Russia and in Siberia bones and skulls of an extinct distant relative of the rhinoceros were discovered. This animal, *Elasmotherium sibiricum,* seemed to resemble the ancient reports even more than does the living rhinoceros. It was noticeably larger than the largest Indian rhinoceros; its horn was much longer and was actually situated in the middle of the animal's forehead. The famous Viennese geologist Melchior Neumayr wrote at this juncture in his *Erdgeschichte (History of the Earth,* Vol. II, 1895): "It is possible that in Siberia man and *Elasmotherium* actually lived together and that *Elasmotherium* was exterminated by man; at least one may explain in this way the ancient songs of the Tunguses, which tell that formerly there lived in their country a kind of terrible black ox of gigantic size and with only one horn in the middle of the forehead, so large that an entire sled was needed for the transportation of this horn alone." But while Melchior Neumayr seems to have been intrigued by the idea that *the* unicorn had at long last been discovered, he was almost certainly mistaken. If he had known the literary history of the unicorn legend—no account existed in his day—he would also have known that *the* unicorn was simply the Indian rhinoceros and that no additional discovery was needed.

So far I have followed the traditional line of the story, from the Bible via the classical authors through the middle ages until the time when alicorn was finally discarded. This is what might be called the "Christian" line of the legend. But it has a Moslem line too, which can be followed quite easily nowadays, thanks to a work by Richard Ettinghausen.[1] Like the "Christian" line, the Moslem branch of the legend ultimately goes back to reports about the Indian rhinoceros, but it assumed a somewhat different shape. There is still some similarity in the fact that the emphasis on the horn was so strong that the horn and its bearer became two separate things, with the animal really occupying second place. The result was that the horns of other animals started intruding, but while the intruding horn of the Christian line was usually narwhal tusk, the intruding horn in Moslem story-telling was usually the tusk of the walrus.

Nor did the Moslem *karkadann* (the name most frequently used, confusing in itself as well as illuminating, because it is also the name for the rhinoceros) assume such a definite shape as the "Christian" unicorn. The karkadann often has the general outline of an antelope; only very rarely, and always quite late, does it resemble the rhinoceros. In between there are endless numbers of bovine, leonine, and canine karkadanns, with the canine shape somewhat predominating. This predominance has a linguistic explanation, relating to the way in which Semitic languages are written—that is, with consonants only. Vowels, if written at all, are represented by little dots and dashes below the consonants, the so-called diacritical marks. Now if in an old manuscript the diacritical marks are missing, a certain word may be read as either *gurg* or *karg*. The latter means "rhinoceros," while the former means "wolf," and is naturally the more familiar word. "To make the issue even more confusing," Richard Ettinghausen remarked, "the text is nowhere precise enough to enable the reader to choose between the two. In the stories of

[1] *Studies in Muslim Iconography, I. The Unicorn,* Freer Gallery of Art, *Occasional Papers,* Vol. I, no. 3, Smithsonian Institution Publication 3993 (Washington, D.C., 1950).

Gushtāsp and Isfandiyār the word is rhymed with *suturg* (large) and *buzurg* (big), thus pointing to *gurg* (wolf), and in the accounts of Iskandar and Bahrām Gūr with *targ* (helmet), *tagarg* (hailstone), and *marg* (death) indicating the form *karg*." The names mentioned in this quotation are those of the four Moslem heroes credited by folklore with having done the impossible: namely, killed a karkadann.

While there was virtually no cross influence between the Christian and Moslem lines of unicorn idolatry, the end was the same:

In the eighteenth century, al-Qazwīnī manuscripts of inferior quality, and thus destined for the simple and impecunious, showed illustrations of the karkadann, in which a kind of dreary resemblance to the rhinoceros emerged. The text, of course, still tells the old tales and superstitions, but the miniatures have now nearly caught up with the actual animal. The encounter with reality is, however, disenchanting. The ferocious and yet impressive character of the old monster has gone and all that remains is an immense and unprepossessing hulk of a body. No new ramifications of the age-old myth could possibly grow up around this sort of an animal.
(Richard Ettinghausen)

Centuries after belief in the unicorn had died there was an unexpected aftermath to the whole. It was a very scientific aftermath, depending on the surgeon's knife. In March 1933 an American biologist, Dr. W. Franklin Dove, then of the University of Maine, performed a simple operation on a day-old male Ayrshire calf. To an outsider this operation must have looked as if it were the direct result of a careful reading of Odell Shepard's *Lore of the Unicorn*. Dr. Shepard mentioned that unicorned sheep exist in Nepal and are even sent to Europe on occasion. It was known that these unicorned sheep were being produced artificially, but the method and reason for such treatment were not clear. There were also reports that the Kaffirs sometimes produced unicorned cattle, and the Dinkas in Africa were also said "not only to manipulate the horns of their cattle as the Kaffirs do but to use this practice as a means of marking the leaders of their herds."

It seems possible, therefore, that what I may call the unicorn idea, the notion that one-horned animals exist in nature, arose from the custom of uniting the horns of various domestic animals by a process which is still in use but still mysterious to the civilized world. Here may be the explanation of the one-horned cows and bulls that Aelian says were to be found in Ethiopia and of the unicorned cattle reported by Pliny as living in the land of the Moors. The cows with single horns bending backward and a span long seen by Vartoman at Zeila in Ethiopia may have been of this sort. The one-horned ram's head sent to Pericles by his farm hands may have been that of the leader of their flock, and so a perfect symbol of that leadership in Athens which, according to Plutarch's interpretation, they wished to prophesy for their master.   (Odell Shepard)

Dr. Dove did not know any of this when he planned his operation. But he suspected that Cuvier's statement about the impossibility of a cloven-hoofed unicorn might not be correct always and under all conditions. Cuvier's contention had been that the bony core of a true horn oculd not grow in the middle of the forehead of such an animal because the frontal bones are joined by a suture. Evidently a protuberance could not be expected to grow from such a spot.

Cuvier was right to a certain extent: horn cores do not grow from this spot under normal circumstances. But he was wrong to assert that they could not grow there. Dr. Dove found, and established experimentally, that the bony horn cores of cattle are not outgrowths of the frontal bones, as Cuvier had believed, but are formed from horn buds which originate in the soft tissue covering the frontal bones. In other words, the bony horn cores do not grow *from* the skull but *upon* the skull and do not fuse with the frontal bones until a certain stage of development is attained.

Anatomical conditions being thus, it is of course possible to transplant the horn buds. The operation performed by Dr. Dove did just that. It consisted of cutting the two horn buds, trimming them flat at their point of contact, and placing them together over the "seam" of the frontal bones. It was expected that they would grow into a single horn spike, sheathed by a single horn, and that this horn would grow to the skull of the animal in exactly the place always reported as the point from which the horn of the unicorn grew.

The experiment was a complete success; in some respects it was even more successful than anyone had dared to dream. Ordinarily this race of cattle has curved horns, but the horn of the artificial unicorn grew almost perfectly straight. Only near its tip did it curve slightly upward. Furthermore, this single horn that covered the single bony spike (which was solidly attached to the frontal bones in spite of the suture) was grayish-white at the base and tipped with black.

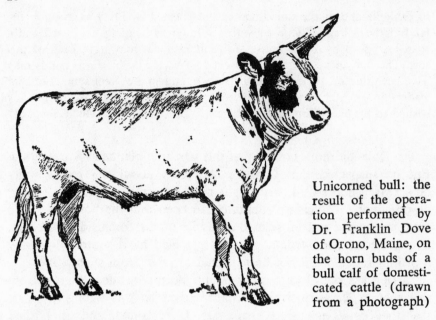

Unicorned bull: the result of the operation performed by Dr. Franklin Dove of Orono, Maine, on the horn buds of a bull calf of domesticated cattle (drawn from a photograph)

The most surprising result, however, was the behavior of this animal. As Dr. Dove reported in *The Scientific Monthly* (May 1936):

True in spirit as in horn to his prototype he is conscious of peculiar power. Although he is an animal with the hereditary potentialities for two horns, he recognizes the power of a single horn which he uses as a prow to pass under fences and barriers in his path, or as a forward thrusting bayonet in his attacks. And, to invert the beatitude, his ability to inherit the earth gives him the virtues of meekness. Consciousness of power makes him docile.

If these sentences were written not in modern English, but in Latin, and if they were printed not in a modern scientific journal of the year 1936 but in a book of about the year 1550, one would probably select them as the shortest and most typical of all the descriptions of the fabulous monster.

The ancient descriptions usually fit the rhinoceros better than the unicorned ox. But at the same time the ancient authors were often emphatic in asserting that unicorn and rhinoceros were not the same. That they afterward proceeded to describe the one in terms fitting only the other is amusing, but excusable. One may be permitted to think that there have always been families that knew and practiced the secret of producing unicorns. One may also amuse oneself by trying to imagine the fanciful tales about long and most perilous voyages invented and told to conceal the real origin of the high-priced animals. In short, one knows much of the story of the unicorn if one knows about the possibility of producing unicorned oxen by a simple operation and if one remembers that the single horn is not only the symbol of the leader of the herd but presumably *makes* the leader of the herd.

One more question is left open for discussion. Do we have reason to assume that the ancients could and did perform this operation, and that the Kaffirs, the Dinkas, and the natives of Nepal can and do today? The last three are known to have produced single-horned domestic animals, and the operation itself is simple. As for the ancients, we know the answer. Pliny, discussing the horns of oxen in the eleventh book of his *Natural History,* gave the recipe for the operation: "Incisions are twisted in several directions so that four horns sprout on the head." Though this concerns multi-horned animals the technique applies to unicorns as well. Pliny must have been unaware of the fact, or surely he would have mentioned it. But it is in any event likely that the people who knew how to manipulate horns also knew how to make a unicorn if they felt like it. After all, we now have proof that it can be done.

Somewhat to my surprise the reaction of some men of letters to Dr. Dove's experiment was quite acid. They did not like it. It seemed to them to spoil all their erudition. Actually, of course, it did not. The literary line of the development of the unicorn legend is still the same. The experiment merely proves definitely how some of the otherwise inexplicable facts mentioned by Odell Shepard should be explained.

The unicorn of the legend is still what it was. But in addition there were some people who could make unicorns. And sometimes they did.

CHAPTER 2

Fairy-Tale Fauna

"THE PEGASUS with its wings and horse's head sounds very much like a legend, just as does the Gryphon in the country of the Moors. Also the Tragopan, of which many say that it is larger than an eagle, that it has curved horns and a red head, while the rest of the body is rust-colored. The Sirens should also be disbelieved, even though Dino, the father of the celebrated Clitarchus, claims that there are some in India and that they lure human beings by their song in order to tear them apart when they come close."

This summary dismissal of legends with a zoological flavor sounds very much as if it had been written by somebody in Italy during the time of the Renaissance, when classical learning was being revived and at the same time subjected to criticism. Well, these sentences were written by somebody in Italy, but long before the Renaissance. The quotation is from the *Natural History* of Pliny the Elder. Pliny was successful with his condemnation, in so far as none of the legends he mentions were taken literally afterward. But he could not anticipate the fairy-tale fauna which would originate after his death or which grew from seeds already in existence when he wrote.

Not counting the unicorn, which is an element of courtly literature and poetry rather than of folk tales and fairy tales, the strange inhabitants of such tales are a foursome. Two are in human shapes, the giants and the "little people" of various kinds. The other two are animals, the dragon and the basilisk. Of these four, the "little people" constitute a special case—dealt with in Chapter 6—while the giants and the dragons belong together, with the basilisk a kind of more intellectual "little dragon."

To begin with the giants, they had two powerful literary documents to reinforce them. One was the Bible—with the single but oft-quoted

28

sentence, "there were giants in those days"—and the other was one of the great epics and the earliest adventure story: the *Odyssey*. These two literary arguments were powerful enough, in fact, to make people look for giants, and as a result giants for several centuries were by no means restricted to fairy tales. Literature, ordinary, serious, and "factual" literature, was full of them. We now know that they were not real but imitation giants, whose existence was borne out by spurious evidence, and belief in them arose from honest misunderstandings.

One of the classical cases of this kind can be found in Merian's *Theatrum Europaeum* of 1647. There is a chapter devoted to the Giant of Krems (a city in Austria) and it begins (translated) as follows:

In the year 1645, around St. Martin's day, when the Swedes occupied the city of Crembs (Krems), those people built, in addition to other fortifications, a stronghold up on the mountain, near the old round tower, but found that rainwater would harm the work: therefore they dug a ditch to carry away such water as it might come. It then happened that they, in that ditch, about three or four cubits below the surface, found in a soil that was yellow but somewhat blackened by the putrefaction of flesh, a gigantic large giant's body, of which (while the work progressed and before it had been recognized as a body) the head and some limbs had been destroyed because everything was soft and rotten with age and decay, but still many parts remained that were looked at by learned and experienced men and were declared human limbs, these parts were salvaged and sent to Sweden and Poland. . . . A few parts, among them a tooth weighing some five pounds, were kept in Crembs, and could be seen in the *Oratorio* of the new church which the Jesuits had built up on the mountain. It is also reported that two other giants' bodies, although somewhat smaller, had been found, but since the digging was pursued only as far as required by the necessity of the fortifications, said bodies were left remaining in the depth of the soil. . . .

Fortunately the author of the book pictured the five-pound tooth, and because of that there can be not the slightest doubt that the Giant of Krems was actually a specimen of *Elephas primigenius,* the woolly mammoth.

A very similar discovery had taken place about a century earlier near Lucerne in Switzerland, whence it is known as the case of the Swiss Giant or the Giant of Lucerne. The remains had been found in 1577 under the roots of an old oak tree, finally felled by a storm.

The local authorities, civil and Church, wondered whether the incomplete corpse was animal or human and whether it, in the latter case, deserved Christian burial. They called in a famous man of their day, one Dr. Felix Platter of Basle. Dr. Platter viewed the remains and pronounced gravely that they had come from a giant nineteen feet tall. They were placed in the town hall, waiting to be seen by a man who really knew anatomy. This happened around 1800 when Professor J. F. Blumenbach of Göttingen paid a visit to Lucerne. One glance was enough for Blumenbach, and the contemporary City Council had to learn and digest the fact that there had once been a member of the elephant tribe called *Elephas primigenius.*

But Blumenbach restricted himself to exposing the Swiss Giant; he had neither the time nor the inclination to go in for a general attack on all similar giants. That was a job which fell to Baron Cuvier.

Cuvier's brilliant battle against the giants was carried on in the French Academy, which had been the battleground for a prolonged and bitter controversy over the "bones of King Teutobochus" ever since their discovery on a plain in the Dauphiné. From olden times this plain had been known as *le champs des géants,* the field of giants, for gigantic bones had been found there repeatedly. On January 11, 1613, someone stumbled over a fairly complete skeleton of *Dinotherium,* an extinct distant relative of the elephant, the bones of which are still in Paris. A "surgeon" named Mazurier excavated the bones and claimed later that he had found them in a stone grave thirty feet long, inscribed with the name of King Teutobochus. Evidently Mazurier's arguments did not sound very convincing, because a number of learned members of the Academy doubted the authenticity of the find. But they did not say that the bones were in reality the bones of a large animal; they only wondered whether they were actual bones or merely a mineral "freak of nature." Cuvier could not only prove that they were bones, but could also say what kind of bones they were. Since 1824, when his *Recherches sur les ossements fossiles* appeared, no one has talked seriously of historical giants.

A great number of similar legends have definitely been traced to remains of large extinct animals. In a number of cases the bones that caused the legends were no longer available, but the stories always pointed to the kind of places in which geologists would expect to find such bones.

To show that Bible-reading medieval Europe did not have a

monopoly on this tendency, I would like to quote just one more case, this time from this side of the Atlantic Ocean. It can be found in the *Extracts from the Itineraries of Ezra Stiles* (Yale University Press, 1916) and is in the form of an entry in the diary of the Reverend Ezra Stiles, D.D., LL.D., president of Yale College, who died in 1795. The entry is dated "June 1764" and reads, maintaining all the vagaries of Dr. Stiles' spelling:

About 1705 Mr. Taylor wrote a poetic Accot. of the Gyant found then at Claveric below Albany—and says that about fourty years before (or perh. 1666) he heard a Story of an Ind. Giant of incredible Magnitude & disbelieved it till he saw the Teeth, which he weighed, one above Two pounds & another full *five pounds.* He was told by the Dutchmen that the Grave or Extent of the Skeleton was *Twenty-five paces,* & they dug up a Thigh bone measuring seventeen feet long & a knee pan a foot Diam. The Ind. has often told the Dutch of this Giant who they said was as tall as the Pine Tree and died Two hundred & fourty years before.

The Thigh Bone was found & took up June, 1705, so he died about 1465.—A Tooth weighed four pound & three Quarters. Grandfather Taylor says: "Two other Teeth after were took up and were Weighed by myself in my house in Westfield; one weighed five pounds, it had three furrows on the Top & was as hard as a stone; the other Two & one ounce. These Bones the Indians about Fort Albany flocked to see, upbraided the Dutch of Incredulity for not believing them who told them about 40 years before that Time they had an Indian as tall as the tall pine Trees, that would hunt Bears till they were treed & then take them with his hands, & wade into Water 12 or 14 foot deep & catch Sturgeons 3 or 4 or 5 at a Time & broil & eat them."

At another place Dr. Stiles quoted from an entry in Taylor's Diary, of 1705, regarding those teeth. It was said there that the teeth "looked like dull Olivant (ivory)" and also that the Indians had always asserted that the giant was "peaceful and would not hurt the little Indians." The description of the teeth, incidentally, poor as it is, indicates that they came from one of the American mastodons.

The tendency to regard any large bones as giant's bones was widespread, as can be seen from these examples, and there can be no doubt that the biblical reference was responsible for that in Christian countries. But that it was not the biblical reference alone is proved by the most classical giant story of them all, that in the *Odyssey.*

After succeeding in breaking away from the land of the Lotus Eaters (now identified as the island of Jerba in the Gulf of Gabes

on the North African coast), Odysseus and his companions sail
for an unspecified but apparently short time:

Unto the Land of the Kyklops, a race overbearing and lawless,
Soon we arrived. Here, trusting the favour of powers immortal,
None with his hands e'er planteth a plant or tills with the ploughshare,
Yet untilled and unplanted, behold, all groweth in plenty,
Wheat and barley and vine; and the vine's luxuriant clusters
Bear rich juice of the grape that the rain of the heaven does nourish.
Neither assemblies for council they have nor laws and traditions,
Dwelling apart on the crests of the highest mountains the Kyklops
Hollow caverns inhabit. . . .[1]

Then follows the well-known adventure with Polyphemus, the son
of Poseidon, mightiest of all the Cyclopes (or, in Greek, *kyklops*).
Odysseus and his men, looking around on the luxuriant isle, enter
a large cave. There are signs of human activity, but nobody is in
sight. But at dusk the Cyclops appears, a gigantic figure with only
one large round eye (as an attribute *kyklops* means "round-eyed" in
Greek) in the middle of the forehead. I might mention here that
Homer had his little joke with the names of these characters, as he
did elsewhere in the *Odyssey:* "Polyphemus" means "the much
talked-about." Such stories must have been daily fare in the harbor
taverns where sailors met and drank and talked.

Polyphemus eats two of the men and then settles down to sleep,
closing the entrance with a boulder too large for human hands to
move. The next morning he again eats two of the warriors and then
leaves, closing the cave behind him. Odysseus and his men sit around
gloomily, thinking of means to overpower the monster. At night
Odysseus greets Polyphemus with heavy Greek wine and, being
asked about his name in the ensuing conversation, tells Polyphemus
that "Nobody called me my mother and nothing but Nobody call
me all my companions" . . . an old ruse often found in ancient literature. When the giant is moaning in drunken sleep Odysseus and his
men heat a pole in the fire and jab it into the single eye. The giant
shouts for help, but when other Cyclopes, assembling outside the
cave, hear him yell that "Nobody tries to kill me" they depart again,
advising him to pray to his mighty and immortal father. Odysseus and
his men escape with the flock of sheep the next morning.

Safely aboard his vessel, Odysseus cannot resist shouting his real
name to the blinded monster. Polyphemus tries to call him back, but

[1] *Homer's Odyssey,* H. B. Cotterill trans. (London: Harrap, 1911), IX, 106–14.

Odysseus very wisely distrusts the pleasant promises and urges his companions to row harder.

> Thereat, with a heart more maddened to fury,
> Breaking a peak clean off from a huge high mountain he hurled it.
> Down on the water it fell. . . .　　　　　　　　(Book IX, 480–82)

Tradition almost as old as the *Odyssey* itself has it that the island of Polyphemus is Sicily, and most commentators saw a perfect description of the giant in lines 190–93, Book IX:

> Yea and a monstrous marvel was he—not fashioned in seeming
> Like to a mortal that liveth on bread but the peak of a mountain
> Covered with forests and standing alone, o'ertopping the others.

It was Vergil who spoke of *Aetnaeos Cyclopas,* indicating that he took the Cyclops Polyphemus to be a personification of Mount Aetna in Sicily. Many of the other features agree well with this explanation. The large *round* eye might well be the crater; the roaring of the giant and the throwing of mountain peaks also speak for a volcano. So do the caves and the fact that the Cyclopes "dwell apart on the crests of the mountains." Even the fertility of the soil, especially for grapes, goes well with volcanism. And in mythology the Cyclopes were the assistants of Hephaistos, the smith, who fashioned the thunderbolts. Pliny the Elder followed that tradition in calling volcanic bombs *cyclopum scopuli.* All in all, it is quite likely that Polyphemus is really Mount Aetna.

But all poetry consists of weaving strands of ideas together, and it is probable that Homer had another thing in mind too, that he referred to living giants (or what were taken to be living giants) in addition to personifying the volcano. Even that thought has a long tradition, and around the middle of the fourteenth century Giovanni Boccaccio announced triumphantly that the remains of Polyphemus had been found in a cave near Trapani on Sicily. He did not forget to mention that this find vindicated Empedocles, who in 440 B.C. had claimed that Sicily had once been the dwelling place of ferocious giants. The bones found in the cave seemed to indicate, Boccaccio wrote, that those giants were close to three hundred feet tall; it must have been distinctly unpleasant to meet them.

Those bones were preserved for centuries, and about three hundred years after Boccaccio's time were seen by the learned Jesuit Athanasius Kircher. Kircher described them as ponderous but added that Boccaccio had exaggerated their size; the giants were not three hundred but only about thirty feet tall, still large enough to enable them to eat two normal humans for one meal.

Unfortunately Kircher, instead of picturing the bones, just printed a fancy "restoration" of Polyphemus, and the bones have not survived. But we can be almost certain what they really were: bones and skulls of elephants are often found in Sicilian caves, and we have seen what happened when elephant bones were found elsewhere in Europe or in America.

But we are not finished with the Cyclopes.

For a long time the chief mystery that remained was why the Greeks believed their giants to be one-eyed, and that one eye placed in the middle of the forehead. Dr. Othenio Abel not only explained that mystery, but even explained it in such a manner as to make it certain that these bones *must* have been the bones of elephants of some kind.

Practically everybody nowadays would recognize an elephant's skull, even if the long tusks were missing. But if you imagine that you never saw an elephant or a picture of one (and the elephant was unknown to the Greeks of the Homeric Age) you'll notice that the skull of an elephant bears some resemblance to a human skull of exaggerated size, especially if the long tusks are missing.

This similarity becomes still greater if you look at it from the front. But in that position, in spite of increased resemblance, you'll also notice an important difference. There are two large holes, which appear to be eye sockets. But they are not separated, they have merged, showing only in outline that there were once two. And that single "socket" is in a position which can only be described in everyday language by saying that it is "in the middle of the forehead." Actually the "socket" is merely the nasal opening, while the real eye sockets are hidden if the skull is viewed from the front.

Sailors of even three hundred years ago, not to mention those of thirty-five centuries ago, would not have noticed such anatomical niceties. The big skulls to them were simply the skulls of big humans, distinguished from others not only by their size but also by the fact that they had "only one single eye in the middle of the forehead." And one can hardly expect these sailors to go home and report in a dry-as-dust manner that there was such a skull in such and such a cave. They would not tell of dried and dead skulls of giants, they would tell of giants that were very much alive and battled with them.

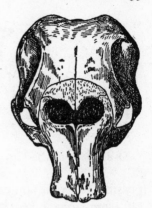

Front view of an elephant skull, showing the
"single eye," actually the nasal opening

And if they had not been victorious in those battles they would not
be sitting in front of the harbor tavern to tell the tale. These tales must
have been numerous . . . "polyphemus"!

If the foregoing examples have given the impression that every
bone of every fossil elephant ever found was converted into a giant,
this impression goes a little too far. If the bones were found in southern France—emphasis on "southern"—or anywhere near the French
Alps, they were often accepted as elephant's bones. This could be
done because there was a ready explanation for them; they were, no
doubt, the remains of one of the war elephants which Hannibal led
across the mountains to attack Rome.

But if the site was too far from any route that Hannibal could
possibly have traveled and if the remains very obviously could
not have come from something with a human shape there was another
way out: they were dragon's bones.

Everybody now knows what a dragon was supposed to look like:
the general body of a crocodile was equipped with bat's wings and
a ferocious head, often (but not always) on a long neck. The whole
was of large size and had one additional special characteristic: it
could, and would, spit fire. But this picture of the dragon did not
come down from antiquity as one can sometimes read; it is a rather
late development and typically North European. Probably the first
dragon picture which conforms to that description is one that an unknown artist drew for a book published in 1598 in Switzerland.

This picture, in turn, was probably derived from a monument
fashioned around the year 1500 in the city of Klagenfurt in Austria.
Othenio Abel traced the story of this monument and of a related
Austrian legend and pointed out that we have here a case—or

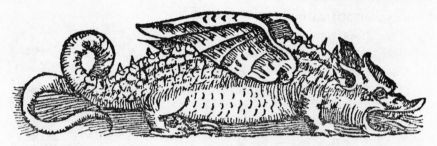

Dragon from the *Cosmographia* of Sebastian Münster (Basel, 1598)

possibly two different cases—where fossil bones became dragon bones but giants were invented to go with the story. The Dragon Monument of Klagenfurt shows a naked giant in the act of slaying a dragon with a spiked club. What is especially interesting is the dragon's head, which, apart from large and incongruous leaf ears, has the outline of a rhinoceros skull. Professor Abel succeeded in finding in chronicles entries which stated that the "dragon's skull" had been found near Klagenfurt about three decades before the monument was erected. Then the skull, after having served the sculptor as a model, was said to have been brought to the town hall to be preserved. Preserved it was; it could still be found there after the First World War. And it proved to be the skull of *Rhinoceros antiquitatis,* a rhinoceros which lived in Europe at the same time as the mammoth and primitive man.

The other legend traced by Abel, which follows very much the same lines, is usually referred to as the legend of the Foundation of the Monastery of Wilten. The underlying facts are insignificant almost to the point of being ridiculous. Near Wilten there is found a natural bitumen which has certain healing properties and has therefore acquired a considerable, though local, reputation. The local name is *Thürschen-Bluet,* an idiomatic term which may be translated as "giant's blood." Originally it was probably "dragon's blood," usually a powerful healing agent in legend. Now, since there was blood, there must have been a battle, a battle in which the dragon was killed, as was the fate of every dragon that ever appeared in legend. To kill a dragon required a powerful adversary, and a giant was the safest assumption, since no particular hero was available for this vicinity. The giant received the name of Heymo, and it was said that when he killed the dragon it had been guarding an orchard with a fence of pure silver and with trees bearing apples of pure gold.

It is evident that the man who first fashioned this legend did not have much original imagination but did have some knowledge of classical mythology, for Heymo's exploit is merely a repetition of one of the deeds of Hercules. Only Heymo, a magnanimous fellow, though a giant, seems to have realized that he owed his victory to God and that an expression of thankfulness was in order. Hence, legend says, he took part of the dragon's wealth to found the Monastery of Wilten.

This legend did not exist in its full form in 1250, the year during which a chronicler mentioned that the bones of the giant (not those of the dragon) were kept in the monastery. The bones later disappeared, but the prior of the monastery had a statute of Heymo made, and two hundred years later the monastery suddenly produced another proof of the great battle. Visitors were told that Heymo after his victory had cut out the dragon's tongue, for which the monks fashioned a silver sheath, presumably with some of the silver from the fence of the dragon's orchard. The sheath was melted down in 1734, but the "tongue" is still to be found in the Museum of Innsbruck. It is the rostrum (sword) of a normal swordfish, probably from the Mediterranean and probably brought home by some pilgrim or crusader.

Critics have taken pains to point out that all these paleontological explanations refer only to late adaptations of an already existing myth. While they admit that the explanations fit the adaptations perfectly, they insist that originally the myth of the dragon must have started with some living animal. Of course it did. And one can see the animal that started the myth in the reptile house of any well-stocked zoological park.

But first let us return for a moment to Konrad Gesner, who can always be relied upon to tell a complete story. Gesner, who carefully neglected to mention giants in his books, did prepare manuscripts for a long chapter on the dragon as part of the fifth volume of his *Historia Animalium*. Although he died before he had a chance to do much more than make a preliminary survey, one Jacobus Carronus edited the half-finished parts he found among Gesner's papers and published them as *"Doctor Konrad Gesner's Snake-Book,* which is: a diligent and thorough description of all snakes and serpents living in the sea, in the fresh waters and on the earth, first collected and described by the highly learned and widely famed Herr Doktor

"Young dragon" of Pierre Belon— in all probability a dried and mutilated specimen of the Javanese tree lizard *Draco volans* (middle sixteenth century)

Konradus Gesnerus and thereafter brought in this order and aggrandized by the very learned Herr Jacobus Carronus and printed in Zurich by Herr Jacob Froschower. . . ."

This essay begins with a few philological remarks about the Latin term *draco,* which, Gesner explains, is in reality the Greek word for "seeing with keen eyes" but was used by the Greeks for "snakes, especially for those snakes that are large and heavy and surpass all others in size." The same is true, said Gesner, for the German word for dragon, namely *Lindwurm,* for *lint* is merely the ancient Germanic word for snake. As a matter of fact, when they spoke of *dracones,* the classic authors meant giant snakes of the python kind. Pliny stated that they lived in India and fell down from trees upon their victims, whom they killed by encircling them in their coils. Gesner added (correctly) that "the dragons have little or no venom." The poets, continued Gesner, often imagined dragons to guard treasures, "probably to symbolize the danger of having possessions of great value. . . ." Gesner himself was poor all his life.

Then abruptly—so abruptly that it is apparent that the hand of the master had not time to knit the excerpts from other authors together—dragons with feet are mentioned. It is said that they possess wings too. Gesner quoted Cardanus, the great physician and mathematician of Pavia, as authority for five "dried" dragons the latter had seen in Paris. There is no doubt that Cardanus saw some dried specimens of some kind in Paris. In his book, printed in 1557, he writes:

Their wings were so small that, in my opinion, they could hardly fly with them. Their heads were small and shaped like the heads of snakes, they were of pleasant color and without feathers or hair and the largest of them was as large as a wren.

The "flying dragon" of Java (*Draco volans*), as it actually looks

These dried specimens were certainly not works of art; "if so, they would have received larger wings to be under less suspicion."

A French author of about the same time, Pierre Belon (Petrus Bellonius), printed a picture which in all probability shows the specimens mentioned by Cardanus. It is unmistakably a picture of the famous "flying dragon" of Java, a harmless little tree-lizard about four inches long. The "flying dragon"—Linnaeus gave it the name of *Draco volans,* in memory of the fanciful tales once told—does not fly; it is one of those "parachute animals" like the flying squirrel. On each side of its body half a dozen "false ribs" protrude and support a skin, semi-circular or triangular, according to variety, which enables the small light lizard to extend its jumps from branch to branch into long glides.

Belon's picture shows only one pair of feet; the lizards had probably been mutilated. Complete specimens of *Draco volans* must have reached Europe later, since in one of the books of Athanasius Kircher (printed in 1678) a *Draco volans* from Java is pictured with only

slight "improvements." The artist evidently used such a lizard for
a model, thinking that it was a newly hatched specimen of the dragon
of legend. Kircher claimed that the picture portrayed the once
famous "Dragon of Rhodos," said to have been killed in 1345 by the
noble knight Deodatus of Gozen. Chronicles relate that the skeleton of
this dragon was found, quite dead and dry, in a cave near the locality
of the alleged battle. Deodatus, it should be said, hailed from Gascony
in France, and Frenchmen have always had their own hardly flattering
ideas about the veracity of their compatriots from that region. What
the dead and dry skeleton was we don't know.

Incidentally, Athanasius Kircher had a beautiful theory about
dragons. In his opinion the earth was honeycombed with caves. All
kinds of monsters lived in these caves, most of them dragons. They
were rare and mysterious only because the surface of the earth was
not their natural habitat; the few that were mentioned in accounts of
dragon battles with famous heroes were simply stragglers that had
blundered into the surface-world and could not find their way back.

Chinese dragons, however, far from being creatures of the subterranean world, come from above. They are "cloud dragons," and the
Chinese say that all the dragon bones and dragon teeth are the remains of such dragons as could not wing their way back into the
clouds for lack of rain.

This sounds, in its own fashion, very much like Kircher's statement; the dragon, since it was so indistinct, was taken everywhere as
an "animal from another world" which had by some mischance
blundered into ours and then could not escape again.

It is said that the outward appearance of the Chinese dragon is
derived from the alligator of the Yangtze Kiang, which is a small
and harmless alligator. Where this statement originated I can't tell;
as far as the Chinese dragon's shape goes, any lizard might have been
its original model—or even a dachshund, if necessary. But be that as
it may, it is quite evident that the Chinese dragon is not the terrible
monster of Western mythology. At its worst it is harmless; as a rule
it is even benevolent.

While there are not quite as many books on the dragon as there
are on the unicorn, their number is impressive. There are probably
more books about the dragon than about any real animal—not counting those libraries of purely utilitarian books on domesticated animals.
There are essays and books on the Chinese dragon (I know of five,

but there are probably fifty). Of course there are essays on the European dragon. All of them contain "explanations" galore, based on straight mythology, on astrological mythology, on folklore, on linguistic developments—and some even on zoology. There are cloud dragons and water dragons in the explanations, and authors permeated with dragon lore have proved to their own satisfaction—especially their own—that the dragon is merely a symbol of the ocean, the snake that girdles the world. Others see in the dragon a symbol of the thundercloud, rainstorms with thunder and lightning—dragons spit fire—and point to the fact that all the dragons of art have wings, something one does not expect from either a marine or a subterranean creature. The Chinese cloud dragons fit this explanation, and so does the fact that the German word for "kite" also means "dragon" (in Russian a "kite" is a "serpent," large, male, and mysterious).

It cannot be doubted that in folklore the dragon is merely a semi-personification of naturally destructive agents, a kind of antithesis to the benign sun which is swallowed by a dragon during an eclipse. Swiss and Austrian peasants say to this day that "a dragon broke out" when one of the wild and destructive mountain streams of the Alps changes its path.

But behind all these mythological and folklore dragons there must be a zoological dragon of some kind. And it does seem likely that the zoological dragon is just the snake, the venomous snake. The fact that such a small and unimportant-looking creature could kill with one swift bite was altogether mysterious, and snake cults have sprung up wherever venomous snakes are found. Idolization naturally increased the size of the idol, and thus the pythons got into the story even though they have no venom. A parallel thought which intensified the dread of serpents was the *Blitzschlange,* the "lightning snake." There was a gigantic and still far more mysterious "snake" in the sky, which was snakelike in shape and luminous, which struck in a swift flash and killed as quickly.

The *Blitzschlange* probably contributed largely to the concept of the winged serpent: since it struck from the clouds it had to have wings. But the wings remained indistinct until *Draco volans* from Java furnished a model.

And with the wings of *Draco volans,* the size of the python, and the swiftness and strength of lightning, the picture-book dragon was finally formed—quite recently, even after the Middle Ages. The discovery of some fossils gave it its habit of living in caves, guarding a treasure or a fair maiden, until a hero came and slew it.

It is a sad fact that St. George acquired world-wide fame for slaying a dragon even though there is no documentary evidence that he actually did so. On the other hand, a man *known* to have slain a basilisk is not at all famous; in fact only a few specialists have heard of him.

This may of course be because the one was a knight and the other just an apprentice to a Master Baker in Vienna, residing at Schönlaterngasse No. 7 in the year of Our Lord 1202. Or it may be because the slaying of a dragon requires boldness, as well as armament and the skill to use it, while the slaying of a basilisk can be accomplished with mere knowledge and a household utensil.

The basilisk may not be too well known nowadays, but it figured in one of the earliest printed books, the *Dialogus creaturarum,* printed by Pieter van Leu in The Netherlands in 1480. The eighth of the dialogues between various creatures is between the basilisk and a fish and begins as follows: "There is a kind of lizard that is called basilisk in Greek and regulus in Latin and Isidorus says that it is the king of all the snakes and serpents. Even serpents flee the basilisk because its breath is deadly and so is its appearance." The Isidorus mentioned is doubtless Isidore of Seville, but the unknown author of the *Dialogus creaturarum* did not have to rely on him for his information; nobody during those days dared to doubt the existence of the basilisk, king of the serpents and of everything alive with the exception of man. The belief in the basilisk was old even then; it had remained unchanged since classical times.

But while the belief persisted, the supposed appearance of the monster had undergone considerable change. Pliny the Elder had described the basilisk simply as a snake, distinguished from others merely by its possession of a small golden crown. The author of the *Dialogus creaturarum* termed it a "kind of lizard," but already there existed a third version that was to become more and more popular. The basilisk, it was said, needed a number of rare events and coincidences to come into existence. It had to be born of an egg laid during the days of the dog star Sirius by a seven-year-old cock. Such an egg was easy to recognize; it did not have the normal ovoid shape but was spherical. Also it had no shell but only a tough skin or membrane. This egg was then hatched by a toad (it was a matter of dispute whether the cock might not also be able to hatch the basilisk). Naturally such an animal combined the features of its various foster parents: while essentially a serpent, it had the habits of a toad and some of the physical characteristics of a cock.

The legend of the killing of a basilisk in Vienna is obviously based on the third and most complicated version of the story. The way it is usually told is that the house mentioned belonged to Master Baker Garhibl, a nasty-tempered widower who could not get along with anybody, not with his neighbors, or his guild, and least of all with his help. The only one who would stay with Master Garhibl was the apprentice Hans, and his reason was Garhibl's daughter Apollonia.

One day, when Master Garhibl was in what for him was an unusually good mood Hans dared to ask for Apollonia's hand. It was in the early morning hours and the cock happened to crow at that moment. Garhibl's mood changed instantly; he threw his apprentice out and screamed after him, "If that cock, which is just as impudent as you are, should lay an egg, you may come back and ask for Apollonia again."

Hans vanished, Apollonia presumably cried, and life at Schönlaterngasse No. 7 continued troubled, as usual. But a few months later there was unusual trouble. In the early morning hours the maid went to a freshly dug well for water but she did not fetch any, for a terrible smell came out of the well and at the bottom she saw something shining and glittering. She told her master what had happened and the master ordered the new apprentice to climb down into the well to see what was going on. The boy did as he was told, but when he was inside the well he fainted. Neighbors hoisted him out and revived him. But they also told the Master of Justice of Vienna, Herr Jacobus von der Hülben, who decided that this was a case requiring his personal attention and who appeared on the scene with several armed city guards carrying halberds and pikes.

First Herr Jacobus listened to the neighbors, who blamed everything, including the wet spring, on Master Garhibl. Then he listened to a scholar who happened to be in the crowd and who explained, mixing as much Latin into his speech as he could, that this indubitably was a basilisk which will paralyze with its glance and kill with its breath. Weapons were naturally of no avail against such a monster, but it could be overcome just the same. Fortunately the sight of a basilisk is so horrible that the basilisk itself cannot stand it. There-

fore a man armed with a mirror can vanquish a basilisk—when the
monster sees its own reflection it will die of fright.

Herr Jacobus von der Hülben did not have to call for volunteers;
a young man in the crowd offered to attack the monster with a mirror.
Hans, of course. And Herr Jacobus, who had heard the whole story
in the meantime, ordered Master Garhibl to do anything Hans might
ask if he succeeded. And while Hans approached the new well, Herr
Jacobus thought about the question of whether he could impose a
fine, the status of the City Treasury being what it was.

Many years after the wedding a brief inscription was carved on
a stone slab next to the door of Master Garhibl's former house. It
read:

ANNO DOMINI MCCII

Kaiser Friedrich II was elected. During his rule a basilisk sprang from a
cock. It was like the effigy above and the well in which it was found was
filled with soil, no doubt because many people died from the venom of
the monster.

Renovated in 1677 by the landlord Hanns Spannring, Bookseller.

Philologists who went to work on the legend assumed that the
account had been "romanticized" and that the names were probably
added or substituted centuries later. But they found, possibly to their
surprise, that the story itself actually dated back to the first decade
of the thirteenth century. Moreover, it was this Viennese legend
which kept the belief in the basilisk alive.

The house was finally torn down and the carved inscription disappeared too (its wording is known from local history books) but the
"effigy," which looked like a clumsy sculpture of a rooster, was
preserved. Around the turn of the century it was examined by the
still famous Austrian geologist Eduard Suess.

Professor Suess saw at once that it was sandstone and that its
shape, though strange, was natural, with only very minor improvements by a sculptor's chisel. In short, it was not an "effigy"; it was the
"basilisk" itself, and that explained why the legend, instead of speaking about a cave, put so much emphasis on a well. The subsoil of
Vienna consists mainly of clay with layers of sandstone, so that a well
has to be dug through sandstone layers in order to reach the underground water. These layers, however, are not solid rock but consist
of roundish pebbles that often cling together in strange shapes. The
water, on the other hand, is not as pure and clean as the inhabitants

The "Vienna basilisk" (after Sebastian Münster's *Cosmographia,* 1598)

might wish it; occasionally it is saturated with hydrogen-sulphur compounds that impart a bad taste and a very bad smell reminiscent of rotten eggs. From these geological facts Suess was able to reconstruct the story as it probably happened. A new well had been drilled which apparently showed a higher concentration of hydrogen-sulphur compounds than even the hardened Viennese were able to stand. After the gases had dissipated somewhat, people climbed down into the well to find out what had caused the "poisoning" and discovered a curiously shaped lump of sandstone that was then declared to be a dead basilisk.

Even in scientific circles the legend of the basilisk survived until about the middle of the sixteenth century. Konrad Gesner of Zürich was the first well-known scientist who thundered against the belief in such a monster. "Women's gossip and false nonsense," he said, and later on stressed the fact that the occasional fainting spells and even deaths occurring in deep shafts and caves were caused by "bad, poisonous, moldy and stinking vitiated air." Though scientists agreed, the belief in the basilisk lingered on for at least two centuries longer with the general public.

But just about in Konrad Gesner's time the story of the basilisk took another turn. There were people who collected sea shells and minerals and "natural curiosities"; Gesner himself started a small museum. The man who already owned several dozen different sea shells, the head of a swordfish, and the rostrum of a sawfish—and an alicorn, if he could afford one—might be intrigued with the idea of acquiring a dead and dried basilisk.

If there is a demand somebody will be pleased to be the supplier. But dead basilisks are difficult to come by; hence there was simply no other way out (in view of the demand) than to manufacture them. The raw material was a fish rarely taken, because it is not edible, but quite abundant: the ray.

Fake monsters made from rays acquired a special name; they came to be called Jenny Hanivers. Nobody knows why or how. Two fish experts, Dr. E. W. Gudger, formerly of the American Museum of Natural History in New York, and Dr. Gilbert P. Whitley of the

Australian Museum in Sydney spent, and as it turned out, wasted, a lot of time trying to find out. The only plausible suggestion anybody ever made was that the word "Haniver" suggested Anvers, the French name for Antwerp. Was Antwerp at one time a manufacturing, or trading, center for fake monsters?

There must also have been a center somewhere in Italy. The Jenny Hanivers that can still be found and examined fall into two groups: those made of North Sea fish and those made of Mediterranean fish. (Two specimens which suddenly turned up in the United States in 1929 and 1933 could be traced; they had been made by simple fishermen who had never heard either of Jenny Hanivers or of basilisks but simply had imagination and time on their hands.)

To change a ray into a Jenny Haniver is not very difficult. Anyone who has ever seen a ray swimming in an upright position near the glass of a large sea-water aquarium will recall the quite unpleasant sensation of having faced an evil living mask. Actually the staring

The earliest known picture of a Jenny Haniver (Gesner, *Historia Animalium*, vol. IV, 1558)

"eyes" of the face are but the nostrils. The real eyes are on the dark back of the fish and are rather inconspicuous, especially on dead and dried specimens. It may be mentioned in passing that a dried ray looks rather harmless if viewed from above. To make it look weird the head has to be accentuated, which is accomplished easily enough by cutting into the large pectoral fins where they are connected to the head. If they are partly severed and pulled somewhat to the sides they give the impression of being wings. There are occasionally adult rays with non-adherent pectoral fins, which are really permanent larval forms. It may well be that such nature-made Jenny Hanivers were the models for the artificial ones that must have sold so well a few centuries ago.

Once having started cutting the pectoral fins, the skillful artisan does not see any reason why he should be restricted to only two incisions. Two more cuts, one on each side, which partly sever a small strip of fin material, are an excellent way of producing forelegs, while the appendages of the pelvic fins of the male fishes need only slight manipulation to be turned into hind legs. Thus the harmless flat ray has already acquired two pairs of legs and a pair of wings. But it is the "face" that really affords an opportunity for the artist to show his skill. The flat mouth is pulled outward a bit to look more curved and to resemble a human mouth more closely. Sometimes the tissue on either side of the mouth is pulled outward to form cheeks or even more weird appendages that would serve no purpose at all if they actually existed. The tip of the head is then pulled so as to become more elongated; after this it is bent over to resemble a pointed hat or a bishop's miter.

This performed, there remained only a few more details for the artisan to finish: to insert artificial eyes into the nostrils, to dry the whole transformation carefully and in such a manner that the distortions would not disappear, and to find a customer.

The latter must have become difficult in time, for the people who collected such items usually also collected books on natural subjects and the books told of Jenny Hanivers. Gesner was the first to do so; in fact he was the first to give a picture of a Jenny Haniver. In volume IV of his *Historia Animalium* he gave short shrift to the whole business:

Apothecaries and other peddlers change the bodies of rays in many ways after their own fancy by cutting, twisting and pulling into the shapes of snakes, basilisks and dragons. I have set such a figure here so that such cheating and deceit may be recognized. I have seen a traveling peddler here [in Zürich] who has shown such a shape for a basilisk but it had been made of a ray.

This was written in 1558. Two hundred years later the basilisk retreated into its last hide-out, the fairy tale.

CHAPTER 3

The Vegetable Animals

THE STORY of the vegetable animals has no proper beginning. Like the strange mixtures of vegetable and animal life of which it pretended to tell, it was begotten by time and by the ocean and slowly grew, with offshoots and misleading results.

Since there is no proper beginning to the legend I think it will be fitting to start with the epitaph of the man whose name combines—by way of a partly true, partly stolen, and partly fictitious book—the two branches of the story of the vegetable animals: the vegetable lamb of the East and the vegetable goose of the northern West. That epitaph is found in Liège in Belgium, and reads:

Hic jacet vir nobilis Dominus Johannes de Montevilla, miles, alias dictus ad Barbam, Dominus de Campdi natus de Anglia medicinae professor devotissimus orator et bonorum largissimus paupribus erogator qui toto quasi orbe lustrato leodii dieam vitae suae clausit extremum anno Domini MCCCLXXII mensis novembris die XVII.

In translation:

Here lieth the noble Lord John de Maundeville, Knyght, also called à la Barbe, Lord of Campdi, born in England, professor of Medicine, illustrious orator, very rich, benefactor of the poor, who travelled over almost all the world and who passed from life in Liège in the Year of the Lord 1372, on the 17th Day of the month of November.

To the inhabitants of Liège the man who was to get this epitaph had been a prominent citizen and a well-reputed doctor who had settled there in 1343. His name was Jean de Bourgogne, but he was also called Jehan à la Barbe (John of the Beard). When he felt his death approaching he called his neighbors and the city notables to-

48

gether and revealed to them that he was not only Jean de Bourgogne, the doctor they knew, but also somebody else, the author of a book most of them had read: that he was Sir John de Maundeville.

After making these assertions he died—leaving to his contemporaries a book which appeared to them the most important travel book they had and which they consequently copied and recopied, translated and retranslated, until it had an incredible circulation. Aside from the book Jean de Bourgogne left an enormous riddle for the historians of posterity and they had to spend much effort and time to unravel at least the main parts of it.

The most important difficulty was that *Monsieur le docteur* de Bourgogne had changed his own story on his deathbed. Earlier in his life he had stated that he had traveled in the Near East, especially Egypt, and resided there for some time. There is no reason to doubt this statement in itself, but what followed is now thoroughly disbelieved. When living in Egypt, in Cairo to be precise, he had met the English nobleman Sir John Mandeville (or Maundeville, Mandevilla, Maundevyl, Mandevylle, or any other spelling that comes to mind). Sir John had been born in England, at St. Albans, but had been forced to flee his native country on the 29th of September, 1322, because he had killed a man in a duel. Sir John embarked on a long voyage which in the end led him to the Far East and which had lasted thirty-four years, all told.

Later on Sir John had visited the doctor at Liège in order to be cured by him, as he was sorely suffering with gout. On that occasion Sir John had given him the manuscript of the famous book, which the doctor had circulated for the first time in 1355. (Strangely enough, it was written in French.)

That was the original story. On his deathbed the doctor suddenly declared that he himself was Sir John de Mandeville, hence an English knight, hence the great traveler, hence the author of the book.

Historians never succeeded in finding an English knight of such or a similar name, save for one Sir Johan Mangevilain, and he, if he traveled at all, did so within the confines of the British isles. Jean de Bourgogne's deathbed admission was only partly true: he was no English knight, but he had written the book, beginning with his actual experiences in Egypt and neighboring countries and then going on an imaginary voyage, stealing information right and left.

His sources could still be traced, five centuries later. One of them was the itinerary of a voyage written by a knight by the name of Wilhelm von Boldensele in 1336. Another one, used almost in full and virtually word for word, was the manuscript of the monk Oderich of Portenau, who had actually traveled to the Far East during the years 1318 to 1330. Needless to say, Marco Polo was among the unknowing contributors to Bourgogne's "life-history," the travel book by Carpini and Vincent de Beauvais' *Speculum* ("Mirror") were used, and the classical authors Eratosthenes and Pliny the Elder became victims.

It is part of Oderich's involuntary contribution which interests us here.

The Mandeville chapter "Of the Contries and Yles that ben bezonde the Lond of Cathay; and of the Frutes there . . ." contains the following marvelous story:

[In Cathay] there growethe a manner of Fruyt, as thoughe it were Gowrdes: and whan thei ben rype, men kutten hem a to [cut them in two] and men fynden with inne a lytylle Best [little beast], in Flessche, in Bone and Blode as though it were a lytylle Lomb with outen wolle [lamb without wool]. And men eten both the Frut and the Best; and that is a great Marveylle. Of that fruit I have eten.

In exchange Mandeville (or Oderich) told his informants a story:

as gret a marveylle to hem [them] that is amonges us; and that was of the Bernakes. For I tolde hem hat in oure Countree weren Trees that beren a Fruyt, that becomen Briddes [birds] fleeynge: and thei that fallen on the Erthe dyen anon: and thei ben right gode to mannes mete [meat]. And here had thei als gret marvayle that sume of hem trowed it were an impossible thing to be.

Oderich did not invent that story in order to "outmarvel" his Asiatic informants; he merely told them something which was then generally believed in the West. Any man of education would have sworn that there was such a tree, growing in England, or maybe Scotland or Ireland, or at any event on some of the islands near England and Ireland, that bore a strange fruit which, if allowed to ripen on the tree, would become a bird and then grow into a small wild goose.

The story had been set down centuries before Oderich made his trip to the Far East and Jean de Bourgogne claimed to have made it. The first reporter was one Giraldus Cambrensis, writing sometime between 1154 and 1189 A.D. But it is obvious that what he wrote in his *Topographia Hibernia* was already a well-developed version of the legend, and not its earliest beginning.

Speaking about birds "which are called Bernacae" and which are numerous in Ireland, he remarks:

. . . against nature, nature produces them in a most extraordinary way. They are like marsh geese, but somewhat smaller. They are produced from fir timber tossed along by the sea, and are at first like gum. Afterwards they hang down by their beaks, as if from a sea-weed attached to the timber, surrounded by shells, in order to grow more freely. Having thus, in process of time, been clothed with a strong coat of feathers, they either fall into the water or fly freely away into the air. They derive their food and growth from the sap of the wood or the sea, by a secret and most wonderful process of alimentation. I have frequently, with my own eyes, seen more than a thousand of these small bodies of birds, hanging down from one piece of timber at the seashore, enclosed in shells and already formed.

After having assured the reader that "nowhere on earth" anybody ever saw these birds lay eggs or hatch them, the author mentioned that "some bishops and clergymen in some parts of Ireland do not scruple to dine off these birds at the time of fasting, because they are not flesh nor born of flesh."

This practice often led to the assertion that the whole story was invented by priests of the Catholic Church in order to have a well-set table even during fast. But things are not as simple as that.

Nobody has the slightest doubt that many individual monks and priests and even whole monasteries gladly seized upon the excuse that these geese were actually vegetables. There was learned argument enough to go even further and extend it to *all* waterfowl, reasserting Abelard's opinion that the sinfulness of an animal could be judged by its feet. That admitted ducks and geese to the table at the time of fasting because they did not have "feet" but "flippers." The learned also quoted a certain line from a Latin poem by Claudius Marius Victor, the line which says *ergo materies avibusque et piscibus una est*—"therefore birds and fishes are of one flesh."

It was somewhat disturbing that the main witness, Giraldus Cambrensis, had condemned the practice himself, arguing that these birds, while not born of flesh, were still flesh themselves, just as Adam, while not born of flesh, was flesh. And the Roast Duck Party quickly lost the first and decisive battle when the highest Council of the Church accepted Giraldus's conclusion and expressly forbade the practice of eating the Bernacae during fast. The Pope himself, Innocentius III, pronounced the *prohibitus est*. That was in 1215.

The next severe blow fell some fifty years later, when another important churchman, Albert von Bollstädt or Albertus Magnus, rejected the story itself. *Omnino absurdum* was his verdict, and others repeated after him, "fully absurd and an impudent lie." Albertus stated that he had observed the birds *in copula* and had watched them lay eggs.

One would expect that the ban on eating the birds, followed by Albert's *absurdum,* would have finished the story. But it did not. The ban on eating the birds was observed, it is hoped, but there was no ban on quoting the "facts" of the case. And they were interesting "facts" and there were many reasons for telling them. One reason was very simply the ingrained *Wundersucht,* the craving for the miraculous, of that age. Another one was that many priests used the story as an example of the greatness of God. Even if it had no gastronomical consequences, it was a proof for the abundance and variety of creation.

In fact it was a contemporary and pupil of Albertus Magnus, and hardly less famous himself, who contributed greatly to the continuation and improvement of the tree geese.

He was Thomas de Cantimpré, or Thomasius Cantipratensis. Following established usage and tradition, Thomas first sought to prove that the vegetable goose was not a recent discovery, but that it could be found in classical writers—more, that the great Aristotle had mentioned it. "The barliates," Thomas wrote, "grow on trees as Aristotle says; they are the birds called barnescas by the common people."

There is one thing wrong with this nice quotation—no later scholar succeeded in finding anything even remotely like that in Aristotle's writings. We now have the choice of believing that Thomas just invented the quotation in order to have Aristotle as his witness, or else that the copy of Aristotle which he used was full of later insertions made by various copyists, not, of course, marked as such. The latter assumption is not only more kind to Thomas, it is also the more likely.

Thomas's book was fated to be translated from the Latin by the Archdeacon of Regensburg, Konrad von Megenberg, and to be (in that form) one of the earliest books which was printed. There were several editions of this Book of Nature (*Puch der Natur*) and all of them carry a paragraph on the tree goose, called *bachad* in that case. The paragraph reads:

This is a bird that grows from wood and that wood has many branches from which the birds sprout so that many of them hang from one tree.

These birds are smaller than geese and have feet like ducks, but they are of black color. They hang from the tree by their beaks, also from the bark and the trunk. In time they fall into the sea and grow on the sea until they begin to fly.

This is not quite the same story as that of Giraldus. Giraldus said that they originate from driftwood which is being tossed around by the sea; Konrad (following Thomas and the spurious quotation from Aristotle) states that they grow on trees like fruit.

This is the version related by Oderich, but it could not last long, because skeptics and credulous alike wanted to know where these trees grew. At first the Flanders coast had been named; that was obviously untrue. One Gervasius Tilboriensis, who wrote around 1210, had said that they could be found in Kent in England. That was untrue too. Ireland was under suspicion, but from there came reports that the birds went north in summer, which made one Sebastianus Munsterus, author of a much-read *Cosmographia,* place them on the Orkney Islands. To people living on the European continent the Orkneys were sufficiently far away to harbor such trees.

The *Cosmographia* was published at Basle in 1598, and that the legend still existed at that time was due to an unusual combination of literary cross-currents and misunderstandings.

Only a few decades earlier Konrad Gesner had written his *Historia Animalium.* Being a well-read and careful and systematic man, Gesner knew that there were many marvelous and interesting stories around which could not necessarily be trusted. The tree goose was one of the stories about which he had doubt. Here was the report of Giraldus, often quoted by others without reservation. But here was Albertus Magnus, just published in a German translation by a certain Ryff. Who was right?

Gesner knew about a priest by the name of Octavius. Octavius was an Irishman, Octavius lived in Ireland. He should know—and Gesner had been assured by others that Octavius was a truth-loving man. Gesner wrote to Octavius and received a reply in due course. "By the religion I serve I swear that everything Giraldus said about the origin of this bird is true." Gesner had no choice but to accept this statement, and others accepted Gesner in addition to Giraldus and Octavius.

And Gesner's book, which appeared for the first time in 1555, only reinforced another book, the *History of Scotland* of Boethius of Aber-

deen, published in Latin in 1527 and translated into English in 1540.[1]
Boethius had no patience with those who believed in birds growing on
trees like fruit:

Some men belevis that thir clakis [birds] grovis on treis be the nebbis
[bills]. Bot thair opinioun is vane. And because the nature and procreation
of this clakis is strange, we have maid na lytyll laboure and deligence to
serche ye treuth and verite yairof [thereof], we have salit throw ye seis
[sailed through the seas] quhare thir clakis ar bred, and I fynd be gret experience that the nature of the seis is mair relevant caus of thair procrea-
tioun than ony uthir [any other] thyng.

Boethius was not only sure that it was mainly "the nature of the
seis" which caused the whole thing, he also had received a rather complete impression of the stages of the development.

All treis that are cassin in the seis be proces of tyme apperis first worm-
eetin [worm-eaten] and in the small boris and hollis thairof growis small
worms. The wormis first shaw [show] thair haid and feit and last of all thay
schaw their plumis and wyngis. Finally, guhan thay are cumyn [come =
grown] to the just mesure and quantite of geis [geese] thay fle in the aire
as othir fowlis dois, as was notably provyn, in yeir of God ane thousand iii
hundred lxxx [1380] in sicht of mony pepyll, besyde the castell of Petslego.

As further proof for his theory Boethius related that once a tree was
found at the seashore and was cut open by means of a saw with the
consent of the "Lard" of the ground. It was found to be riddled with
"a multitude of wormis," "mony" of them with "baith heid, feit, and
wyngis." However, they had no "fedderis" (feathers).

Two more reports, both originating in England, have to be cleared
out of the way first before an attempt can be made to disentangle this
multiply intertwined coil of beliefs, adopted prejudices, and real
observations.

The first of the two, in spite of Boethius's hammering at the belief
that there is a specific goose-bearing tree, defends just that point of
view. The book in which it appeared, in 1597 in London, was called
Herball, written (or better compiled) by one Gerard who is called a
"Master in Chirurgerie."

[1] *The Hystory and Croniclis of Scotland, with the cosmography and dyscription
thairof, compilit be the noble Clerk Maister Hector Boece, Channon of Aber-
deene.—Translatit laitly in our vulgar and commoun langage be Maister Johne
Belleden, Archedene of Murray, and Imprentit in Edinburgh, be me, Thomas
Davidson, prenter to the Kyngis nobyll grace.*

In the north parts of Scotland, and the Ilands adjacent called Orchades (Orkneys) are found certaine trees, whereon doe growe certaine shell fishes, of a white colour tending to russet; wherein are contained little living foules whom we call Barnakles, in the north of England Brant Geese, and in Lancashire Tree Geese; but the other that do fall upon the land, perish, and come to nothing: thus much by the writings of others and also from the mouths of people of those parts . . . they spawne, as it were, in March or Aprill; the Geese are found in Maie or June, and come to fulnesse of feathers in the moneth after.

A Relation Concerning Barnacles even found its way into the *Philosophical Transactions of the Royal Society* of the year 1677/78. The *Relation* was, of course, much more carefully worded than any of the other books quoted, either because it was written for such an important scientific society, or else because the reporter, Sir Robert Moray, was "lately one of his Majesties Council for the Kingdom of Scotland." He wrote:

Being in the Island of East (Uist), I saw lying upon the shore a cut of a large Firr tree of about 2½ foot diameter, and 9 or 10 foot long; which had lain so long out of the water that it was very dry: And most of the shells that had formerly cover'd it, were worn or rubb'd off. Only on the parts that lay next to the ground, there still hung multitudes of little Shells: having within them little Birds, perfectly shap'd, supposed to be Barnacles. . . . The Shells hang at the Tree by a neck longer than the Shell. It [the neck] is made of a kind of filmy substance, round and hollow, and creased, not unlike the Wind-pipe of a Chicken; spreading out broadest where it is fastened to the Tree, from which it seems to draw and to convey the matter which serves for the growth and vegetation of the Shell and of the little Bird within it. . . .

The most important sentence of all this, good as the description of the observation is, is the last. It reads:

All being dead and dry, I did not look after the Internal parts of them, nor did I ever see any of the little Birds alive, nor met with anybody that did. Only some credible persons have assured me they have seen some as big as their fist.

It is clear from this last sentence that Sir Robert had his doubts whether the strange forms he saw actually *were* little birds—and the readiness to accept them as such is actually the error which held the whole story alive.

From the zoological point of view the "Barnacle Goose" is fully explained, and has been since about 1700. To begin with, there exists such a bird as was always described; it is the *Anser bernicla* of Linnaeus's system, the name being a deliberate allusion to the legend. Of course Albertus had been perfectly correct when he said that he had seen these birds breed and multiply in precisely the same manner as any other bird.

What Giraldus and all the others after him had reported as the "young" birds—today we would say "larvae"—were not birds at all, but specimens of a strange-looking member of the crab family. The scientific name of the creature is *Lepas anatifera* and, when fully grown, it looks very much like Sir Robert Moray's description. A tough leathery "stem" clings to a piece of driftwood, while the main part of the animal is enclosed in a shell resembling the customary bivalves. A thicket of appendages protrudes from the shell, looking very much like the wet plumage of a bird.

Boethius had brought a third animal into it, the much-feared Teredo or shipworm. To express it in modern terms: he took Teredo to be an early stage of Lepas and Lepas to be the undeveloped bird. Three different creatures were thought to be connected by a marvelous and weird metamorphosis; small wonder that the result was fantastic.

Unfortunately this perfectly satisfactory zoological explanation is only one of the various explanations required. There are still some unanswered questions. One of them is why Giraldus, who has to be regarded as the first reporter simply because we don't know anything about his probable predecessors, accepted the idea of a bird growing out of a piece of wood at all. The other is why this legend, once it existed, was concentrated upon the wild goose which Linnaeus dubbed *Anser bernicla*.

The latter question was answered some time ago by a professional linguist, Professor Max Müller, whose book *Lectures on the Science of Language* was published in London in 1864. Müller thought—and so far nobody had any better suggestion to offer—that it was merely the result of a linguistic confusion.

The birds in question, he said, became known first from Ireland and were therefore referred to as Irish Geese. The Latin name for Ireland being *Hibernia,* Irish Geese would logically be *Hibernicae* or *Hiberniculae.* The barnacles, the Lepas of zoology, were called *Bernaculae.* All that was necessary was to shorten the word *Hiberniculae* to *Berniculae,* and birds and crabs differed by one letter only. Misunderstandings were easy, but would have been cleared up quickly and would have failed to do any harm if it had not been that the

Lepas anatifera

Bernaculae had a shape in which the imagination could "recognize" an "unripe bird."

This leaves only one question, the question of whether the "recognition" of Lepas was, so to speak, the fulfillment of an existing legend or belief, with purely incidental fixation on the Hiberniculae for linguistic reasons.

That question has not received any satisfactory answer so far, but there is a possibility that there was such a legend, of the same order as the other legend that certain tropical flowers, at a certain stage of their development, separate from the plant that bore them and fly away as butterflies.

One Dr. Carus, author of a German *History of Zoology,* thought that he might be able to point to Semitic sources. He said that the Jewish book Sohar contains a reference to a Rabbi Abba who told that he had seen a tree with fruits from which birds emerged. Such a short reference might, of course, be understood or misunderstood in many ways and does not sound too convincing. However, it is true that Jewish and Arabic literature do contain more conclusive statements of that sort.

The tales of Sindbad the Sailor provide one possible source. Among the marvels he saw in the Indian Ocean Sindbad mentions "a bird that cometh forth from a sea-shell and layeth its eggs and hatcheth them upon the surface of the water, and never cometh forth from the sea, upon the face of the earth" (Lane translation). That these tales were not translated in their entirety until the first decade of the eighteenth century has no bearing on the question. The Sindbad tales, when carefully analyzed, are found to contain so little original material that it can be assumed that each incident was known earlier and could be found somewhere, and therefore might have made its way to Europe separately.

What "Sindbad" actually meant is not quite certain. The lines may refer to the strange breeding habits of the paper nautilus (*Argonauta argo*), an octopus which, like the real nautilus (*Nautilus pompilius*), produces a shell that resembles a large snail shell. But while Nautilus and its shell are inseparable, Argonauta and its shell are not—or, I should have said, *her* shell, since in the case of Argonauta only the female produces a shell. That shell serves as a brood chamber for the eggs and is discarded when incubation is over and done with. That, of course, would be a "bird" which "comes forth from a sea-shell" but since it occurs in the Mediterranean Sea too, it is hard to see why it should be mentioned as a marvel of the Indies.

Pliny, who often was the source of the storyteller of the Sindbad tales, mostly second and third hand, mentions the nautilus "or, as some say, pompilos" really meaning Argonauta, without saying anything about the habits of incubation just discussed.

Since there were such stories around in the Near East, Carus may have guessed correctly in thinking that the literary origin of the tree geese is to be sought somewhere along the shores of the southeastern Mediterranean, but that it remained uncertain and groping until a zoological fixation on Lepas and a geographical fixation on Ireland and England took place. But we must not forget that such exchanges of natural-history lore of the marvelous, as evidenced by Oderich, often go both ways, and that Ireland was in as nebulous a distance to the peoples of the eastern Mediterranean as the East and India were to the North Europeans.

It is perfectly possible that this rather stable bit of natural lore did start with Lepas, and in the North, and that it made its way to the East, where for lack of Lepas it had to be projected onto something else.

The East was all the more receptive, since it also had a more or less indigenous share of semi-vegetables, of which the vegetable lamb of

Brother Oderich was only the most outstanding example. One, little known to naturalists, is described in an interesting book which was privately printed in 1858. Its author was one Dr. L. Lewysohn, who called himself "Preacher of the Israelitic Congregation of Worms." The title of the book is *Zoologie des Talmuds* (Zoology of the Talmud). It consists of a systematic arrangement and identification of all the animals mentioned in the Talmud; with special indices of the Greek, Hebrew, Latin, and German names. The section on "Fabulous Animals" tells of the *Jidra,* "an animal whose bones are used to perform magic." It is described as being of human shape; whether it is also of human size is nowhere stated. The Jidra grows from the soil "like a pumpkin" and is attached to its roots by the umbilical cord. It eats the plants which are within reach and is mobile within the radius given by the length of its umbilical cord. Any animal or human which enters its circle is killed at once. In order to kill a Jidra the hunter has to take hold of the cord and pull it out of the ground or else break the cord by shooting at it with arrows.

This fable influenced one version of the story of the "vegetable lamb" and also seems to have contributed a few features to the legends around the mandrake plant.

Later books on natural history had a simple and pat explanation for the vegetable lamb: they blamed it all on the existence of a certain fern that grows in many Asiatic countries and which represents an interesting oddity. The fern develops a thick and heavy horizontal semi-root which runs a few inches below the surface. The real roots descend from this pseudo-root. Occasionally it happens that there are two pairs of vertical roots descending from the horizontal pseudo-root so that the whole, especially when dried, bears some resemblance to a four-legged animal with a tuft of greens in lieu of a head. As if to increase the similarity, the whole root system, particularly the thick pseudo-root, is covered with fibers which suggest a pelt. And the sap of those roots is reddish, like thin blood. It may be remarked that the plant is not edible.

Western naturalists, when examining specimens of this fern, felt that here they had found the solution to the bothersome riddle of the "vegetable lamb" or *barometz* popularized by Oderich via "Mandeville." It was for this reason that Karl von Linné, or Carolus Linnaeus, the great Swedish systematician, called the fern *Polypodium barometz,* though the name was later changed to *Cibrotum glamescens.*

It seemed to be at least as good a vegetable lamb as Lepas was an unripe vegetable bird, and one version of the story itself is probably explained by it. That is the version in which the barometz grows out of the ground, being attached to its root system by its umbilical cord and capable of feeding only as far as that cord will reach—a perfect counterpart to the Jidra of the Talmud.

Traders who brought the fur called Persian lamb to the West claimed that it owed its wonderfully fine wool to the fact that it was not really the fur of an animal, but the fur of such a vegetable lamb. This story also accounts for the name of barometz, which is a corruption of the diminutive of the Slavonic word for sheep. It would be wrong to conclude that the fur traders invented the story "out of thin air" in order to protect their trade secret—namely, that these furs came from just-born or even unborn lambs. Most probably they just adapted an existing story of a vegetable lamb, and the Talmudic legend may have been the starting point.

The other version of the tale of the barometz is not quite so fantastic; it merely claims that there are certain trees growing somewhere in the East which bear fruit from which little sheep emerge. It was never made clear whether those little sheep then grew up, separated from the tree, and ran away, or whether they remained part of the plant.

Because the strange fern root does not account for this latter version

Vegetable lamb plant (from a printed edition of Sir John Mandeville)

some authors have felt that it is not a fully satisfactory explanation and that another and more comprehensive one was needed. Whereupon the British naturalist Henry Lee made a survey of all the offshoots of the tale that he could find and, after digesting the material and tracing its sources, announced an explanation of his own.[2]

It is a startling explanation and can be expressed in one sentence: The barometz is really the cotton plant!

"In tracing the development of the early and truthful accounts of the cotton plant," he wrote, referring to the reports rendered by Herodotus, Theophrastus, and Julius Pollux, "into the complete fable of the compound plant-animal we shall find it, as is the case with some other myths of the Middle Ages, attributable to two principal causes: 1) the misinterpretation of ambiguous or figurative language, and 2) the similarity of appearance of two actually different and incongruous objects."

The latter refers to the similarity in appearance and texture of cotton and wool, the former to figures of speech like "the fleece that grows on trees," a perfectly good simile for cotton, provided it is not taken literally.

The error seems to have started with the choice of one particular word. Theophrastus, one of the very first authors to mention cotton, needed a word for the unripe cottonseed pod and chose *melon*. This word covered well what he had in mind because it has several meanings. One of the meanings of *melon* is "apple," or any other tree fruit; the other meaning is "sheep." It is easy to see why he should have chosen such a term, which indicated not only that the thing under discussion was a tree-fruit but also that it was, figuratively speaking, a sheep, a wool-bearer.

Unfortunately this choice made life difficult for translators, who did not have a word to cover both meanings. They had, in their respective languages, the choice of translating it either as "spring apple" or as "spring sheep," and since wool, or a vegetable substitute for wool, was under discussion it is not hard to guess which word they used. Then all that was necessary was to take literally what was probably still figurative language . . . and the sheep that grows on a tree came into being.

[2] Henry Lee, *The Vegetable Lamb of Tartary* (London, 1887).

CHAPTER 4

The Sirrush of the Ishtar Gate

W<small>HEN</small> on June 3, 1887, Professor Robert Koldewey of Germany, on a hurried two-day visit to the site of ancient Babylon, picked up a fragment of old brick, one surface of which was covered with a bright blue glaze, he probably expected to make an archaeological discovery, but he did not dream how big a discovery it would turn out to be. And he certainly did not imagine that it would pose a zoological puzzle which is still as provocative today as it was a half-century ago.

In any case Professor Koldewey did not return to this site for more than ten years. This time he spent the last three days of the year 1897 looking for more bits of old glazed brick. The administrators of the Royal Museum in Berlin and of the German Orient Society had hinted that they had funds available for excavations in Babylon, provided that interesting results could be expected. The evidence Koldewey collected on his second trip proved sufficiently conclusive to convince even these stay-at-home gentlemen.

Everything turned out as neatly as it does in novels. "Excavations were commenced on March 26, 1899, on the east side of the Kasr to the north of the Ishtar Gate," Professor Koldewey wrote later. Then, in 1902, after being buried many centuries, the famous Ishtar Gate itself emerged once more into the sunlight. Although partly ruined, it proved to be a most impressive sight. The Ishtar Gate is an enormous semicircular arch flanked by gigantic walls and opening toward a procession way of considerable length, which is also flanked right and left by walls. The building material is brick, glazed bright blue, yellow, white, and black. To increase the splendor, the walls of the gate and the procession way are covered with bas-reliefs of unusual beauty, showing animals in very lifelike positions. Rows of gravely walking lions grace the walls of the procession way. The walls of the gate are covered from top to bottom with alternating rows of two other animals, one of them a strong and fierce bull (the re'em; see page 15); the other—here is where the zoological puzzle begins.

That other animal is commonly referred to as the Dragon of Babylon and it is the same "animal" that is mentioned by that name in the Bible. The Babylonian name for it has been preserved in cuneiform inscriptions, but there is some slight doubt as to the correct pronunciation. At first the sign (it denotes the plural of the word) was read *sîr-ruššû;* the name would, therefore be *sirrush.* But it has also been read *muš-ruššû* (*mushrush*) and translated loosely into German as *Prachtschlange.* This could be just as loosely rendered in English as "Splendor Serpent" or "Glamour Snake." However, until one of those terms is generally accepted, it is better to use sirrush, which is the term Koldewey preferred.

To give an impression of the size of the whole brick structure I quote from Koldewey's description:

The rows are repeated one above the other; dragons and bulls are never mixed in the same horizontal row, but a line of bulls is followed by one of *sirrush.* Each single representation of an animal occupies a height of 13 brick courses, and between them are 11 plain courses, so that the distance from the foot of one to the foot of the next is 24 courses. These 24 courses together measure almost exactly two meters (6 feet 8 inches) or four Babylonian ells in height.

Originally there were thirteen rows of animals, beginning with a top row of sirrush; each of the eight lower rows contained at least forty animals and each of the five upper rows at least fifty-one, so that the grand total of animal pictures on the gate amounts to about 575.

It is certainly an impressive structure, and it is not at all surprising that King Nebuchadnezzar, who was responsible for reconstructing the Ishtar Gate, was very proud of it. When it was finished he composed an inscription which was written down in cuneiform characters for all to read. With the lack of modesty then customary it began:

Nabû-ku-dúr-ri-u-ṣu-úr [Nebuchadnezzar], the King of Babylon, the pious Prince, ruling by the will and grace of Marduk [the supreme god of the Babylonians], supreme ruler of the City, beloved by Nebo [son of Marduk, supreme god of the neighboring city of Borsippa], of clever cunning, who never tires . . . and ever works for the welfare of Babylon, the wise one, first-born son of Nabopolassar, King of Babylon, this is I.

Nebuchadnezzar's sirrush (from a photograph of the reconstructed Ishtar Gate)

The inscription then goes on to tell that owing to a repeated heightening of the road to Babylon the clearance of the gates had steadily diminished, so that Nebuchadnezzar finally ordered a complete reconstruction. All this is in perfect keeping with the archaeological findings, so that there is no reason to doubt either the veracity or the genuineness of the inscription, which is, incidentally, not quite complete. The inscription does not neglect to mention the pictures of the animals:

Fierce bulls [the original says *rimi*] and grim dragons I put onto the gateyard [meaning its walls] and thus supplied the gates with such overflowing rich splendor that all humanity may view it with wonderment.

Humanity did view it with wonderment for centuries—and now does so again, after excavation and reconstruction—and the pictures of the *rimi,* or re'ems, were even copied elsewhere (see Chapter 1). In ancient Greece, too, the Ishtar Gate was well known by name and reputation, but the name used was the "Gate of Semiramis."

Of course no one of those who saw the Ishtar Gate in those days was plagued by zoological scruples. The lions on the walls of the procession way were lions, the bulls on the gate were bulls—even if they

Sirrush, redrawn in modern style from the Ishtar Gate bas-relief, assuming the "headdress" to have been fleshy appendages

did look slightly unusual; and that King Nebuchadnezzar's artisans had seen fit to add a monster of their own invention did not trouble anyone. They had also occasionally pictured eagles with the heads of bearded men, and other hybrid monsters. In short, the pictures of the sirrush caused no astonishment. It required the tremendously enlarged knowledge of the later age that excavated and reconstructed the Ishtar Gate to feel astonishment about those pictures.

The bas-reliefs of sirrush are very definite in outline and show a slender body covered with scales, a long slender scaly tail, and a long slim scaly neck bearing a serpent's head. Although the mouth is closed, a long forked tongue protrudes. There are flaps of skin attached to the back of the head, which is adorned (and armed) with a straight horn—possibly a pair of horns, since the pictures of the re'em also show only one horn. "It is remarkable," wrote Koldewey, "that, in spite of the scales, the animal possesses hair. Three corkscrew ringlets fall over the head near the ears; and on the neck, where a lizard's comb would be, is a long row of curls."

Most remarkable, however, are the feet. The forefeet are those of a catlike animal, say a panther, but the hind feet are those of a bird. They are very large and four-toed, covered with strong scales. And in spite of the combination of so many different characteristics the sirrush looks tremendously alive, at least as much so as the re'em shown next to it, if not more so.

If the Ishtar Gate had been excavated a century earlier, this combination of catlike forefeet and birdlike hind feet would have been sufficient proof that the "Glamour Snake" was no whit more credible than the winged bulls and man-headed birds of Assyrian and Babylonian mythology. During these hundred years, however, Georges Cuvier had become the "Father of Paleontology," Professor O. C. Marsh in America had earned the title of "Father of Dinosaurs," and our conceptions of what was biologically possible had changed greatly. Paleontologists had discovered fossil animals that sported incredibly long necks and tails, big bodies and small heads, serpent heads with horns on them (and possibly even forked tongues, although unfortunately tongues do not fossilize), and similar attributes. They had even found a type of dinosaurs that walked upright on their birdlike hind legs, waving smaller five-toed forelegs in the air. They had even found some that seemingly had been undecided whether to walk erect or not and that probably used both types of locomotion alternately, according to fancy or to circumstances. A living and fairly large lizard from Australia (*Chlamydosaurus*) had come to light, which walked on all fours under normal conditions and on its hind legs only when in a hurry.

Consequently, the sirrush suddenly began to look very real and quite possible. It was thought at first that it might be a picture of a saurian. Professor Koldewey, who had given more thought than anyone else to the identity of sirrush, wrote in 1913 that the Babylonian dragon corresponds in most features to extinct saurians. "The *sirrush* . . . far exceeds all other fantastic creatures in the uniformity of its physiological conceptions," he stated, and then concluded with a sigh: "If only the forelegs were not so emphatically and characteristically feline, such an animal might actually have existed." Knowing that the Bible explicitly asserts the existence of sirrush, he ventured the guess that the priests of Babylon kept some reptile and exhibited it in the semi-darkness of a temple chamber as a living sirrush. "In this case there would be small cause for wonder that the creature did not survive the concoction of hair and bitumen administered to it by Daniel." [1]

This is from Koldewey's first comprehensive report about his Baby-

[1] In the Apocrypha Daniel is said to have killed the "dragon" by giving it a pill made of bitumen and hair.

lonian excavations. In 1918—five years later—he wrote a beautifully illustrated folio tome on the Ishtar Gate and had to wage another struggle with the dragon. This time he grew bolder. Although still somewhat bothered by the very catlike formation of the forelegs, he cited lists of extinct saurians showing one or another feature of the sirrush and concluded that the animal, if it did exist, would have to be classified as a bird-footed dinosaur. After approaching his conclusions cautiously he suddenly stated: "The Iguanodon of the Cretaceous layers of Belgium is the closest relative of the Dragon of Babylon."

This development in the attitude of a top-ranking expert is interesting and significant. He started out by finding something he was not looking for—especially since it was not even in his field of knowledge—and when he realized what it was he had found, he had many entirely justified doubts. But the uncanny biological credibility of the ancient bas-relief compelled him to dismiss those doubts one by one until he had to state that the picture showed an animal closely resembling a known fossil saurian.

The story is surprising in more than one respect. The Ishtar Gate was enlarged and adorned with those bas-reliefs by order of a king who is known mainly because he is repeatedly mentioned in the Bible. And the two most mysterious biblical animals appear side by side— or rather, one on top of the other—on that gate: the re'em which should not be trusted even though his strength is great, and the dragon that was kept in a temple in Babylon and worshiped by the inhabitants of that city until it was killed by Daniel.

The re'em was finally identified as the urus. How about the sirrush? Why not consider it simply an invention? Koldewey himself said that this seemed unlikely if only for the reason that the picture of the sirrush remained unchanged for thousands of years, a fact which does not apply to the other fantastic creations of the Babylonians. The sirrush appeared in recognizable form in the earliest Babylonian art and was still pictured under the reign of Nebuchadnezzar, about 604–561 B.C.

Modern science has little trouble in identifying the type of saurian to which sirrush belonged, despite the facts that fossil remains of the exact variety are not known and that the artist seems to have made some minor mistakes. Now, it is certain that the Babylonians knew nothing of paleontology. Their sirrush is either a direct portrayal of something they knew or a miracle of correct imagination, but it is certainly not a "reconstruction." Besides, there is no known site of fossil dinosaur bones anywhere near Babylon.

Since we do not know of a living or recently extinct animal that could have served as the model for the sirrush, we have the choice of either giving up at this point or proceeding under the assumption that the sirrush actually *is* a direct portrayal of an animal unknown to present-day zoology. We do not need to be troubled by the fact that it would have been a most unlikely animal for the vicinity of even ancient Babylon. The re'em was also extinct in Mesopotamia at the time but it lived on in Europe for about twenty centuries. To the Babylonians the re'em was a "monster from afar"; the same might easily have applied to the sirrush.

But from where?

Let us assume that it is an animal, one we still have not discovered. The only place where it could still exist without having been found is Central Africa, the area of the Rainy Forest and the Congo Basin. And it is suspicious, to say the very least, that rumors about a large unknown and ferocious animal come from just this area. One such rumor was picked up, quite accidentally, by the big-game hunter Hans Schomburgk, years before Koldewey wrote his first comprehensive work.

Hans Schomburgk was employed by Carl Hagenbeck, a dealer in wild animals for zoological gardens who maintained an enormous but "transient" zoological garden in Stellingen near Hamburg. Following up a different rumor, Hagenbeck had sent Schomburgk to the interior of Liberia. There were stories of an animal which the natives referred to as a "large black pig," and it was likely that this was either an actual wild pig unknown to science or else that the term referred to the pygmy hippopotamus. As for the latter, there were two schools of thought, one that it was just a legend, the other that it was extinct. Hans Schomburgk in 1911 found that the pygmy hippopotamus was neither legend nor extinct (see Chapter 22).

In 1912 Schomburgk returned to Hamburg and to Hagenbeck with this information, and brought back with him another astonishing tale. He mentioned it with hesitation and was both relieved and surprised that Hagenbeck did not laugh at it. Instead he informed Schomburgk that he had repeatedly received similar reports from other sources. These reports were of native tales about a large animal, "half dragon, half elephant," which was supposed to live in inaccessible swamps.

Hagenbeck added that it was difficult to obtain a more detailed description, and Schomburgk knew precisely what this meant. There is, or used to be in the days of colonialism, one major problem which Schomburgk, at a later date, described in a lecture as follows: "The natives, wishing to please the white visitor and hoping for a valuable gift at the same time, are only too ready to assert that they know of an animal in their territory with blue skin, six legs, one eye, and four tusks. The size is entirely up to the questioner; the native will tell him what he thinks the white man wants to hear."

Such an exaggerated desire to oblige makes experienced hunters careful. In this case, however, even without specific questioning, the informants usually mentioned that the animal had a single horn.

Schomburgk apparently had never heard of this animal when he went to Liberia. But when he arrived on the shores of Lake Bangweolo, an environment that seemed ideally suited for hippopotamuses, and asked why there were none, the natives answered matter-of-factly that there was a good reason. They—I am quoting now from Schomburgk's book, *Wild und Wilde im Herzen Afrikas*—

reported that there is an animal living in this lake, which, though smaller than a hippo, kills them and feeds on them. It must be fully amphibian in its habits; it never comes to the shore and its footprints were never found. Unfortunately I thought this story to be a fairy tale and did not investigate further. Later I spoke to Carl Hagenbeck about it and I am now convinced that it must be a saurian of some type. I am of this opinion because Hagenbeck received reports from other sources that fully agree with my own observations and with the reports of the natives questioned by me. Hagenbeck sent a special expedition to Lake Bangweolo; unfortunately this expedition did not even find the lake.

In 1913, the German government sent an expedition under the leadership of Freiherr von Stein zu Lausnitz to make a general survey of its colony in the Cameroons. The official report of this expedition, which is still in manuscript, contains a fairly extensive section dealing with Schomburgk's unknown animal. It is only natural that Captain von Stein worded his report with the utmost caution, referring guardedly to a "very mysterious thing," which "possibly does not exist except in the imagination of the natives," but which is "probably based on something more tangible." Captain von Stein's evidence consisted, as he expressed it, of "narratives of natives of the former German colony" (Cameroons) about a "creature feared very much by the Negroes of certain parts of the territory of the Congo, the lower Ubangi, the Sanga, and the Ikelemba rivers." He stressed the fact that the narratives came from "experienced guides who repeated characteristic features of the story without knowing each other." The natives named the creature *mokéle-mbêmbe,* but whether the name had any special meaning was uncertain. Captain von Stein wrote:

The creature is reported not to live in the smaller rivers like the two Likualas, and in the rivers mentioned only a few individuals are said to exist. At the time of our expedition a specimen was reported from the non-navigable part of the Sanga River, somewhere between the two rivers Mbaio and Pikunda; unfortunately in a part of the river that could not be explored due to the brusque end of our expedition.[2] We also heard about the alleged animal at the Ssômbo River. The narratives of the natives result in a general description that runs as follows:

The animal is said to be of a brownish-gray color with a smooth skin, its size approximately that of an elephant; at least that of a hippopotamus. It is said to have a long and very flexible neck and only one tooth but a very long one; *some say it is a horn.* A few spoke about a long muscular tail like that of an alligator. Canoes coming near it are said to be doomed; the animal is said to attack the vessels at once and to kill the crews but without eating the bodies. The creature is said to live in the caves that have been washed out by the river in the clay of its shores at sharp bends. It is said to climb the shore even at daytime in search of food; its diet is said to be entirely vegetable. This feature disagrees with a possible explanation as a myth. The preferred plant was shown to me, it is a kind of liana with large white blossoms, with a milky sap and apple-like fruits. At the Ssômbo River I was shown a path said to have been made by this animal in order to get at its food. The path was fresh and there were plants of the described type near by. But since there were too many tracks of elephants, hippos, and other large mammals it was impossible to make out a particular spoor with any amount of certainty.

It is a pity that Baron von Stein did not have more time; he might have suceeded in actually finding the mokéle-mbêmbe.

As for the animal in Lake Bangweolo which Schomburgk was told about, an Englishman, J. E. Hughes, got little more information. In his book *Eighteen Years on Lake Bangweulu* (he preferred this spelling) he reported a conversation with the son of the chief of the Wauschi tribe about the animal which is called *chipekwe* by this tribe. The young man proudly told that his grandfather had taken part in or at least witnessed a chipekwe hunt.

[2] This refers to the outbreak of the First World War.

A good description of the hunt has been handed down by tradition. It took many of the best hunters the whole day spearing it with their large Viwingo harpoons—the same as they use today for the hippo. It is described as having a smooth dark body, without bristles, and armed with a single smooth white horn fixed like the horn of a rhinoceros, but composed of smooth white ivory, very highly polished. It is a pity that they didn't keep it, as I would have given them anything they liked for it.

Hughes also knew a Rhodesian administrator who said that one night he heard a tremendous splashing in the lake near which he was camped, and the next morning found a spoor which he had never seen before.

During the interval between the World Wars news dispatches carried a story of a Monsieur Lepage, said to have been a Belgian, who was quoted as saying that he had seen two "dinosaurs" from a distance and that they looked like the famous Iguanodon, the remains of which had been found on Belgian soil. Lepage said that he had a powerful rifle, but with two animals he did not dare to use it. He just kept quiet until the animals made off, and then he advanced to the place where they had been, where he found large three-toed spoors, such as an Iguanodon would make and as have actually been found fossilized in England.

Scientists were unanimous in saying that this was simply a story and nobody had to believe it. (This is my personal feeling too.) But a few zoologists went on to say that it must be untrue solely for the reason that Africa was now well enough known to make the existence of an undiscovered large animal impossible. These statements produced another witness. This was Frau Ilse von Nolde,[3] who said that she had lived for ten years in the eastern part of Angola, in the area of the Kuango river, and that she had talked to "innumerable" natives about an unknown animal which they called *coje ya menia.* I suspect that Frau von Nolde's spelling of the native name is influenced by the official language of Angola, which is Portuguese. The translation, in any event, is "lion of the water."

All the reports were as follows: It is a very large animal, only a little smaller than the hippopotamus. It lives in rivers and in stagnant waters but it does go on land, just like the hippopotamus. During the rainy season when the water is high, it comes out of the Kuanza to go into the smaller

[3] Her article appeared in the *Deutsche Kolonial-Zeitung* (German Colonial Gazette), 1939, No. 4, pp. 123–24.

tributaries and lagoons. At night one can then hear its mighty roars. It will pursue the hippopotamus relentlessly and hippopotami flee it and leave the area. . . . Often there is a wild chase of pursuer and pursued hippopotamus which will be in the water or on land. The coje ya menia will kill it [the hippo] but does not eat it by any means. According to the stories the hippo will be torn apart with claws or teeth with unexplained bloodthirstiness. Once I met a native at the banks of the Lui, a tributary of the Kuango and noticed that he wore sandals made of hippopotamus skin. I asked him whether he had hunted the hippo himself and he replied matter-of-factly, as if it were the most natural thing in the world, "No, I found it; it had been killed by a coje ya menia." . . . All the people dwelling along the tributaries of the Kuango know about the coje ya menia; they had heard it roar during the night but none of them has ever seen one—at least none of those I talked to—and they say that it will come ashore during the night only and hide in the water during the day.

These are the highlights from the article by Frau von Nolde, who filled the remaining space with assertions that this could not be a case of mistaken identity with a known predator, quoting all the native names for the larger animals of the area to show that the words coje ya menia are used exclusively for this unknown animal.

All this taken together hardly permits any conclusion but the one that there *is* a large and dangerous animal hiding in the shallow waters and rivers of Central Africa. Something which might be called a "reptilian flavor" in the descriptions made Carl Hagenbeck say that he conceived of the unknown animal as a medium-sized dinosaur.

Hagenbeck, unlike M. Lepage, probably did not use the word "dinosaur" in its strict zoological sense. He meant a large reptile— large as compared to the normal reptiles of our time, and some of them are sizable. Hagenbeck himself at one time had a 30-foot snake for sale and he knew of crocodiles which were almost as long. A reptile can be both large *and* extinct and still not be one of the dinosaurs; many reptiles that lived when the dinosaurs flourished were not, strictly speaking, dinosaurs themselves.

The next question is, naturally, whether a large reptile could have survived in Central Africa. The answer is that if any survived anywhere it would *have* to be in Central Africa.

Here are the facts on which this statement is based.

The true dinosaurs, and the other large reptiles associated with them, became extinct at the end of the Cretaceous period, about sixty million years ago. We do not know precisely why life forms which had flourished for many millions of years suddenly disappeared from the scene, but all the theories blame climatic changes. One of the first theories advanced, so to speak the classical theory, postulated a slight lowering of temperature, which could have reduced the volume of vegetation, principally of those plants that furnished food to the large plant-eating dinosaurs of the *Brontosaurus* tribe. Thus these dinosaurs were reduced in numbers. As a result the carnivorous dinosaurs, that preyed on the plant-eaters, also had difficulties in finding enough food, and there began a relentless hunt for the herbivorous survivors until the last of them had been killed. Then the flesh-eating dinosaurs became extinct, too—partly from starvation, partly from fighting among themselves. Such mammals as existed then could not furnish a dinosaur's normal meal, being usually about the size of rats. Besides, they made their homes in places inaccessible to dragons: in burrows, in hollow tree trunks, in nests in tree tops, or between the roots of trees.

This explanation sounds convincing, for there is little doubt that, once a reduction in the number of large plant-eaters took place, such a cycle was inevitable. Plant-eaters can often turn flesh-eaters in a pinch, but normally it fails to work the other way round. The other explanations for the disappearance of dinosaurs that have found support proceed along much the same lines, differing only in the point at which the cycle begins. For example, it is an established fact that there existed a number of small dinosaurs, about as large as small dogs, that made their living by feasting upon the eggs laid by the big dinosaurs. Also it seems likely that a few varieties of birds of that time developed a fondness for dinosaur eggs; and doubtless some of the early mammals were skilled in that pursuit, too. An increase of small egg-robbers might well have made life miserable and very uncertain for the large egg-layers. As soon as conditions were no longer just perfect for them, they could not maintain themselves against new enemies.

More recently some field work with living reptiles has provided another clue as regards the extinction of the dinosaurs. These experiments have shown that the "thermal tolerance" of reptiles is surprisingly low. They don't mind cold half as much as one would expect, but when they are subjected to the direct rays of the sun their blood temperature, lacking any regulation by sweat glands, shoots up rapidly, inevitably ending the life of the specimen. These experiments also suggest how a comparatively small change in climatic conditions could have ended the life of all the large forms. All that was needed was the change of a swampy forest into drier plains. The dinosaurs, exposed to sunlight and without cooling water, would have died off literally from heat stroke. In fact, this may account for some of the large accumulations of dinosaur bones which have been found.

The enormous dinosaur beds near Tendaguru in East Africa show that something like this also happened in Africa. There can be no doubt that, there as well as elsewhere, the largest forms are gone. But for medium-sized forms the story is somewhat different.

Elsewhere in the world the last sixty million years were marked by all kinds of geologic changes. Large areas were flooded by shallow seas; other areas dried up. Land bridges formed and disappeared again. Mountains were piled up by tectonic forces; volcanism was active. But Central Africa proved to be geologically stable: the African land mass of today is essentially the same as it was sixty million years ago.

Finally, the continents to the north and to the south of the 50th parallels in both hemispheres went through a series of glaciations, but although these did affect the climate between the tropics of Cancer and Capricorn to some extent, the change was not dramatic. Central Africa, then, has not undergone any geological upheavals since the Cretaceous period, and has had only minor climatic changes. If large reptiles from that time did survive, Central Africa is the most likely spot to look for them.

And this brings to an end the story of the dragon of the Ishtar Gate. It is by no means a complete story. It exhausts the available and reliable material, but the available material is by no means satisfactory. It merely points to the existence of a zoological puzzle of fantastic dimensions. As regards the solution, we'll just have to wait and hope.

CHAPTER 5

The Abominable Snowmen

Somewhere in the high valleys north of India, next to and between the highest mountain peaks of our planet, there is something unknown, or, at the very least, something unexplained. What evidence there is consists mainly of footprints. They are, as is logical, considering the high altitudes, footprints in snow. For that reason they are not only rather impermanent evidence, but have the further inconvenience that under the action of the sun's rays they will change both shape and size.

The natives of the region claim that these footprints are made by beings frightful and inimical; beings unknown to the white visitors and therefore unnamed in the visitors' languages. The white visitors would much prefer to think that the footprints were made by bears, which can be frightful and inimical if hungry enough. But this the natives energetically contradict. Not bears but "snowmen" left these footprints, and the visitors were very lucky that they came across the footprints only and missed encountering their originators.

The visitor to the Himalayas, after his return, is usually asked whether he heard anything about the snowmen and feels moved to write an article about either his or other people's experiences. The article, as a rule, begins more or less as follows: "The mystery originated very fittingly with the first Mount Everest expedition, the reconnaissance of 1921. . . ." This refers to the now famous report by the leader of that expedition, Colonel C. K. Howard-Bury, who, accompanied by five other white explorers and by twenty-six native porters, made an attempt at the north col of Mount Everest in September of that year. Using the Kharta glacier as the best means of approach, the expedition headed for the Lhakpa La, a pass at a height of 22,000 feet. There, in soft snow, they saw the tracks of

75

hares and of foxes and also, to their intense surprise, a track which could well have been made by a barefoot man.

The porters, Colonel Howard-Bury reported, at once said that these were the tracks of a *metohkangmi*.[1] He also added that this word is translatable—other terms used by the natives for the same creature, *mirka, yeti,* and *sogpa,* are not—and stated that *kangmi* means "snowman," while *metoh* is a term of disgust or revulsion which can be rendered as "abominable" or "foul." Though Colonel Howard-Bury himself made light of the idea of the existence of a special and unknown race of "snowmen" (he suggested that the tracks might have been wolf tracks), the daily press would have none of his explanation. A report from an expedition which was a preliminary survey for a later climb to the peak of the world's highest mountain made good copy all right, but the possibility of encountering a hitherto unknown race of "wild men"—that was a *story!* And the newspapermen did have a very good point: it was the natives' calm assertion versus Colonel Howard-Bury's guess, and although the colonel was an able and experienced man, just who had lived there all his life and could be expected to know what else lived in the same area? This, of course, has remained the argument ever since.

Actually Colonel Howard-Bury was not the first to report either on mysterious tracks or on the natives' assertion that there were snowmen. The earliest source known at the moment is a book by one Major L. A. Waddell, who, on the title page, is identified as having been a member of the India Army Medical Corps. The book is entitled *Among the Himalayas;* it was published in London in 1899, but his journey—from Darjeeling to northeastern Sikkim—took place in 1889. On page 223 occurs the following passage:

Some large footprints in the snow led across our track and away up to the higher peaks. These were alleged to be the trail of the hairy wild men who are believed to live amongst the eternal snows, along with the mythical white lions whose roar is reputed to be heard during storms. The belief in these creatures is universal among Tibetans. None, however, of the many

[1] In magazine and newspaper articles you can find this term in a variety of spellings, as *metoh-kangmee, metchkangmi,* and *Metch-kangmi,* substituting a "c" for an "o" in a critical place. I am following the usage of W. H. Murray, who was a member of the 1951 Reconnaissance Expedition to Everest and who seems to have some familiarity with the native tongues.

Tibetans I have interrogated on this subject could ever give me an authentic case. . . .

Major Waddell, for want of a better explanation, suggested that the tracks may have been made by a bear, most likely of the species *Ursus isabellinus.*

Another, though somewhat dubious source, which probably antedates Colonel Howard-Bury's report, is a book by a French author, Jean Marquès-Rivière. The title of his book is *L'Inde secrète et sa magie*—it is probably my fault that this title alone makes me wrap myself in several layers of the finest skepticism available. Monsieur Marquès-Rivière, in any event, says that a pilgrim assured him that the creatures were a race of human giants, neither bears nor monkeys, and that they spoke an unknown language. The pilgrim claimed to have been a member of an expedition of natives who followed a track of footprints and finally saw the snowmen. Ten "or more" of them sat in a circle; they were "10–12 feet high, beating tom-toms, oscillating and engaged in some magic rite. Their bodies were covered with hair; their faces between man and gorilla; quite naked at that great altitude, and a sadness expressed on their frightful visages."

Nobody is under any obligation to believe any of this, but whether or not the witness or the writer of the book embellished the story, it can still be taken as an independent report on the existence of such a belief among the natives.

Confirmation on the universality and casual acceptance of the belief, if it actually was still needed, came in 1922 from the leader of the second Everest expedition, General C. G. Bruce. When General Bruce stopped at the Rongbuk Monastery, located to the north of the mountain, he used the opportunity to ask the Head Lama whether he had ever heard of the metohkangmi. The Head Lama reacted to the question as if it had been about a herd of yak or something else equally generally known, and said, yes, five of them lived farther up in the Rongbuk Valley.

General Bruce apparently felt that he could not spare either the time or the manpower to go after the snowmen. In retrospect his decision to keep to the main task looks wrong, since his expedition did not climb Everest and a diversion of forces might have led to a discovery. But in recent decades expeditions have always had very specific and definite goals, just as if they were military operations.

This probably is a fundamental mistake; the earlier explorers who
went out to see what they could find seem to have been more successful on the whole. Of course it is also possible that General Bruce
simply disbelieved the whole story.

In 1925 a report appeared in Bombay, privately published and
not causing any stir discernible from a distance. Its author was an
Italian, N. A. Tombazi, who had then returned from a photographic
expedition to the southern portions of the glacier area of the
Kanchenjunga. Signor Tombazi stated simply that he had actually
seen a snowman, at an elevation of about 15,000 feet.

Intense glare prevented me seeing anything for a few seconds, but I soon
spotted the object referred to two or three hundred yards away down the
valley—unquestionably the figure in outline was exactly like a human
being, walking upright and stopping occasionally to uproot some dwarf
rhododendron. It showed dark against the snow and wore no clothing.
Within the next minute or so it had moved into some thick scrub and was
lost to view. I examined the footprints which were similar in shape to
those of a man but only 6–7 inches long by 9 inches wide at the broadest
part. Marks of five toes and instep were clear but trace of heel indistinct.
I counted five at regular intervals from 1 to 1½ feet. The prints were undoubtedly of a biped.

A stride of 12 to 18 inches is about normal for a man who is
not in a special hurry. As for the dimensions of the footprints, it
might be that the heel did not touch the ground, or at least not firmly
enough to leave an impression.

Just as Colonel Howard-Bury's report on mysterious tracks proved
not to have been the earliest, so Tombazi's report on a sighting
turned out not to be the first. An earlier one had been transmitted
by one H. J. Elwes, a Fellow of the Royal Society, to the Zoological
Society of London and had been published in the *Proceedings* for
1915. The actual witness was not Mr. Elwes himself, but a forest
officer named J. R. P. Gent, who was stationed in the vicinity of
Darjeeling and who said that he had seen humanoid creatures, called
sogpa by the local people, above the treeline. They looked more
apelike than manlike to Mr. Gent, who went on to say that they
were covered with long yellowish-brown hair. Their stride measured
from 1½ to 2 feet on reasonably flat ground. But in steep places
they seemed to "walk on their knees" so that the toe marks seemed to
point backward. This last remark is important if only because quite

a number of people have made fun of an alleged belief of the Tibetans that the feet of the snowmen point backward.

Chronologically, a story told by the English explorer Hugh Knight lies between the Elwes–Gent report and Tombazi's publication. Unfortunately I have not been able to find Knight's original story, so that the following is very much second- or even third-hand and is given essentially for the sake of completeness. Hugh Knight is reported to have seen a snowman (who was unaware of his presence) from as close a distance as twenty paces. The snowman had the size of a big man, with a barrel chest and overlong arms. His skin was yellow and covered with blondish hair. He had the high cheekbones of the mongoloids and splayed feet. Though apparently without clothing the creature carried a primitive bow. He is reported to have suddenly run off, as if in pursuit of something which Knight could not see.

The next man to write in defense of the snowmen is a famous geographer and explorer, Ronald Kaulbach. He stated that, in 1936, he had come across tracks "looking exactly as though they had been made by a barefooted man" in a pass between the valleys of the Chu and Salween rivers. There were not just one set of tracks but five of them. Kaulbach had four Sherpa porters with him. All four were agreed on the existence of the metohkangmi, but only two said that these particular tracks had been made by them; the other two were willing to admit that they *might* have been made by snow leopards. Though Kaulbach stressed that "there are no bears in that part of the country," he was told later that the tracks must have been made either by bears or by giant pandas or by an unknown species of monkeys. Kaulbach replied that neither bears nor giant pandas occur in this area, that there are no monkeys there either, and furthermore that any monkeys living there would not go above the snowline. He might have added (but didn't) that "an unknown species of monkeys" would be a very interesting discovery too.

The species of bear usually credited by far-away experts with really having made the tracks is the one known to zoologists as *Ursus arctos pruinosus*. It does occur in the Himalayas—but not everywhere, and this is a large area—and it is a large animal, growing to the dimensions of a big American grizzly. In color its fur is pale and can be nearly white, and when it is striding normally the hind feet more or less obliterate the tracks made by the front feet, producing a strange compound spoor. The telltale sign is that in addition to the five toe marks in front there are two additional marks on either side of the track, caused by the innermost and outermost toes of the hind feet.

A case of this kind of confusion was told by Frank S. Smythe in his book *The Valley of Flowers* (New York: Norton, 1949):

About four inches of snow had fallen recently, and it was obvious that the tracks had been made the previous evening after the sun had lost its power and had frozen during the night, for they were perfect impressions distinct in every detail. On the level the footmarks were as much as 13 inches in length and 6 inches in breadth, but uphill they averaged only 8 inches in length, though the breadth was the same. The stride was from 18 inches to 2 feet on the level, but considerably less uphill, and the footmarks were turned outward at about the same angle as a man's. There were the well-defined imprints of five toes, 1½ inches to 1¾ inches long and ¾ inch broad, which, unlike human toes, were arranged symmetrically. Lastly there was what at first sight appeared to be the impression of a heel, with two curious toelike impressions on either side. . . .

My photographs were developed by Kodak Ltd. of Bombay under conditions that precluded any subsequent accusation of faking and, together with my measurements and observations . . . were examined by Professor Julian Huxley, Secretary of the Zoological Society, Mr. Martin A. C. Hinton, Keeper of Zoology at the Natural History Museum [London] and Mr. R. I. Pocock. The conclusion reached by these experts was that the tracks were made by a bear. At first, due to a misunderstanding as to the exact locality in which the tracks had been seen, the bear was said to be *Ursus arctos pruinosus,* but subsequently it was decided that it was *Ursus arctos isabellinus* which is distributed throughout the western and central Himalayas. The tracks agreed in size and character with that animal and there is no reason to suppose that they could have been made by anything else.

It would be very nice, even though somewhat disappointing, if Mr. Smythe's photographs proved more than just this single case. But they do not; even though his porters had been fooled by the tracks, the Sherpas, as a rule, are well acquainted with the bear's compound spoor. Besides, bear tracks and "snowman" tracks have been found together.

More stories about strange tracks came in shortly before the outbreak of the Second World War temporarily interrupted interest in Mount Everest. In 1937 Eric Shipton and H. W. Tilman ran a survey expedition in the Karakorum. One member of their expedition and two Sherpas visited a known but remote area which is referred to as Snow Lake, and promptly found tracks: "They were roughly circular, about a foot in diameter, 9 inches deep and 18 inches apart. They lay in a straight line without any right and left stagger, nor was there any sign of overlap as would be the case with a four-footed beast. The Sherpas diagnosed them as those of a yeti. . . . A few days later, in another glacier valley, bear tracks were everywhere and were quickly recognized as such by the Sherpas." Eric Shipton had seen elsewhere such circular tracks, which indicate some melting of the snow. And Tilman, who had originally considered the whole matter as a collection of silly superstitions, openly reversed his opinion.[2]

Though these circular tracks did not show any detail, it is important that they were in a straight line. Bears can't walk that way. It is true that smaller predators, like the European fox, occasionally manage to put all four of their footprints in a straight line—in Europe they say that the fox has been "stringing"; that is, you can stretch a string over the the prints—but only small four-footed animals can do it. A large creature either needs legs like a camel's to produce such a track, or else it has to be bipedal.

One particular Sherpa who accompanied Shipton repeatedly must be mentioned now: Sen Tensing. He not only saw yeti prints on quite a number of occasions, he also once saw a yeti. In November 1949 a large group of Sherpas gathered in front of the Thyangboche Monastery for a religious festival. The monastery is located on a hilltop at an elevation of about 13,000 feet, not too far from Mount Everest; in fact, the mountain can be seen from the monastery. The Sherpas assembled in a meadow which is bordered on one side by a forest. It was out of the forest that a yeti suddenly appeared. The nearest of the Sherpas were about 80 feet away; they said that it was of the same size as they are themselves—they average 5½ feet in height—and that its whole body, except the face, was covered with reddish-brown hair.

Because Sen Tensing was known personally to Eric Shipton, W. H. Murray, and other explorers, they saw to it that he was thoroughly questioned later in the same month. The occasion was a cocktail party at the British Embassy at Katmandu. The Sherpa was brought in, still wearing climbing boots and heavy breeches, and several

---

[2] Tombazi had also been skeptical originally, referring to the yeti as a "delicious fancy" until he saw one.

Nepalese cross-examined him for half an hour. They later said not only that Sen Tensing stuck to his story all the way through but also that he could not have done so if he had not spoken the truth.

Then came the expedition of 1951, and, as W. H. Murray put it, more news of the yeti. Writing in *The Scots Magazine* (vol. LIX, no. 2, May 1953), he told the following story:

Early in November we withdrew from Everest into Sola Khombu in Nepal, and thence explored the unsurveyed ranges which lie 30–40 miles westwards. Our party split up. Shipton and Ward penetrated into the heart of the Gaurisankar range—a wild tangle of high and icy peaks—by crossing a pass of 20,000 feet, now called the Menlung La. Bourdillon and I followed them a few days later (after explorations of our own farther north). From the Menlung La we dropped 2,000 feet onto a long, westward-flowing glacier. At 18,000 feet, on its snow-covered surface we came upon the tracks of two bipeds, which were quite distinct from the tracks of Shipton and Ward. Like the latter before us, we followed the strange tracks for two miles down the glacier, because they had chosen the best route through the crevasse system. Where broad crevasses barred the way, the tracks struck sharp left or right to avoid them or dodged around little ice cliffs and pinnacles. They were the tracks of an animal using its intelligence to choose a good, safe, and therefore (in its detail) complex route. Apart from that very important observation our evidence at the best corroborates Shipton's, for the prints had been enlarged by melting and so were the round shapeless prints typical of two previous reports.

After two miles the glacier became excessively riven so the tracks diverged rightwards onto the stony morain and there we lost them. We, too, had to take to the morain. We followed it one mile to rough grazing grounds which support small herds of wild goat and sheep and presumably yetis too. On meeting Shipton and Ward we found them still in a state of subdued excitement over the tracks for they had come on them several days earlier than we, when the prints had been no more than a few hours old. Where the snow lay soft and heavy the yetis had left only the deep outline of the foot, but where it lay thin and frozen the pad marks and the five toe marks had been distinct within the print. Where the yetis had jumped the smaller crevasses the scrabble marks of their toes could be clearly seen on the far side. The prints were 6 inches wide by 12½ inches long, the gap between the prints was 9 or 10 inches. The Sherpa, Sen Tensing, who accompanied Shipton was able to identify the prints as those of two yetis. He knew well the spoor of bear and could say at once that these were not bear tracks. . . .

Eric Shipton, who had come across the tracks when they were still fresh, took a photograph which proves that, no matter how

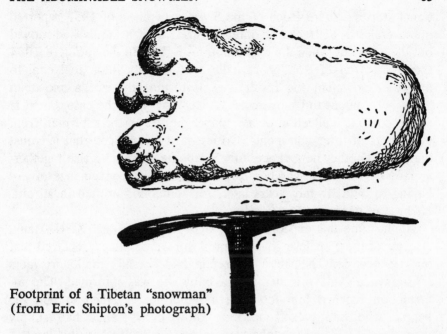

Footprint of a Tibetan "snowman"
(from Eric Shipton's photograph)

many "yeti tracks" were really made by bears, these were decidedly
not. There is no mammal known to science in this area which leaves
such tracks.[3] And although they resemble human tracks they are as
decidedly "un-human." The latter fact is important too, for in addition to the customary explanations citing two kinds of bears, loping
wolves, loping snow leopards, giant pandas, and monkeys, several
people have held that the snowmen were simply men: Hindu ascetics
or outlaws. Of course both Hindu ascetics (who go naked, or very
nearly so, in the snow) and outlaws do exist, but if they leave footprints they are still human footprints, about 10 inches long and at
most 4 inches wide.

The conclusion appears inevitable that the prints were made by
something other than outlaws, bears, or snow leopards. W. H. Murray concluded his article rather lightheartedly: "What, then, is the
Abominable Snowman? In my own judgment it is no other than
the metohkangmi, mirka, yeti or sogpa."

But what is the metohkangmi, or rather what could it be?

Before embarking on speculation I want to list quickly a few addi-

[3] Dr. Lawrence W. Swan of San Francisco State College has called attention
to the strong similarity between the footprints photographed by Shipton and the
cast made by Carl Akeley of the foot of an African mountain gorilla (*Science*,
vol. 127, 18 April 1958).

tional stories. André Roch of the Swiss expedition of 1952 reported on several sets of tracks of different sizes, as if a family had moved out of the valley when the expedition moved in. In the spring of 1954 the *Daily Mail* of London actually sent an expedition to Nepal to find the snowmen; the result was, unfortunately, not a snowman but a book about the snowman.[4] It does not settle the case, but it is a nice compact collection of newspaper stories on the snowman from the papers of three continents. Critics have complained that it is just that, plus another newspaper story wrapping everything else together; apparently only a researcher can appreciate the convenience of *not* having to hunt, twenty years later, for something printed in an out-of-the-way newspaper.

At the time this expedition was under way, Colonel K. N. Rana, director of the Nepalese government's Bureau of Mines, reported that on two occasions Nepalese tribesmen had actually made prisoners of snowmen. One prisoner was a baby, he was informed. The information reached him too late; a search party failed to find the people who had picked up the "snow baby"; they had simply vanished. This, it was emphasized, is not too unusual in this land of glaciers, towering peaks, and high snowy passes, but it was annoying just the same. In the other case a male snowman, presumably full-grown, was taken prisoner by tribesmen. They trussed it up securely but the specimen refused to eat what they offered and finally died on the long journey. Not realizing that a dead specimen would be almost as valuable as a live one, the tribesmen abandoned the carcass and arrived with nothing but the story of their adventure. Unfortunately for Colonel Rana mere stories are not always believed.

The most tangible piece of evidence is an object of animal hide, strangely peaked and furry, which is kept at the Thyangboche Monastery and which is stated to be the scalp of a yeti. Ralph Izzard quotes several people who have seen it as going on record that it is not a cap but must be a scalp, since no seams could be detected. It is as understandable as it is deplorable that the Lama does not wish to part with this item, though he will show it to serious visitors. In 1953 Navnit Parekh of the Bombay Natural History Society visited the monastery and was accorded by the Lama the privilege of being shown the scalp. Taking some slight advantage of the old man's friendliness, Mr. Parekh pulled out a few strands of hair, which he sent to Dr. Leon A. Hausman of New Brunswick, N.J., for examina-

[4] *The Abominable Snowman,* by Ralph Izzard (New York: Doubleday, 1955).

tion and possible classification. Doctor Hausman tends to think that the "scalp" is actually a cap, made of fur from the back or shoulder of a large mammal. The strands of hair are definitely not from a langur monkey (*Semnopithecus roxellanae*), or from a bear, or from any animal closely related either to the langur or to the bear. The strands are quite old; their age possibly may have to be measured in terms of centuries. Finally Dr. Hausman pointed out that, if it *is* a cap, the animal which grew the fur need not be native to Nepal or Tibet.

In 1957 the snowman hunt of the *Daily Mail* was repeated by a private expedition, again without tangible result. Later in the same year a member of a Soviet expedition to the Pamir Mountains reported having seen a snowman from a distance. These mountains are in the Tadzhik Republic in Central Asia, and the purpose of the Soviet expedition was to survey water resources. One day one of the specialists with that expedition, A. C. Pronin, saw a snowman on a rocky summit and watched it for about five minutes. The creature was stocky, Mr. Pronin told the reporter of *Komsomolskaya Pravda,* had long arms and a body covered with grayish-brown hair. Three days later Pronin saw it again briefly in the same spot. These sightings occurred in August 1957; the exact dates were not given.

I don't know what the Russians thought about snowman stories as long as these reports reached them from "capitalist" countries, but apparently a sighting by one of their own nationals spurred them into activity. A special "collective" has been organized to track it down; among the members are the geologist and explorer Sergei V. Obrutchev and the historian Professor Boris F. Porshev. In November 1958 the collective made a kind of interim report in which two things were asserted: that the "existence of the snowman was confirmed little by little" and that its habitat was in the deserts of Tibet and in Sinkiang province in northwestern China. One of the Russians said that the failure of the various expeditions made by Englishmen and Americans was probably due to the fact that they had looked in the wrong place, to the south of the Himalayas.

"Many Tibetans have met this creature," the Soviet scientists stated. "They speak of it as an animal moving on two legs, with brown shiny fur and long hair on its head. Its face looks like both ape and man. Hunters often find remnants of its food, for example, bits of rabbit. But, according to them, the wild man also eats plant roots."

Now that the reports and sightings have been brought up to date,
a few tentative conclusions can be drawn. The explanations which
have been advanced are the following:

1. It is just the langur monkey.
   This is the weakest of all. Langurs walk on all four legs, they
   are not large enough, and, furthermore, where they occur they
   are well known to the local people.
2. The tracks were made by bears and since bears often rear up
   and sometimes walk on their hind legs the whole thing was
   caused by bears.
   There is no doubt that some yeti tracks probably were bear
   tracks. But bears only sometimes walk upright, not all the time.
   And Shipton's footprint most decidedly was not that of a bear.
3. The tracks were caused by *Mylodon,* the giant sloth.
   This explanation is the weirdest one and is advanced essentially because the Mylodon *seems* to have walked upright and
   did have a heavy fur which would protect it from the cold. But
   all sloths, giant or otherwise, extinct or living, are New World
   animals.
4. The yeti is either a very primitive type of Man, possibly the
   supposedly extinct "giant man of China," or an anthropoid ape.
   This is the only idea worth considering.

Right now there are three kinds of living apes, quite different in
type and appearance. Two of them live in Africa, the chimpanzee
and the gorilla; the third, the orangutan, in Sumatra. All three of
them can and do assume an upright stance and walk on their hind
legs only. The chimpanzee can do it better than the gorilla and the
gorilla better than the orangutan. But none of them walks on its
hind legs exclusively; they all revert to a special variety of four-legged
walk whenever it is convenient. The mountain gorilla can stand rather
cold temperatures and happens to be the least hairy of the trio, while
the orangutan, living in the warmth of Sumatra, has exceptionally
long hair, though the fur is not very dense.

One can see that the puzzle would not be completely solved simply
by postulating the existence of a hitherto unknown ape of Central
Asia. Not that such an ape would be impossible. Apes did live in
Asia in the geologic past and they might well have shared the experience of two animals which have been mentioned in connection
with the snowmen. Both the giant panda and the langur monkey

were originally inhabitants of a near-tropical area. As the mountains slowly rose and the area cooled off, the giant panda—a fairly close relative of our raccoon—adapted to changing conditions rather than migrate elsewhere. The food problem was resolved in a somewhat peculiar manner: the panda lived exclusively on bamboo shoots. The bamboo, normally a warm-climate plant, had proved to be rather cold-resistant too. The langur monkey, itself long thought to be a fable until it was discovered by Père Armand David, also chose to remain in the cooling mountain forests, perplexing later zoologists with the surprising spectacle of a monkey roaming snowy branches, and causing itself to be actually named "snow monkey" for a while. Naturally neither of these animals lives above the snowline, where there is no food for a vegetarian or partly vegetarian animal.

What happened to the panda and the langur might also have happened to an ape. But simply postulating the existence of a Central Asian equivalent to the African mountain gorilla does not solve the problem fully. One would have to postulate an ape with some special characteristics, the most obvious of which would be the adoption of a bipedal walk all the time. Why an ape, staying with its cooling forest, should have done that is hard to understand; cold or not, it is still a forest. In addition, it would have to be an ape that has taken to a partly carnivorous diet, which, considering the circumstances, is easier to understand. Finally, if Hugh Knight's story can be trusted, it would be the only "ape" to carry a tool.

The reasoning narrows on something that is closer to "Man," bluntly speaking a very primitive type of Man—"proto-Man," if you like. And that is where the suggestion of the "extinct giant man of China" comes in. During the interval between the two World Wars interesting things transpired in East Asia. Quite a long time ago, in October 1891, a Dutch physician, Eugène Dubois, found a skull (jaws missing) and a femur some distance from Ngawi, near Trinil on Java. The owner of these bones was named *Pithecanthropus erectus* (the "upright [walking] ape-man"), and the long controversies that arose all centered around the unanswerable question whether this being had still been essentially an ape or already essentially a man. The probability was that it actually stood halfway, but the more sensible people stayed away from the argument and said that more evidence was needed to make a decision.

That new evidence took a long time to come. In 1929 Dr. Davidson Black turned up with very primitive skulls from the vicinity of

Peking. They were named *Sinanthropus* (China Man) and were considered human. Just the same, there were numerous similarities between the skulls of Sinanthropus and that of Pithecanthropus, indicating that Pithecanthropus might also be considered human. Soon after the finds near Peking, Java began to yield more Pithecanthropus material. The man who did most of the work, both in the field and in the laboratory studying the material, was Dr. G. H. R. von Königswald. In January 1939 Dr. von Königswald went to Peking, where the late Dr. Franz Weidenreich was working at the time. Doctor von Königswald brought a part of an upper jaw with him. It had well-preserved teeth which were indubitably human. But it also had a gap between the front teeth and the canines, which had always been considered typical for the anthropoids and was therefore called the "simian gap." In spite of the simian gap both scientists accepted the jaw as human, because of the teeth, and in spite of the fact that it was unusually large for a human jaw.

After some hesitation the new type was called *Pithecanthropus robustus.* Then Dr. von Königswald found two more jaws, both near Sangiran on Java. The first could not be classified because many of the teeth were missing completely and what there was left of some was so worn down that it was impossible to tell the difference between man and ape. The other was undoubtedly human. And it was large, large even for Pithecanthropus robustus. Dr. von Königswald decided that it had to be a still different type and named it *Meganthropus palaeojavanicus,* the "big man from old Java." Speaking of it in a lecture, Dr. Franz Weidenreich declared, "We shall not err in estimating that Meganthropus reached the size, stoutness, and strength of a big male gorilla."

A point of doubt was permissible. There have always been individual "giants," pathological specimens with malfunctioning glands, usually weak and sickly not in spite of but because of their size. Their lower jaws are especially large if the pituitary gland is unbalanced, and that has even received the special name of "acromegalic giantism." What proof was there that the jaw fragment found was not such a pathological case?

It would have been a reasonable question, but Dr. Weidenreich forestalled it by looking for such a possibility himself. Now, in an acromegalic giant the thickening is pronounced only in the lower portions, accompanied by an enormously prominent chin. The jaw of Meganthropus is thick all the way through and it has no chin at all.

Furthermore, the teeth of a pathological case of giantism are of normal human size. The teeth of Meganthropus are of the proper size in relation to the bone.

There was, the experts declared, nothing pathological about that jaw. It is just big, indicating a primitive man with the size and strength of a gorilla but with much higher intelligence.[5]

All of which, taken together, means that several types of proto-human or very primitive human types existed in Asia and Indonesia in the past. And as regards the yeti, the two most likely possibilities are these: either it is an anthropoid ape which differs very considerably from the other anthropoid apes which have easier climates to contend with, or else descendants of a very primitive near-human type are still around and are now known as "snowmen."

---

[5] An even more astonishing find was made by Dr. von Königswald a little later. The Chinese call all fossils *lung-tchih* or *lung-koo,* "dragon bones" or "dragon teeth," and ascribe high pharmaceutical value to them. For that reason they used to keep secret the localities where such bones could be found, and Western scientists had to buy their fossils in pharmacies. Paleontologists spoke half-jokingly of a "Chinese drugstore fauna." In such a drugstore Dr. von Königswald acquired, one by one, three large molars (roots missing) which seemed to be human but had six times the volume of the corresponding molars of modern man. Dr. von Königswald referred to them as *Gigantopithecus* (giant ape) but Dr. Weidenreich said they should be called *Gigantanthropus* (giant man). If one can assume the same proportions now prevailing the creature must have had twice the size of a male gorilla! But it may be wise to wait for more fossil material before a verdict is attempted.

CHAPTER 6

The Little People

TAKE a map of the North American continent and look for Hudson Bay. It connects with the Atlantic Ocean to the east by way of Hudson Strait, which, on the inland side, ends at a large island: Southampton Island. To the north of Southampton Island you'll find Foxe Channel, to the east of Foxe Channel the Foxe Peninsula, which is a part of Baffin Island. To the north of Foxe Channel, finally, there is Foxe Basin. As the spelling suggests, these names have nothing to do with an arctic variety of the well-known carnivore but are derived from the name of a man: Captain Luke Foxe of Hull, who explored this region in 1631 and 1632. Like many another sailor of his time he tried to find the so-called North-West Passage through which, it was hoped, one could sail into the Pacific Ocean across the northern part of North America.

When Captain Luke Foxe published the journal of his voyage (in 1635) the book bore the title

NORTH-VVEST FOX;
or Fox from the North-west Passage

Much later it was reprinted by the Hakluyt Society as volume 88/89 of its publications. On page 319 of the second volume of the Hakluyt Society edition there is mention of an island which had just been visited by an exploring party:

The newes from the land was that this Iland was a Sepulchre, for that the Salvages had laid their dead (I cannot say interred), for it is all stone, as they cannot dig therein, but lay the Corpes upon the stones, and well them about with the same, coffining them also by laying the sides of old sleddes above, which have been artificially made. The boards are some 9 or 10 ft long, 4 inches thicke. In what manner the tree they have bin

90

made out of was cloven or sawen, it was so smooth as we could not dis-
cerne, the burials had been so old. And, as in other places of those countries, they bury all their Vtensels, as bowes, arrowes, strings, darts, lances,
and other implements carved in bone. The longest Corpes was not above
4 foot long, with their heads laid to the West.

The printed book does not say more about this most astonishing find, except for stating that "their Corpes were wrapped in Deare
skinnes" and that the sailors left them undisturbed, but took the
wooden boards for firewood. But a hand-written copy of the original
manuscript contains an additional sentence: "They seem to be people
of small stature, God send me better for my adventures than these."
This, I am sorry to say, is all that is known about the case of the
stony graves of "little people" in the Western Hemisphere. Captain
Foxe wrote that "this Iland doth lie in 64 d. 10 m. of latitude," but
there is no island in this geographical position. There are, however,
a number of small islands at the southern end of Foxe Channel, any
one of which may be meant. Of course one can disbelieve the whole
story and be done with it; but it is hard to see why Captain Foxe
should have inserted a few paragraphs of completely useless lies in
an otherwise trustworthy narrative. If he did tell the truth, he is the
only witness to the only known case of "little people" in the Americas.

Of course every country has its own legends and stories about
"little people." Details vary, but always, in addition to being small,
these people are described as living either deep in the forest or else
in caves in the mountains. The folklore of some countries includes
both types of habitat and provides different names; German folklore, for example, distinguishes between the gnomes who live *in* the
mountains (not *on* the mountains) and the *Ellenmännchen* of the
forest. The latter term is virtually self-translating; all that needs to
be added is that, while the English "ell" was standardized early as
being 3 feet in length like the yard, elsewhere an ell was usually
somewhat longer—about 4 feet.

How the "little people" got into folklore is by no means certain,
but the fact that there exists a long literary tradition about them no
doubt helped. Anybody who asked the learned men of his time about
the gnomes and the ell-men did receive confirmation of some kind,
since small-sized people had been mentioned in various highly regarded works that had been preserved from the classical age. Herodo-

tus told in the second book of his work about an adventure of five
Nasamonians which had been related to him in Egypt. Five young
men of this tribe decided to learn something firsthand about the
unknown parts of Africa.

After journeying for many days over a wide extent of sand, they came at
last to a plain where they observed trees growing; approaching them and
seeing fruit on them, they proceeded to gather it. While they were thus
engaged, there came upon them some dwarfish men, under the middle
height, who seized them and carried them off. The Nasamonians could not
understand a word of their language, nor had they any acquaintance with
the language of the Nasamonians. They were led across extensive marshes,
and finally came to a town, where all the men were of the height of their
conductors, and black complexioned. A great river [probably the Niger]
flowed by the town, running from west to east, and containing crocodiles.

But the literary tradition about the "little people" had begun even
earlier than Herodotus, with Homer's *Iliad,* which acquired its final
shape in about 600 B.C., or possibly earlier. The hexameters of lines
3–7 of the third book of the *Iliad* read:

Like to the unending screeching of cranes which fly overhead then
When, having fled from the unceasing rains and the cold of the winter,
Screaming they fly down the path to Okéanos' far-flowing waters,
Threatening death and destruction to races of small-bodied pygmies,
Swooping on down from the high dusky air to do terrible combat. . . .

Egyptian or Cretan sailors must have reported that somewhere,
far to the south and almost at the rim of the world, there lived
"small-bodied pygmies." To those who might be distrustful of a
poet's assertion the *Natural History* of Aristotle served nicely:

The cranes fly from the Scythian plains [Russia] to the swamps situated
beyond Upper Egypt, whence the Nile comes. These areas are inhabited
by pygmies. This is no myth, there actually exists a small tribe, and even
their horses are small, their habits are said to be those of Troglodites [cave
dwellers].

Later, in Europe, Homer was not known directly but people did
know Aristotle, and also Pliny, who had copied that particular paragraph from Aristotle. An amusing side-thought cropped up later in
the writings of Albert von Bollstädt (Albertus Magnus) in the
thirteenth century. After quoting Aristotle, he adds that the pygmies
stand one ell tall, that they have children when they are three years
old, and that they die in their eighth year. After stating this, he

suddenly paused to ask *utrum pygmaei sint homines?* (whether the pygmies are people?). His answer is a firm "no." They can speak and presumably think, but they merely live together without forming a community; they have neither art nor philosophy, neither a moral code nor decency. Although they can make things they are not people. Since Albertus cannot have known such details (and since, moreover, his assertions are wrong on every count), all this must be the result of "pure thought." But his reasoning certainly became food for German folklore: the ell-men can speak and practice some crafts, but pictures awe and worry them, and they are not people because they lack immortal souls.

It is difficult to imagine what a scientist of, say, the first half of the eighteenth century might have answered when asked about the pygmies. Most likely he would have asserted that they were merely folklore—Greek, Egyptian, Latin, and European—which was helped along by an occasional midget, a freak born to normal parents and having normal offspring, if any.[1] But during the latter half of the eighteenth century some stories, emanating mostly from Portugal, began making the rounds. Portuguese sailors, returning from Africa, swore that they had been told by reliable Negroes about "little men" in the forest, and "hairy men" in the forest, and "big hairy men" in the mountains. All this remained rumor, possibly true but most likely not, for another century.

The man who furnished the first definite proof was born on July 31, 1835, in France, probably in Paris. His name was Paul Belloni du Chaillu and he came to the United States when he was twenty years old. Because he already had some African experience the Academy of Natural Sciences in Philadelphia sent him on an expedition to equatorial West Africa. On this expedition du Chaillu discovered the gorilla, once and for all time ending the ancient confusion between gorilla and chimpanzee. (The latter had been called "gorilla" and the real gorilla had been thought mythical.) Naturally such a successful man was sent on another expedition, which he later described in a book called *Journey to Ashangoland.* On that expedition, made during the years 1863–65, du Chaillu encountered the pygmies.

[1] I remember reading somewhere (and quite some time ago) that a king of France once tried to establish a "tribe" of small people by caring for a number of midgets and generally unusual small people, on condition that they would marry and have children. They did, but the result was disappointing—almost all their children "grew up."

They were of the tribe of the Obongo, and du Chaillu reported that apparently they were not "real Negroes." Their skin was neither dark brown nor black, but a pale yellow-brown, "like imperfectly roasted coffee beans." They did not have much beard and not much hair on their heads, but "a great growth of body hair," especially when contrasted with the neighboring Negro tribes, which had virtually none, much less than even a relatively hairless white man. Of course he measured them and found the average height of the males 4 feet, 7 inches, the females some 6 inches shorter.

Du Chaillu's discovery settled the question of whether pygmies existed at all, but it did not clear up the problem of the pygmies mentioned by Homer and Aristotle. *They* were supposed to live in or beyond the Nile swamps, somewhere near the Mountains of the Moon, and not in West Africa. Geographers had already settled the problem of the Mountains of the Moon by the time du Chaillu made his voyages. High mountains had been discovered in equatorial Africa; the ancients probably meant the ones now known as the Ruwenzori range. And a linguist had also found the explanation for the intriguing and ancient name "Mountains of the Moon." In Arabic this is *Jibal el-qamar,* but what the Arabs had said and written originally was *Jibal qomr,* meaning "bluish [distant?] mountains."

To establish the "classical" pygmies was the lot of a German, Dr. Georg August Schweinfurth, who was born in Riga on December 29, 1836. Schweinfurth, a gifted artist and an ardent student of plant life, followed a course which could be expected to lead him to the sources of the Nile. He penetrated the territory of the Niam-niam, discovered the Welle River and established that it was not a tributary of the Nile, and, in 1870, saw his first pygmy.

This was Adimokoo of the tribe of the Akka, a fairly old man and rather tall—4 feet, 10 inches. Schweinfurth had read du Chaillu's books and knew of the Obongo. His Akka seemed to be about the same size; they had the same skin color; but they did not have more body hair than their tall neighbors. Their physical proportions were not extraordinary: they were slightly short-legged, especially when compared with the usually long-legged Negroes; they had a tendency to a "pendulous abdomen" and rather large shell-like ears. Schweinfurth stressed that point as indicative of a racial difference, because "all Negroes have beautiful ears." Adimokoo, questioned with the aid of interpreters, rattled off the names of seven other pygmy tribes.

Schweinfurth's notes and sketches were destroyed later when his camp caught fire, but he remembered having measured a male Akka who was only 4 feet, 4 inches, tall and a female Akka 4 feet, 1 inch.

In spite of Aristotle's two mistakes about these pygmies—they are not cave dwellers and they don't have horses, either large or small—they are undoubtedly the ones he meant, as is indicated by the fact that they were known to the Egyptians. The Cairo Museum preserves an old (but apparently undated) statuette of a typical pygmy, and three pygmies appear on a frieze in the Festival Hall of Osorkon II in the Temple of Bubastis. In addition to this pictorial evidence we have direct information from the Sixth Dynasty. An Egyptian named Harkhuf had traveled south to "Nubia" repeatedly, and on his fourth trip he secured a pygmy. This was important enough information to be sent to the ruling pharaoh, who immediately dispatched an enthusiastic and detailed letter to the traveler.

Come northward to the Residence immediately. . . . Leave [everything?] and bring this pygmy with thee, which thou has brought living, prosperous, and healthy from the land of Akhtin [unknown southern

Ancient Egyptian statuette of a pygmy, in the Cairo Museum

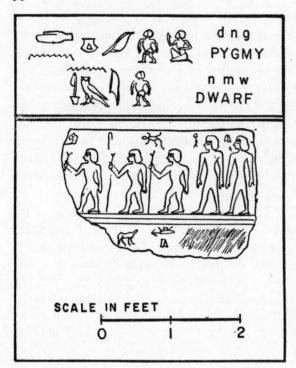

A frieze from the Festival Hall of Osorkon II in the Temple of Bubastis, showing three pygmies. *Above,* the hieroglyphs for "dwarf" and for "pygmy"

people] for the dances of the god to rejoice and gladden the heart of the King of Upper and Lower Egypt Neferkerē, may [he] live forever. When he [i.e., the pygmy] goes down with thee to the vessel, appoint trusty people who shall be about him on each side of the vessel; take care lest he fall into the water. When he sleeps at night, appoint again trusty people who shall sleep about him in his tent: inspect ten times a night. My Majesty desires to see this pygmy more than the produce of Sinai and of Pwenet. If thou arrivest at the Residence, this pygmy bring with thee alive, prosperous, and healthy, My Majesty will do for thee a greater thing than that which was done for the Treasurer of the god Werdjedba in the time of Isesi, in accordance with the heart's desire of My Majesty to see this pygmy.

Harkhuf must have been successful in bringing the pygmy "alive, prosperous, and healthy" to the Residence, because he himself was later prosperous enough to have the ruler's letter reproduced on his tomb—which is how we know about it.[2]

[2] Some of the representations on Egyptian tombs and other monuments which have been referred to as pygmies in literature are actually dwarfs, midgets. The Egyptians distinguished between the two; there were different words and different symbols for them.

Hard on the heels of Schweinfurth's report came some detailed information about Asiatic pygmy tribes, the earliest mention of which was in the famous, though mutilated and fragmentary book of Ctesias, the personal physician of Artaxerxes II. The ones about which Ctesias had heard were probably the forest pygmies of the Malayan peninsula; the pygmy-like natives of the Andaman Islands, the Aētes of the Philippine Islands, and others were discovered much later.

Anthropologists now call the African pygmy tribes Negrillos, and the Asiatic tribes Negritos. The distribution of the Negrillos and Negritos on a map of the world is spotty in detail, but the general features of this distribution can be easily described. It is all Old World, from Africa around to the Philippines, generally between the equator and 20 degrees northern latitude. In all cases the pygmies live in undesirable surroundings, usually in dense forests, though some of the island Negritos are obvious exceptions. It certainly looks as if they had been pushed into areas which their taller and stronger neighbors did not covet for themselves. As soon as that fact was realized a question came up which sounds rather like a conscious paraphrase of Albertus Magnus. But the question was no longer whether the pygmies are people; that had been settled. It was now whether the pygmies might not be the "original people." Did they by any chance represent the early human stock, now scattered and pushed into odd corners, surviving as small and generally browbeaten leftovers?

Scientists toying with this idea around the year 1910 recalled to themselves and to their audiences that the ancestors of the horse had been much smaller than present-day horses, and that, in general, most large mammals of today had smaller ancestors. Why should this not apply to people too, especially in view of the fact that all our living, though distant, relatives are far smaller than Man, with the single exception of the gorilla? It was a nice and logical idea which suffered only from one serious drawback: it was not supported by fossil evidence anywhere.

At that time a number of human fossils were already known. There was the famous Neanderthal skull, found in 1856 in the Neander Valley, a short distance above the Düssel River and not far from the industrial city of Düsseldorf. That Neanderthal skull, after a long-drawn-out and rather silly controversy, had finally been accepted as human. Its owner was not particularly tall, as proved by later and more complete finds. He stood around 5 feet, 3 inches, to 5 feet, 4 inches—not very tall as present averages go, but certainly not a pygmy.

Then there was the "Heidelberg jaw," found on October 21, 1907, in a sand pit near the town of Mauer, not far from Heidelberg. Its owner is still unknown as far as complete skeletons go, but two things about him were realized within weeks of the discovery itself. He was considerably earlier than "Neanderthal" and he was a big man. Recent estimates say about 6 feet, 2 inches, with a probable leeway of 2 inches in either direction. Certainly not a pygmy.

And there was *Pithecanthropus,* from Trinil on Java, found in 1891 by the Dutch physician Dr. Eugène Dubois. Only a skull cap and a femur were found, and for a long time it was doubtful whether they belonged together or not. But either way you took it Pithecanthropus worked out to be over 5 feet. No matter what else he was, he was well within the size range of modern Man.

In addition to all these forms, which differed considerably from modern Man in many particulars, there were the Cro-Magnon, later than Neanderthal and no doubt the direct ancestors of many Europeans. The name comes from the place of the supposed first discovery in 1868, Cro-Magnon at Les Eyzies, Departement de Dordogne, France. It later turned out that these Cro-Magnon had been discovered before. In 1823 Dean Buckland of Oxford University had unearthed a fine skeleton from the Paviland Cave, on the seaward side of Bristol Channel, England. He had thought it to be the skeleton of a Briton lady of the Roman period and because it was stained with red ochre it was later referred to as the "Red Lady." In 1912 the "Red Lady" was re-examined and proved to be a Cro-Magnon, and male at that. And in 1852 a small landslide near the village of Aurignac, France, had exposed a cave in which the skeletons of seventeen persons were found. The mayor of Aurignac was informed about this, looked at them, regretted the accident which had overtaken the party of indubitably nice people, and laid the case before the local abbé. They were given a Christian burial, of which the victims of an accident are deserving. They proved to be Cro-Magnon too, the men averaging 6 feet, 1 inch, the women around 5 feet, 7 inches.

In 1921, at Broken Hill, Northern Rhodesia, a skeleton generally resembling the Neanderthal type was found. This man's weight, when he was alive, must have been around 210 pounds, and he must have stood 5 feet, 10 inches, tall. His case also spoiled some contentions about the degenerate state of modern people, whose appendixes act up, whose teeth decay, and whose little toes are being reduced because of their habit of wearing shoes. We don't know about the appendix and the little toe of *Homo rhodesiensis,* but he must have had toothaches which surpassed description. He had a mastoid breakthrough, too, and literally died of the septic condition of his mouth.

But no pygmies had been found anywhere.

There had been a loud noise emanating from Switzerland in about 1910 concerning whole villages of pygmies from the period of the Late Stone Age. The noise had been all the louder because the artifacts had become somebody's private property and were commercially exploited. But a Swiss anthropologist, Dr. Franz Schwerz of Berne, had traced everything still available and found that the men had been 5 feet, 3 inches, on the average, and the women 4 feet, 11 inches. While he was at it he also determined the average size of the Late Stone Age populations of France and of Denmark, finding it in France 5 feet, 5½ inches, for the males and 5 feet, 1 inch, for the females, and in Denmark 5 feet, 7 inches, for the males and 5 feet, 5 inches, for the females. These sets of figures were still approximately correct for the populations of the two countries in 1914 when he made his study.

Just as a scientist in 1814 would have been highly skeptical about the existence of living pygmies, in spite of some rumors, so a scientist of 1914 had every reason to be highly skeptical about the existence of prehistoric pygmies. But the rumors would not die. Prehistoric Man had not become known only because of his bones. One might almost say, on the contrary. The first indications of his existence had been the tools he had made, the now so well-known flint implements of early Man. They had come to light piecemeal all through recorded history, the first to guess at their meaning being a British antiquary named John Frere. That was in 1797, but it was another half-century before everybody had become used to the simple concept that Man, before he learned how to smelt and work metals, made his tools and weapons of stones.

As more and more material was amassed, scientists first distinguished between the "Old" and the "New" Stone Age, the implements from the "New" Stone Age being far superior in workmanship. Later this scheme had to be broken down further, into types of weapons and into localities—there were regional differences even then. But all stone implements, whether "old" or "new," came from the same geological period, the period immediately preceding our own, which is known as either the Pleistocene or the Ice Age. The latter name is not quite as good as the former, for the big glaciations from which the term Ice Age came comprised only a comparatively small portion of the total time of the Pleistocene.

But along with the collections of primitive stone implements a kind of small side collection began to form. If the artifacts which comprised this side collection had been found in any of the deposits which could be dated as having been the "interglacial periods," the long stretches of time between the glaciations, there would have been very little fuss about them. They would have been taken as belonging to a very primitive tribe, one which even the gentleman from the Neander Valley would consider far beneath his notice (except as food) and that with justification. Or they might have been considered the first attempts of an apprentice boy, learning the craft; or discarded pieces, just begun when an interruption took place and not recovered afterward. As these remarks indicate, they show very little workmanship, so little that a layman would hardly think they had been worked on at all. Even the experts are often doubtful, and some of the pieces, as some of the experts claim, may have been chipped accidentally by natural causes. Their whole relationship to Man may consist in having been stepped on once by somebody.

But these pieces are *not* from the Pleistocene. They are from deposits of the Tertiary Period, with a minimum age of one million

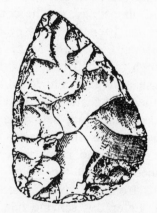

Undoubted stone tools of primitive Man, found at various sites in France

years. They have been named "eoliths" (dawn stones) and will be
fought over for many years to come. What is important here is that
some, found by Professor Rutot of Brussels, are not only old but
also small. Professor Rutot sent some of them to a German naturalist, the late Wilhelm Bölsche, who, in reply to a question, wrote
me that one thing is absolutely certain: *If* the eoliths which he had in

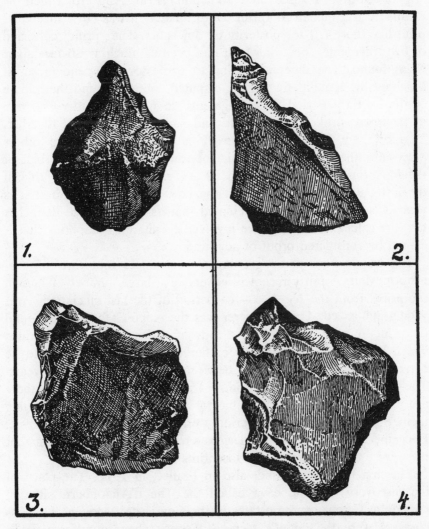

Of these four stones, two (2 and 4) are known to be stone tools, fashioned
within historic times by the now extinct Tasmanians. The other two, similar
in general appearance, are "eoliths" from Europe

his collection actually were tools they were made for the hands of small children or pygmies. And he, as well as Rutot, felt sure that the marks they bore were not accidental but the result of admittedly primitive and clumsy workmanship.

In addition to these doubtful and violently debated eoliths, Belgium produced another find along the same lines. During the last year of the First World War a German professor from the University of Göttingen discovered something near Antwerp which he claimed was a human footprint. Unfortunately it was not a nice clear print like those left for posterity by dinosaurs. The "print" consisted of five fragments, some of which had been as much as 30 feet apart when found. The date, according to Professor Freudenberg, must be about the same as that of the disputed eoliths, around the middle of the Tertiary Period. The fragments do not fit together and one of them was broken when found and had to be cemented together. Two of them Freudenberg himself called "doubtful." The others *may* show the imprint of the big toe, the little toe, and the ball of the foot, but you don't have to be a case-hardened skeptic to call the last one doubtful too. From the size of the big toe—if that is what it is—the discoverer calculated that its owner stood 30 inches tall; the calculation must have involved so many assumptions that it cannot be considered proof of any kind.

But we do have some genuine and complete footprints of prehistoric Man. A fairly recent discovery of a large number of human footprints from the Ice Age—the period of the last glaciation—was widely publicized. The discoverer was the Abbé Cathala, who found the prints in a side cave of the Grotto of Aldène in southern France which had been overlooked by earlier explorers. The age could be determined rather well—it is between 15,000 and 20,000 years. The people who made the prints carried staffs and torches—there are marks on the walls where the torches were rubbed for cleaning them. Some pictures of these prints were published in *Life* magazine, December 6, 1948. But the newspapers were wrong in saying that these were the first prehistoric footprints discovered.

The first had been found, also in France, in 1912. The place of the discovery was the cave called the Tuc d'Audoubert, situated near Saint Girons on the estates of the Comte de Bégouen. The discoverers were the count's teen-aged sons. They found a cave in which prehistoric men had made clay sculptures with enough artistry to stand even tough present-day competition. The material was clay, scooped up in an adjoining cave. And that clay, where it was scooped up, showed handprints and footprints, deep impressions, covered with a thin veneer of lime.

All the books say that these prints of the Salle de Danse (as this cave of the Tuc d'Audoubert has been named because of the footprints) are "small and delicate," but none I read gave any measurements. Of the new prints in the Grotto of Aldène the measurements were provided by Norbert Casteret in Saint Gaudens. The length of a step, he wrote, where it can be established, is 50 centimeters (about 20 inches); the length of the footprints varies from 18 to 25 centimeters (between 7 and 10 inches). The little toe shows signs of reduction, to the same extent as that of modern Man. Like the septic teeth of *Homo rhodesiensis,* this demolishes another tenet of those who warn of degeneration and doom; the Aldène people did not wear shoes, as we can clearly see. How tall were they?

Since they are rather modern we can assume that their proportions were about the same as ours. Among white people of today there is a well-known relationship between foot length and height. Males, we find, are between 6 and 6.5 times as tall as their footprint is long. Among women the variation is somewhat greater; it usually lies between the figures 6.5 and 7, but some especially long-legged and small-footed individuals may be almost 7.5 times as tall as the length of their footprints.

Taking the largest of the Aldène footprints and assuming that it was made by a man—which is highly probable, of course—you arrive at a height of 5 feet, 3 inches. The smallest footprint, taken to be female and calculated with the upper end of the female ratio (to make her as tall as possible) results in a woman 4 feet, 4 inches tall, but actually the print was probably made by a child. For comparison: if you take a 6-foot man who wears a size 10 shoe (which means that his foot is a foot long) and scale him down to a height of 4 feet, his footprint would measure 20.3 centimeters, or just about 8 inches. The Aldène prints point to a small race, where apparently only a few individuals "towered" over 5 feet—presumably the same race (or at least the same size) as the sculptors of Tuc d'Audoubert.

This discovery makes for a rather varying-sized humanity in Europe after the last glaciation. The big 6-foot, 2-inch "Neanderthalians" [3] of the Mauer-Heidelberg type were probably no longer around, but the equally tall Cro-Magnon were. The short Neanderthalians had probably just disappeared, but the still smaller modern Aldène type seems to have flourished. And elsewhere in Europe these was a type intermediate in size, the men running about 5 feet, 7 inches, the women about 5 feet, 3 inches. Except for possible remnants of short Neanderthalers these were all modern types; but now we know that the same variation in size, even more pronounced, prevailed in South Africa at an earlier stage.

The story of the discoveries of early men and of somehow related prehuman or near-human forms in South Africa will be told one day by somebody in a massive work. A good deal has been written already, but it must, of necessity, be incomplete because the sites are not yet exhausted and impressive new discoveries may take place any day.

The locality of the first finds was the district of Taungs, some 80 miles north of the Kimberly diamond fields. There, in the valley of the Harts River in Taungs, the Reverend Mr. Neville Jones had collected implements indicating human habitation for the last 500,-000 years. They began with primitive stone weapons of the Early Stone Age, went on through more finished types right down to the coming of the Bushmen (in what would be very early historical times if the location were Egypt and not South Africa), and on from then to the hammer and spade of the Reverend Mr. Jones himself. In 1924 Professor Raymond A. Dart discovered most of the skull of something very much ape but also human. Unfortunately it was the skull of a child, corresponding in development to a human six-year-old. Professor Dart called it *Australopithecus,* which translates as "southern ape" (*austral* means south) but is apt to make the layman think of Australia ("Southland"), which never had any monkeys or apes. Other scientists felt inclined to talk about "Dart's child," partly because it was a child, partly because Dart behaved very much like a proud father. He said that this was the most important find since Pithecanthropus. By now everybody knows that he was

[3] This term was invented by the late Dr. Franz Weidenreich of the American Museum of Natural History. He suggested just three subdivisions of human beings: (A) the early human, Homo erectus, comprising Pithecanthropus and Sinanthropus (Peking Man); (B) Homo neanderthalensis, the "Neanderthalians," comprising a wide variety of primitive groups above Homo erectus but not yet Homo sapiens; and (C) Homo sapiens, Cro-Magnon and all living forms.

right, but at first only two important experts, Dr. Robert Broom of the Transvaal Museum in Pretoria and Dr. William King Gregory of the American Museum of Natural History, believed him.

Nothing else happened for a long time, but the inhabitants of Transvaal were convinced that there had to be important things in their ground. It is a matter of record in serious scientific journals that soon after the First World War a Mr. Cooper, who owns a number of caves near Sterkfontein, wrote a guidebook containing the sentence: "Come to Sterkfontein and find the Missing Link."

Dr. Robert Broom did just that, although one may say that it was not a missing "link" which was finally uncovered, but a missing chain. First he obtained the major portions of a skull, a fine mixture of ape and human characteristics, from those caves. Originally he thought it closely allied to Dart's *Australopithecus africanus* and called it *Australopithecus transvaalensis*. Then he reconsidered—they were not that closely related—and substituted the name *Plesianthropus* or Near-Man. That was in 1936. We now have all the bones of Plesianthropus, but they come from many individuals; so far no single complete or near-complete skeleton has turned up. In 1938 a schoolboy picked up some fossils at Kromdrai, about two miles away, which came into Broom's hand and proved to be remains of still another early type. It was named *Paranthropus* ("manlike") *robustus*.

A number of years later at a site at Swartkrans, three-quarters of a mile west of Sterkfontein, a jaw fragment of a truly gigantic type came to light, and a few years later skull fragments of still another type, which has been named *Telanthropus capensis*. As has been said, the complete story of these finds cannot be written yet, and it would therefore be useless to go into detail. But they all have been dated in the Pliocene, the most recent of the five subdivisions of the Tertiary Period. It is hard to say just what this means in years: if we consider the very end of the Pliocene it would be slightly less than a million, but the Pliocene itself lasted 6 million years and the fossils might well fit anywhere into its latter half. As regards the fossils themselves, present opinion seems to be that Paranthropus and Plesianthropus and the giant "Swartkrans Man" were divergent forms, not in the direct line of human evolution. But as for Telanthropus, Dr. J. T. Robinson of the Transvaal Museum in Pretoria has gone on record in calling him "a very primitive euhominid"—the last word meaning "true man."

But let's return to Australopithecus, who is of special interest to us here because of his small size. Among the variegated near-human forms inhabiting South Africa at that long-ago though somewhat uncertain date he was the pygmy. The most important finds were made by Dr. Dart some distance from the place where Plesianthropus and Telanthropus were uncovered. The Sterkfontein of Plesianthropus and the Swartkrans of Telanthropus lie not far from Krugersdorp, about 30 miles southwest of Pretoria. Dart's site of Australopithecus lies 125 miles from Pretoria in a northwesterly direction. Its name is Makapaansgat and the nearest town is Potgietersrust. These two places are named after people with an interlinked fate. Makapaan was a native chieftain who attacked a caravan of Boers. The Boers, led by Potgieter, drove Makapaan and his men into a cave, piled brushwood into the entrance, and set it afire. Makapaan and his men were killed, but so was Potgieter. When Professor Dart came to those caves near Potgietersrust he saw that the breccia forming the roof of one of the caves contained charred bones.

It was worth investigating.

It turned out to be very much worth investigating.

The entire deposit had been consolidated by a calcareous cement. It was that dream of an archaeologist, a so-called "sealed site." There was evidence of fires, repeated fires. There were bones of Australopithecus. There were skulls of an extinct species of baboon, *Parapapio,* from the Pliocene period. And these skulls had been smashed, but not from above, as might happen in a cave because of falling rocks. The skulls were smashed on their left, as if from a right-handed blow with a weapon, which may have been a thigh bone of some kind. (Specimens just like them were also found later in the Sterkfontein-Krugersdorp area.) To Professor Dart the whole picture built up to that of an erect little creature, about 4 feet tall, weighing between 80 and 100 pounds, knowing fire and wielding weapons, usually right-handed, and having a brain volume of 650 cubic centimeters, which is equal to that of the largest gorilla, half that of the average Homo sapiens, and only about 125 cubic centimeters less than that of the much larger Pithecanthropus.

These carnivorous hunters were therefore familiar with the use of fire and bludgeons and apparently used crude long bones as implements in similar fashion to *Sinanthropus.* Some of the penetrating puncture wounds which are also found may have been caused by the dagger-like horns of antelopes, and it is noteworthy that up to the present ungulate heads retaining their horns intact have never been found in the dumps. . . . These intelligent, energetic, erect and delicately proportioned little people were as competent as any other primitive human group in cavern life made comfortable by the use of fire, in the employment of long bones as lethal weapons, in the cunning and courage of the chase and in internecine strife. They had conquered the most formidable beasts of the field; they were already in the toils of an ever-accelerating evolutionary process occasioned by their intellectual struggle with the forces of nature and with their fellows.[4]

One expert, Dr. Sollas, expressed his regret that this astonishing early creature had received such a clumsy name as *Australopithecus prometheus;* he said that it should have been Homunculus. Renaming something in science is difficult and tedious—justly so—and it did not happen in this case. If it had, it might have been wrong.

In 1954 Dr. Kenneth P. Oakley, anthropologist of the British Museum in London, examined the Makapaansgat sites and took samples with him. His position is almost precisely opposite to that of Professor Dart. The blacking of the bones, he declared, may be due to manganese dioxide instead of fire. And the ash, he stated, is not the remains of a wood fire. He admitted that it might be burned bat guano, since the guano of insect-eating bats consists mainly of insect wings and is highly inflammable. He even admits that a fire user who lives in caves might use bat guano at hand rather than carry wood over some distance and across possibly difficult terrain. But he does not think so:

The doubtful evidence of fire in the *Australopithecus* layer at Makapaan is still *sub judice,* and even if confirmed could most readily be accounted for by a natural grass fire outside having ignited inflammable bat guano at the entrance to the cave—there are in fact records of comparable fires having occurred in recent times. (Kenneth P. Oakley, in *American Journal of Physical Anthropology,* 1954, 12, 9.)

In short, we can't tell yet. We need more finds and we need more reliable dating. With the dating we have now it looks as if quite a number of clearly distinct species of sub- or pro- or para-humans lived simultaneously in the same area. Maybe they did—until finally the true humans won out.

---

[4] From "The Makapaansgat Proto-Human *Australopithecus prometheus,*" by Raymond A. Dart, *American Journal of Physical Anthropology,* September 1948.

It has even been suggested that one of these forms—interestingly and significantly again a pygmy form—is still alive in Africa. The idea is based upon a rumor of something the natives are said to call *agogwe*. The British writer Frank W. Lane, after an extensive correspondence with British colonial officials, finally succeeded in finding two men who were willing to go on record with their observations. The following is quoted from Lane's *Nature Parade* (revised edition, London, 1944):

The first account, written by Captain W. Hichens, runs:

"Some years ago I was sent on an official lion hunt to this area (Ussure and Simbiti forests on the western side of the Wembare plains) and, while waiting in a forest glade for a man-eater, I saw two small, brown, furry creatures come from the dense forest on one side of the glade and disappear into the thickets on the other. They were like little men, about four feet high, walking upright, but clad in russet hair. The native hunter with me gaped in mingled fear and amazement. They were, he said, *agogwe*, the little furry men whom one does not see once in a lifetime. I made desperate efforts to find them, but without avail in that wellnigh impenetrable forest. They may have been monkeys, but, if so, they were no ordinary monkeys, nor baboons, nor colobus, nor Sykes, nor any other kind found in Tanganyika."

The other account was written by a Mr. Cuthbert Burgoyne:

"In 1927 I was with my wife coasting Portuguese East Africa in a Japanese cargo boat. We were sufficiently near land to see objects clearly with a glass of twelve magnifications. There was a sloping beach with light bush above, upon which several dozen baboons were hunting for and picking up shellfish or crabs, to judge by their movements. Two pure white baboons were among them. These are very rare, but I had heard of them previously. As we watched, two little brown men walked together out of the bush and down amongst the baboons. They were certainly not any known monkey and yet they must have been akin or they would have disturbed the baboons. They were too far away to see in detail, but these small human-like animals were probably between four and five feet tall, quite upright and graceful in figure. . . ."

After what Dart has said about his Australopithecus, these *agogwe* suddenly look very familiar. And since two reputable men have gone on record as having seen them, we'll have to accept the fact that there is something living in East Africa that looks from a distance like a furred small man. Judging from the experience with the other pygmies, we can hope that we'll find out one day what it is.

But Captain Foxe's "corpes" are likely to remain a riddle forever.

PART TWO

RECORDS IN STONE

Archaeornis (reconstructed), eating the seeds
of a cycad tree

CHAPTER 7

Footprints in Red Sandstone

ONE OF the stories a professor of mine liked to tell had as its central character a minor Russian nobleman who owned an estate at the seashore in the vicinity of Riga. Said nobleman, the report ran, was in the habit of inviting artists, writers, composers, and scientists to his estate for the summer months. One summer one of the guests asked why Professor so-and-so, an astronomer, had not yet arrived. "Because," replied his host, "I did not invite him this year." The guest, feeling that something was amiss, merely said "Oh," but he did not have to wait long for an explanation. "That man," the host continued, "is an outrageous liar. Last time he was here he tried to tell me that he could measure the height of the mountains on the moon."

Measuring the height of the mountains on the moon (from the length of their shadows) is a rather elementary problem in trigonometry, but let's not go into that here. I recount this story merely because the one I am going to tell may sound equally incredible. It has to do with footprints, fossil footprints of an unknown animal, nicely preserved in red sandstone from the Triassic period, but without any bones to go with them. The problem was to determine not only the size but also the shape and the type of the animal which caused them, without any clue other than the footprints themselves. Just to make things a little more baffling, these footprints happened to have a highly misleading shape.

The first specimens of such prints were found a little more than a hundred years ago and the case made its entry into scientific literature in the then customary form of a printed "Open Letter." Its author was a Professor F. K. L. Sickler and the letter was addressed to the very famous anatomist Johann Friedrich Blumenbach, pro-

fessor of medicine at the University of Göttingen. It was published
in 1834 and the title deserves to be quoted in full, not because it is
a very good title but because it contained virtually all the information
then available. It read in translation: "Open Letter to Professor
Blumenbach about the very strange reliefs of tracks of prehistoric,
large, and unknown animals, discovered only a few months ago in
the sandstone quarries of the Hess Mountain near the City of
Hildburghausen."

Hildburghausen is an old and small city, situated some 40 miles
south of the better-known Erfurt in Thuringia. The sandstone quarried there is a rich deep red color; the castle of Heidelberg and the
cathedral of Strasbourg are built of stone of that type. Quite often
this stone splits naturally into thick slabs, as if there had never been
a natural fusion between layers but only a kind of superficial hanging together because of the weight of the layers piled on top. It was
in such places, where the stone split naturally, that the prints were
found, usually the lower slab with the original imprint and the upper
slab with a precisely fitting raised cast of the print.

I have not seen the originals which caused Professor Sickler to
write his Open Letter, but I have seen the specimens that were in
the collection of the Natural History Museum in Berlin. They made
the sense of suprise and wonder which is apparent even in Sickler's
deliberately stiff wording quite understandable. The dark red stone is
flat, sometimes with a faint "wavy" contour which is more apparent
to the touch of the hand than to the eye. And in the middle of such
a flat stone there is suddenly the perfectly clear and rather deep
print of a hand. Usually that handprint is somewhat too large for
a human hand to fit well and when you try it you also find that the
proportions are not quite the same. The fingers are much thicker
and heavier, and so is the thumb, while the palm is too wide near
the fingers and too narrow at the other end.

Still, the similarity, at first glance, is almost breathtaking. The
differences do not show until one proceeds from general "looking"
to detailed examination. In many of the better specimens, there
appears a tiny handprint, like that of a child, immediately in front
of the large handprint. And a good number of such slabs are over-
laid with an irregular network of criss-crossing ridges—"ridges"
because this is usually clearer on the "casts" on the upper slabs—
which do not puzzle a trained observer for a minute. They can be
seen almost anywhere now after a succession of hot days when

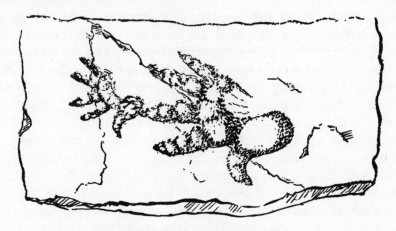

Prints of *Chirotherium barthi*

puddles have dried out and the left-over mud has cracked. With enough material it was easy to find specimens where a print had been ripped apart by such a crack and other specimens where the print had been made over an already existing crack.

The general picture was clear almost from the outset. The area where workmen now quarried red sandstone from the flanks of the Hess Mountain had once been desert, wind-blown sandy desert. Either it rained occasionally, or else a river flooded the area periodically, as the Nile has done all through human history, and then there were places where a footprint could be preserved, at first temporarily, in hardening mud. And if wind-blown sand covered these prints deep enough so that the next moistening, whether a river flood or a rainfall, did not soften the old hardened mud again, the prints lasted to our time, the sand becoming sandstone under the pressure of other deposits piled on top of it.

Considering the shape of these tracks it is not surprising that discussion began at once, *furioso e fortissimo*. To Friedrich S. Voigt the whole case was perfectly simple. These were the tracks of a giant ape—let's call him *Palaeopithecus*. Others shook their heads, especially Alexander von Humboldt. Apes are rare and tropical and Hildburghausen was not in the tropics. More likely the tracks belonged to a large marsupial, something like the kangaroo of today. One Professor Link, who wrote in French, preferred to believe that it might have been a large toad—quite large, since a large track is about 9 inches long. Then Voigt revised his opinion in part. He had a large track, presumably one where the imprint of the thumb had either broken off or happened not to show, and he declared that this must have been a bear, "possibly the famous cave bear itself." But he also had much smaller tracks of somewhat different shape; these must have been made by a monkey, "probably" a mandrill.

Nine different papers on the "Hess mountain quarry tracks" appeared in 1835, the year after the publication of Sickler's Open Letter. One of these nine, written by a Dr. Kaup, made the one lasting contribution of that year: he named the tracks, or rather the animal that had caused them. Of course nothing was really known about them except their shape. But that was enough for a name—after all, by order of the school commission one had spent six years learning Greek; now apply what had been learned. The tracks looked like hands; the Greek word for hand is *cheiros*. Unfortunately all safety stopped at that point. Did the animal that had made the tracks belong to the reptiles? If so, since *sauros* is Greek for "lizard," the name would be *Chirosaurus*. But if it was a mammal the name would have to be *Chirotherium*. Dr. Kaup believed with von Humboldt that it had probably been a marsupial and hence a mammal, but he still was careful. The title of his paper read: "Animal tracks of Hildburghausen, Chirotherium or Chirosaurus."

Later usage dropped the "Chirosaurus" so that the tracks came to be called "Chirotherium tracks" in all books in any language. It is unfortunate that the wrong term was the one retained. We now know that the animal was a reptile, but the name is still Chirotherium.

For a few years it seemed as if the mystery surrounding these tracks would remain centered on Hildburghausen. But in 1839 there appeared in the *London and Edinburgh Philosophical Magazine* a report by P. G. Egerton, with the title: "On Two Casts in Sandstone of the Impressions of the Hindfoot of a Gigantic Chirotherium, from the New Red Sandstone of Cheshire." Egerton's article dealt in the main with the tracks to which the title refers and which had been discovered near Storeton in 1838. But he could point out that Chirotherium tracks had actually been discovered first in England. Some had been found in 1824 in the standstone of Tarporley (near Chester, also in Cheshire) but had been neglected until the Storeton tracks came to light. Of course the Storeton find, two "handprints," each about 15 inches long, was impressive because of its size. The Tarporley tracks were smaller and apparently not very clear.

France was brought in when Daubée, in 1857, published a contribution in the *Comptes rendus* of the French Academy of Science, dealing with the *découverte de traces de pattes de quadrupèdes* in Triassic sandstones of Saint-Valbert, near Luxeuil (Haute Saône). Between these two dates, the second English and the first French, more tracks had been found in Germany, in Hildburghausen as well as in other places. That the mysterious hand-animal had also lived in what is now Spain was reported for the first time in 1898 by Calderón in the *Actas de la Sociedad española de Historia natural.* Several years later Chirotherium tracks were found in America; the reason they were discovered so late is clear from the place names occurring in the following short quotation, taken from a recent authoritative publication:

> Well represented in North America in Lower and Upper Moenkopi of Little Colorado River region by total of eight species. Chirotherium occurs as far east as Snowflake, Arizona, and as far west as Rockville, Utah, a lateral distribution of 250 miles. . . .[1]

The main problem all through the history of the Chirotherium tracks was, of course, "What kind of animal made those tracks? How did it look?" But before we go into that we should gain a better idea about the age of the tracks. (See chart of geologic periods in the Appendix.) Before our planet entered the Present and Recent periods, there was the Pleistocene period, also known as the Ice Age, lasting about one million years. Before that there was the Tertiary period; before that the Cretaceous (it lasted about 65 million years), and before the Cretaceous the Jurassic—of about 35 million years. And before the Jurassic there was the Triassic period, also estimated to have lasted 35 million years.

The word "Triassic" itself hints that it has three clearly distinguishable subdivisions, usually called Lower, Middle, and Upper Triassic, the last, of course, being the most recent. It so happened that German geologists went to work on this period first and they naturally gave the divisions German names. They called the Lower Triassic *Buntsandstein,* which is simply a contraction of the two words *bunter Sandstein,* meaning "colorful sandstone." Part of this has been adopted into geological English so that an English or American geologist will calmly say—to stick to our theme—"Chirotherium tracks occur mainly

[1] Frank E. Peabody, "Reptile and Amphibian Trackways from the Lower Triassic Moenkopi Formation of Arizona and Utah," *Bulletin of the Department of Geological Sciences,* vol. 27, no. 8 (Berkeley and Los Angeles: University of California Press, 1948).

in the middle Bunter." The Middle Triassic was called *Muschelkalk* by the German geologists. *Muschel* means any clam, while *Kalk* does *not* mean chalk, but limestone. That particular word is used in full if there is need to refer to this specific formation in Central Europe. The Upper Triassic was called *Keuper* by the Germans (a miner's term), and this, too, is used in English when the European formation is under discussion.

All finds of Chirotherium tracks in continental Europe can be dated as Bunter, or Lower Triassic, which makes their average age about 190 million years. Only in England have Chirotherium tracks been found in the Keuper—25 to 30 million years later than those in continental Europe. Nobody can tell whether tracks may still be found in continental Keuper too, or whether Chirotherium actually lasted 25 million years longer on English soil. I have the feeling that Englishmen would be the first to subscribe to the latter hypothesis.

Naturally there were several species in Europe too. If the number of tracks is an indication of the abundance of a species, and not just an indication of some special habits which produced more tracks in places where they might be preserved, the most common variety was *Chirotherium barthi,* so named by Dr. Kaup. Sickler himself established a smaller form which he called *Chirotherium minus.* Later his own name was attached to still another species, *Ch. sickleri,* which is the smallest yet known. Its prints are only 3 inches long, as compared to the 9 inches of *Ch. barthi* and the 15 inches of Egerton's *Ch. herculis.*

All this, however, would have been prettier by far if the red sandstone had been kind enough to yield some fossil bones too. Scientists hovering around the quarries of Hess Mountain were quite certain that it would, sooner or later. After all, a Chirotherium must have died somewhere, sometime, in the area where it had lived. Even if one assumed that it could defend itself most effectively against attackers, there was still old age. And there was thirst—remember the area was a desert.

Whether the corpse of an animal in a desert area will fossilize depends entirely on circumstances, which most of the time are against it. The likely thing to happen is that the body will be torn apart by hungry carrion eaters and all the soft parts gulped down as fast as possible. The bones will be gnawed; some of the smaller ones swallowed, the larger ones carried about. What is left will be dried by the sun and eroded away by wind-blown sand. But just in the desert the

precise opposite is also possible. If an animal is not killed by a predator or does not die "on the surface" from natural causes, but is killed
by a sandstorm and left dead and deeply buried, the chances for
preservation are excellent. The body will desiccate rather than decom-
pose and will fossilize as a "mummy."

True desert animals do not succumb to sandstorms as often as one
might think, simply because they are adapted to a life where sandstorms form a part of the environment. While they may be buried
alive by a sandstorm they usually manage to stay buried *and* alive
until the danger has passed. Occasionally they do die. That this did
happen in the past as it happens now is demonstrated by a unique
find which brings us back to the neighborhood of Chirotherium, both
in time and space. This is a sandstone slab, measuring about 3 by
6 feet, found about half a century ago at Hesslach near Stuttgart. Its
geological age is Keuper, the youngest of the three subdivisions of
the Triassic, and very young Keuper at that.

On that slab you can see the remains of twenty-four small reptiles
of crocodile shape. The largest of them is, as well as it can be measured, 34 inches long. They must all have perished together in the
same sandstorm. This little *Aëtosaurus,* as it has been named, belonged
to a group of reptiles now completely extinct, the *Pseudosuchia.* Like
the equally extinct *Parasuchia,* they were related to the crocodiles, but
of a different branch of the family. One may translate the technical
terms as "pseudo-crocodiles" and "para-crocodiles" without being too
far off. It is worth noting that the little pseudo-crocodile Aëtosaurus
was completely encased in armor, each plate with a neat little decora-
tion. An armor-encased body should fossilize easily, but in spite of
this feature only this one slab of Keuper sandstone with Aëtosaurus
on it has ever been found. Obviously their customary mode of death
was accompanied by destruction of the body—say some other reptile's longer teeth and stronger jaws—and death in a sandstorm was
a rare exception.

The scientists who were patiently waiting for Chirotherium bones

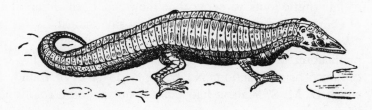

Aëtosaurus

from the Hess Mountain quarries did not then know about this particular instance, but they knew quite well what desert conditions would or would not do and their hopes were not too farfetched. But unfortunately the hopes are still unrealized.

In addition to hoping, one could guess a little more. It became clear just at that time that large mammals had not existed in Triassic days. That ruled out all guesses about apes, bears, and monkeys. But there was still a choice. Chirotherium could have been a reptile, or it could have been a large amphibian. In the periods preceding the Triassic there had been large amphibians, grotesque, heavy, and large-headed salamanderlike monsters of crocodile size. And in 1841 the then very famous Professor Richard Owen in England thought that he could point his finger at a specific group. Because of the strange labyrinthine structure of their usually enormous teeth one group of these ancient giant amphibians had been named labyrinthodonts. Remains of them had been found in England. Chirotherium tracks had been found in England too. They did not occur together, nor was it certain that tracks and bones belonged to the same reasonably short time interval. But Owen thought that they might and he announced that the creature that had made the tracks was in all probability a labyrinthodont.

Some other paleontologists shook their heads and decided that they would not believe anything for a while. But the word of Owen happened to be the word of authority and many patiently tried to fit the known bones and the known tracks together. The whole episode culminated in a drawing published by Charles Lyell showing a 6-foot-long toadlike labyrinthodont walking cross-legged. Some consecutive tracks which had been found indicated that the "thumb" was on the outside. Lyell therefore had to postulate that the right foot was put down to the left of the left foot in walking.

It was a bit strong for most informed observers, but the best they could do was to keep quiet. They had to admit that 6-foot labyrinthodonts had existed. They had to admit that some of them were generally toad-shaped. They could not show how the originator of the handlike tracks had really looked. Nor could they produce tracks of labyrinthodonts to show that they had been different from those of Chirotherium. All they could really say against Lyell's picture was "We don't like it." The result was that between 1855, the date of publication of that drawing, and 1915, the choice lay between acceptance or resignation. No bones had yet been found, and a fact which D. M. S. Watson had pointed out in the *Geological Magazine*

Richard Owen's labyrin-
thodont walking cross-
legged

(December 1914) was in itself not conclusive. Watson had noted that whenever there were consecutive tracks the trackway proved to be quite narrow. This pointed to an animal of narrow build, probably tall. Probably a reptile. But those that were not yet tired of the discussion could say with at least equal justification that a trackway resulting from a cross-legged walk would of necessity be quite narrow.

In 1917 a graduate student, K. Willruth, who devoted the thesis for his doctorate to Chirotherium, came up with another idea. His thesis was based in part on a paper written in 1889 by a geologist named J. G. Bornemann but for some reason never published. Bornemann had emphasized that a single spoor might teach something but that a trackway would teach much more, like length of stride, etc., etc., and that study should, therefore, be concentrated on trackways.

The advice was good, but you then could not avoid running into the difficulty of having the "thumbs" on the outside. Willruth tried to find a way out of this problem; it may have been due to the fact that he had *not* read Owen's paper that he evolved a novel idea.

There is no law that says that there have to be five toes on a reptile's foot. Very many reptiles do have five toes but geological history is full of three-toed forms. And since the mammals can have anything from five toes (monkey) to a single toe (donkey), and since there are even some forms where the number of toes on the hind feet does not agree with the number of toes on the front feet (tapir), there was nothing to prevent one from assuming that Chirotherium was four-toed. The four "fingers" were its true toes. But the "thumb" was no toe, it was a fleshy appendage of some sort, possibly the lower end of a heavy skin fold, which made the impression on the ground. Willruth's teacher, Professor J. Walther, not only accepted his student's thesis, he also agreed enthusiastically with the conclusions. Everybody had been fooled; we had here an animal of narrow build, progressing normally in a natural manner on hind feet which were several times the size of its forefeet. If it had not been for that accidental appendage which produced a false thumbprint on the ground all this would have been clear from the outset.

As regards the restoration of normal walk to Chirotherium, Willruth's thesis was a long step forward. As for the fleshy appendage, one can only say that many a pretty hypothesis has been ruined by an evil fact. The fact in this case consisted of the great clarity of many Chirotherium prints. It is not only possible to count the fingers, it is sometimes even possible to count the joints. And on such specimens one can see that the "thumb" has joints too, just what it should not have if it were a fleshy appendage. It also spoke against this idea that the "thumb" was always as deeply impressed as its two neighboring "fingers." That, in itself, indicated an internal bony stiffening.

In short, Willruth's brave guess miscarried. But it took only a few more years to bring the case of the unknown fossil to a conclusion. In 1925 there appeared a small book, only 92 pages, devoted to Chirotherium tracks.[2] Its author was Professor Wolfgang Soergel, then professor of geology and paleontology at the University of Tübingen, near Stuttgart. Professor Soergel, as became evident from his book, had spent years in a concentrated study of all the tracks he could find in museums and collections in southwest Germany. While he did not neglect other types he worked especially on tracks of *Chirotherium barthi,* the most common form and a rather large one.

The "thumb," Soergel saw soon, was on the outside of the foot and was a toe. Anatomists number fingers and toes in the same manner in which musicians mark piano scores, from the inside out, beginning with the thumb and ending with the little finger. The only difference between an anatomical picture and a piano score is that the piano score counts 1, 2, 3, 4, and 5, while the anatomical picture uses I, II, III, IV, and V. The "thumb" of Chirotherium, therefore, was not I, it was V. This is not so surprising as it may sound. If you look at the foot of any lizard—well, almost any lizard; it does not apply to some—you'll see that the outside toe V is spread apart from the remainder of the foot to a fair degree, while I on the inside is usually more or less parallel to the others. Once you realize this the whole picture becomes clear; the long confusion had been due solely to the fact that everybody who saw such a track succumbed to the impulse of putting his own hand into it for comparison, putting the right hand into the left footprint.

Looking around among fossils for a skeleton of a reptilian foot which looked about the way the foot of Chirotherium must have looked, Soergel found that there was one which "fitted" closely, except for size.

[2] W. Soergel, *Die Fährten der Chirotheria* (Jena: Gustav Fischer, 1925).

In Triassic layers of South Africa the fossil foot of a small pseudo-crocodile (*Euparkeria capensis*) had been found. It was definitely, as one could tell from the bones, a right foot. Digits I to IV are roughly parallel, but digit v on the outside is spread away from the remainder of the foot. Soergel drew a picture of the probable footprint of an Euparkeria; it resembles that of a Chirotherium but not quite closely enough to be confused with one. And the foot length of Euparkeria is only about 2 inches.

This settled, Soergel went on, looking for fine detail. Did Chirotherium have claws? One print showed one clearly, on digit IV, and when others were examined closely faint marks of claw tips could be found, including one on digit v, the "thumb." In fact, Chirotherium had possessed very strong and long claws which were carried in such a way that they were not worn by touching the ground. This strongly suggests carnivorous habits.

The next step was to examine the prints and their casts for skin structure. Folds of the "sole" were quite apparent on some pieces; scaly skin showed clearly on these and on many others. This proved that Chirotherium was a reptile. A British zoologist, Richard Lydekker, had always insisted on that and had started writing "Chirosaurus" in 1890, but unfortunately he had been unable to break the established habit.

Next step: check the impressions of a number of consecutive tracks for the probable sequence of movement. Soergel concluded that it must have been left foreleg, right hind leg, right foreleg, left hind leg —the normal gait of a four-legged animal. Next step after that was to measure the depth of impression, especially the relative depth of "foot" and "hand" of the same individual. It has been mentioned earlier that the "hand" is much smaller than the "foot." By measuring the depth of impression Soergel also found that the foot carried all the weight, while the "hand" just touched the ground.

From this fact alone the shape of the unknown animal could be reconstructed. If a four-legged reptile manages to carry virtually the whole weight of its body on its hind feet the body must be built in such a way that it almost balances. This means that Chirotherium must have had a long and massive tail, heavy and stiff enough to serve as a counterweight for the body. For the same reason it cannot have had a very long neck, especially since a carnivorous reptile has to have a reasonably large head. This general shape—massive hind legs with large feet, weaker forelegs with small "hands," fairly short neck with a

Chirotherium as it probably looked in life

relatively large head, and long and massive tail—is very well known
to paleontologists. It is the shape of all the later dinosaurs that took to
walking upright. Obviously Chirotherium was evolving in the general
direction of bipedal walk; it did not quite balance on two legs only,
but it came close. Of the late forms of Chirotherium which left tracks
in British Keuper we can be virtually certain that they did walk upright. Of the earlier forms there exist a few suspicious tracks where
the small prints of the front legs are unaccountably lacking. Maybe
Chirotherium could do what the Australian collared lizard (*Chlamydosaurus*) still demonstrates. When undisturbed it walks in the same
manner as any other lizard, but when angered or frightened it will
put on bursts of speed, holding the body stiffly curved backward and
running on its hind legs only.

How big was Chirotherium? Or, since there were a number of species, how big was *Ch. barthi?* It is easy to measure the length of the
stride, but not quite as easy to draw conclusions from it. The length
of the stride is determined not only by the length of the legs but also by
their angle of "swing." Weighing carefully all the possibilities and especially all the possibilities of error, Professor Soergel concluded that the
body of *Ch. barthi* must have been about 3 feet long. The tail, in order
to balance the weight in front of the hind legs, must have been equally
long or somewhat longer, while neck and head together measured
probably a little less than the body. This, then, would make the over-
all length 8 feet for *Ch. barthi,* while the total length of the smallest

known varieties, *Ch. bornemanni* and *Ch. sickleri,* would work out to 14 inches.

Because it was a carnivore, Chirotherium cannot have been very numerous—in any given fauna the carnivores are and must be a small minority. Because of the quantity of tracks, some early paleontologists unthinkingly concluded that it was very common. They forgot that they were not dealing with a few hundred fossil foot skeletons but with several hundred footprints, and a single individual can make any desired number of footprints. One Herr Winzer, for many years the owner of the sandstone quarries near Hildburghausen, made himself a large drawing of his quarry in which each footprint was entered as it was discovered. They all fitted the pattern of *four* long trackways and it is not even certain that these were made by four individuals.

After all this was settled, Professor Soergel still had to decide where this family of reptiles belonged in the system, and which other reptiles were its closest relatives. The answers had occurred to Soergel while he was working on the whole complex of problems. The one fossil foot which most closely resembled the reconstructed foot of Chirotherium belonged to a pseudo-crocodile. The general proportions of Chirotherium, especially the relationship between body length, tail length, length of hind legs as compared to forelegs, all pointed just to these pseudo-crocodiles, the Pseudosuchia of the paleontologists, the sub-order believed to be ancestral to the dinosaurs and the flying saurians. There was just one main reason for avoiding the outright statement that "the Chirotheria are pseudo-crocodiles." Only *Ch. bornemanni*—which Sickler had called *Ch. minus*—was of about the same size as the other known pseudo-crocodiles of European Triassic deposits. All the others are considerably larger.

Soergel's book was received with much surprise, much enthusiasm in selected circles, and without dissent. So it had been possible, by dint of hard work and sound reasoning, to make something out of these tracks for which no fossil bone was ever found. A few dozen handbooks were rewritten and the "family" of the Chirotheriidae was established.

More than ten years later an interesting addition to the story was provided by another German paleontologist, Friedrich Freiherr von Huene. He had been in Brazil in the early 1930s with another paleontologist, one Dr. R. Stahlecker. Their interests had been well known, of course, and one day a Brazilian named Vicentino Presto told them about a site of fossils near a place called Chinquá. The two Germans not only found the site promising, they could also determine its age. The fossils belonged to the Upper Rio-do-Rasto formation of Brazil, Upper Triassic and equivalent in age to the German Keuper. The main find was a rather large saurian, which von Huene named, in honor both of the original discoverer and of the place, *Prestosuchus chiniquensis.*

Of course one is quite careful with fossils in the field. Most especially nobody in his right mind will try to separate the fossil bone from the stony matrix to any larger extent than is absolutely necessary for recognition. Fossils are taken out with much of the surrounding stone sticking to them. They are then usually wrapped in burlap that has been soaked in fresh plaster of Paris, more plaster of Paris is smeared on, and the whole is nailed into stout boxes for transportation. The detail work of separating bone from matrix and of mounting the bones (if they are in a shape to be mounted) is decidedly an indoor job and may take years.

Doctors von Huene and Stahlecker packed their Prestosuchus and returned home. When the fossil was in a sufficiently advanced state of preparation to be examined it was found to be a pseudo-crocodile, of a size far surpassing all the forms from the same group that had been found in Europe. Its total length was 15 feet, 6 inches, and it stood 3 feet, 6 inches, tall. The shape of Prestosuchus was almost precisely what Professor Soergel had drawn as the "calculated" shape of Chirotherium. And the foot of Prestosuchus agreed with the foot of Chirotherium as Soergel had reconstructed it from the prints.

Prestosuchus is considerably larger than *Ch. barthi* and also considerably later. And, of course, it lived in the Southern Hemisphere, while all Chirotherium tracks known were found quite far north of the equator. But it does prove that the pseudo-crocodiles could not only attain the size required for Chirotherium but even grow much larger.

As for fossil remains of the European Chirotherium, it is still true that there are none. But this is not so disappointing any more, because we can be quite sure that if they are ever found they will merely confirm what could be deduced from patient detail studies and by careful thinking.

CHAPTER 8

The Dragon from the Lias Epsilon

In my mind it is literally just one step from Chirotherium to another extinct animal which did not resemble it in the least.

This may sound highly illogical, but it is based on a circumstance in my past. In the Berlin Museum of Natural History there was a special hall devoted to paleontology and in that hall there was a whole wall of Chirotherium prints. Almost all the way to the high ceiling it was "paneled" with large slabs of red sandstone which was even more intensely red because of the sunlight that struck slantwise through tall windows. In the days I have in mind Dr. Soergel's book was still in the process of being written and Dr. von Huene had not yet been led by Senhor Presto to the remains of his Prestosuchus. One turned away from that wall of red sandstone with a sense of mystery.

And when one had turned away one faced a tall partition, also covered with stone slabs. But this stone was black, black slate, and on that black slate there showed in beautiful bas relief the bodies of fishlike animals, some 7 feet long. To anybody who knew anything about them, these slabs came as a relief from the mystery of the red sandstone. There nothing was known; here it was hard to think of a question for which there was not at least a tentative answer. These slabs showed specimens of ichthyosaurs.

That particular arrangement was probably due to the accident of available space, but it happened to work out into a fine lesson in geology. The few steps the visitor to the Museum had to make in order to progress from the red sandstone to the black slate transported him through a whole geological period, from the Lower Triassic of the Chirotherium tracks to the Lower Jurassic of the ichthyosaurs. Expressed in terms of time, these few steps represented approximately 35 million years. They also represented a complete change of environ-

ment. It so happens that both the Chirotherium tracks and the bodies
of the ichthyosaurs were found in the same general area in southwestern Germany. In the Museum they were separated by some 15
feet of distance; the actual localities from which they came are about
100 miles apart. But since Jurassic slate is younger than Triassic
rocks, it would even be possible for both to be found in what looks
on a map like the same spot, with ichthyosaurs near the surface and
Chirotherium tracks at the bottom of a mine shaft. The ichthyosaurs
swam in over what had once been a desert.

When the Romans crossed the Alps from Italy into Switzerland
they could see, in the distance, still another chain of mountains. These
mountains were much lower than the Alps themselves and they were
darkly forested. Somebody coined the name which was to be entered
on the good Roman road maps. It was *Mons Jura.* Much later this
name was asserted to be a Celtic word in Roman garb, namely the
word *jor,* meaning forest. Whether this derivation is correct or not
does not matter much. "Jura" became the name of these mountains,
at first in Switzerland only, though a continuation of the range, after
an interruption, sweeps through German Swabia and then curves up
into Franconia.

In 1795 young Alexander von Humboldt journeyed to Switzerland
and saw the Mons Jura of the Romans. At first it probably had mostly
classical connotations to him, but then he realized two things. One
was that the rock of which it was made was one that he had already
seen in southern Germany. The other was that this "Jurassic" rock
differed from any other he knew. Presumably it had formed during a
specific geological period of its own, different from the other periods
that had formed other rocks and other mountains. The name of the
Swiss mountains was thus extended both to the German mountains
and to the geological period during which they had formed. Like the
Triassic, the Jurassic has three definite subdivisions. Their names are
now in international use, as are the German names of the Triassic
subdivisions, but those of the Jurassic are British.

The lowest and oldest of the three is characterized by its decided
black color. It can be called either the Lower Jurassic, or the Black
Jurassic, or by its special name, Lias. The Middle Jurassic, again for
reasons of color, is often called the Brown Jurassic, but it too has a
special name, Dogger. And finally the Upper Jurassic is either that, or
White Jurassic, or Malm. At some time somebody made the guess
that the color shades might simply be the result of difference in age,

that the Lias had turned black from sheer age. We now know better, though apparently this simple idea stuck in some people's minds.

The actual reason involves that change in environment I mentioned earlier. The landscape of the Chirotherium sandstones at the beginning of the Triassic was decidedly desert. We are not quite sure how far to the south this desert extended. The Alps, of course, did not exist; they were formed much later, during the Tertiary period; but we do know that there was an ocean in the south. That ocean, a kind of enlarged and glorified Mediterranean, seems to have reached around the whole earth; it is technically known as the Tethys Sea. During the subperiod of the Bunter, something, presumably a coastal mountain chain, kept it out of the "Danube area," which interests us here. I am using the word Danube here in an exaggeratedly broad sense; what I mean is the area just to the north of the present-day Alps, but I don't like to mention their name since they did not exist then.

But whatever restricted the Tethys Sea during the Bunter finally gave way, thereby causing the end of that subperiod. The Tethys broke in and formed a probably shallow local sea, the result of which is the second subperiod of the Triassic, the Muschelkalk—or "clam limestone." But it was a temporary sea only, which in due course of time became land again. In the third subperiod of the Triassic, the Keuper, it was land, some of it at least even desert, as the mass death of little Aëtosaurus has proved. However, the victory of the land over the "Muschelkalk Sea" hardly counted in the long run. With the end of the Keuper, which marked the end of the Triassic period as a whole, the Tethys Sea won out.

All through the 35 million years of the Jurassic period and the following 65 million years of the Cretaceous period most of Europe was under water. For about 100 million years Scandinavia must have been the largest of the islands of the "European archipelago." Everything from Scandinavia south to about the present-day northern shore of Africa was flooded by the Tethys. The sea, while lasting for a long time, was probably never very deep anywhere, perhaps even shallower than the present Mediterranean.

The climate was warm and so was the water. The many small islands of the European archipelago must have looked very much like the South Sea archipelagos of today. There were "high islands," remains of former mountains and otherwise solid blocks of land which the sea could not wash away easily. Near them corals built reefs and formed "low islands." On those islands grew tree ferns and the now tropical cycads. On others, the remainders of old land, there grew ginkgo trees and early redwoods.

The Jurassic European sea must have been small at first, a little bay here, a minor breakthrough there, large islands with not too much water between them. The sediments that settled in that sea were essentially mud, now hardened into the black slate of the Lias. As the water surface increased and the land area shrank, the sediments changed character. They were no longer typical black mud, but brown Dogger instead. And finally they were the sediments of the high seas, consisting largely of the hard remains of microscopic animals—white Malm.

As for the ichthyosaurs, their early forms appeared during the Triassic period. As far as time alone is concerned, they might have been found in the South-German Muschelkalk Sea that formed when the Tethys broke in from the southeast, through present-day Bohemia. Actually things did not work out quite that beautifully. In fact most of the early ichthyosaurs now known were found in California. But the first specimen came to light, about a century ago, in strata from the Muschelkalk level of Spitsbergen, that group of icy islands far to the north of the northernmost capes of the Scandinavian peninsula. The name of the type became *Mixosaurus nordenskjöldi*. By the time Mixosaurus was found, the later Jurassic ichthyosaurs were already well known. One might say that they had become the special friends of many scientists who sometimes became each other's enemies because of them.

Nobody can say whether ichthyosaurs were found, or how many, in times antedating the development of modern science. But for a long time paleontologists believed that the first find of which there is literary mention was made in 1708. However, the late Professor Samuel Wendell Williston, originally an assistant of the famous dinosaur hunter Othniel C. Marsh, and later of the University of Chicago, found a source about twenty years older than the one which had been believed to be the first. It is a big and beautifully illustrated book by a Welsh naturalist named Lluyd. The illustrations it contains are mostly those of fossil fishes, and ichthyosaur remains appear among them. Why Lluyd thought them to be fishes is very easy to understand; the vertebrae of the ichthyosaurs have the same typical shape—a biconcave lens—as the vertebrae of true fishes. This was a mistake for which he can hardly be blamed. What makes a reader of today gasp is the explanation Lluyd gave, but even that was not completely

*Mixosaurus norden-
skjoldi,* one of the early
ichthyosaurians

his own invention; he took his pick from a variety of existing ideas.

Fossils, if not specifically ichthyosaurs, had been found ever since the time of classical Greece. Since they did not interfere with philosophy they had not caused much of a stir and the worst misinterpretation was that they were thought to be the bones of former tribes of giants. But later, during the Christian Middle Ages, somebody had to say something definitive about fossils. Most theologians seem to have been quite happy to forget all about them, after stating that these things, which sometimes looked like bones, and sometimes like clamshells, and sometimes even like animal skulls, but which were always stone, were merely accidental formations—strangely shaped stones. Others, toying with astrological thought, were willing to discourse at length on the influence of the constellations on inanimate matter. I don't recall right now whether the devil was ever blamed for their existence, but a few theologians thought they might have been preliminary models which the Lord created prior to the creation of the living forms.

Lluyd happened to come in at the tail end of much discussion of this kind. He apparently did not like any of these ideas but picked up one more trend of thought which had been handed down from the Greek philosophers. Theophrastus of Lesbos, who died in 284 B.C., had known fossil fishes and had also known where they had been found. There were rivers nearby and Theophrastus considered that these rivers might have flooded the surrounding countryside sometime in the past. During that flood fish from the river must have swum about over land and laid their eggs before the flood retreated. For some reason these eggs had not died off, but grown up in sand instead of water. Hence they were "stony fishes." Lluyd elaborated only slightly on Theophrastus. He abolished the river flood. The eggs had been laid in the sea and had been carried up to the clouds with moisture, ultimately falling on the land as rain.

A Swiss naturalist, Johann Jakob Scheuchzer, also a professor of mathematics and a doctor of medicine, and in some respects Cuvier's forerunner, fought against such ideas. To him a fossil fish was precisely what it is to us, a once-living fish which, after its death, had been somehow preserved. The only trouble was that fossil fishes were usually found many miles from any body of water. But Scheuchzer had an answer: Didn't the Bible tell of the Flood? Didn't everybody know this? Didn't everybody know, too, that this Flood had been caused by the sins of Man? Those fossil fish, which had died in the Flood, had lost their lives because of Man. And now Man, in deep wickedness, was not even willing to accept them as visible proof of the Flood and as reminders of the sins of his forefathers, but insisted that these fossils "are engendered by stone and marl." Scheuchzer's convictions took the shape of a book—or should one say a sermon? —entitled *Piscium querulae,* "The Complaint of the Fishes," which appeared in 1708. Among the pictures there are two vertebrae of an ichthyosaur. Strangely enough, the learned doctor did not even make Lluyd's mistake, but described the vertebrae as human, belonging to one of those sinners who had drowned in the Flood. It must have been Scheuchzer's obsession to find the bones of one of these "sinners"; some twenty years later he pictured the skeleton of a fossil giant salamander as *Homo diluvii testis,* adding (in German) "bone-skeleton of a man drowned in the Flood."

The way Scheuchzer got the two ichthyosaur vertebrae is known; he himself told the story. One evening in 1708 he accompanied a friend named Langhans for a walk near Altdorf, a village not far from Nuremberg. Philosophizing as they walked along, they came to the local gallows hill, which then was precisely what its name means. Langhans noticed a piece of black slate on the ground and picked it up. Looking at it more closely, he saw eight vertebrae in a row and, struck by sudden panic terror, he hurled the stone away. Scheuchzer, being a physician, was less scared of human bones, which he thought he had recognized. First he walked his frightened friend home, calming him as well as he could. Then he returned for the piece. He kept two of the vertebrae and pictured them on Plate III of his book.

Strangely enough, another picture of ichthyosaur vertebrae appeared during the same year, in a book called *Oryctographia Norica.* It was written by one Johann Jacob Bayer who had found the bones in Jurassic deposits in Franconia and who calmly labeled them "vertebrae from a large fish." Scheuchzer grew indignant. True, Bayer at least had not taken these vertebrae to be mineralogical accidents, and thereby, in Scheuchzer's opinion, acknowledged the Deluge. But Bayer should have seen by their size that they had to be human, coming from a drowned sinner. However, in spite of Scheuchzer's insistence, other anatomists of the time quietly but firmly said "fish" when confronted with the evidence.

Things remained reasonably quiet for a century, as far as the ichthyosaur was concerned. In 1814 the "skull of Lyme Regis" was found at a coastal town on Lyme Bay of the English Channel. It was a fine ichthyosaur skull and it was described by the Scottish surgeon Sir Everard Home. Other finds followed quickly and after some years Sir Everard began to wonder what kind of an animal it was that kept cropping up down there in Dorset. If he had also concluded that it was a large and peculiar fish, it would not have been too surprising. But he made a different mistake instead, mostly because a peculiar little animal had just then achieved some zoological glory.

Beginning about the year 1700 stories about a strange creature had emerged from Austria, usually originating in the mountains inland from Trieste. The peasants had said at first that the creatures were young dragons. To a calmer observer they could hardly be that, but they were strange enough for anybody's taste; up to 10 inches in length (but usually measuring only 8), they had the general shape of an eel. But instead of fins they had four small legs. They had two bundles of pinkish feathery gills sticking out from their heads. They were blind. And they were pale whitish in color. The mystery of their sporadic occurrence actually had the same cause as their weird appearance. The rare visitor was a newtlike animal which had adapted itself to life in waters in dark caves. Only when the caves were flooded was it occasionally washed up into surface rivers. The first complete description of this animal appeared in 1800 and the scientific name given to it was *Proteus*.

Like the real newts and the salamanders, this Proteus is an amphibian. Sir Everard Home thought that the animal from the Lias of Lyme Regis was an amphibian too and, impressed by the recent description of the Austrian mystery, named it *Proteosaurus*. The name was in use—or, let's say, it stayed uncontradicted—for just two years, from 1819 to 1821. Even though Sir Everard became the first president of the Royal College of Surgeons during the latter year, critical characters from other departments of knowledge shelved the name just then. The curator of mineralogy of the British Museum, Koenig by name, had gone over the material he had received and if there was anything he failed to find it was amphibian characteristics in the skulls or skeletons. The animal, it seemed clear to him, was either half-fish and half-reptile, or else something with different proportions of the same ingredients. *Sauros,* as we already know, is the Greek word for lizard. The Greek word for fish is *ichthys.* Koenig suggested *Ichthyosaurus.*

During those same years another Englishman, William Daniel Conybeare, had prepared a careful description of the finds. Conybeare (probably predestined to zoology by his name) accepted Koenig's suggestion and called the animal *Ichthyosaurus communis.* And then Cuvier, "Father of Paleontology," began to write *"Ichthyosaurus communis* Conyb." That made it definite; the name has been in use ever since. Recently paleontologists have been forced to invent several different names for the different types, but they still say ichthyosaurs when they mean the whole group.

Cuvier himself had characterized the old saurian as "a creature with the snout of a dolphin, the teeth of a crocodile, the skull and the chest of a lizard, the paddles of a whale, and the vertebrae of a fish"—but in spite of these various similarities a reptile. Professor Richard Owen in England agreed.

Three years after Conybeare's monograph on ichthyosaurs a small book appeared in Germany. Its author, one Georg Friedrich Jaeger, was a man of the old school, who wrote in Latin. And he said that one did not have to make a trip to England and brave the unpleasantness of a Channel crossing if one wanted to see an ichthyosaur. They could be found in fine condition in Swabia, in the vicinity of the places called Boll and Holzmaden by their vulgar German-speaking inhabitants. They were located in the co-called Swabian Alb—originally of course the Roman *Mons albus,* the "white mountains." Since none of these names appears on unspecialized maps I may add here that Holzmaden, which was to become the most famous, is 20 miles from Stuttgart in a generally easterly direction.

At the same time it became known that a fine skull of an ichthyosaur (probably from Boll) had been kept in the City High School of Stuttgart since about 1750. Nobody connected with the school had any idea what it was; nobody not connected with the school knew it was there.

Careful investigation followed quickly. The white crown of those not very high mountains which gave rise to the Roman name *albus* is, of course, White Jurassic, or Malm. Fossils can be found there, but no ichthyosaurs. They occur in what may be called the foothills, where black Lias forms the surface. The Lias, in turn, rests on Triassic, just as one should expect; mostly on Keuper. Underneath that Keuper there might be, in places, the much older Bunter with Chirotherium tracks. It forms the surface 120 miles to the northeast. Examining the black Lias deposits carefully, experts gradually began to discover subdivisions inside the Lias. Of course not every one of them was present everywhere, but relative ages could be assigned to them. And it became customary to designate them with Greek letters. The oldest was the Lias alpha. Then followed the Lias beta and gamma, above that the Lias delta. Ichthyosaurus occurred in the Lias epsilon.

The wonder was the quantity. Every visitor to the places where ichthyosaurs could be found returned with the same simile in mind: "They are as tightly packed in that slate as herrings in a barrel." And that held true for other localities too. There was (and is) a pile of ichthyosaurs near Holzmaden. Another one near Castle Banz in Franconia. Another one in Dorset in England. But there is not a single one in the "original Jura" in Switzerland. That the ichthyosaur came to be identified with Holzmaden in later years is due to several factors. One is that the Holzmaden specimens are especially well preserved—quality always helps. Another is that this particular "ichthyosaur catacomb," as it has been called, was closer than any other to a large city with a natural history museum and a staff of scientists. This was Stuttgart, of course. And finally one of the men whose grounds yielded ichthyosaurs, one Herr Bernhard Hauff, turned into a very specialized specialist and into a craftsman of the very first order. It was no accident that almost every ichthyosaur on exhibit, if it came from continental Europe, had a little label attached to its frame, reading *"Ichthyosaurus quadriscissus, Dr. B. Hauff. Holzmaden, Württ."* The last word is the abbreviation for the former kingdom, later the state, of Württemberg.

But I am getting ahead of my own story.

There was another factor which contributed to the fame of the Holzmaden deposit. The slate itself was quarried for commercial purposes, for garden walks, for tops of outdoor tables, for blackboards in schools; in general, for all the purposes for which natural black slate was used a century ago. There were numerous small open quarries, and a few of them (those that happened to cut into the epsilon stratum) yielded ichthyosaurs—two hundred of them per year! Every year. Of course all the workmen knew that they might find slate slabs which were not just sold by weight. Old Professor Oskar Fraas, of the Museum of Natural History in Stuttgart, knew all the details of the "ichthyosaur business" and wrote a report about it in 1866. Before quoting a section in free translation I have to mention that the same Lias epsilon also yields on occasion specimens of *Teleosaurus,* an armored Jurassic marine crocodile. Fraas wrote:

There they lie in their stone coffins of many millennia, wrapped in slate, and one can just discern a rough outline like in a wrapped-up mummy. One may see the head stick out, the spine, the position of the extremities, the over-all length of the animal, and even the workman needs only a glance to see whether it is an animal with paddles or one with "paws" [Teleosaurus]. One with "paws" is worth three times as much. But this is not the only criterion for the price . . . a complete animal may bring as much as a hundred guilders. The workman does nothing about selling, he quietly puts his find aside in the secure knowledge that prospective buyers, representatives of scientific institutions, will call every week. No horse trading was ever performed with more zeal, with such an expenditure of eloquence and tricks, and nothing requires as much knowledge and cleverness. Since you buy "packaged goods" to begin with, you can very easily lose a good deal. And then, of course, no sale is ever final, unless the buyer obligates himself, in addition to the cash involved, to throw a wine-drinking party in celebration of the death of the old reptilian hero.

But then comes the most difficult part of the business. It is then necessary to "clean up" the saurian, meaning to free him from his slate wrapping and expose his old bones to the light of the sun. This job can be given only to experienced people; an unskilled hand will "flay" the animal. Occasionally this work takes months and the stone is taken from the bone not by means of hammer and chisel, but with engravers' tools and fine needles.[1] Nobody who has not done it himself can imagine the joy of the expert when he follows the line of a bone in the slate and, every day progressing a little bit, finally can look at the whole.

By the time this was written, scientists had had enough time to study the animal and enough material for their study so that they knew a good deal about it. The original knowledge that this was a reptile which had taken on many of the external characteristics of the fishes did not indicate in what kind of water it swam. The dolphins and the porpoises, mammals by descent and organization, have also approached the fish type in their habits and general appearance. But

[1] Long after Fraas a few progressive technicians began to wield dentists' drills with both enthusiasm and success.

that does not mean that they have to be marine. Mammals breathe air; hence it does not matter to them whether the water is fresh or salty. A fresh-water dolphin is possible; in fact there *is* a fresh-water dolphin. The ichthyosaurs, being reptiles, were air breathers, as are the water-loving reptiles of today, turtles, crocodiles, and some snakes. Looking at the living water-loving reptiles merely confused the issue. The water snakes of our time live in the Indian Ocean. The crocodiles live in rivers and lakes but don't shun a stretch of salt water. The bigger turtles are marine forms, the smaller fresh-water forms.

Whether ichthyosaurs were marine or fresh-water reptiles could be decided only by looking at the fossils associated with them. Of course, Teleosaurus, a crocodile, left the question as open as the ichthyosaurs did. But the other fossils were definite. At Holzmaden one can often find "sea lilies"—in technical language, crinoids. These crinoids are now a rather rare tribe of marine animals. They are related to the sea stars (miscalled starfishes), but while the sea stars are mobile, the sea lilies took to attaching themselves by means of a long stalk to something, in the manner of the present-day sea anemones, to which, however, they are not related. None of the living crinoids can survive in fresh water and all the very numerous fossil sea lilies from all geological periods have always been found in deposits which were definitely marine.

The sea lilies from Holzmaden, usually found clinging to pieces of driftwood, alone decided in favor of salt water. In addition to them, numerous extinct relatives of our squids and cuttlefish have been found. They are mostly forms with shells; of the living octopi, only the nautilus of the Indian Ocean still has a permanent shell. This nautilus is not in any way closely related to the octopi of the Lias Sea, but it demonstrates that octopi can form shells. Again, there is no living fresh-water octopus, and no fossil octopus has ever been found in deposits not of marine origin.

The gradual advance of the Tethys Sea, described earlier, has actually been determined mostly from the distribution in space and in time of those crinoids and the shelled octopi, the ammonites and belemnites.

The ichthyosaurs, then, were marine reptiles.

The next question was: how did they look?

Conybeare had drawn a nice skeleton with a dotted line around it, showing the probable outline of the missing fleshy parts. Cuvier had reproduced this drawing in his own works with only a few minor changes. It showed the long-snouted head with its hundreds of crocodile teeth and its rather large eyes. The body attached to that head can only be called lizardlike. Of course, instead of four legs it had four paddles, the front paddles quite large, the hind paddles very small by comparison. Then came a long tail, tapering to a point. As for the over-all size, it was usually about 7 feet, some specimens going up to 10 and 11 feet. Smaller ichthyosaurs, of an over-all length of about 3 feet, showed relatively larger heads, and were obviously young individuals. A few vertebrae of much larger size had come to light, presumably of another and much larger variety.

The large number of fossils indicated that the ichthyosaurs probably lived in "schools" like our dolphins, and a few scientists made an additional guess. Being reptiles, the ichthyosaurs were apt to lay eggs, like crocodiles and marine turtles. Marine turtles come ashore for this purpose; the ichthyosaurs probably did too. Of course they would have been quite clumsy on land because of their paddles. But so are the large seals whose legs have almost changed into paddles. And the turtles that do have fully changed paddles somehow manage. So why not the ichthyosaurs?

This about sums up the ideas about the ichthyosaurs as they were held during Cuvier's lifetime (he died in 1832) and for a number of years afterward. The next step was taken by Richard Owen in 1838. Owen, during his long life, repeatedly devoted his attention to the ichthyosaurs, as did most of the German paleontologists during the nineteenth century. In fact one might say that both German and English paleontologists developed a proprietary attitude; the ichthyosaurs were their saurians and if any discussing was to be done they were well equipped to do it, both with material and with eloquence. They fully acknowledged each other, and science is, of course, international. But as regarded ichthyosaurs and the paleontology of the Lias formation, Russians, Italians, Frenchmen, and Spaniards were not qualified to butt in. They didn't have any good Lias.

Owen, in looking at the British saurians from Lyme Regis, noted a number of facts. The front paddles were large, the hind paddles small. That reminded him of the whales. The whales, while mammals themselves, resembled the ichthyosaurs in their emphasis on the front paddles. So did, incidentally, the marine turtles. But the whales had gone a long step further. They had dispensed with their original hind feet completely. To make up for the loss they had developed an enormous tail fin. And from all reports one could find it seemed as if that large horizontal tail fin of the whales did all the propelling, that the paddles in front served for steering without adding a noticeable amount of propulsion. If the ichthyosaurs resembled the whales in habitat and habits—well, of course, they didn't have to. The whales were mammals; the ichthyosaurs had been reptiles. But supposing that they did resemble them, wouldn't it be logical to assume that they might have evolved a tail fin too? Having no bones, the tail fins would not fossilize. But if there had been tail fins, there must have been muscles to move them. And the muscles had to be attached to the bones somewhere. And this produces very typical marks on the bones and one should be able to find them.

Professor Owen did find them. The marks indicated that the ichthyosaurs had indeed resembled the whales by having a tail fin. But they also indicated that there had been a decided difference. The tail fin of the whales is horizontal; the tail fin of the ichthyosaurs must have been vertical. And there was additional evidence. In almost all specimens found, the pelvic region very neatly marked the halfway point of the total spinal column. The half from head to the pelvic region showed a curvature; from then on it was virtually straight—except that in a good many specimens the last third of the tail appeared to have been broken.

It is always the simple things which require careful thought. The last third of the tail appeared to have been broken. One should have asked, broken before or after fossilization? And if that question had been answered "before," then the next question should have been, before or after death? The men who stripped the superfluous slate from the bones and who had developed a remarkable skill for this job had failed to ask these questions. They had simply assumed that any breaks they came across had happened by pressure in the rock, long after not only this particular ichthyosaur but also all other ichthyosaurs had died. So they had straightened the breaks out, producing the long, straight, tapering tail.

Owen, having found evidence for the existence of a vertical tail fin, had reasons to think differently. That break had obviously occurred before fossilization. But presumably after death. He imagined that an ichthyosaur, having died for any one of a large number of possible reasons, would have drifted at the surface of the sea, slowly decaying. After a while the tissue had weakened enough so that it could no longer support the weight of that large tail fin. Then the tail fin's weight broke the tail. And then the drifting dead body, if luck was with the scientists, fossilized. Fortunately that had happened quite often, because, Owen assumed, the ichthyosaurs probably had habits similar to those of the seals and sea lions of today which spend much of their time at the shore. Being near the shore, a dead saurian, when its body finally sank to the bottom, stood a good chance to be covered by mud from a nearby river.

Now the scene shifts to Germany and more specifically to Holzmaden. I have already mentioned the name of Bernhard Hauff. He was the son of the owner of one of the local slate quarries and had to help with the quarrying when he was still a boy. Since this particular quarry bit into the Lias epsilon he grew up with fossils. He became interested. Conversations with visiting naturalists, among them Oskar Fraas, deepened this interest. His parents finally agreed to let him go to Stuttgart to learn taxidermy. But only half a year later his father had to call him back; he could not make ends meet without his son's help. Still, Bernhard had learned enough during those six months to go on by himself. He began to work with his hands on a poor fossil specimen, trying his skill in peeling the slate from the bone. His skill, as became apparent quickly, was simply unheard of. It was not the skill of a man who had mastered a skilled trade; it was the rare skill of an artist which cannot be taught. The fossils of Holzmaden, the beautiful complicated sea lilies, the rare fishes, the large and delicate shells of those extinct octopi which are known as ammonites, seemed to come to life again under Hauff's hands and tools. Of course they were still just fossilized bone on smooth slate when Hauff was finished. But I remember some slabs with sea lilies that had come from his workshop; it needed little imagination to believe that one saw them alive, attached to a piece of driftwood, floating in black muddy water.

To Hauff all these were incidentals, changes which were welcome because they were changes. His main work was, from beginning to end, Ichthyosaurus, his beloved dragon from the epsilon layer. I am not quite sure when he began—it must have been around 1885. But I do know that he finished his three hundred and twentieth ichthyosaur in 1920. This means that he must have judged over three thousand specimens, since it was his own estimate that only about 10 per cent of all the ichthyosaurs found at Holzmaden were worth the large amount of work involved in "cleaning" them. Among the "incidentals" during this period had been twenty-five teleosaurs.

The big discovery was made in 1892. On his work table Hauff had a large slab of slate, broken in two places. That was nothing to worry about; the slabs usually broke in quarrying and as long as nothing was missing it did not matter. But it was practical to ascertain for the purpose of the work itself just where these breaks went through the skeleton. In this case, one break cut through the tail about at the point where the spine might be broken for the reasons which Professor Owen had worked out. The other break was much worse; it seemed to go right through the skull. But since the two pieces fitted together the damage could be repaired. Hauff went to work on the specimen and after about a week's work a good number of the larger bones showed. At that point a glass of water was accidentally spilled on the specimen. No harm done; slate is waterproof. Just wait till it dries. But it did not dry evenly. Hauff saw that the pattern of drying water seemed to suggest an outline around the bones, like the outline of a gigantic fish.

A day or so later some gentlemen from the Natural History Museum in Stuttgart came to Holzmaden. Hauff told them about his experience, asking whether soft parts might have fossilized in some manner and whether he should try to bring them out more clearly. This, the men from the Museum declared, would be a waste of time. They did not see how soft parts could fossilize. They also were very well satisfied with Mr. Hauff's work as it was. The water must have dried in such a pattern by pure chance. Then the conversation turned to business, specimens were nailed into boxes for transportation, and gold coins clinked prettily. But after they had left, Hauff decided that he would forget the conversation. He would follow those black shadows which became visible when one spilled water on the slab.

A month later, when Professor Fraas came for another visit, Hauff confronted him with a finished specimen, complete with skin! Fraas was enthusiastic. Old Owen (who happened to die during the same year) had been right about his vertical tail fin. Here it was, clearly visible. Detail, however, was different. It was not a symmetrical tail fin like that of the whales. It had not broken the spine by its weight. Instead, that bend in the spine was normal; it supported the lower lobe of the tail fin, which, on the whole, looked like the sickle of the moon just before it has reached the stage of being a half-moon. A fin of similar construction existed in the living world. The shark's tail is built in the same manner, except that in the case of the shark the bone structure supports the upper lobe.

In addition, this extraordinary specimen showed something neither Professor Owen nor anybody else had suspected: a large triangular dorsal fin. All of a sudden, the shape of Ichthyosaurus had been changed completely. What had appeared to be essentially a large swimming lizard with paddles instead of feet had turned out to look very familiar. In general appearance it came closest to the dolphin. Of course there are many differences. The dorsal fin, for example, does not have the shape of the dorsal fin of living marine mammals but rather of that of some living sharks. The head is different too. But what one may call the large features, the general shape, the smooth skin, and probably the coloration, too (no doubt dark above and whitish below) are all quite similar to those of the dolphins. If the ichthyosaurs were still alive nobody would mistake one for a dolphin or porpoise when seen close by. But from a distance one might not be sure which was which.

Unfortunately the first skin specimen had been somewhat damaged by pressure before it was found. The skin of the back between the large dorsal fin and the tail had been torn to pieces. Hauff could not recover a continuous skin line from this specimen because it was not there. And Professor Fraas, keeping in mind that the ichthyosaurs were reptiles, and probably remembering the dorsal spikes of a number of living lizards, thought that there were six small dorsal fins of irregular shape behind the main fin. That was quickly recognized as a mistake because, fortunately, more skin specimens came to light. In fact every *well*-preserved Holzmaden specimen turned out to be a skin specimen. And because there were younger and older specimens the growth of both dorsal and tail fin could be observed. Individuals which were obviously not only fully grown but old, possibly old males only, showed something else which was as unsuspected as the dorsal fin. They had a rather small throat pouch, or at least a fleshy appendage that is in the place where a throat pouch would be. Whether it actually was a pouch is still uncertain. At any event it was rare.

The skin specimens had definitely killed one of the earlier ideas. With a fish shape like that the ichthyosaurs could not cavort on the shore like seals. They were as decidedly animals of the high seas as our whales, large and small. Ashore they must have been as helpless as our whales—and presumably as doomed. Admitting this, however, produced another difficulty. The original assumption had been that the ichthyosaurs, like our marine turtles, came ashore to lay their eggs. But if they could not go ashore, what did they do?

Fossilized droppings of ichthyosaurs have been found; they have a special scientific name: coproliths. They show that the mainstay of the ichthyosaur's diet was octopods of many kinds. They also show that the saurian's lower intestine had a curious spiral twist. If we are informed about such intimate details we certainly are justified in asking about fossilized eggs. None is known. The lack of fossilized eggs made scientists scan the short list of living marine reptiles once more. The black iguana of the Galápagos islands is called marine, but actually it just swims out to eat seaweed. One could not learn anything from that example. The turtles—well, their method obviously did not apply. The sea snakes of the Indian Ocean? They do form eggs, being reptiles, but they don't lay their eggs. Instead the embryo develops inside the body of the mother and is "born alive," *not* in the manner of the mammals which by way of the placenta furnish nourishment for the embryo. The method of these sea snakes can best be understood if you imagine a bird keeping a ripe egg inside its body until the egg is hatched.

Logic alone decreed that the ichthyosaurs used this method too. The next problem was to find evidence as to whether or not the logic applied.

Bernhard Hauff did his part. He was not only able to locate the position of the stomach in some individuals by way of undigested parts of shelled octopi; he also showed that there were tiny ichthyosaurs inside of big ichthyosaurs. By 1908 he had a total of fourteen such cases. Of these fourteen, seven had one young inside, two had two each. One each had three, five, six, and seven young, respectively, and one had either ten or eleven, depending on whether one wanted to count a very small batch of tiny bones.

The unborn young differed greatly in size. The largest of them was about 2 feet long, which is considerable if you know that the female in question was only an inch or so over 7 feet. The smallest measured around 7 inches and were usually in a curled-up position. The bigger ones were more or less straight. In the majority of cases the heads of the young pointed in the same direction as the heads of their mothers. The large embryos were perfectly clear and sharp, as clear as the bones of the mother. The smaller embryos had often decayed pretty badly before they fossilized.

The preceding paragraph gives the "statement of fact" issued by Hauff and the paleontologists in Stuttgart. But elsewhere that statement was received with a faint sneer. "Decayed?" "Did you say decayed before fossilization? Digested, you mean." These were embryos all right, but they were not unborn embryos. They had been eaten by others, not excluding their own fathers. We know that many fish will gobble up their own young. Some reptiles do it too. Ichthyosaurs presumably lived in the state normal for many marine animals: perpetual hunger. They grabbed and gulped down what they could get, without looking or caring what it was.

Offhand there was nothing one could say against this idea. It certainly was a possibility. Nor was it advanced without some proof. There was, first of all, the predominant position of the embryos: head forward. This did not look like a probable birth position. It looked much more like a "pursuit position": if a full-grown ichthyosaur chased a smaller one which could not swim as fast as the big fellow it would be likely to be caught by the tail and swallowed tail first. Still better proof was offered by one specimen where a young ichthyosaur was lying alongside the hard parts of octopi; obviously it had been in the stomach together with gulped belemnites.

About this last case no doubt was possible. But in the other cases there were no traces of food from which the location of the stomach could be determined. All one could do was to trace, with the aid of those specimens in which the location of the stomach was known, where it should have been and then determine whether the embryos were near that probable position of the stomach or not. At that point the discussion adopted two war cries. One was: too far forward to be an unborn young. The other: not far enough forward to be in the stomach. Of course there were incidental remarks, such as, we don't know what allowance to make for individual variations, and, we can't be sure that the location of the stomach of an individual may not change with pregnancy. Much of this fight dealt with one particular specimen in the Berlin Museum. Then somebody had an idea. If an adult ichthyosaur ate a young one it would swallow it whole—reptiles eat that way. But the process of catching and turning it into proper position for swallowing should leave teeth marks. The specimen did not show teeth marks upon examination. But maybe those bones which happened to show also happened not to have marks.

The Museum's saurian was taken from the wall and X-rayed. The photographs were greeted with shouts of triumph: at least some of the embryos were damaged in a way which might be explained by teeth marks. And that proved that!

It is quite easy to lose sight of the whole picture if you find your pet theory confirmed by evidence. The evidence did prove that ichthyosaurs, like fish, occasionally ate their own young. But the young still had to be born first even if they were eaten later. Did anybody know of specimens of young ichthyosaurs unassociated with big ones, either "uneaten" or "unborn"?

Bernhard Hauff had a nice one hanging in his own living room; it was so pretty that he had not sold it. Its length was a little over 2 feet. One or two others like it were in various museums. But nothing smaller was known, except for one piece, in a curled-up position, less than a foot long. The point was that, with the exception of this one case, all "unassociated" young that were known were quite large. So were some of the "associated" ones. In Berlin there was a 6-foot-plus specimen with a young one inside, the latter about 2 feet long. The head of the young one pointed forward but only its head was in a position where the big one's stomach might have been. And the state of preservation of old and young was very much the same.

The solution was finally provided by a Stuttgart specimen, and it is possible that commercial reasons had delayed that solution for a number of years. Ever since Hauff had found his first skin specimen the market had been wide open for skin specimens. Consequently Hauff subjected each new find to the water test he had discovered accidentally. If the water test indicated the presence of tail fin and dorsal fin, the specimen had a very high priority in the "cleaning" schedule. The Stuttgart specimen in question had given a negative water test; it had no skin. I don't know when it was found; it did not go on exhibit until several years after the end of the First World War. The specimen is 219 centimeters long, which means 7 feet and slightly above 2 inches. There are three small and very poorly preserved embryos inside the abdominal cavity. And there is a large one, 59.5 centimeters long (half an inch short of 2 feet) with its head in the pelvis of the large one. The remainder of the body is outside. Quite evidently it is in the process of being born, tail first.

Mother and young died together before this birth process was quite finished. Their bodies were covered by a mud which, as that type of mud is even today, was virtually free of bacteria. They fossilized without decaying in the usual sense of the word. But the three very young embryos inside, probably still in their egg sacs, were not in a sterile environment and did decay to a considerable extent before fossilizing. One could read these things off that specimen without needing any additional information. But there happens to be a parallel among living animals. I am quoting the following from a work by Dr. Othenio Abel.

According to information received from Chr. Lütken it is well known to the Greenland Eskimos that in the case of the white whale (*Delphinapterus leucas*) the tail of the unborn young will protrude from the vagina of the mother four to six weeks prior to actual birth. During this whole period the pregnant mother will carry its young with the tail hanging for a considerable length from her body. At first the tail of the young is still curled but soon straightens and when it is strong enough so that the young can maintain itself swimming the real birth takes place. The birth, therefore, takes place not head first but tail first.

The ichthyosaurs, being adapted to the same environment, obviously functioned in a similar way. This, of course, completely col-

Ichthyosaur with young: *Stenopterygius quadriscissus,* from Holzmaden in Württemberg, Germany. This is a restoration of the Stuttgart specimen, which fossilized during the long-drawn-out birth process

lapses the idea of "pursuit position." It explains why "unassociated" young are always fairly large, 2 feet long or more, because that was their birth size. It may be that one mating fertilized several ova which then developed to full birth size one by one. On rare occasions there may have been an abortion of a true egg, which would account for the single small curled-up specimen known. And the X-rayed teeth marks in the Berlin specimen may not be teeth marks after all. Or else a few ichthyosaurs tore up a pregnant female which had died from some other cause.

All along, scientists who investigated the ichthyosaurs and tried to piece their life history together were, needless to say, greatly pleased with the excellent material that came from Holzmaden. But its very excellence, both in quality and in quantity, brought up another question: what had happened at Holzmaden? How had this wonderful deposit formed?

A few facts were clear. The European Lias Sea must have had a shore nearby when the epsilon deposits formed. The type of sediment speaks in favor of this. So do occasional plant fossils, which are remains of land plants such as may be torn off by wind and blown out to sea. So does the fossil of a small flying saurian which may have been out fishing. Scientists, in fact, speak of the Bay of Holzmaden. Fishes seem to have been rare in that bay; the few that were found— in an excellent state of preservation—are of the type of our living sturgeon. The field is dominated by the large fossils. Ichthyosaurs by the ton. The skull of a much larger type of ichthyosaur, called *Leptopterygius,* which must have measured 40 feet over-all length. Considerable numbers of the marine crocodile Teleosaurus. An occasional long-necked plesiosaur. And, of course, those shelled octopi. Also one small shark, which, to Hauff's satisfaction, turned out to be a skin specimen.

The generally excellent state of preservation is explained by the nature of that black mud. The mystery is that the black mud almost invariably had sound specimens to enshroud. Those which we now consider poor turned into poor specimens afterward, torn apart, broken and ground up by pressure in the stone. But even these, as far as it is possible to judge, were fine specimens when they fossilized.

And that is unnatural, because among animals death is normally violent and does not leave unmutilated bodies. Also one would expect that a dead ichthyosaur that drifted ashore would have been torn apart at the seashore by large numbers of small carrion eaters, especially crabs. Well, that probably happened all the time elsewhere. But not at Holzmaden. With understandable reluctance scientists had to assume that there was something in the Bay of Holzmaden which killed the larger visitors without mutilating their bodies and which at the same time was inimical to crabs; crabs are very rare in the Holzmaden deposits.

There is only one answer: poison. Just such "foul mud," as the Germans call it, is apt to form a rather potent poison, hydrogen sulphide. Of course no crabs or marine worms would or could live in such mud, which made the carcass of a larger animal safe for fossilization. We not only have examples of such hydrogen sulphide mud now, we also know that the slate of the Lias epsilon contains considerable quantities of sulphur compounds. So do the similar deposits of Boll and of Castle Banz. The evidence for a submarine death trap is quite strong.

Now we don't have to imagine that the shallow waters of the Bay of Holzmaden were poisonous all the time. It was not necessarily a dead sea. There probably was life all the time for 10 feet of depth or so from the surface. But when a storm broke or when a large "school" of ichthyosaurs, in pursuit of a swarm of fishes or darting octopi, thundered into the bay, the thick layer of poisonous bottom mud was disturbed. The gas was released in large quantities and the bigger intruders were overcome by the poison. Those that did not accidentally escape died and finally sank to the bottom to be covered by the settling mud. The mud was impartial. It killed and preserved without discrimination: fish and ichthyosaurs, plesiosaurs and marine crocodiles, sea lilies and sharks.

In this story of the life and death of the ichthyosaurs I could and did behave as if there were only one kind. That, of course, is not the case. I simply related the researches into the life history of the best-known form. And because Koenig and Conybeare originally called it *Ichthyosaurus communis* I have used the term ichthyosaur. Its scientific name is now *Stenopterygius quadriscissus*. There was a good reason for the change, too.

I have mentioned that an early type of ichthyosaur was found in Triassic deposits of the Muschelkalk level of Spitsbergen—the small three-foot Mixosaurus. Several decades later an early type of ichthyosaur, from levels of corresponding age, was found in Nevada. It was named *Cymbospondylus* for reasons which will become understandable when the name is translated. The Greek word for "boat" is *kymbion,* while *spondylus* is Greek for vertebra. If the early type from Spitsbergen was rather small for an ichthyosaur, the one from Nevada was exceptionally large; its over-all length must have exceeded 33 feet. But in general appearance the two resembled each other. Additional fossil finds made it clear that there had been quite a number of quite different marine reptiles of the order Ichthyosauria when the Jurassic period began. They entered the Jurassic with at least three sharply distinct "tribes." But paleontologists had fallen into the habit of naming anything Jurassic Ichthyosaurus, behaving more or less as if the existing differences were merely between closely related species.

Eurhinosaurus longirostris, a late form of the ichthyosaurians

Quite some time ago, in 1904, Professor O. Jaekel began to say that things could not go on in this manner. He set an example by coining a new name for a new type. But a revision of the existing names involved a thorough study of all the available material and literature. To say that this was a formidable job is using gentle language and it was not until 1922 that another paleontologist, Friedrich Freiherr von Huene, got it done.

The best and easiest way of telling the ichthyosaurs apart was to examine the skeleton of the paddles. In the course of adaptation to life in the seas the ichthyosaurs, originally land reptiles, had changed the construction of their extremities considerably. The originally elongated bones of the fingers had turned into small round thick disks. They had also increased in number: where there should have been three bones there were ten or more disks in a row. And when you started trying to label the fingers by the I, II, III, IV, V method, you saw that even that had been changed. The numerous Holzmaden type, for example, had four fingers in the front paddle but only three toes in the hind paddle. That was bearable, but in one type you could count to eleven "fingers."

Since the paddles served as a criterion the new names referred to them. There is a Greek word *pteryx* which means both "wing" and "fin"; it could serve for "paddle" too. And "broad" in Greek is *europs,* "narrow" is *stenops,* and "slender" is *leptos.* Consequently the names of the three main types became *Europterygius, Stenopterygius,* and *Leptopterygius.*

The last of the three is the 40-foot giant from Holzmaden which has been found in England too. The second is the well-known original Ichthyosaurus, the first the one with multiple "fingers." Of this type there existed a strange offshoot, called *Eurhinosaurus,* for which one need only point to the illustration on page 147.

Of course the end of the Lias formation did not mean the end of the ichthyosaurs. There just don't seem to have been any more such reliable death traps as the Bay of Holzmaden. But such ichthyosaurs as have been found in more recent deposits show interesting trends. There is one from the White Jurassic of England which has been named *Nannopterygius* (Greek, *nanodes,* "dwarfish") because of its tiny paddles, the hind paddles being so small that they look useless. But it has an exceptionally long tail. Apparently one trend was to increase speed, which could be accomplished by a more elongated shape. Another ichthyosaur, also from the White Jurassic of England, had a more conventional shape, with two outstanding characteristics. One is expressed in its name, *Ophthalmosaurus. Ophthalmos* (Greek again) means "eye"; it had enormous eyes, indicating, probably, that it hunted at night and hid during the day. Its other characteristic was that it was virtually toothless. The shelled octopi of the early Jurassic had mostly died out for unknown reasons and for eating the soft octopi teeth were unnecessary. The soft octopi were also faster.

It looks as if the ichthyosaurs had adapted themselves to speedier prey. Their early Triassic forefathers had entered the seas well armed and with considerable armor. In the early Jurassic the armor had been shed, the armament was still there. In the late Jurassic the armament was gone too, which is probably the reason why we have no ichthyosaurs left in our oceans. In the early Cretaceous the sharks, themselves a far older type than any reptile, produced a number of very large, speedy, and heavily armed forms. The ichthyosaurs, having specialized on a diet of small and speedy squids, had in the process become helpless prey themselves.

Sharks are still with us. But the last of the ichthyosaurs lived during the Cretaceous period.

CHAPTER 9

The Mammal from the Permafrost

Of all the animals of the past none is better known by name to a wide public than the woolly elephant of the Pleistocene: the mammoth. And of all the animals of the past there is none which has so persistently intruded on human history as this very mammoth. The resurrections of other extinct animals, like the gigantic dinosaurs of the Atlantosaurus beds of Wyoming, or the fish-shaped ichthyosaurs of the German and English Lias, were purely intellectual adventures, requiring an advanced science to accomplish. But the mammoth was always part of human history, even when people had no conscious idea of its existence. Because of that ignorance it sometimes appeared in strange disguises. Or it cropped up in a curious roundabout manner. Or it appeared in places which were so far outside the realm of normal activities that even professional geographers had to consult maps to identify the strange place names with which it was associated.

At first the relationship between mammoth and Man was simple and direct. Primitive men of the type we now call Neanderthal men hunted it. It must have been a difficult and dangerous hunt, but no other animal rewarded success with such mountains of meat and fat. A less primitive type of Man which came somewhat later, the small and graceful Aurignac people, not only hunted it, they also left its portrait on cave walls. There is no disagreement about the reasons for these paintings; they figured in ceremonial rites which were to assure hunting luck in days to come. The animal which had been "captured" in a picture would not escape in the flesh. But it is quite difficult to date these paintings, even ignoring the obvious fact that they certainly are not all of equal age. A reasonably well-founded estimate for the best of these artistic efforts seems to be 50,000 B.C.

But from then until modern historical times there is an enormous gap in the direct relationship. When the famous Cro-Magnon men appeared in western Europe the mammoth apparently was no longer there, although another race of mammoths still inhabited the tundra of northeastern Siberia. The successors of the Cro-Magnon, the ancestors of the modern peoples of Europe, never knew the mammoth.

Yet they were haunted by it all through recorded history. When a river changed its course, large bones were likely to come to light. The people in the vicinity presumably kept quiet about the occurrence and avoided the spot for a while until erosion had done its work and made the bones disappear again. But that was not always easy; often there were too many witnesses present. A king ordered a palace built, and large bones were found in the ground when the foundations were put down. Monks broke the ground for an addition to the monastery and their shovels struck big bones. Many an abbot was faced with deciding whether these bones deserved Christian burial, or should be quietly thrown away, or should be saved.

But not only large bones came out of the ground as mysterious reminders of something past and unknown. Many an old chronicle or description of a town or landscape contains a remark about fossilized hands of monkeys. If some accounts did not include pictures, or if the "stone hands" themselves had not been saved, we could never puzzle out just what the chronicler meant. The stone hands were mammoth molars, found separately because the jaw bone in which they had grown had eroded. The strange designation was caused by the fact that such a mammoth molar had several roots, often five, which were taken to be the fingers.

And then there was, of course, the *unicornum verum* which was found in the ground and which was the ultimate remedy for any sickness. That it was also mammoth tusk was not yet known.

But then there came a time when large bones found in the ground no longer frightened people, when it was considered doubtful whether those things that looked like stuffed gloves were actually fossilized monkey hands, and when the remaining specimens of *unicornum verum* began to gather dust in dark corners of old pharmacies because both doctors and patients had lost faith in their remedial value.

Just at this time the mammoth began to appear in a new form, this time coming from the east. In 1611 a British traveler, Josias Logan, returned to London, bringing with him the tusk of an elephant. That would have been commonplace if Logan had been in India or Africa. But he had been in Russia, and the tusk was not a hunting trophy, but had been bought from Samoyede tribesmen who lived near the shore of the Arctic Ocean (more precisely the Barents Sea) at the mouth of the river Petchora. It was not the tusk itself which was marvelous, it was the climate of the area from which it had come.

Almost precisely a century later a Dutchman, Evert Ysbrandszoon Ides, came with a similar tale. He had journeyed across Siberia and a member of the party, a Russian, had told him that he had once found the frozen head of an elephant and also a frozen elephant's foot, which had been taken to the village of Turukhansk on the Yenisei River. From more recent and better-authenticated experience one may conclude that the find was probably made on the banks of the Yenisei itself.

There followed confused reports about ivory found in Siberia and large bones sticking from the frozen ground. The reason these reports were so confused is now easy to explain: mammoth and walrus were mixed together and described as one and the same animal. But the tribesmen, mostly Tunguses and Yakuts, not only failed to distinguish between the two animals, which had in common only that they both furnished ivory, they also added their own reasoning. When they came across one of these beasts it was always partly in the ground. And it was invariably dead. Their conclusion was that the animal lived underground like a gigantic mole, burrowing all its life. But sometimes it burrowed up instead of down, or it came out on the bank of a river. When it saw the light it died.

The hodgepodge of several sets of facts and native legends was not accepted in full by the scientists of the Western countries. But it did indicate that there was something large and interesting in Siberia. A name had filtered through too. It was *maman, mamont,* or something like that. Englishmen, Germans, Frenchmen, Dutchmen, and Swedes decided that it had to be a Russian word. The fact is that it isn't, at least not originally. It was the name given by the tribesmen and just possibly means something like "large," though it is probably safer to say that the meaning is unknown. The reason the word was believed to be Russian was that the Russians, in referring to the indubitably existent Siberian ivory, had adopted the name in a Russianized version and called the ivory *mamontova-kostj.* The last syllable means bone as well as ivory, but when used in such a construction it usually refers to ivory.

In 1722 a Swedish officer, Baron Kagg, colonel of the Royal Swedish Cavalry, returned home from Siberia, where he had been not as

"Russian mammoth" of 1722.
A copy of the picture Baron
Kagg brought from Russia

an explorer but as a prisoner of war. One of his fellow prisoners,
Philipp J. Tabbert von Strahlenberg, had spent whatever time he had
in inquiring about those rumors of a large ivory-bearing creature,
possibly of subterranean habits, and had found a Russian who claimed
to know about it and who drew him a picture which is reproduced
here. It was this picture which von Strahlenberg handed to Kagg to
take with him to Sweden, where it is still preserved in the library of
Linköping. It is hard to decide whether the Russian who drew this
clawed and twisted-horned super-cow was sincere in his belief or
whether he was indulging in a heavy-handed joke on his imprisoned
enemy.

Baron Kagg obviously believed in the picture. Scientists didn't.

Nor were the Russians themselves too sure about those Siberian
rumors. Czar Pyotr Alekseyevitch, known as Peter the Great, had sent
a naturalist, Dr. D. G. Messerschmidt, to Siberia, for general exploration but with the injunction to keep his eyes open for those supposed
elephants. The Czar knew about Ides' story, for Ides had been a
member of his own ambassadorial party to China. Doctor Messerschmidt was lucky. A mammoth had come to light in the steep banks
of the river Indigirka in eastern Siberia and he came in time to examine it before wolves had devoured all the fleshy parts and the rapid
decay of the hot Siberian summer dissolved what even the wolves did
not want. He reported on the large bones and on big pieces of skin
with long hair, resembling the fur of a goat, if different in color.
Messerschmidt ended his report: "No doubt this is the animal mentioned in the Bible as behemoth."

Since the biblical behemoth is actually the hippopotamus, Dr.
Messerschmidt very nearly succeeded in adding a third ingredient to

the mixture that already included an extinct elephant and the living walrus. That danger was avoided mostly because few people then believed in the identification of the behemoth and the hippopotamus. But another confusing element was added by a generally very reliable man, the German explorer Peter Simon Pallas, who traveled through Siberia in 1768–74 at the expense of Catherine II of Russia. In 1771 Pallas came across an incomplete skeleton and large pieces of heavy fur of an animal which had thawed from the banks of the Vilyui River, a tributary of the Lena River, a number of miles to the west of the village of Vilyuisk. The fur consisted of thick woolly hair, "of conspicuously dark coloration." Protruding from this woolly hair there were bunches of stiff bristles, about three inches long, almost black in color. On the head of the animal the fur was reddish brown and in places a brownish-black. But this animal—and it did not need Pallas's training and experience to recognize it—was most certainly a rhinoceros.

The one thing which prevented Western scientists from giving up in resignation was the fact that they could find the same animals on their home grounds, in Germany and France. The Siberian finds were superior in producing whole carcasses which had frozen when the animals had succumbed in treacherous muck or broken through thin layers of new snow covering rifts in the ice. In Germany and France the dead animals had been covered by sand and had decayed, so only bones and teeth were left. But they had some advantages just the same. They were not 4000 miles away. And one did not have to carry a shovel in one hand for the work and a rifle in the other for the wolves.

The first European rhinoceros bones had been collected from Pleistocene deposits in England in 1701. They had been turned over to Professor Nehemiah Grew, who had recognized them for what they were and put the case on record. But since he was a botanist he had not pursued the matter any further. Precisely half a century later, in 1751, a similar collection of bones was handed to Professor Samuel Christian Hollmann of the University of Göttingen. They had been found at Grubenhagen near Herzberg in the Hartz Mountains. Professor Hollmann saw quickly that they too were rhinoceros bones and described them in detail. But he also refrained from drawing conclusions. That was left to his younger colleague, Johann Friedrich Blumenbach, who became professor of medicine at the same university after Hollmann's retirement.

Blumenbach began to collect large bones from the sand pits, which were a special kind of sand that later received the name of loess. Some of the bones were certainly rhinoceros bones, just as Hollmann had said. Others just as certainly were not. They were elephant bones, but not quite the same as the bones of the two living types of elephants. In 1799 Blumenbach felt that he had his evidence complete and he announced that there had once been a kind of elephant in Europe which was different from the living types. And it was also, obviously, much older. Hence he proposed the name of "first" elephant, or *Elephas primigenius*. The name, we now know, was a bit enthusiastic—the mammoth was by no means the "first" elephant. Blumenbach also could not know that it had had a heavy fur. But, as was mentioned in Chapter 2, he traveled around and looked at various "giant's bones," preserved in churches, castles, town halls. All *Elephas primigenius*. He ferreted out old pieces of *unicornum verum*—*Elephas primigenius,* too.

Then he turned his attention to the rhinoceros bones. They too closely resembled those of living species of rhinoceros, but again were not quite the same. By 1807 Blumenbach was sure that this was a species apart and he named it the "old rhinoceros," *Rhinoceros antiquitatis* (now *Tichorhinus antiquitatis*). A little later a second type of extinct rhinoceros was identified; in honor of Goethe's friend, the privy councilor, writer, and literary critic Johann Heinrich Merck, this was named *Rhinoceros merckii* (now *Coelodonta merckii*).

Meanwhile another mammoth had thawed from a river bank in Siberia, in the delta of the Lena River. This was found in 1799, the same year in which Blumenbach proposed the name *Elephas primigenius*. A Tungus ivory collector, Ossip Shumakhoff, saw it first, but he did not know at once what it was. It looked like a small dark-colored icy hillock. But it also looked unusual, so that Shumakhoff returned to the place in the following year. He still could not be sure. But one year later, in 1801, one of the tusks protruded from the ice. Shumakhoff was much less happy than one would think. The Tunguses think nothing of picking up tusks which they find lying around by themselves. But to find a whole *mamont* is, for some reason, bad luck. Indeed it prophesies the death of the finder and of all his family. And Shumakhoff actually fell sick; he had worried himself into a psychosomatic condition of some kind. But matter triumphed over mind in his case, and he recovered, from his illness and also from the superstitious fear. He had not died, in spite of everything people always said. Now for some money.

There was a Russian in a neighboring village, one of the men who traveled through Siberia for the purpose of buying *mamontova-kostj,* and also furs on occasion, from the tribesmen. The Russian, whose name was Boltunoff, followed Shumankhoff to the place which the latter had kept carefully secret. During the third summer, the carcass had really thawed. The two men pried the tusks loose and then Boltunoff handed the tribesman fifty rubles. He also made a drawing which a few years later was acquired by Blumenbach, was seen in Blumenbach's study by Cuvier some time prior to 1812, and later belonged to Ernst Haeckel. Blumenbach made a notation at the bottom of the picture which reads (translated): *"Elephas primigenius,* which in Russia is called *Mammut,* dug up with skin and hair in 1806 at the mouth of the Lena River at the Ice Ocean. Badly drawn, just as it was found, mutilated and all dirty."

The date 1806 refers to the year when a special expedition under Professor Adams reached the place to salvage the whole skeleton and much of the pelt. The drawing itself does look funny, mostly because there is no trunk and the tusks are in an impossible position. But one should not judge too harshly. Boltunoff most likely had never seen an elephant and the mammoth's trunk probably had been torn away by wolves before Boltunoff got there. Presumably the whole face had been torn away, because Boltunoff placed the eyes of his drawing in what must be the ear openings. There were probably no ears left— the mammoth had rather small ears anyway—and the remaining holes looked as if they might be the eye sockets. I believe that Boltunoff was as careful as he could be under the circumstances, because above his picture he placed a sketch of the grinding surface of the mammoth's molar.

This find, often called the "Adams mammoth," converted Blumenbach's "first elephant," assembled from bones only, into the "woolly mammoth." The skeleton which Adams had salvaged was mounted in the museum in St. Petersburg (now Leningrad) with the skin on the feet and a number of tendons still attached to the skull. Cuvier printed a picture of this mammoth in his large work on fossil bones. With that picture the mammoth finally and definitely entered the world of science.

Nevertheless, there was still some feeling of uncertainty. Thanks to Mr. Boltunoff of Yakutsk and Professor Adams of St. Petersburg on the one hand, and Professor Blumenbach of Göttingen and the Baron de Cuvier of Paris on the other hand, the woolly mammoth was nicely nailed down. So was the woolly rhinoceros, thanks to Pallas and Blumenbach. The other rhinoceros, which had been named after Goethe's friend Merck, was summarily taken to be woolly too. From all we know now this was a mistaken conclusion, but what applied to the one was logically thought to apply to its contemporary too. The question was, why had they been woolly? By then scientists had good pictures and descriptions of the elephants and rhinoceri of Africa and India, and many of them were even in a position to visit the steadily improving and growing zoological gardens where they could see these animals alive. The modern animals were not completely hairless: the rhinoceros had some few hairs on face and ears; the elephants had some around the mouth, on the trunk, and on the tail. The Indian domesticated elephant even has something like a sparse baby fur which does not last long and of which the few hairs one can see later are the remains.

All of which showed that it was not impossible for an elephant or a rhinoceros to grow a fur. The living types just happen not to; the extinct types, as was established beyond any doubt, had done so. Why?

To this question a troublesome Frenchman added another. It was now known that the mammoth had, without being recognized, intruded on human history as far back as there were records. This Frenchman, Jacques Boucher de Crèvecœur de Perthes by name, claimed that at one time in the past Man had intruded on the mammoth. Monsieur de Perthes, in his younger years a diplomat in the service of Napoleon I, later economist, playwright, novelist, and self-styled archaeologist, had dug up things fashioned of stone. They were really just pieces of flint, chipped around the edges. Such things were no novelty in themselves. They had "always" been found, and the population had called them "thunderbolts" and many other names. Oh no, one didn't know what they were. One had to admit that they did resemble some implements which travelers had brought back from certain backward tribes beyond the seas. Monsieur de Perthes insisted that they were tools and weapons of a primitive race of Man which had once inhabited France.[1] Maybe so, maybe so, but he certainly

---

[1] Boucher de Perthes arrived at that idea independently, but he was not the first. Some decades earlier a British antiquary, John Frere, had anticipated him. Frere had collected such flint implements in England and sent a selection to the Society of Antiquaries in 1797, accompanied by a letter in which he wrote: "I think they are evidently weapons of war fabricated and used by a people who had not the use of metals."

went too far. He said that those primitive men, our own ancestors, had hunted mammoths with such weapons!

Of course not! That was just the kind of idea one could expect from a man who had written novels, not even using a pen name, a man who had written stage plays and probably even associated with actors and actresses. What Monsieur de Perthes apparently did not know was that the mammoth and the woolly rhinoceros and primitive Man (whatever *that* term was supposed to mean) had not been contemporaries. More, that they could not have been contemporaries, because the mammoth and the various European rhinoceri had lived during the preceding geological period. In that period there had been no men because men belonged to our period.

The name most frequently quoted in all attacks on Boucher de Perthes' *chimères* was, quite naturally, that of Cuvier. Cuvier had said that he had never found a fossil animal in more than one period. Sometimes similar forms, yes. The mammoth had existed in one period, while the Indian and the African elephants lived in another. They were similar. But they were not the same. And most especially, Cuvier had emphasized that no fossil man had ever been found. This was not true, as was learned later, but the Cro-Magnon skeleton found by Dean Buckland in 1823 was then believed to be the skeleton of a British lady of the Roman period.

Boucher de Perthes kept quiet. He was not looking for a professorship anywhere, he had some income, derived in part from those novels and plays that were cited against him. He went on collecting his chipped flint implements, meanwhile resolved not to believe in Cuvier's world-wide catastrophes. Johann Wolfgang von Goethe in Germany did not believe in them either, but he was another playwright and novelist and one did not have to believe his scientific reasoning even though he also held a high position in society and in politics. But somebody else who did not believe in them was Sir Charles Lyell in England, a professional geologist. He collected all the geological evidence he could find. But he could not find any evidence for world-wide catastrophes. Tectonic forces built mountains; rains and rivers washed them away again. Rivers filled seas with sediments and made them shallower and shallower. On the other hand the surf nibbled at coastlines and slowly moved them inland. Wherever Lyell looked, he saw only those forces which are still operating, day and night, day after day and night after night, through weeks, months, years, centuries, and millennia.

There was no longer any reason for disbelieving that a species of animals or plants had survived from one geological period into another. In fact later on scientists began to look very avidly for such "living fossils." There was no longer any reason why the mammoth should not have survived into the present geological period (then called the Alluvium). Conversely, if the mammoth had died out with the end of the Pleistocene there was no reason why Man should not have lived *then*. Sir Charles Lyell himself considered this not at all improbable. And one day, in 1859, old Boucher de Perthes, living reasonably contentedly at Abbeville in the beautiful valley of the Somme, received a visitor, an English gentleman by the name of Sir Charles Lyell. He wanted to see the stone implements which Monsieur de Perthes had collected. After that he wanted to see where they had been found. He checked carefully, not saying much. But when he did open his mouth he began with the words, "Monsieur de Perthes, you are correct."

With that, one of the two questions which had been answerless in 1830 had been disposed of. Theoretically, at least, man and mammoth could have been contemporaries. It took the remainder of the nineteenth century to show that they actually had been, and also that they had lived in the same place at the same time. This was not as easy as it sounds nowadays. Fossil remains of man not only had to be found, which in itself was mostly a matter of luck, they also had to be established as unmistakably fossil. That took time, and many people did not want to go along with these new ideas. Not only that, some individual scientists, being human, were reluctant to abandon theories which they had treasured as valuable property. They were even justified in being skeptical; skepticism is a prime requirement in scientific work. To us, who see everything brightly illuminated in the light of afterknowledge, some of the skepticism looks exaggerated, stubborn, and blind. All that was the case on occasion, but essentially the skeptics were merely wrong.

I'll just touch upon a few cases. When the first skull of Neanderthal Man was found, the eminent medical authority Professor Rudolf Virchow tried to show that its differences from a modern skull might be explained as individual pathological differences, caused by battle wounds in youth and by *arthritis deformans* in old age. It was nonsense, but as long as only one such skull was known the possibility existed. When a place where ancient man had obviously eaten mammoths was discovered near Předmost in Bohemia, the Danish zoologist

Japetus Steenstrup said that this still was no proof for contemporaneous existence; the men might have found frozen carcasses, as Tunguses and Yakuts still do. When the first cave paintings came to light in France, they were suspected of not being genuine. But fossil Man, or his modern champions, won all along the battleline.

Before that victory could be complete, something fundamental had to be learned, which had to do with that other question already posed: why had the mammoth been woolly? The Siberian finds indicated a fur from 6 to 9 inches thick.

It was a question about which one could think in circles for any length of time. If one took the fur to be a special adaptation to Siberian conditions, from the example of the Siberian tiger which has a heavier fur than his Bengal brother, one got into the dead-end problem of why the mammoth no longer walked the Siberian tundra. If one did not take the fur to be a Siberian specialty, one had to assume Siberian climate in Europe, all the way from England to Bohemia. There was one suspicious indication in Switzerland, relating to the glaciers, which became a tourist attraction after the invention of the railroad simplified travel. A glacier is essentially a slowly flowing river of compacted snow. When rocks are dislodged by the glacier itself, or by other causes, they are carried by the glacier. If it should at some later time melt faster than it can advance, these rocks are left as a telltale mark, called a moraine. But a glacier not only carries rocks on its back, it also moves them with its sole, scraping another telltale mark into the rock over which it flows. Nobody who had looked at the evidence could doubt that the glaciers of Switzerland had been much larger in the past. In 1829 Goethe himself, after looking at them, stated thoughtfully, "For all that ice [of the larger glaciers] we need cold. I hold the suspicion that a period of great cold has passed at least over Europe."

But the scientific world did not pay too much attention to the Swiss glaciers. It had another and geographically larger puzzle on its hands. All over North Germany and the corresponding areas of Poland and Russia one found large blocks of stone, from pieces a man could still move to boulders weighing hundreds of tons. They were scattered without rhyme or reason over a landscape which was largely sand, with bedrock hundreds of feet below the surface. Nor did that bedrock correspond to the boulders on the sand. Geologists comparing rock samples had established something at least as surprising as the presence of the boulders themselves. Their material perfectly matched the mountains on the Scandinavian peninsula. How did large pieces of Scandinavian mountains get to Pomerania and Poland?

Lyell's answer, incorporated in his big work, seemed to explain all this nicely and was fully accepted for about half a century. Let's assume, he began, that all of Europe north of the Alps was lower by a certain and comparatively small amount. Then a shallow sea would cover the plains of Germany quite far inland, at least to the Hartz Mountains. The Scandinavian glaciers would then have flowed directly into the sea. When a glacier flows into the sea its end breaks off periodically to form icebergs. Drifting southward, these icebergs, probably smaller to begin with than the monsters which float down into the Atlantic from Greenland, would slowly melt. The rocks they had scooped up as glaciers would drop to the bottom. As the European mainland slowly rose, the sea became shallower and shallower and simultaneously iceberg production in the north would stop because the Scandinavian glaciers no longer reached the shoreline.

Building on the foundation of that theory, one could even explain the larger size of the Swiss glaciers. If the sea was that much larger, a lot more water could evaporate from it, causing more snow in Switzerland in winter and thereby increasing the size of its glaciers. That that sea apparently had not covered France was somewhat awkward, but France did not seem to have any of those boulders from Scandinavia, so obviously it had not been flooded.

Any doubts anybody might have harbored could not be voiced for lack of evidence. But in 1875 there was a meeting of the German Geological Society in Berlin. Among the invited guests was the head of the Swedish Geological Survey, Otto Martin Torell. Torell did not just come, deliver a speech, and rush home again; he made a few excursions, looking at boulders from Scandinavia resting in the rye fields in the vicinity. And there is a place named Rüdersdorf, about an hour's train ride from Berlin, where bedrock actually breaks through the sand and forms very modest mountains. The bedrock is Muschelkalk. Torell had to see that. When he did, he also saw the typical glacier scrapes which he knew so well. (Later a boulder from Sweden was placed near that spot as a memorial.) The same night Torell spoke to the assembled geologists. Europe had not been covered by a shallow sea with icebergs from the Scandinavian glaciers, he said. Europe had been covered by the glaciers. Wherever there was bedrock at the surface their marks would be found.

Goethe's forgotten remark of more than forty years before about the period of great cold that had passed at least over Europe suddenly seemed prophetic. The idea of a large portion of a continent flooded by a shallow sea was not a rare concept to geologists. Europe had been flooded like that during the Jurassic and Cretaceous periods. And during the Cretaceous at least, the North American continent had been split in two in the same manner by a shallow sea extending from the Gulf of Mexico through the central plains to Hudson Bay.

It was a different proposition to be asked to imagine large portions of a continent buried under glacier ice. That concept could not be assimilated quickly, not just because it was new, but because it seemed to involve a very profound climatic change. You could imagine a sea breaking through from the Gulf to Hudson Bay, or one connecting the North Sea with the Adriatic Sea, without a climatic change at the outset. Of course the presence of the sea, once it existed, would influence the climate. "But for all that ice we need cold." Something like relief resulted when Melchior Neumayr published a calculation which said that the whole Ice Age could be explained by a reduction of the average year-round temperature of from 8 to 10 degrees Fahrenheit. If every day and every night, Neumayr said, were 8 degrees cooler than it is now, the snow and ice of winter would fail to melt away as completely as it does now. The snow line of the mountains would be lower, for one thing. Next winter more ice and snow would accumulate in these places. If this went on for a sufficiently long time the glaciers could grow large enough to cover all of Europe.

Meanwhile the glacier scrapes which Torell had so confidently predicted had actually been found. Once geologists knew what to look for, it seemed a wonder that they had ever been overlooked. From a mass of data maps were made, showing the extent of that past glaciation. There was one large area of which so little was known that one could not tell. That happened to be Siberia. We still don't know about Siberia, but the expedition under Roy Chapman Andrews established definitely that the ice shield did *not* reach the Gobi and the high land of Tibet. But from the Ural Mountains west, the picture was quite clear. The glaciers had covered Russia to points south of Moscow, Poland to south of Warsaw, and Germany to Berlin and beyond. From there on the "glacier line" ran through Belgium, crossed the Channel, cut across the southernmost portion of England to the vicinity of Bristol, and then ran westward through the Irish

Sea. Everything north of that line was covered by the ice shield, including all of Ireland. That is the reason there are no snakes in Ireland. Probably there were some before, but after the glaciers which had killed them had melted away, no snakes could get back.

In the Western Hemisphere the glacier line began at the shore of the Atlantic Ocean somewhat south of the fortieth parallel, ran west south of the Great Lakes to the Dakotas, turned north there, and then followed approximately the present United States–Canadian border to the Pacific Ocean. Naturally it was not quite as straight as that political boundary. Here in America the areas not covered by the ice shield were comparatively large, including everything south of Pennsylvania in the east and everything south of the state of Washington in the west. In Europe the Mediterranean countries and all of France had escaped. So had the extreme south of England, much of the area of the English Channel (then probably dry land), western and southern Germany, southern Poland, and southern Russia. Austria and Czechoslovakia had not been reached by the Scandinavian glaciers. But the Alps, as Swiss guides had pointed out to the visiting Goethe, had produced large glaciers of their own.

The evidence seemed to leave little room for early men and mammoths, but there was an ameliorating factor. It was a pardonable mistake of the geologists to have thought at first that there had been just "the Ice Age." Then they discovered evidence that two glaciations had successively gone over the same spot, with an interval during which plants grew there which can now be found in Italy. With eyes sharpened once more, they continued to search, finally arriving at the conclusion that there had been about four glaciations, with "interglacial periods" between. The "glacier line" first established belonged to the time of the maximum glaciation, the third. The others had been of somewhat lesser extent; it is hard to say just how much less. For easier reference the glaciations have received names which as names mean very little, because they are actually just the names of small rivers. In chronological order, the names are Günz, Mindel, Riss, and Würm, and the majority of the experts believe that the last of the four, the Würm glaciation, had two distinct phases.

How much the glaciers receded during the warmer interglacial periods is an especially hard question to answer. Since the first of these warmer periods was quite long in duration one may be justified in thinking that the glaciers had receded to at least their present status, which leaves only the extreme north of America, Greenland, and the Siberian rim still in the Ice Age. As for the recession in the other warmer periods, almost any guess will do, but it must have been a good deal, because one can clearly see that each time a fauna geared to a somewhat warmer climate moved in. When the glaciers advanced, spreading tundra and cold steppes ahead of them, cold-proof mammals appeared on those tundras. The mammoth itself. The woolly rhinoceros. The heavily furred musk ox. The reindeer. The gigantic cave bear. Wolves.

When the glaciers receded and the steppes warmed up, forests spread and with the forests came a different group of animals. There was the "old" elephant, the majestic *Elephas antiquitatis* with its long tusks. (Because it was not particularly old, scientists later referred to it as the "forest elephant," in spite of the meaning of its Latin name.) There was Merck's rhinoceros, most likely a hairless form. There were bears, lions, lynxes, stags, fallow deer, deer, and wild hogs.

This seesaw between a temperate forest fauna and a cold-resistant tundra fauna had started with a fairly stable condition in the late days of the Tertiary period. At that time the area which was to be invaded by the northern cold had a fauna which, if anybody saw it now, would make him think that he had been transported to Africa. In fact, in a manner of speaking he would have been transported to Africa's fauna, except that it was not yet on African soil. The north European fauna of the late Tertiary, leaving the slowly cooling continent, largely escaped via the Balkan peninsula (which had somewhat different geography then) into Africa, where they survived with comparatively little change. During the time when the first glaciation was slowly building up there were only a few apparently more hardy forms left.

A species of hippopotamus was still around for a while and so was a rhinoceros which is called the Etruscan rhinoceros. There was a large elephant, called the "southern" elephant (*Elephas meridionalis*). There was a type of moose which is considered to be the direct ancestor of the living form, and another which was the ancestor of a form that flourished all through the Pleistocene and became extinct in very early historical times; it seems to have survived longest in Ireland. There was a very large beaver which has been named in honor of Cuvier and there were large numbers of a wild horse, possibly zebra-striped.

In putting down these names I am relying on a list prepared by Professor Wolfgang Soergel of Chirotherium fame. Professor Soergel had long been interested in a specific problem. Because of animal bones burned in fires, large bones split open for the sake of the marrow, and lots of similar evidence, everybody was sure that primitive Man had been largely a hunter. The problem which busied Soergel was no longer *whether* the men of the Old Stone Age, the Neanderthalers and the later men of the small Aurignac race, had hunted. The problem was *how* they had hunted their game. But that problem, in turn, rested on the question of what kind of game was available. By about 1910, when Soergel started this work, enough material had been amassed to enable him to draw up tables showing which animals had occurred when. Some ten years later he brought his tables up to date once more. An adaptation of his second table appears in the Appendix, with my own translations of some of the scientific names.

These tables show clearly how that "temperate forest fauna" which was to become so typical for the interglacial periods moved in during the first of them. The earliest known fossil of a man, the so-called Heidelberg jaw, indicating a 6-footer of the Neanderthal type (the later "true" Neanderthalers were a good 6 inches shorter), is also dated as belonging to the first interglacial period. During the second glaciation, the mammoth's ancestor (*Elephas trogontherii*) appeared on the scene, along with the reindeer, an early form of the cave bear, and so forth. The transition from the remains of the Tertiary fauna which somehow managed to hold on for a while to the fauna that "belongs" to the Ice Age was complete.

Man did not have easy hunting in these surroundings, which he could endure only because of his possession of fire. There was much competition from carnivorous mammals, some of them of considerable size. The hunter often enough became the hunted. Even more often he must have lost to wolves game which he could not kill at a stroke.

And, as the remains of his meals show, he was handicapped in other ways too. We do know that the forests of the interglacial periods, as well as the tundra and steppes fringing the glaciers during the glaciations, were inhabited by many small mammals which, being rodents, were probably numerous. There were also flocks of birds, many of them types still living in the northern countries. But in the refuse heaps of ancient Man the bones of small mammals are a great rarity, and there is not a single well-established case of bird-bones as remains of a meal. This seems to indicate at least that Man in the Old Stone Age had not yet learned how to build traps and snares, and that he had no missile weapons—slingshots, bows and arrows, etc.—with which he could kill a bird. He probably relied entirely on what are known as impact weapons: spears, clubs, and related armament which required a close approach. Small animals were difficult to approach and not worth the trouble. With equal effort the hunter could kill a reindeer or a horse.

Anthropologists have often tried to give helpful hints to paleontologists by pointing out the methods of hunting used by primitive tribes in comparatively recent times. They have told how natives use brush fires to stampede animals in a certain direction so that they are forced to jump down steep cliffs. They have told how natives, armed with several spears per man, isolate a single animal from the herd, corner it, and then dispatch it either by means of throwing spears or by using the spears as close-range weapons.

Such hints are helpful, but whether or not they are applicable is another question. The so-called fire drive requires not only fire (and a suitable locality), but also large numbers of hunters. The anthropologists who told about such hunts stressed that hundreds and sometimes even thousands of natives took part in them, with enough yield for every hunter and his family. But primitive Man, at least during the Old Stone Age, simply was not numerous enough to conduct such hunts. Later, in Cro-Magnon times, the fire drive was probably used; in fact, there is one place in France where everything speaks in favor of the theory that herds of animals (especially horses) were stampeded over a cliff, not just once, but many times. Neanderthal Man, however, did not live in tribes, in our meaning of the word. There were just large families; maybe two or three families getting together on occasion. They were not numerous enough to stampede herds, either by means of the fire drive or by plain noise-making.

Separating a single animal from a herd and cornering it was probably practiced, but what weapons they used was another problem. Those primitive tribes about which the anthropologists told had already acquired iron; their spears were tipped with pointed and sharp blades of considerable size and fatal power. Stone blades of equivalent deadliness were a late invention. A German archaeologist, Otto Profé, borrowed a number of stone artifacts which were indubitably "Neanderthal," attached them to wooden handles in a manner probably superior to anything Neanderthal men could have managed, and then tried to "kill" a freshly butchered calf with these weapons. Try as he might, he could not even penetrate the thin skin of the belly. Only where the skin was underlaid by strong muscles did the flint implements break through the skin at all. Even if wielded by a powerful man, these weapons could not have inflicted fatal wounds. They were just not sharp enough.

It was a different matter to use the Neanderthal implements to cut the carcass apart. For operations like separating the skin from the flesh, splitting the flesh off the bone, and even for cutting the tendons from the bone, these stone knives were almost as effective as modern tools. One could not cut across the muscle, but Neanderthal man probably did not care whether his meat was sliced into steaks or roasted as chunks. Profé concluded from this experiment, and Soergel agreed with him, that the stone weapons were not hunting weapons at all, with all due respect for Boucher de Perthes' pioneer work. The stone weapons were household tools. They may have been weapons of war, where the situation is different, but they were useless for hunting.

Then what was used for hunting? A weapon was needed which would penetrate deeply with relative ease, causing a wound that did not permit the animal to get far away. Soergel concluded (in 1922) that Neanderthal Man's hunting weapon was probably a spear not tipped by anything. Just a straight stick, either a straight branch or more likely a sapling tree, with the tip hardened by fire and then sharpened. Such a spear would be effective in a more or less individual hunt on reindeer and horse and animals of similar size, and with luck even on larger game. Soergel's prediction was borne out in 1948 when such a wooden spear was actually found near the Aller River in northwestern Germany. It was broken into ten pieces, but nothing was missing. It had been 8 feet long, fashioned of the tough and heavy wood of the European yew (*Taxus baccata*), and examination of the tip showed that it had been hardened by fire. It was pointed and showed no traces of having had anything attached to it, but clear traces of the strokes of stone knives that had been used to sharpen it.

The spear could be dated as having been made and used during the last interglacial period, and it was found imbedded in the rib case of a forest elephant. Nearby a dozen flint scrapers lay about. The whole effect was precisely like that of a hunting method still in use in Africa by the pygmy tribes of Cameroon. There, a solitary hunter, armed with a spear longer than himself, carefully approaches a solitary feeding or dozing elephant from behind. If his approach fails to be noiseless enough, the elephant usually just moves on. If the hunter does succeed in getting close, he pushes his spear into the elephant's abdomen from below and behind. The animal, fatally wounded, rarely seems to turn around for an attack on the hunter but races away in terror and pain. Finally it breaks down exhausted, often a considerable distance away. It worked that way with the African elephant in the last century; it worked that way with the forest elephant during the last interglacial period in Europe.

But it could not have worked that way with the mammoth. The skin of the elephant, while thick, has soft spots. So, presumably, did the skin of the mammoth. But the long hair protected those softer areas. Before a spear could touch the inch-thick skin it had to penetrate some 8 inches of wool. And under the skin there were some 6 inches of fat. A high-powered rifle bullet would be needed to get through all this to the vital organs. No spear could ever do it; no man could put enough driving force behind it.

The only thing we can think of now—and primitive man certainly thought of it too—is the pit. That had always seemed the most likely method, but it was one about which quite a number of archaeologists were very skeptical. They said a pit large enough to catch a mammoth was impossible for primitive man to make. The only digging tool Neanderthal Man could have had was the so-called digging stick. It would take a whole tribe many weeks to dig a large enough pit.

It sounded like a very strong argument, but in view of the evidence it had to be wrong. There were several answers. One was that the men would not have dug the entire hole; they would have started with a natural hole of some kind. Another was that it was not necessary to make a hole into which a full-grown mammoth would disappear; it was enough to render it helpless. If only the forelegs or the hind legs were caught, even a mammoth could be clubbed to death by incessant attack. I may add here that I personally doubt very much that the digging stick was the only digging instrument of Neanderthal Man. He dealt with fairly loose sand and for such material nature provided a ready-made digging tool: moose antlers. They may be somewhat awkward to handle, but I can testify that they work in loose sand.

Still and all, the mammoth probably was exceptional game which was hunted only under special circumstances. But there was Předmost in Bohemia, where, as mentioned earlier, Man had evidently eaten mammoths. This place, like so many such finds, was an accidental discovery. The ground belonged to a Czech landowner who could not help noticing that his farm hands quite often came across large bones. To the mind of the landowner there was just one use for old bones: he had them ground up as fertilizer for his fields—until one day somebody who knew better saw what was going on and screamed for help, invoking the Academy of Science, the police, the Ministry of the Interior, and everybody else he could think of in a hurry. The practice of fertilizing fields with mammoth-bone meal was stopped and an investigation started.

There were numerous remains of people. There were also numerous remains of mammoth. And the people, it could not be denied, had had some sense of order. Here was a pile of shoulder blades, there was a pile of leg bones. Over there some skulls. Since nobody could tell how many bones had been ground up there was immediate disagreement on the number of mammoths that had been eaten there. First estimates said "at least a thousand"; that was revised downward to about half in the course of time. Soergel, on the other hand, at first refused to believe in a number higher than about 300, but doubled his estimate later on, so that we can't be far wrong in saying that the Předmost site contained the remains of about 600 mammoths.

As I mentioned, the Danish zoologist Japetus Steenstrup (justly famous for other work) held that all these mammoths had just been frozen carcasses, such as had been found in the Lena delta and along the Indigirka River. If he had stopped at that point we would now say, "Old Steenstrup was a good judge." But he elaborated on the case, "proving" that primitive Man had never hunted or killed a mammoth. Very soon afterward overwhelming evidence that primitive Man had hunted and killed mammoths was found in many places. Steenstrup's reputation collapsed, he was ridiculed, and those who had originally sided with him kept very quiet about it. Primitive Man was acclaimed as a great hunter.

But it is now accepted that in the specific case of the Předmost mammoths what primitive Man actually did was to stuff himself with the flesh of dead animals. No doubt he could kill 600 mammoths in time. But he could not have dragged the heavy bodies to the same place. And if he made a mammoth trap of some kind near Předmost, the animals would not have patiently walked into the same trap year after year. Obviously something, probably a blizzard of unusual severity, had killed the mammoths there. Only a natural catastrophe can account for the presence of 600 mammoth carcasses in one place.

Six hundred elephants, however, is a very large herd. And that naturally brings up the question of how numerous the mammoth was. It cannot have been rare. The teeth (molars) of more than 200 individuals have been found in a most unlikely spot: they were dredged up with oysters from the Dogger Bank in the North Sea. In the German state of Württemberg alone, remains belonging to about 3000 individuals have been found during the time interval from 1700 to 1900. The number of remains from Austria and Czechoslovakia must be about the same. And the total of the tusks found so far in Siberia, where the mammoth lasted longest, points to 50,000 individuals.

As to the appearance of the mammoth, there are absolutely no doubts left. We have numerous complete skeletons, we have the Siberian specimens preserved by what engineers now call "permafrost" (permanently frozen ground), and we have, almost more important, the very lifelike drawings left by men of the later Stone Age. These show something one could not have deduced from the skeleton: the mammoth had two humps, like the Bactrian camel. These were indubitably humps of fat for the foodless season. One of these humps was placed above the shoulder blades, as one should expect; the other, strangely enough, was on top of the head. These two humps, combined with the long fur and the enormous tusks which apparently never were put to any use, made the shape of the mammoth quite different from that of living elephants. The color of the fur looks quite red now, but it is supposed that it has faded, so that in life the mammoth was probably clothed in reddish-black. One special adaptation to the cold climate, revealed by the Siberian finds, is worth mentioning. The mammoth carried, at the root of its tail, a strange skin flap which protected the anal opening against the cold. Its tail was quite short and the ears were small, smaller even than those of the small-eared Indian elephant.

And not all mammoths were of "mammoth size." There is really only one type to which this word would properly apply: the race or sub-species which occurred in Württemberg and which has been named after Professor Fraas. "Fraas's mammoth," as it may be called, stood a full 3 feet taller than the largest African elephant

Mammoth

known. And that measurement disregards the hump, which may have added another foot or two. The most common type was somewhere between the African and the Indian elephant in size, and the Siberian species was smaller than the Indian elephant, just half as tall as the mammoth's ancestor, the admittedly enormous *Elephas trogontherii*. Whether that Siberian species—named *Elephas beresovkius* for reasons which will quickly become apparent—is to be considered a degenerate version of the European species is an unanswered question. But it probably was.

It is usually said that the European mammoth "died out" at the end of the glacial period. But it is more likely that it did not die out but moved out. As soon as the last glaciation in Europe had come to an end the forest moved in again. And apparently the mammoth just did not like forest. It probably behaved much the same as did another typical animal of the glacial periods—the reindeer. The reindeer also just moved away, with the one difference that it stayed alive in the extreme north and the mammoth did not. One may imagine, therefore, that the mammoth, like the reindeer, stuck to the cold steppes and tundra, following them northward as they receded, and then going east, to Siberia, where conditions were still most like those to which it had adapted itself.

How those Siberian permafrost mammoths which started all the excitement had found their individual end became clear in 1901.

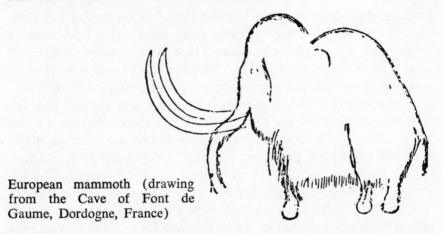

European mammoth (drawing
from the Cave of Font de
Gaume, Dordogne, France)

During that year the Russian Academy of Science in St. Petersburg
received news from Yakutsk that another mammoth had come to
light, this time in the extreme northeast, near the Beresovka,[2] a tributary of the river Kolyma. Because of an old ukase originally issued
by Peter the Great, the Czar had to be notified about the find and he
ordered an expedition to go after the mammoth. The leader of the expedition was Dr. Otto Hertz.

When the expedition arrived, wolves and dogs had already done
their work, and much of the skull was bare of flesh. But it was still a
virtually complete mammoth, since everything but the head was still
solidly frozen. The decayed portions of the flesh emitted such a terrible stench that the scientists more than once felt that they might
have to give up. But they always succeeded in persuading themselves
to stand it for a few more days. And as the work progressed, their
professional enthusiasm dulled their noses, to the great benefit of
science.

The mammoth apparently had been feeding in freshly fallen snow
which covered a deep crevasse in its path. When it fell in it was fatally
injured, having broken both the right foreleg and the pelvis. It is quite
probable that it struggled for some time in spite of the injury, pulling
down tons of loose snow under which it finally died. There was still
food in its mouth, and from the frozen stomach the scientists extracted
27 pounds of chewed but undigested food. Botanists could still
classify the food: it consisted of larch, fir, and pine, some ground-up
fir cones, sedge, wild flowers of various kinds, wild thyme, and two

[2] The name signifies "Birch River" and the proper pronunciation (not with-
standing the spelling) is Berózovka, with the accent on the "ro."

kinds of moss. Except on the head and one foreleg, the fur was complete, consisting of a thick yellowish undercoat and a thick mass of guide hairs, up to 14 inches long. There were manelike patches of long guide hairs on cheeks, chin, shoulders, flanks, and belly. The fat layer under the skin was pure white and on the average 4 inches thick. The meat was dark red, suggesting horse meat, and marbled with fat. The dogs ate it avidly; the men could not quite steel themselves to try it too. Some of the dark frozen blood was saved; a serological test made later indicated the Indian elephant as the closest living relative.

The scientists who did the work were not only hampered by the stench of the decayed parts, but after they had skinned the mammoth and cleaned up the skeleton they were faced with distance. It took ten sleds to carry what they had salvaged, for a 2000-mile journey over a snowy landscape, ending with the city of Irkutsk and the Trans-Siberian railroad. Both skeleton and skin were finally mounted in the museum in St. Petersburg, the skeleton in normal position, the skin in the half-sitting position in which the animal had died.

The mammoth was an American animal too in its time. Together with other elephants, it had crossed over from Asia into Alaska and found its way south. But it was not very numerous in the Western Hemisphere, much less so than the American mastodon which, in spite of early guesses to the contrary, was probably a hairless type.

For a long time there was a rumor that the woolly mammoth might still be alive in Alaska. Nobody knows just when or how that rumor originated but it is more than a century old. And every once in a while something happened to strengthen it. One of the most widely believed props of the rumor was a piece of fiction describing the "killing of the last mammoth," which appeared in *McClure's Magazine* in 1899 and was taken seriously by a large percentage of the magazine's readers. Obviously it is an appealing idea that the mammoth of the Ice Age, unwilling companion of Man since the earliest days of recordless prehistory, is still alive somewhere. Unfortunately it is not true.

But there must be mammoths in Alaska—frozen mammoths, undisturbed in permafrost like their Siberian kin. A tiny one was found some years ago and made the journey to New York in a deep-freeze unit. It is a promising beginning. Scientists are eying the frozen muck of Alaska. Somewhere in it there must be specimens which will teach us a lot about the mammoth in America—and possibly about early Man in America too.

CHAPTER 10

Prelude to Aviation

Again my thoughts go back to the hall in the Berlin Museum of Natural History which contained the red sandstone slabs with the footprints of Chirotherium and the black slate with the ichthyosaurs uncovered by Bernhard Hauff.

But I am now thinking of another stone slab, which was whitish-yellowish in color. Its size, as I remember it, was not quite that of a sheet of ordinary typewriter paper. There was a similar slab next to it, but this one had a label stating that it was a copy of a fossil which the museum did not possess. These two slabs were on a flat table—under glass, of course—but I cannot truthfully say that they were being exhibited. They were in a niche which one could easily pass without ever realizing that one had missed something important. Originally the table had stood with its back against an enormous plate-glass window, on the other side of which was the glass-roofed inner courtyard of the museum. Some time in the past this window presumably had furnished enough light on a bright day to see the fossils clearly. But other exhibits had been placed in the inner courtyard, cutting off the light, so that it took good eyes and patience even to read the label.

No artificial light was provided.

All this would have been surprising in the case of any exhibit. It was almost incredible in view of the fact that this particular fossil was unique, that it was one of the most important fossils ever discovered, and, moreover, one of the most expensive items in the whole museum.

This poorly displayed item was the *Archaeopteryx,* the earliest known bird, from the white Jurassic of Bavaria, somewhere between 125 million and 135 million years old.

Black Jurassic slate from the Lias is prominent in Württemberg; the classical place for white Jurassic from the Malm is just about 100 miles due east from the ichthyosaur quarries in Bavaria. It is located just north of the Danube River in the general vicinity of the city of Ingolstadt. It was a classical place in every respect; the Limes of the Roman Empire once ran through it, following more or less the course of the Danube. The Romans had early discovered that a light-colored slate [1] of exceptional quality was to be found near a tributary of the Danube. It was hard and strong, almost impossible to break but easy to split. The Romans had used it for the *castelli* which guarded the empire against any far-reaching ideas some chieftain beyond the Limes might conceive after the third horn of mead. The first slate quarries in the mountains were worked under the supervision of the legions for their own immediate needs, both military and otherwise; archaeologists have found a Roman military bathhouse floored with such slate.

It may be supposed that the local inhabitants continued to work the quarries for their own needs after the legions left. Very little is known about the local history of the area until the time of Wynfrith of Devonshire, better known as St. Boniface, who preached in Bavaria with authorization from Pope Gregory II and who, in 748 A.D., became the Archbishop of Mayence. St. Boniface's connection with the white Jurassic slate is rather indirect: one of his pupils, St. Sola, went to the valley of a tributary of the Danube to live there as a hermit. Later this tributary received the name of Altmühl (Old Mill) River; it empties into the Danube at Kelheim, a short distance upstream from Regensburg. A town which is at or near the site where St. Sola lived named itself Solnhofen, which may be translated as "St. Sola's courtyard."

Solnhofen—until 1900 the name was spelled Solenhofen—later became the most famous of all the places where white Jurassic slate was quarried, with the result that slate from the whole Altmühl Valley was often labeled Solnhofen slate. Actually the quarries of Eichstätt, Pappenheim, Zandt, Pfalzpaint, Langenaltheim, and other places in the valley are older—the Solnhofen deposits were not even discovered until 1738. Some quarries must have been in operation far back in historic times, as is proved by the slate roofs and slate floors of many very old houses in the area. We also have documentary evi-

[1] The stone is actually limestone but is called slate because it has a smooth surface and splits well.

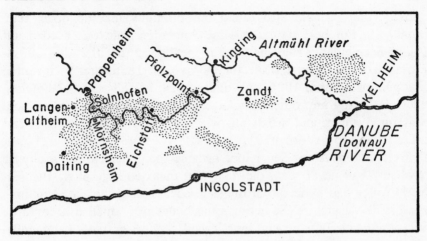

The Altmühl valley in Bavaria. Dotted areas indicate "lithographic slate"
at or very near the surface

dence in the form of an edict, of *Fürstbischof* Marquard of Eichstätt,[2]
dated 1674, regulating working conditions in the quarries of Mörn-
sheim, five or six miles south of Solnhofen.

The quarry owners—at Solnhofen the owner was the municipality
itself—presumably considered themselves prosperous and their business thriving all through the eighteenth century. But the heavy demand for Solnhofen slate—real Solnhofen slate from the municipal
quarry—was still to come. The benefactor of the city was one Aloys
Senefelder, who was born in Prague in 1771. Aloys Senefelder's
father was an actor; the son thought he would be a composer. In any
event he wrote music. I don't know whether he tried his hand on
cantatas or sonatas or fugues, but whatever it was one may have
doubts about the quality, since he could not find a publisher. He decided to engrave his music himself but found the price of copper
plates too high. He happened to have a slab of Solnhofen slate for
mixing paints. Most likely he was unaware that the Romans had used
the same kind of slate for mixing salves, but whether he knew this or
not he discovered some qualities of the slate which the Romans had
missed—its properties as a medium for printing. In short, he invented
lithography.

The year was 1796. The news of the invention, and its use, spread

[2] The now obsolete title of *Fürstbischof*, Prince Bishop, designated church-
men who were men of the high aristocracy. They had jurisdiction over worldly
affairs as well as religious matters and were sovereign over certain areas.

rapidly, and printers also found out promptly that no other slate
would do. For best results genuine Solnhofen slate was needed. Of
Aloys Senefelder it may be further mentioned that the king of Bavaria made him Royal Inspector of Maps in 1806, that he invented
color lithography in 1826, and that he died in 1834. In Solnhofen—
there is hardly any other way of expressing it properly—the boom
was on. Printers and artists all over the world needed its slate and
were willing to pay for it.

Even before Aloys Senefelder became the benefactor of a city he
probably had never seen, the men who quarried slate along the Altmühl valley had noticed that the slate occasionally showed something
almost like a picture. Sometimes the bones of a small fish could be
seen, more rarely a strange long-legged crayfish or even a dragonfly.
It was only natural that at least the better pieces were kept as curiosities. Sometimes they were sold to travelers and sometimes they were
passed on to a local priest. Gradually scientists learned about the
occasional fossils in the white Jurassic slate. Their interest, in turn,
made the quarry workers and foremen more attentive.

Thus a scientist named Collini acquired a slab of slate with a
strange fossil soon after it had been found in a quarry at Eichstätt.
The vertebrae and the neck of this fossil could be seen clearly, one
rather long leg with an apparently three-toed foot showed up well,
and there was a rather small skull with an enormously long beak
which bore tiny teeth in front only in both the upper and lower jaws.
Then there were several long bones which probably belonged to the
forelegs. Collini did not quite know what to make of it, but in 1784
he published a description of what could be seen, calling the fossil
the remains of an "unknown marine animal."

Not surprisingly, it was Cuvier who realized what it was that had
been found. His first publication about it stated even in the title that
it was, or had been, *un reptile volant,* a "flying reptile." And it was,
as Cuvier suspected from the outset and as was made definitely clear
by later discoveries, an actual *flying* reptile, not just a parachute animal like *Draco volans.* Cuvier called it *Pterodactylus,* from the Greek
words *pteron* for "wing" and *daktylos* for "finger," which is one of
the comparatively few really good names in paleontology. An over-all
description of the "flying finger" cannot very well avoid comparison
with the bats, especially since the various flying reptiles of the Pterodactylus type also showed about the same size range as the present-
day bats. But there is a fundamental difference, even apart from the

Reconstruction of *Pterodactylus suevicus* from the Solnhofen area. In size these flying reptiles ranged from that of a sparrow to that of a raven. Their habits must have been like those of the present-day bats, such as sleeping with their heads hanging down

other fundamental fact that the bats are mammals and Pterodactylus was a reptile. The skeleton of the bat wing shows, except for over-all size and proportions, a surprising resemblance to a human hand. The thumb is fairly short and usually equipped with a strong claw; the four fingers are enormously elongated and support the flying membrane which also encloses the legs and the tail. Of the four long fingers the equivalent of the index finger is usually the shortest, the equivalent of the middle fingers the longest, and the equivalent of the little finger somewhat longer than that of the ring finger. The skeleton of the Pterodactylus wing is entirely different. Thumb, index finger, and middle finger are short and usually clawed; the little finger is lost, but the ring finger is longer and stronger than the bones of the arm. While, as with the bats, the flying membrane encloses arms and legs and tail, only the one finger stretches it and is, to borrow a term from aeronautics, the main wing spar.

Because of Cuvier's work the first fossil of a flying reptile to be discovered in a place other than the Altmühl valley was recognized at once for what it was. This one was found in 1828 by Miss Mary Anning in the Jurassic strata of Lyme Regis in Dorsetshire. The Jurassic of Lyme Regis is black Jurassic or Lias; consequently the

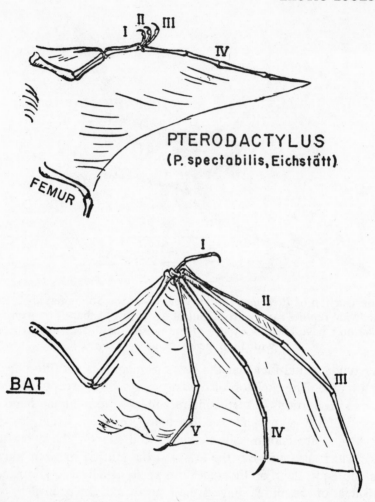

The wing structure of a flying reptile and that of a flying mammal. The digits are numbered in the customary manner, so that the "thumb" is no. I

fossil is a good 20 million years older than the Pterodactylus from Eichstätt. It was first described in 1835 by the Very Reverend William Buckland, D.D., Dean of Westminster, who was a very fine geologist though not one of the top luminaries of this science. Dean Buckland entitled his report: *On the Discovery of a New Species of Pterodactyle in the Lias of Lyme Regis*. As this title shows, he believed it to be a fairly close relative of the type from Eichstätt, but he did point out that it had a long tail while the tail of the Bavarian specimen was ridiculously short. In fact, the tail of the Lyme Regis specimen accounted for almost half of the total length of the animal. There were also differences in body build and in skull shape.

About fifteen years later another fossil of a flying reptile turned up at Eichstätt, this time a long-tailed form from the white Jurassic. The skeleton was not quite complete but the fine-grained slate of the Altmühl valley had done something which the Lias of Lyme Regis had failed to do: it had retained the impressions made by the wing membranes. And these wing membranes had been long and narrow, of the shape of a swallow's wing, while those of Pterodactylus must have been fairly short and wide triangles. (Later finds proved this to be correct.) Most surprisingly, the long tail, thin and naked, ended in a rhomboid skin "rudder." Professor Hermann von Meyer, who described it, decided that this was not just another species of Pterodactylus but a different genus. He proposed the name of *Rhamphorhynchus.* Since the two Greek words *rhamphos* and *rhynchos* which make up this name must both be translated as "beak," a translation would read "beak of beaks." Sometimes scientific names are of that kind; the well-known swordfish of the Atlantic Ocean is *Xiphias gladius* in zoological terminology, the first part being the Greek word for sword and the second part the Latin word for the same weapon.

Professor Richard Owen in England was a bit reluctant to accept Hermann von Meyer's name, but after re-examining the Lyme Regis specimen he fully agreed that the new find belonged to another genus. It was clear then that there had been two entirely different types of true flying reptiles during the Jurassic period. (A third type, *Pteranodon,* was later added from the American Cretaceous.) Both apparently ranged far. Since any flying animal has, of necessity, a high rate of "fuel consumption," they all need concentrated food: seeds, insects, other animals. A grass-eating flier is an impossibility; besides, the grasses did not yet exist in the Jurassic period. A lot of circumstantial evidence has led paleontologists to conclude that both Pterodactylus and Rhamphorhynchus of the Jurassic, and Pteranodon of the Cretaceous as well, led a life that can be compared with that of the fishing birds and fishing bats of our time.

With such interesting things coming to light from the slate of the Altmühl valley it is easy to understand that many scientists looked forward to new announcements as one waits for the daily mail. But in spite of much commercial quarrying the news did not come fast.

Pteranodon ingens, from the Cretaceous of North America. With a wing span of about 20 feet, this was the largest flying animal that ever lived

If one wanders through the paleontological exhibits of a modern museum of natural history the steady repetition of the names of Eichstätt and Solnhofen may easily conjure up a picture of slate quarries stuffed with beautifully preserved and rare fossils. It would be nice if this picture were correct, but it isn't. The visitor to a museum momentarily forgets that he is dealing with a highly artificial concentration of remains which took a long time to accumulate. One might as well conclude after a visit to the meteorite collection of the Hayden Planetarium in New York that the earth is daily being pelted by iron meteorites weighing between 3 and 15 tons apiece.

But apparently the impression that the Solnhofen slate was about as full of fossils as a herbarium is of dried plants prevailed for some time. In 1922 Professor Othenio Abel felt obliged to issue a kind of warning. He stated that, for one thing, the municipal quarry of Solnhofen was virtually exhausted, and continued, "Whoever undertakes a trip to Solnhofen and the neighboring quarries of the Altmühl valley in the hope of finding an impressive number of beautiful and valuable fossils will be bitterly disappointed. After climbing around in the quarries for several days he might have found, especially in the vicinity of Eichstätt, a number of the free-floating crinoid

Saccocoma, a few ammonites, and several Leptolepis, a small fish of about the size of a sardine, but it would be a case of very special good luck if he had found even one somewhat larger or more valuable fossil. The wealth of fossils in the slate is . . . caused by the intensity of commercial operations and the special attention of the quarry owners and all their workmen who immediately salvage every fossil which comes to light in the course of their daily labors."

The special attention which Professor Abel mentioned fortunately also existed in 1850; everybody from the owner down to the youngest apprentice was steadily on the lookout for fossils. Nothing was broken except accidentally, and then the pieces were saved; nothing was thrown away. And a special class of middlemen began to form, people who did not have any scientific training but who had acquired an eye for fossils, who knew what was relatively common and could therefore recognize something as rare, and who went around the quarries at intervals, buying up what had been found and offering their "interim collections" to scientific institutions in turn.

In 1860 a piece of slate showing an impression of a single bird feather was found. I don't know how it looked when it was taken from the Solnhofen quarry, but when I saw it on exhibit some 60 years after its discovery the slate had been neatly squared off, measuring about 2 by 4 inches, with the feather in its precise center. The size of the feather was such that it might have come from the breast of a pigeon. Within a short time the fossil came to the study of Professor Hermann von Meyer, who was understandably excited. A feather, even a single one, proved the existence of birds. Hermann von Meyer described it in the *Jahrbuch für Mineralogie* (*Annual of Mineralogy*) for the year 1861 and provided a scientific name for the bird which had left a feather in the lithographic slate. The Greek word *archaios* means "very old" and *pterinos* means "feathered"; using these words von Meyer coined the name *Archaeopteryx lithographica*.

A single feather, however, was not completely beyond what lawyers call reasonable doubt. The impression did look like a feather, but one could question it on several counts. The feather itself had not been preserved, but its impression only—could it be the impression of a leaf which just looked like a feather? If so, it could not be considered proof of the existence of birds during the Jurassic period, since it was the *only* proof. Then, even if the impression actually was that of a feather one could not be really certain that it belonged to a bird.

Anatomists were reasonably certain even then that feathers had evolved from reptilian scales. But if this was so who could deny that at one time in the past, say during the Jurassic period, there had been feathered reptiles?

Before anybody got around to formulating elaborate theories and learned arguments the discussion was cut short by the announcement that the bird that had to go with the feather had been found, just one year after the feather. It had not come from Solnhofen but from the Ottmann quarry in Langenaltheim, about one hour's walk to the west from Solnhofen. It had been bought, at an unstated price, by one Ernst Häberlein, *Landarzt* (county doctor) in nearby Pappenheim and was for sale as a part of a collection of unusual "lithographic fossils." Until a buyer was found, Dr. Häberlein would be glad to show the fossil to any scientists who cared to come to Pappenheim. Because of the uniqueness of the find, Dr. Häberlein could not permit anyone to photograph the relic, or make drawings; he allowed only personal inspection in his presence. Of course after a sale had been made the new owner could do as he pleased. As regards the price, Dr. Häberlein felt that $4000 would be quite reasonable.

Professor Albert Oppel did not lose any time in visiting the business-minded county doctor. Of course he flinched when he thought of the local equivalent of $4000, but he himself did not intend to spend more money than the trip would cost. Professor Oppel and Ernst Häberlein met, and after a few preliminary remarks Häberlein put the fossil on the table. There were impressions of the feathers of two wings, a long feathered tail, the skeleton of a bird's leg complete with foot. The foot of the other leg was missing, as were the skull and large portions of the body.

The finest description of what it looked like was given later by Professor Richard Owen. He wrote:

The remains . . . as preserved in the present split slab of lithographic stone recalled to mind the condition in which I had seen the carcase of a Gull or other seabird left on estuary sand after having been a prey to some carnivorous assailant. The viscera and chief masses of flesh, with the cavity containing and giving attachment to them, are gone, with the muscular neck and perhaps the head, while the indigestible quill-feathers of the wings and tail, with more or less of the limbs, held together by parts of the skin, and with such an amount of dislocation as the bones of the present specimen exhibit, remain to indicate what once had been a bird.

Professor Oppel looked at the slate. Häberlein was satisfied that he did not sketch it, and there were then no cameras small enough to be concealed. But to a specialist like Oppel a bone was not just a bone, it was the specific bone of a bird, dislocated from the position it should be in in such and such a manner and to such and such an extent. Examining the plate, feather for feather and bone for bone, as an anatomist would, Oppel simply memorized it! Then he went home and made a fine drawing.

The drawing was published by Andreas Wagner, who furnished the first preliminary description and a tentative name. Here, it seemed to Professor Wagner, was what some people had guessed at from theoretical reasoning: a feathered reptile. Some of the bones were rather birdlike but others pronouncedly reptilian. Too bad that the head was missing, but to make up for this there was the long reptilian tail. No living bird has an external tail; what is called a long tail, as in pheasants and peacocks, is simply long tail feathers. The actual bony tail of a bird is inside the body, and usually a number of tail vertebrae are even fused into a special bone, called the plowshare bone, which is the support for the tail feathers. To Wagner the long tail alone was proof of the essentially reptilian nature of the fossil.

Andreas Wagner would have liked to go to Häberlein's residence himself for a personal examination of the fossil, but he was too sick to travel—he died soon afterward—and had to rely on Oppel's drawing and personal report. Since a feathered reptile reminded him of the mythological griffin which is customarily drawn as something like a feathered dragon, he named the fossil "griffin-lizard," *Griphosaurus*. A zoologist named Giebel was the only one to contradict sharply; everybody else had the good sense to wait until more became known. Giebel declared the whole thing an absurdity. Feathers, he said, were feathers and scales were scales. And lizards are lizards and birds are birds. So if this plate shows lizard bones it is a fossil lizard. It cannot show feathers too because lizards don't have feathers. But if it does show feathers the feathers must be faked. And science does not deal with fakes, except to expose them. Now that he, Giebel, had exposed this fake, let's get back to genuine fossils.

Meanwhile Richard Owen, who a few years earlier had been appointed superintendent of the Natural History Section of the British Museum, quietly discussed with the trustees the desirability of buying the fossil. The trustees agreed that if Professor Owen said it was desirable, the next move was to find out about condition and price.

Accordingly the Keeper of the Geological Department of the museum, George Robert Waterhouse, wrote to Dr. Häberlein, asking whether he was willing, in principle, to sell his collection of Solnhofen fossils to England. That letter was written on the last day of February 1862. Doctor Häberlein replied under the date of March 21 and began by saying that Professor Louis Agassiz had come from America to look at his collection and that the Duke of Buckingham and Lord Enniskillen had also been there. They had all been interested in his collection. Then he said that it would be best if Mr. Waterhouse or some other staff member of the British Museum would come to Pappenheim to look at it. The letter made some statements about some of the pieces in the collection, and delivered a short description of the slab with the *gefiederte Thier* (feathered animal). No price was mentioned.

Mr. Waterhouse wrote back and asked what the whole collection would cost. The reply said that the whole collection would cost £750 (then about $3570), but if the British Museum did not want all of it there would be a proportionate reduction. The trustees, Waterhouse, and Owen had a meeting and decided to send Waterhouse to Pappenheim. He was to pick out the pieces the British Museum wanted and to go as high as £500.

The outcome of that trip is described in Owen's diary with the date of July 17, 1862.[3] "A visit from Mr. Waterhouse, just returned from Pappenheim, where he has been in treaty for the collection of fossils, in which is the curious fossil with the alleged feathered vertebrate tail. The old German doctor is obstinate about his price, and Mr. Waterhouse has come away empty-handed. We ought not to lose the fossil."

But on July 10, 1862 (letters took a long time to get from Bavaria to England), Dr. Häberlein had written to the British Museum that his lowest price for the whole collection would be £700. His lowest price for the pieces selected by Mr. Waterhouse would be £650. Professor Owen recommended buying the whole collection and paying for it in installments: £400 was immediately available, and the other £300 could be paid out of the following year's budget. The trustees said "no" to this idea; after all next year's budget had still to be voted by Parliament. But Owen and Waterhouse did not give

[3] Quoted in Chapter I of *Archaeopteryx lithographica*, by Sir Gavin de Beer, Director of the British Museum (Natural History), published by the Museum (London, 1954).

up. They wrote Häberlein that they would buy a selection, including
of course the *gefiederte Thier,* at once for £450, and the rest during

Archaeopteryx: first specimen, later called the London specimen

the following year for £250. He agreed to this arrangement and the feathered fossil arrived in London on October 1, 1862.

The only remaining details of this part of the story are that the trustees did make the additional £250 available the following year, that the whole collection consisted of 1703 fine fossils, that the British Museum never regretted the purchase, and that Häberlein gave the £700 to his daughter as her dowry.

Some of the German scientists were decidedly unhappy with the idea that the unique specimen had gone to London, but none of them, or the institutions they represented, had the equivalent of $3300 liquid and ready. Richard Owen, in any event, could be trusted to produce the best scientific description possible.

Richard Owen did. His report *On the Archeopteryx of von Meyer* appeared in 1863 [4] and made it clear once and for all that there had been a bird in Jurassic times. Owen compared it in size with the peregrine falcon, and (this more by accident) the one foot matched the foot of the peregrine falcon best both in size and in shape. In spite of the long tail and the reptilian cast of a number of the bones, Owen was convinced that this was a true bird. A bird with reptilian characteristics, yes, but a flying bird, not just a feathered reptile. Since it was indubitably a bird Owen rejected Wagner's name of Griphosaurus—*sauros* being the Greek word for lizard—and re-established von Meyer's name, Archaeopteryx. But since the single feather which had been found in 1860 did not match any of the feathers on the London specimen, as it came to be called, Owen thought that the feather had belonged to a different species. Since Solnhofen and vicinity had yielded both short-tailed and long-tailed flying reptiles, Owen said that the area might also yield short-tailed and long-tailed Jurassic birds. Possibly the single feather came from a short-tailed bird which, when found, would take von Meyer's full name *Archaeopteryx lithographica*. The London specimen was most obviously long-tailed (*macrura* in Greek) and should be called *Archaeopteryx macrura*.

Richard Owen had spoken the last word for a long time in matters relating to Archaeopteryx, largely because he had said everything that could be said. Only old Professor Giebel kept remarking that all this was nonsense, nobody had ever seen either a feathered lizard or a

---

[4] In *Philosophical Transactions of the Royal Society of London for the year MDCCCLXIII*, vol. 153, pt. 1, pp. 33–47, with several beautiful (lithographic) plates.

long-tailed bird, and this was just a case of one Englishman trying to prove another Englishman (meaning Darwin) right—something that wasn't Owen's intention at all. Giebel's colleagues grew annoyed at times, but in general they let him talk and waited—for another Archaeopteryx, one that had not been three-quarters eaten by something else. And, hopefully, one with a head.

The years went by and there were all kinds of developments. Scientific discoveries were made: one could now tell the chemical elements composing the stars just by analyzing their light. Technology progressed: the telegraph and the railroad became common. There were political changes: the German states fought France and a German empire resulted. In the more specialized field of paleontology a new name and a new continent began to intrude: Professor Othniel C. Marsh in America sent the most amazing reports about the most incredible fossils he had discovered in the American West. But still no new Archaeopteryx.

Finally, in 1877, Herr J. Dürr, owner of a quarry near Eichstätt, found a slab of slate which was imperfect from the point of view of a builder. A piece had split off so that at one corner the slab had only about half its thickness. But on the exposed inner surface something like a small bunch of feathers showed. In some never-explained manner Ernst Häberlein learned about this fossil at once and bought the piece from Dürr for a never-revealed price. Then he went home and with the skill that he had acquired in many years split the slate to expose the imbedded fossil. It was an Archaeopteryx, complete with head! At first glance it even looked as if it were complete in every detail. Later examination did not support this view; a few minor portions were missing and had presumably been eaten by crabs. But it certainly was a much better specimen than the first.

Häberlein's reasoning was simple-minded and straightforward. This was a much better specimen; therefore it ought to be more valuable. Translating his thought into the new unified currency of the new German Empire, he asked for 36,000 marks ($8560); he would add a small collection of other lithographic fossils as a friendly bonus. No drawings or photographs were to be made, but accredited scientists representing scientific—preferably solvent—institutions were invited to inspect the find. Häberlein probably had in mind to see to it that these inspections did not last too long, just in case somebody else with the memory and artistic ability of Professor Oppel should appear.

At various institutions there were conferences between scientists and trustees. In London not much mental arithmetic was needed; Häberlein's new price amounted to an even £1800. The British Museum decided to say nothing for a while. When a representative of a Munich museum said to Häberlein that the price was somewhat high, Häberlein replied that he was a reasonable man; in fact, he was just contemplating an offer from Professor Marsh of Yale University of just $7500. (Whether Marsh ever made such an offer is not known.) Häberlein felt quite secure in his position. He could count on various factors. The British Museum, having bought the first specimen, would certainly like to have the second one too. And the British Museum had money. As for Professor Marsh in America, it was hard to guess just how deeply he would be interested in a European specimen, but Professor Marsh had worked on fossil birds of lesser age from American sites—and the Americans had money. Häberlein's main trump card, however, was the fact that the first specimen had been sold to the British Museum. German scientists would do everything to keep Number 2 in Germany.

Häberlein's reasoning proved to be perfectly correct.

There was a foundation in Frankfurt-on-the-Main—it bore the untranslatable name of *Freies deutsches Hochstift*—which had the purpose of saving German antiquities and items of historical interest. It had, for example, saved Johann Wolfgang von Goethe's house in Frankfurt from destruction by the simple expedient of buying it. Although the foundation was not normally interested in fossils, the second Archaeopteryx was obviously a special case. Moreover, the chairman of the foundation, Dr. O. Volger, happened to be a geologist. The foundation did not have the money on hand, but Dr. Volger approached Häberlein, and they signed a contract which stipulated that the foundation would take the specimen under its care for a period of six months. During these six months the foundation would either raise the money for a direct purchase or else would act as an agent for another German institution or foundation. The other conditions were those Häberlein had always made: no drawings, no photographs, no casts.

Contract signed and specimen under his care, old Dr. Volger first approached the German government. But there were difficulties. The German Empire was deeply interested, Dr. Volger was told. But it was a new empire and therefore had no equivalent of the British Museum—no Empire Museum, so to speak. But the Empire was a federation of kingdoms, principalities, and such, and these had museums of their own. The discussions with officials of the German Empire no doubt enriched Dr. Volger's knowledge of constitutional and administrative principles and problems, but that was all. The alternative seemed to be to raise the 36,000 marks from various sources, but the six months ran out before even a fraction of the sum had been pledged.

Häberlein was asked whether he would grant an extension of the agreement for another three months. He agreed, but Dr. Volger was still unable to get the money. Häberlein, after waiting a few more months, took his specimen back with him to Pappenheim and started to negotiate directly. At first he corresponded with the University of Geneva. The man in charge of the department of geology was old Professor Karl Vogt, a German exile for political reasons and a devoted follower of Darwin. There was no doubt that Karl Vogt wanted the fossil, but the university simply did not have that much money. Next Häberlein approached the museum in Munich. Since Archaeopteryx had actually been found in Bavaria, the people in Munich, the capital of Bavaria, were most interested—one might even say that to them it was more a question of regional patriotism than of scientific prestige. But they did not have enough money either.

Häberlein wrote to Berlin, which was a dual capital, of the German Empire and of the Kingdom of Prussia. After he had been rejected twice because the price was too high—and Häberlein knew that this was really the reason—he asked for 26,000 marks. And, having learned about Dr. Volger's negotiations, he approached an institution of the Kingdom of Prussia: the Royal Mineralogical Museum of the University of Berlin. Its paleontological collection was not impressive at that time and Berlin was eager to acquire such a unique find. But no matter how eager the curator might be, there was a procedure to be followed, especially when such a large sum was involved. The museum had to pass its recommendation on to the university, and the university had to pass it on to the place the money came from, namely the Royal Prussian Ministry of Education. And the ministry had its own procedure, which required, first of all, expert testimony about the genuineness and the value of the items to be purchased. Privy Councilor Professor Dr. E. Beyrich was delegated to travel to Pappenheim, examine the collection, and report.

It would have been difficult at that time to find a paleontologist, geologist, or zoologist anywhere in the world who had a kind word to say about Ernst Häberlein. The second Archaeopteryx had been found in 1877. Privy Councilor Beyrich traveled to Pappenheim early in April 1880. Three years had gone by and all anybody knew was that the thing existed. No description was available, not even a picture. And Häberlein, while negotiating with the Prussian Ministry of Education, continued to negotiate with America, or at least said he did. During the same week that Dr. Beyrich spent in Pappenheim examining the fossils somebody told the story to the industrialist Werner von Siemens, famous designer of electrical equipment and part owner of the gigantic Siemens and Halske factories. He listened, asked a question or two about the value, and acted.

Within a few days Ernst Häberlein accepted 20,000 marks in cash and disappeared from the scene; he presumably retired. The fossil was now the private property of Werner von Siemens, who immediately made a formal offer to the Berlin museum at the price he had paid himself. And a month or so later scientists could at long last go to work on it.

Even those brief glances that some of them had caught of the fossil while Häberlein was holding out for a high price had shown to them that it—the Berlin specimen, as it soon came to be called—was not quite the same as the London specimen. It was generally smaller, about the size of a pigeon, and less sturdily built. There were other differences too, and it therefore had to have a different name, which fact, I am sorry to report, caused some more trouble. The Germans had never ceased to call the London specimen *Archaeopteryx lithographica,* insisting on the name coined by Hermann von Meyer. The news of the discovery of the first specimen had reached von Meyer just before his report on the single feather was published, and without seeing the specimen he had assumed that his feather had come from it. In reality the specimen which lost the single feather is considered unfound (and it may never have fossilized), but while Hermann von Meyer had been wrong, his name, in German eyes, still had priority over Owen's *Archaeopteryx macrura.*

The name of *Archaeopteryx siemensii* was proposed for the Berlin specimen to honor Siemens for his fast and successful action. But there were opposing voices (Siemens had been reimbursed, hadn't he?)—and the next suggestion was to accept Owen's name for the London specimen and to establish *Archaeopteryx lithographica* for the Berlin specimen. Then the whole problem resolved itself for several decades because the men who made a special study of the Berlin specimen decided that the differences were sufficient to warrant a different generic name.

The Berlin specimen was called *Archaeornis* ("ancient bird") but in the meantime the most important publications had appeared with Archaeopteryx in the title. Now the latest publication on the London specimen—by Sir Gavin de Beer, published by the British Museum in 1954—bears the title *Archaeopteryx lithographica,* because the author came to the conclusions (1) that Hermann von Meyer's name does have priority over Owen's name, and (2) that

Archaeornis: the Berlin specimen

the London and the Berlin specimens both belong to the same species. No doubt the Germans in charge of the Berlin specimen will presently have something to say about this—I expect some 300 pages of rebuttal. In the meantime I am going to refer to the Berlin specimen as Archaeornis and to the London specimen as Archaeopteryx, as convenient labels to tell the two apart.

Archaeornis was examined down to the minutest possible detail at least three times, the first description coming from Wilhelm Dames, who worked in Berlin. Archaeornis and Archaeopteryx were alike in many features—always keeping in mind that Archaeopteryx is somewhat larger and more sturdily constructed. For example, the one foot of Archaeopteryx that is preserved is larger and stronger beyond the difference in scale; it must have had more grasping power than the feet of Archaeornis. But the feet of the two specimens are alike in construction in that, though looking quite similar to a bird's foot of the present, they are actually closer to the construction of the feet of some reptiles. Both Archaeornis and Archaeopteryx have the same long reptilian tail, that of Archaeopteryx having twenty-one vertebrae, that of Archaeornis only twenty; both have the same type of vertebrae, which even among reptiles can be found only in old forms, as, for example, in the still-living Hatteria of New Zealand. Archaeornis showed ventral ribs, also an ancient reptilian attribute; as to Archaeopteryx, it was impossible to be sure, since the specimen had been too mutilated—and had also partly decayed before fossilizing.

While Archaeopteryx had clearly displayed the feathered long tail and bunches of feathers showed where the wings had been, Archaeornis gave information about most of the plumage. The wings were virtually intact and it could be seen that the legs had been feathered too. There was a clear ruff of feathers around the base of the neck. The neck itself seemed naked, and as for the body it was at first difficult to decide. Old Professor Karl Vogt in Geneva, who had wanted to buy Archaeornis, was much impressed with this information. Feathers showed on tail, legs, and wings, but nowhere else except for that ruff around the base of the neck—this, he mused, probably meant that body and neck had been covered by scales. Maybe, he said, Andreas Wagner had been right after all and the animal had actually been a feathered lizard. But Wilhelm Dames and later Gerhard Heilmann contradicted this, pointing out that if you looked at the original instead of at photographs you could make out where the body feathers had been.

The wings were one of the features in which Archaeornis differed most from modern birds. There were still three "fingers," with large claws which must have been helpful in climbing on the rough trunk of a cycad tree. But Heilmann could show that two of the three fingers had grown together in a highly surprising manner; they could not have been as freely movable as had originally been thought. Of all living birds only the South American hoatzin still develops something like that for a while when young. As William Beebe and others have observed, the wing claws of the young hoatzin do help in climbing. The wing fingers of Archaeornis probably could not do much better; as Heilmann wrote, "Nature's attempt at producing an organ for both climbing and flying purposes seems to have been anything but suc-

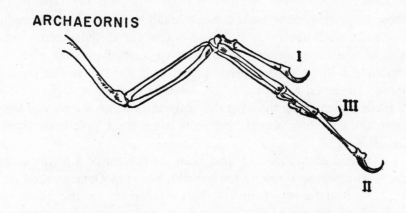

ARCHAEORNIS

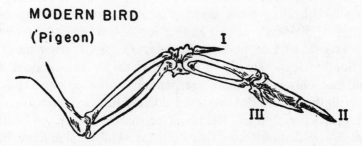

MODERN BIRD
(Pigeon)

The wing bones of Archaeornis and of a modern bird. Note how the second and third "finger" of Archaeornis are connected and that the same bones in the wing of a present-day bird are reduced to small stubs.

cessful and it is not surprising that the grasping power of the wing was lost."

That the flying power of the Archaeornis wing was not too advanced was obvious almost at first glance. Not only are the wings small compared to the body size; they could not have had much power behind their strokes; Archaeornis still lacked the enormously developed breastbone of the modern birds, which is the anchor for the flying muscles. Nobody doubts that Archaeornis had the power of true flight, but the flight must have been fairly slow, the wing strokes "weak," and the duration of each flight rather short. That the feathered legs helped, that they were "pelvic wings," was for a while a minority opinion of one man, but was discredited by Othenio Abel and fully demolished by Gerhard Heilmann. If the legs had been "pelvic wings" they could never have assumed the position in which they show in the fossil.

Last but not least, Archaeornis demonstrated the type of head those early birds possessed. It was a small head with little room for a brain and without the horny bill so typical for all living birds. And it still bore a large number of tiny sharp teeth. From the size of its mouth it is quite evident that Archaeornis must have fed on either insects or seeds, or perhaps both. But its powers of flight were not sufficient to catch on the wing the dragonflies which are so well known from the Solnhofen slate; the insects it ate must have been crawling insects.

The head of Archaeornis had been the subject of a highly enlightening disagreement among the experts. Wilhelm Dames called it "all bird," except for the teeth. Gerhard Heilmann, on the other hand, stressed all its reptilian characteristics and provided a drawing of the skull which he had made directly from the fossil, accompanied by drawings of the skulls of two extinct reptiles, *Aëtosaurus ferratus* from the Triassic of Europe and *Euparkeria capensis* from the Triassic of South Africa. He could show that they matched bone for bone, and not only could the corresponding bones of one skull be found in both the others, but they even differed little in shape and had the right proportional sizes. Heilmann proved his point, of course, but Dames's slip demonstrates that even the skull of a modern bird still shows a good many reptilian characteristics. In general, Heilmann concluded that Dames's original contention—that "Archaeornis was already a bird but still endowed with many reptilian features"—was wrong, although it had been accepted by most zoologists at the time

Reconstructed head of Archaeornis, actual size. The long feathers of the crest are *not* indicated on the fossil but are a likely adornment of the male at mating time

it was made. Instead, Heilmann wrote, "we may now stop talking about the 'missing link' between birds and reptiles; so much so is Archaeornis this link that we may term it a warm-blooded reptile disguised as a bird."

Heilmann's comparison of the skull of Archaeornis with those of the two reptiles shed much light on the ancestry of Archaeornis and the ancestry of the birds in general. Both these reptiles belonged to the same extinct order, the Pseudosuchia or "pseudo-crocodiles," and while it was still thriving another extinct order, the Parasuchia or "para-crocodiles," also existed.

Paleontologists suspect that both branched from the same stem, the para-crocodiles adapting to life in water, the pseudo-crocodiles to life on land. The order of the crocodiles, still well represented by living forms, probably sprang from the pseudo-crocodiles, which were rather prolific. Quite a number of spectacular later "dinosaurs" are known to have evolved from the pseudo-crocodiles. So did the flying reptiles of the types Pterodactylus and Rhamphorhynchus. And so did the birds.

In old books with titles like "Marvels of the Fossil World," written at a time when little was known and that imperfectly, you can find remarks to the effect that the flying reptiles were somehow on their way to becoming birds; these remarks sound rather like Gesner's statement that the bat is the middle-animal between the birds and the mice.

Of course in this form the statement is nonsense. Pterodactylus, after it had grown its wing membrane, did not sprout feathers. And the ancestors of the birds that did sprout feathers never had a wing membrane. Indeed, for many millions of years the membrane must have seemed a better solution; Rhamphorhynchus was obviously a far better flier than Archaeornis. But the old, mistaken thought happened, by sheer accident, to contain a grain of truth; the flying reptiles and the birds, though going, or rather flying, their strictly separated ways, both came from the same ancestral group, the pseudosuchians.

The reptiles belonging to the line that led to the birds must have acquired a more or less bipedal walk, with the forelimbs thus left free for other tasks, and have had the feet modified in such a manner that they resembled bird feet in appearance. But we know from countless fossil examples that the reptiles which took to walking on their hind legs only—either to widen their horizon in the literal optical meaning of the word, or for greater speed—simply had their forelimbs reduced because they did not make *any* use of them. It is obvious therefore that the pseudosuchians which were to become the ancestors of the birds must have been bipedal but must have used their forelimbs vigorously just the same. This could happen only with tree-dwelling forms which had a need for grasping hands—*and* for a parachute. Of course only small animals can be tree dwellers, but most pseudosuchians known to science were small, some tiny.

The pseudosuchians used by Heilmann for skull comparisons were found in deposits from the Upper Triassic period; Archaeopteryx and Archaeornis come from the Upper Jurassic. They are roughly 40 million years apart in time, during which interval the evolution of the birds must have taken place. The same interval, incidentally, applies to the evolution of the flying reptiles too. The conquest of the air occurred during the earlier part of the Jurassic period.

So far the luck which paleontologists unfortunately need has failed to produce a specimen of "pro-avis," the name used by Heilmann for the "feathered reptile" that preceded Archaeopteryx. However, a third specimen of Archaeopteryx was found at Langenaltheim in 1956. For various reasons no one even looked at the find until late fall 1958, when the Archaeopteryx was recognized. Regrettably it is a very poor specimen, much less complete than the London one, but the bones that have been preserved are precisely the same size as the corresponding bones of the London specimen.

We still need a fine fossil of "pro-avis."

PART THREE

OCEANIC
MYSTERIES

The "Great Wall Snake" (Gesner's *Historia Animalium*,
vol. IV, 1558; Olaus Magnus's "Sea Orm")

CHAPTER 11

The Curious Case of the Kraken

THE WORDS which should go at the head of any piece dealing with that famous sea-monster, the kraken, were provided a little over two hundred years ago. In 1753, when Erik Pontoppidan, Bishop of Bergen, wrote the second volume of his big and beautiful *Natural History of Norway,* he began the discussion of the kraken with the sentence: "Among all the foreign writers, both ancient and modern, which I have had opportunity to consult on this subject not one of them seems to know much of this creature, or at least to have a just idea of it. . . ."

It would surprise the good bishop if he could learn that even now, two centuries later, he is still largely right.

We still know very little about the "kraken," the gigantic relative or relatives of the small and medium-sized squids, calamaries, and cuttlefish. And the story of that truly awful monster of the sea is still mostly one that is founded on uncertainty, put together by way of hearsay, designed by the imagination, and embroidered and polished by literary splendor.

Still and all, the story somehow holds together, mostly because there *are* some facts. They are scattered and many of them are insufficiently documented, but they are *facts.* And while a twenty-foot piece of foot-thick tentacle vomited in death struggle by a dying whale cannot very well replace the whole giant octopus that went with that piece of tentacle, it at least proves that there *is* a giant octopus of such size.

To myself, and to almost anybody I have ever met, east and west of the Atlantic Ocean, the giant octopus is a literary acquaintance from early childhood, encountered for the first time in the exciting pages of Jules Verne's *Twenty Thousand Leagues Under the Sea.* It is in the latter part of the novel that the submarine *Nautilus* is suddenly at-

tacked by giant octopi. One man is carried off and the tentacles reach
down into the boat for more prey. But by chopping off the tentacles
with an ax the crew of the mysterious Captain Nemo save themselves
and the boat.

Being of the impressionable age of ten at that time, and being eager
to learn more about these unusual creatures, I went to the Supreme
Authority of boys at that age: I asked my teacher. Little did I know
then that grade-school teachers hardly know the things they are supposed to teach, and that they hardly ever feel the urge to acquire any
information not required of *them* by their superiors.

I did not get the information I expected. Instead I was informed that
I was too young to read Jules Verne to begin with, that it was not nice
of me to read books by a Frenchman, and how was my collection of
cherry and plum pits coming (this was in the winter of 1916, and
German schoolchildren were ordered to collect all such pits they could
find, for machine oil), and that the whole novel was, of course, only
Gallic imagination. There were no such things as giant cuttlefish—I
often had the feeling later on that he would have denied the existence
and possibility of submarines too, if the German press had not just embarked on a vigorous publicity campaign for the German submarine
fleet.

Years later I came across the giant octopus again, this time in Victor
Hugo. (I was still reading books written by Frenchmen.) By that
time I knew that one can look things up in libraries; the only trouble
was that the library at my disposal was poor and small. It did not contain any of the few books in which the theme is discussed at any
length—as I know now, because they are fairly scarce and all written
in French or English. But the library did contain a few zoology books
and a German counterpart of the *Encyclopaedia Britannica*.

The zoology books were silent on the subject of the kraken, as more
than ninety per cent of *all* zoology books are, but the encyclopedia did
contain a short paragraph stating that "there is evidence for the existence of very large octopi even though they do not attain the fabulous
proportions ascribed to them by old authors like Olaus Magnus and
Erik Pontoppidan."

That was of little help to somebody who did not even know the
names of Olaus Magnus and Erik Pontoppidan, much less their writings.

It took a lot of omnivorous reading to produce even a clear mental
image of the sequence of the story of the kraken. It seemed that a

Swedish archbishop, Olaus Magnus, or Olaus the Great, had been the first to mention the kraken, during the early part of the sixteenth century. He did so in a book on the history of the northern nations. Later it turned out that this history, while highly imaginative, was not too reliable.

Olaus had also spoken about other sea monsters "off the coast of Norway" and had had an artist picture them. There were whales squirting fountains of water into frail ships, other whales with a whole mouthful of elephant's tusks, chewing up similar ships with evident enjoyment, big fish of some kind eating a fisherman's net full of fish and the fisherman along with it. The pictures were such that Konrad Gesner, when he wrote his gigantic folios on natural history around the middle of the sixteenth century, reprinted them without description and with a general heading stating: "Such monsters were put on plates by Olaus, how well and right is his responsibility to bear."

Just to make things more pleasant, Olaus himself was confused by many writers with his brother Johannes; they were near the same age, being only two years apart, and they were both archbishops.

A little more than a century later the kraken found its next historian in the Norwegian bishop Erik Pontoppidan. Again, half a century later, the scene of action shifted to France, where Denys de Montford devoted the greater part of his book on mollusks to the kraken (with hand-tinted illustrations). That was in 1802.

Kraken in action (adapted from Denys de Montford)

In spite of de Montford's fluent French rhetoric, and in spite of the brightly colored illustrations—or maybe because of them—all books became unanimous in asserting that "there ain't no such animal." From about 1810 to, say, 1860 nobody believed a word of all this and any mention was purely derogatory.

Then, unfortunately, the "kraken" began to appear in person.

Huge carcasses, some of them still semi-alive, were washed up in Scotland and Denmark, and a little later the waters around Newfoundland were found to be infested with them.

The Danish naturalist Japetus Steenstrup had collected some of the evidence that had come to light and published it. Unfortunately Steenstrup, otherwise a man of merit, had just pulled his enormous boners on the question of whether the woolly mammoth and Man had ever been contemporaries. For a while Mr. Steenstrup's opinions were not apt to be very impressive.

But then the Newfoundland cases proved him right after all, and zoological science now admits the existence of gigantic octopi, even though the theme is still treated in a curiously diffident manner in most zoology books. The so-called "manuals" usually fail to list the gigantic varieties after listing the well-known types. Lydekker's enormous *Library of Natural History* (I have the edition of 1904) does not devote a single paragraph on any of its 3556 large-size pages to kraken. The even more enormous German *Tierleben,* originally written by one Dr. Alfred Brehm and now a compendium of fourteen volumes, encyclopedia size, has just *one page* about it.

Of course there is a reason for this.

The strict zoological information on hand still consists mainly of the fact that giant octopi exist. Body weights of a ton or more, tentacles of a length greatly surpassing 20 feet, staring eyes 10 inches in diameter, coloration ranging from dark green to bright brick red . . . these are the facts on record.

Places where such creatures have been found or observed are the North Sea, especially its northern parts, along both the Scandinavian and Scottish coasts; the Atlantic Ocean west of the Strait of Gibraltar; the Atlantic Ocean around Newfoundland; the Caribbean Sea; the Pacific Ocean around the Philippines; northeastern Australia; the Antarctic Sea.

It is fairly well established that there are several varieties. There is little doubt about their food: anything alive provided that it is not vegetable in nature.

But the two things for which we really want to know the answers still have question marks. One is: what are these giant varieties? Are they special varieties of which we know nothing except chance specimens or pieces of chance specimens? Or are they simply incredibly old individuals of known varieties? There is some reason to believe that at least some varieties of octopi grow as long as they live. Most individuals, of course, meet a violent end before they get very old. Some fish like octopus. Whales, especially the toothed varieties, seem to hunt especially for octopi; in fact, octopi appear to be their favorite food. Then, of course, larger octopi eat smaller octopi, as has been observed often enough in aquariums. Are the giants just individuals that managed to escape all mishap for centuries? Do we have their "young" in our museums without knowing it?

The other unanswered question is: where do the giants usually live? In the South Seas they are often encountered emerging from the cracks of coral reefs, in water shallow enough to be accessible to human pearl and sponge divers. It seems likely that submarine caves, in water of two hundred fathoms or less, are their favorite haunts. The sudden abundance of giant octopi around Newfoundland has been explained, for example, by saying that something happened to their submarine caves in about 1870. Tectonic events may have forced them to the surface into the open sea for a number of years at that time. Or it may have been just a shifting of currents of the sea, which made the old haunts uncomfortable.

Or are the ones encountered near the shore all chance specimens? Are they essentially animals of the high seas, living an unsettled life at a depth of one hundred fathoms or thereabouts? The facts that they are unlikely to encounter a sufficient amount of large prey at greater depths and also that they are so successfully hunted by whales (mammals which have to come to the surface for air) are against the oft-advanced hypothesis that they normally live at the bottom of the sea.

That is the outline of the story. Now for some detail. When I came to New York in 1935, and found an entirely new large library at my disposal, I decided to go in for some literary research, and the kraken was one of the subjects on the list. The New York Public Library, I have been told, has a little over two million volumes. The Prussian State Library in Berlin, to which I was used, had close to three million, before large sections were destroyed during the Second World War or confiscated by the Russians afterward.

The interesting point is that the two libraries overlapped to such a slight extent that it was surprising. Especially as regards older books you could almost count on finding in the one what was lacking in the other.

The first thing I looked for and found was Olaus Magnus, an English edition (the original is in Latin) printed in London in 1656 and entitled: *A Compendious History of the Goths, Svvedes & Vandals, and Other Northern Nations: written by Olaus Magnus, Arch-Bishop of Upsall, And Metropolitan of Svveden.*

It is in Chapter V of the Twenty-first Book that the kraken appears:

There are monstrous fish on the Coasts or Sea of Norway, of unusual Names, though they are reputed a kind of Whales, who shew their cruelty at first sight and make men afraid to see them; and if men look long at them, they will fright and amaze them. Their Forms are horrible, their Heads square, all set with prickles, and they have sharp and long horns round about, like a Tree rooted up by the Roots. They are ten or twelve Cubits long, very black, and with huge eyes: the compass whereof is above eight or ten cubits: the Apple of the Eye is of one Cubit, and is red and fiery coloured, which in the dark night appears to Fisher-men afar off under Waters, as a burning fire, having heirs like Goose-Feathers, thick and long, like a Beard hanging down; the rest of the body, for the greatness of the head, which is square, is very small, not being above 14 or 15 Cubits long; one of these Sea-Monsters will drown easily many great ships provided with many strong Mariners. . . .

The description is not at all bad, with its emphasis on the large size of the head compared with the size of the body, the gigantic eyes, the tentacles looking like the roots of a tree—there can be no doubt that Olaus, even if he had never seen a giant octopus himself, had eyewitness accounts to go by. And, if his remarks mean anything at all, accounts from eyewitnesses who had been badly frightened.

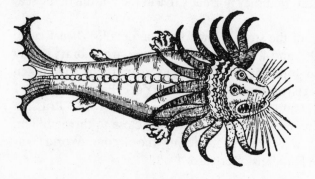

How Gesner's artist pictured Olaus's Kraken from the description. Living in Switzerland, he had never seen an octopus of any type (*Historia Animalium*, vol. IV, Zurich, 1558)

So this was history's first account of the giant cuttlefish.

I looked for the second, Pontoppidan's, and found that too, an English edition of his *Natural History of Norway,* published in London in 1755 in a very big, well-printed, perfectly bound, and neatly illustrated folio volume weighing some ten pounds. The first volume of the Norwegian original had been written in 1751, the second in 1753.

Well, Bishop Pontoppidan did lay it on somewhat thick. His kraken lies in water of eighty or one hundred fathoms offshore, but sometimes the fishermen find only twenty fathoms. When they do, they know that they will have an overabundant catch, but they also watch the depth, because it means that the kraken is rising to the surface. Sometimes it does not actually come up, but when it does, it looks at first like a number of small islands. Finally the whole back appears "about an English mile and a half in circumference—some say more but I chuse the least for greater certainty."

These are fishermen's stories, as admitted by the bishop. But there is one little paragraph, tacked on like an afterthought, which looks as if it were a report of an actual event:

In the year 1680 a *Krake* (perhaps a young and careless one) came into the water that runs between the rocks and cliffs in the parish of Alstahong. . . . It happened that its extended long arms caught hold of some trees standing near the water, which might easily have been torn up by the roots; but besides this, as it was found afterwards, he entangled himself in some openings or clefts in the rock, and therein stuck so fast, and hung so uncomfortably, that he could not work himself out, but perished and putrefied on the spot.

Having finished with Pontoppidan, I sat on one of the stone benches in front of the Public Library and wondered. Something was not quite right with all this. It was not the obvious exaggerations of Pontoppidan's fishermen's tales. It was modern commentary. Why did they all say, probably copying from one another, that Olaus and Pontoppidan were the earliest two sources for the giant squid? I seemed to remember something much older.

Roman?

Gaius Plinius Secundus?

Yes, of course, Chapter Forty-eight of the Ninth Book, where the old cavalry colonel told the story of the "polypus" of Carteia, a place in Spain, just outside of the entrance to the Mediterranean. "It was only with the greatest difficulty that it could be dispatched with the

aid of a considerable number of three-pronged fish-spears. The head
of the animal was shown to Lucullus; it was as large in size as a cask
holding fifteen amphorae of wine"—a considerable cask, since an
amphora was about nine gallons.

The tentacles of that octopus, amusingly called "beard," were so
thick that a man could not reach around them with both arms and
were thirty feet long. Some remains were preserved for some time; they
weighed seven hundred pounds.

I don't know why Olaus, who wrote in Latin himself and certainly
had access to a copy of Pliny, failed to mention him in order both to
prove his erudition and bolster his own case. I know even less why
later writers kept harping that Olaus and Pontoppidan were the first
to mention the giant octopi.

But even Pliny did not satisfy me. He was a much older source all
right, but not what I had vaguely in mind. There was still another one
—after Pliny, contemporary, or older than Pliny? It was the thought
of "still older" which proved fruitful. After all, there were not too
many: there was Strabo, then Herodotus, and Hesiod, the probable
contemporary of Homer . . . of course, Homer's *Odyssey,* the story
of Odysseus's encounter with Scylla.

The description given in the epic itself is clear enough:

> . . . but her form is a sight portentous that no one
> E'er would gladly behold, not even a god if he met her.
> Round her a dozen of feet she is always waving suspended
> Six long sinuous necks outstretching before her and each one
> Beareth a head terrific with teeth in a threefold order,
> Many and thickly arrayed, where gapes death's cavernous blackness.
> Up to the midmost parts she is hid in the depth of the cavern
> Whilst from her lair in the fearful abyss six heads she extendeth
> Hunting for fish at the foot of the rock and peering around it,
> Dolphins to catch or dogfish, or haply another and greater
> Beast. . . .[1]

It contains all the now familiar elements, the cavern in which the
monster waits, the nervous play of the tentacles, some of which are
invisible as a rule, the generally terrifying appearance which would
dismay "even a god if he met her." The "teeth in threefold order" are
probably the sucking disks of the tentacles and that their total number
is wrong (twelve instead of the possible maximum of ten) proves nothing against the story itself.

[1] *Odyssey,* XII, 87ff., Cotterill's translation, op. cit.

Here we have an old, a very old, account of an encounter with a giant squid, written at the latest in about 650 B.C. but probably a century or two earlier.

Homer, not Olaus, had introduced the giant octopus into literature.

Later it occurred to me that Scylla is not the only mythological monster which can be traced back to the frightening appearance of the kraken. There is another one: Medusa.

She too appears for the first time in the *Odyssey*, mentioned as a monster of the underworld—the *Mythological Lexicon* contains an explanatory note saying that the Gorgon lived in the realm of the dead, the Far West, which then meant the coast of the Atlantic Ocean and Spain.

Hesiod knew three Gorgons: Stheno (the mighty), Euryale (the far-springer), and Medusa (the queen). They were the daughters of the sea-god Phorkys and of Keto. Medusa especially was very beautiful and finally attracted the attention of Poseidon. During their liaison they defiled one of the temples of Athena; and Pallas Athena, armed and armored as always, and eternally on tense terms with Poseidon, changed Medusa into a monster of extreme ugliness, with writhing snakes for hair. The king Polydectes (needled by Athena?) sent Perseus to slay Medusa. Whether Athena had caused Perseus's punitive expedition or not, she gladly aided him and gave him the advice which saved Perseus from the petrifying stare of Medusa. The two sisters tried to kill Perseus in turn, but their pursuit was ineffectual.

Before we go on, it must be mentioned that the classic picturizations of Medusa acquired the shape of a coldly beautiful woman with snakes for hair rather late. The early picturizations are different. They show the head only—it was used to fill round spaces, like shields, coins, and later even doorknobs—but it is a face which has little resemblance to a human face. It is round, with large eyes and a cleft tongue protruding from the open mouth. Instead of snakes there are only scroll lines, which may be taken for hair, or for snakes, or merely for space-filling lines.

When one examines the story it becomes clear that it is a sea story. Medusa is the daughter of one sea-god and the beloved of another one. She dwells in the Far West, in or at least near the ocean. Perseus's trip is a sea voyage; he kills Medusa at the seashore. Her sisters, who are immortal—i.e., who were not killed by Perseus—pursue him ineffectually, since he is on land and under the protection of the (land) goddess Athena.

Medusa, in short, was a sea monster, of a type which looks as if it were only head, with staring, terrifying eyes, with writhing "snakes" surrounding the face.

I said earlier that nobody around the middle of the nineteenth century believed in the existence of large octopi or squids any more. The kraken had been finally "unmasked" as a product of the imagination of Nordic fishermen, of a time, be it noted, when heart- and body-warming rum had already been introduced along the Scandinavian coastline with outstanding success.

This opinion was still firmly grounded in 1860.

In 1861, a few weeks before Christmas, the French corvette *Alecton* made port with a very unusual report. The *Alecton* had been about 120 miles northeast of Tenerife on November 30th, in a calm sea and with a clear sky, the air being unusually warm, when the lookout man sang out that there was "a large body, partly submerged, drifting at the surface."

The commander of the corvette ordered approach and investigation, thinking that it might be a half-submerged wreck. It turned out to be a gigantic squid. The bright brick-red body was about 18 feet long, the tentacles another 18 feet or more. The eyes, which were coal-black and had a cold, glassy stare, measured 10 to 12 inches across.

Since the *Alecton* was a war vessel there was no lack of armament. Solid cannon balls were shot at (and through) the animal, which, though lazily drifting, was unmistakably alive. Harpoons were thrown at it. Ship and kraken were immediately alongside (which made the estimate of the measurements so accurate); there was no way of missing. But apparently there was also no way of hurting the creature. The cannon balls penetrated without causing much of a reaction; the harpoons did not hold in the flabby flesh.

The monster did not even seem greatly disturbed by the furious attack. The giant squid disappeared under the surface three or four times, but always reappeared after intervals never exceeding five minutes. After several hours of intensive naval action one of the cannon balls hit a vital spot; the monster vomited large quantities of messy mucus and half-digested food, producing an intense and oppressive stench, even more oppressive because of the heat of the day.

At about that time one of the men succeeded in throwing a noosed rope around the squid. It slithered along the body but caught at the big fins at the rear end. The men, in an incredible display of bravery, tried to haul the still living monster aboard, but the flesh was so soft and the weight so great that the rope severed the tail end of the kraken. That part was salvaged; the main part disappeared under the surface for good. But even the salvaged section quickly became so "high" that it had to be thrown overboard—when the *Alecton* made port, there was no proof except the word of her commander and the affidavits of her whole crew.

The case was put down as a case of mass hallucination!

Captain Bouyer's reply is, unfortunately, not on record.

The encounter of the *Alecton* (which prompted the famous kraken scene in Jules Verne's story of Captain Nemo and the *Nautilus*) had been preceded by all the cases which Denys de Montford had collected, among them one in which a kraken had actually reached up into the shrouds of a vessel and torn a sailor from his perch. One of the tentacles had been hacked off in the battle; it measured 23 feet.

Only a few years before the *Alecton* case (in 1854) a large specimen had stranded on the Danish coast. The fishermen cut it up for bait, but the 9-inch beak was saved. Some three or four years later a 7-foot calamary stranded in the Shetlands. It was badly mutilated but could still be measured, the eight "short" tentacles were 8 feet long, the two long tentacles 16 feet each.

These were the two cases which made Steenstrup undertake his investigation—but it did need the "Newfoundland series" to clinch the case.

In 1873 three fishermen off the Newfoundland coast saw a shapeless mass floating upon the water. Hoping for salvage they rowed up and struck it with their boat-hook. At once the shapeless mass opened up into what looked like an umbrella, two green eyes stared at the men, and two tentacles gripped the boat. When one of the fishermen severed both tentacles with his hatchet, the monster ejected a large amount of black fluid and disappeared. One of the tentacles was cut up for bait before a Reverend Mr. Harvey (the reporter of this case) saw it. The other, lacking 6 feet used up for bait, still measured 19 feet, while the fisherman swore that another 10 feet had been left on the kraken.

Soon afterward another one caught itself in a fish-net, the body measuring 8 feet in length and 5 feet around, the long arms 24 feet, the short arms 6 feet. The eyes were 4 inches in diameter. Only a short time later one was taken alive at Coombe's Cove, Fortune Bay; the eight short arms measured 6 feet on the average, the two long arms

42 feet, the body 10. A specimen cast ashore in 1877 was brought to the New York Aquarium; it was 9½ feet long and 7 around. The long arms measured 30 feet each, the eyes had a diameter of 8 inches.

During the same year a specimen of similar size was washed up at Trinity Bay and was observed struggling desperately and fearfully to escape from the shallow portion into which it had been deposited by the tide. "In its struggles," an eye-witness reported, "it plowed up a trench 30 feet long and of considerable depth, by means of the stream of water that it ejected with great force from its siphon."

For a few more years giant cuttlefish and calamaries of many types were fairly frequent along the Newfoundland coast. Then they became rare again.

Some more and less direct evidence has been furnished by whalers. Toothed whales, vomiting in death struggle, have shown evidence of still larger kraken; in one case a 6-foot piece of tentacle, *with a diameter of 2 feet,* has been claimed. Another claim goes for marks on the skin of such a whale, looking like the mark of a sucking disk over 2 feet in diameter.

There is no longer any doubt that cephalopods of truly gigantic size do exist. But the knowledge that they do exist is only the fundamental item on the long list of things which we would like to know about them.

CHAPTER 12

The Great Unknown of the Seas

THE STORY of the Great Unknown of the Seas begins somewhere in the cold waters off the northern Norwegian coast, where the midnight sun sheds a reddish light on eternal glaciers which in winter are illuminated by the bluish fire of the aurora borealis.

It was in these surroundings of sea and spray, cliffs and ice, that stories of the great sea serpent were first told. Hardy Norse fishermen and sailors knew that the monster stuck its small head and long neck out of the water of the fiords and the boulder-dotted coastal waters between the mainland and the open sea. And, they said, the appearance of the sea serpent was an evil omen. When the fiery eyes of the sea serpent shone through the mist and spray, tragic news was sure to follow.

The "chronicler of sea monsters and midnight marvels," Archbishop Olaus, became the first chronicler of the sea serpent too. But Olaus, as has been stated, was a credulous and careless man; moreover, when he wrote his book, he was very old and living in Rome, far from what he was writing about. As soon as these facts had been thoroughly realized by more skeptical people elsewhere, everything Olaus had ever mentioned began to be discredited on principle. Olaus had told about the kraken, of course there was no such thing. Olaus had told about the sea serpent, naturally . . . oh, well, Olaus Magnus of Uppsala . . .

That Erik Pontoppidan also got mixed up in the story of the sea serpent was another negative asset—Bishop Pontoppidan, wasn't he the one with the kraken a few miles in extent?

But then there came those real kraken, still very much alive and as tangible as a shark or seal. And with the real kraken there came— unfortunately no live sea serpents, but more and still more stories

211

about live sea serpents. And some people began to wonder whether it is so absolutely correct that "skepticism cannot be overdone." Maybe there was, after all, something in those sea-serpent yarns. But many who started thinking along that line learned to their sorrow that most people begin to smile the moment the words "great sea serpent" are even mentioned.

There exists a well-authenticated story about a sea captain of a passenger liner who was just having lunch when the officer of the watch sent a seaman to his cabin, asking him to come to the bridge "if you have the time, sir," because a sea serpent had been sighted. The captain flatly refused to go to the bridge or even on deck and kept his eyes on his food and away from the portholes of his cabin until another dispatch informed him that the sea serpent had passed. Later he explained: "Had I said that I had seen the sea serpent, I would have been considered a warranted liar all my life after."

It is a matter for great admiration, therefore, that there have been many sea captains who did not avoid looking at sea serpents, but who did their best to get an accurate impression of size, shape, and probable nature of the animal and did not hesitate to report what they had seen and to enter their observations in their logbooks. These captains gained nothing by doing so but ridicule and reproach; in fact they sometimes risked their positions for so simple and basic an emotion as the love of truth.

During the last five decades the number of men of solid reputation and standing (including some speaking for scientific institutions) who are willing to be at least open-minded about the sea serpent has steadily grown. And it is very important to fix in one's mind that these men use the term "sea serpent" with great reluctance and merely as a label, since this happens to be the established name. None of them is willing to believe in a real "serpent," that is, in a large marine snake (beyond those sea snakes of the Indian Ocean which are in zoology books and aquaria). They all use "sea serpent" to mean something in the seas which is in all probability a large animal, undiscovered and unknown, and probably even of mammalian nature.

The first professional zoologist who had the courage to come out openly and say, "Yes, I believe that there is a large undiscovered animal in the seas and here are my reasons for this belief," was Professor A. C. Oudemans, director of a zoological park in Holland and Member of the Royal Dutch Zoological Society. In 1892 he published a large-sized book of 592 closely printed pages, called *The Great Sea Serpent*.

Dr. Oudemans's book contains two hundred reports of encounters with, or observations of, this unknown animal. It is doubtless true that some of these reports are erroneous interpretations of fact, and some are even deliberate hoaxes, but it is equally true that at least half of them are sincere and trustworthy reports of observations made by men who grew up on or near the sea and, even in bad weather, knew the difference between a shark, a seal, a whale, and something else.

One of the favorite "explanations" of many people who do not take the time to acquaint themselves with the material amassed by Professor Oudemans, as well as that later compiled by Lieutenant-Commander Rupert T. Gould of the British Royal Navy,[1] is that the sea serpent is only an optical illusion caused by a school of dolphins or porpoises. These "interpreters" say that ten dolphins leaping one behind another may well give the impression of being ten coils of one large black serpent winding its way through the waves. This school-of-porpoises-swimming-in-a-line theory has a striking air of plausibility, except for two weaknesses. It assumes, first, that old salts do not recognize porpoises when they see them; and, second, that the reports of these observers speak of a gigantic snake. But they do not.

Much of the resistance to the seemingly obvious consideration that after all some observers may actually have seen an unknown animal is the result of a mistaken application of an otherwise sound rule: that for any controversial story one should always go back to the original source. In this case, the original source is—or so it is believed—the account by Olaus Magnus, usually quoted in the version given by Konrad Gesner. Now the descriptions by Gesner of the "Great Wall Snake" and by Olaus of the "Sea Orm" actually speak of enormous snakes, 300 feet long, "rolling their coils in gigantic spirals," attacking small ships (see illustration on page 197), and snapping sailors out of the vessels that passed close to their caves. It may be hard to prove, but I have the feeling that it was the Scylla of the *Odyssey* that caused Olaus Magnus to introduce these man-eating habits into the classic sea-serpent lore, for the hodgepodge nature of which he is largely responsible.

Yet the sea serpent is not merely a literary tradition requiring that one go "back to the original" for its explanation. The persistent stories

[1] *The Case for the Sea Serpent* (London, 1930).

Gesner's "Lesser Sea Snake" (*Historia Animalium,* vol. IV, 1558; source
unidentified, but presumably not Olaus Magnus)

of sea serpents are mostly based on obviously sincere eyewitness reports and not on the continuity of a tradition. Therefore each of these
reports should be treated as an "original." And the point upon which
they all agree is the existence of an animal that is *not* a gigantic snake,
nor a sea orm. Even the very earliest report of a man who claimed to
have seen the "monster" with his own eyes does not repeat any of the
details that have brought so much justified ridicule on Olaus Magnus's
sea orm.

That earliest eyewitness on record was also a priest, Hans Egede,
"the Apostle of Greenland," who sailed from his native Norway in
1740. His ship was still off the west coast of Greenland when it met
with the most remarkable adventure of the whole trip. Egede carefully recorded it in his journal (without undue emphasis, it might be
remarked), and possibly supervised the drawing of a picture of the
animal encountered, which was later used by his son Povel as the
frontispiece of the printed edition of the journal. The entry reads:

Anno 1734, July. On the 6th appeared a very terrible sea monster, which
raised itself so high above the water, that its head reached above our main
top. It had a long sharp snout, and blew like a whale, had broad large
flappers, and the body was, as it were, covered with a hard skin; and it
was very wrinkled and uneven on its skin; moreover on the lower part it
was formed like a snake, and when it went under water again, it cast
itself backwards and in so doing it raised its tail above the water, a whole
ship-length from its body. That evening we had very bad weather.

Critics have said that the last sentence of this entry proves that
Egede's sea serpent was the offspring of Olaus's midnight monster, but
the whole tenor of the entry belies this interpretation. What Egede
meant to say with this sentence is most probably that at the time of
the encounter the weather was not bad. This seems to be important
because of all the later well-authenticated sea-serpent reports only a
very few (roughly two per cent) mention bad weather. This may indicate that the sea serpent does not come to the surface unless the water
is smooth and the weather good. As a matter of fact, it would be more

Hans Egede's sea serpent (from his book *A Full and Particular Relation of a Voyage to Greenland in the Year 1734*)

in keeping with the tradition of superstition if the sea serpent did come to the surface in bad weather—presumably to prophesy doom—while the good-weather habits point strongly in the direction of a real animal.

Hans Egede's story is perfectly simple and clear. An animal with a large body and long neck (reaching to a height of about 30 feet [2]), with large flippers, of which two were seen, is something that is biologically possible. (Egede also described and pictured several varieties of whales to be found off the coast of Greenland; therefore, his sea serpent cannot have been a whale, as has been suggested.) Under no circumstances does it fall into the same class as Olaus's famous "midnight marvels" which Gesner reproduced but declined to be held responsible for.

The very next eyewitness report after Egede's takes the last remnants of "otherworldliness" out of sea serpents. This report dates from

[2] Unfortunately the dimensions of Egede's ship are not known.

a day near the end of August 1745. It was made by Commandant
Lorenz von Ferry and was preserved in the *Natural History of Norway*
by the famous Erik Pontoppidan. Commandant von Ferry was traveling in a small sailing vessel from Trondheim to Molde, along the coast
of Norway. The day was very hot, the sea smooth as a mirror, and the
air completely calm. When they were still about a mile from Molde:

> I heard a kind of murmuring voice from amongst the men at the oars,
> who were eight in number, and observed that the man at the helm kept
> off from the land. Upon this I inquired what was the matter, and was in-
> formed that there was a sea serpent ahead of us. I then ordered the helms-
> man to keep the land again, and to come up with the creature, of which
> I had heard so many stories. Though the fellows were under some appre-
> hensions, they were obliged to obey my orders.
>
> In the meantime the sea snake passed by us, and we were obliged to
> turn the vessel about in order to get nearer to it. As the snake swam faster
> than we could row, I took my gun, which was loaded with small shot, and
> fired at it; on this it immediately plunged under water. We rowed to the
> place where it sank down (which in the calm might be easily observed)
> and lay upon our oars, thinking it would come up again to the surface;
> however, it did not. Where the snake plunged down, the water appeared
> thick and red; perhaps the small shot might have wounded it, the distance
> being very little.

If this report had been written by Olaus Magnus, he would probably have told how the sea serpent seized and devoured at least four
of the crew of eight. Actually nothing happened. The animal, upon
discovering itself attacked, simply disappeared under the sea. This
type of behavior is also noted by a number of later reports. It seems
that the Great Unknown of the Seas pays surprisingly little attention
to the ships and boats of Man. Again the weather was good and the sea
calm. There might after all be some connection between the hot days
of summer and the sea serpent, but in a sense other than has often
been jokingly asserted.

The next important chapter in the story of the Great Unknown
of the Seas appears under the title of the "New England Sea Serpent
of 1817." This chapter exhibits many of the perennial elements of
the history of the sea serpent: first, a number of sincere and generally
trustworthy reports; second, a confession of inability to explain what
has been observed; third, a complete absence of the kind of conclusive
evidence nonobservers like to have, which, in the case of the sea
serpent, must be nothing less than a captured specimen, dead or

alive—preferably the latter; and, finally, a fearful blunder which provided an excellent excuse for poking fun at the unfortunate people who had enough backbone to insist that they had actually seen what they had described.

The locality frequented by the New England sea serpent was Massachusetts Bay, especially the harbor of Gloucester; and the whole matter of its investigation was handled very expertly (save for the last-minute blunder) by a committee appointed by the Linnaean Society of Boston. This committee laid down some rules to guide its research: it would examine only persons who claimed to have seen the creature for themselves; these persons were to give their testimony in writing, either before the committee or before the Honorable Lonson Nash, Justice of the Peace; and they must answer twenty-five questions prepared in advance by the committee.

The earliest date obtained in these statements is that of a mariner named Amos Story who saw the "strange marine animal" for the first time in the harbor of Gloucester on August 10, 1817. Story was also the last witness, for he saw it again (apparently while it was asleep) early in the morning of August 23, 1817. As an example of the general tenor of these affidavits, that of Shipmaster Solomon Allen may be quoted in part:

I, Solomon Allen 3d, of Gloucester, in the County of Essex, Ship master, depose and say; that I have seen a strange marine animal, that I believe to be a serpent, in the harbor in said Gloucester.

I should judge him to be between eighty and ninety feet in length, and about the size of a half-barrel, apparently having joints from his head to his tail. I was about one hundred and fifty yards from him, when I judged him to be of the size of a half-barrel. His head formed something like the head of the rattle snake, but nearly as large as the head of a horse. When he moved on the surface of the water, his motion was slow, at times playing about in circles, and sometimes moving nearly straight forward. When he disappeared, he sunk apparently directly down, and would next appear at two hundred yards from where he disappeared, in two minutes. His color was a dark brown, and I did not discover any spots upon him.

This mysterious ability to sink "directly down" is also mentioned in the affidavit of Matthew Gaffney, one of the men that tried to settle the sea-serpent problem with a gun:

I, Matthew Gaffney, of Gloucester in the County of Essex, Ship carpenter, depose and say: That on the fourteenth day of August, A.D. 1817, between the hours of four and five o'clock in the afternoon, I saw a strange marine animal, resembling a serpent, in the harbor in said Gloucester. I was in a boat, and was within thirty feet of him. . . . I fired at him, when he was the nearest to me. I had a good gun, and took good aim. I aimed at his head, and think I must have hit him. He turned towards us immediately after I had fired, and I thought he was coming at us; but he sunk down and went directly under our boat, and made his appearance at about one hundred yards from where he sunk. He did not turn down like a fish, but appeared to settle directly down, like a rock. . . .

Lonson Nash, who officially collected all these affidavits, was also one of the witnesses. He saw the mysterious animal twice through a glass, for a short time, and at other times with the "naked eye."

All in all, the animal was seen for several weeks by many hundreds of people, at ranges varying from 20 feet to 2 miles. That all these people should have banded together to perpetrate a hoax is well-nigh impossible. There can be no doubt that *something* was swimming around in Massachusetts Bay in August 1817. Many plans were made to kill or capture the animal, but the time was apparently too short to put these plans into operation.

One feature that keeps cropping up in these New England reports (and in other reports as well) is the "humps" or "bunches" on the back of the animal. This feature was emphasized again later in the accounts of the Reverends Twopenny and Macrae from Loch Hourn in Scotland and also in the Loch Ness reports, although it is rarely mentioned in observations made on the high seas. It seems that the back of the Great Unknown shows (or may form under special circumstances) a series of bunches. There is no agreement as to their number, but eight or ten seems to be a fair average. It is likely that these bunches, whatever they may be, are responsible for the name of sea *serpent,* being interpreted as the visible parts of the coils of a gigantic snake. Such an explanation is, of course, nonsense, if only for the reason that no snake moves in vertical coils as some caterpillars do. In fact, there are reports that mention these bunches and horizontal loops in the same breath.

It was because of these bunches that the sea-serpent committee of the Linnaean Society of Boston committed the blunder to which I have already referred. The learned members must have wondered considerably about the humps, or serrations, as they preferred to call them, and when a man named Beach brought them a three-foot snake with a number of small humps on its back they believed they had ample reason for feeling elated. The snake had been found and bravely slain near Cape Ann, about a month after the sea serpent had left Gloucester harbor.

The date of the serpent's departure is fairly well established. Amos Story, the last of the Gloucester witnesses, saw it on August 23, but five days later an animal of the same type was observed 2 miles east of Cape Ann by the captain and crew of the schooner *Laura*. It seems reasonable to conclude that it was the same animal; and it is probable that two sea-serpent reports from Rye Point on Long Island Sound, dating October 3 and October 5, 1817, also refer to the same individual.

To go back to the committee of the Linnaean Society, the residents of Gloucester had agreed among themselves as to the reason they had been visited by the sea serpent. Most probably it had to come to shore, like the big marine turtles, to deposit its eggs. Some lucky person might find the eggs and settle the question. If anyone looked for sea-serpent eggs—as many doubtless did—he did not mention it, to avoid ridicule. Whether the boy who found the three-foot humped snake and the man, his father, who slew it with a pitchfork thought of a "young sea serpent" at once is doubtful, but they must have thought along these lines later on, else they would not have presented the Linnaean Society with the cadaver. The members of the committee did not reject this suggestion; when they found a number of small humps on the back of the snake they accepted it with joy. Without hesitation they stated that their 3-foot specimen and the observed 70-foot creature agreed in every respect, except in size, and that they "felt justified in considering them individuals of the same species." They gravely named it *Sciolophis atlanticus* and published two plates illustrating it. Then every expert saw at once that the "young sea serpent" had been a slightly diseased common black snake.

It was a bad blow. A committee that made such a mistake did not seem very trustworthy in other respects. Consequently the sea serpent, inexplicable as it was, was quickly termed "American humbug" and disregarded by men of science, while a few practical jokers thought this a good opportunity for some juicy sea-serpent hoaxes.

The most famous of these, the "mystery of the fossil sea serpent," was perpetrated in New York in the early summer of 1845. "Dr." Albert C. Koch exhibited on Broadway a large skeleton of a fossil animal, labeled *Hydrarchus sillimanni*. Koch claimed that, though extinct, it was most certainly related to the sea serpent of our present time, and was probably an ancestor of the present group or family. The skeleton certainly looked it. It was 114 feet long, definitely of serpentine form, consisting mainly of a long row of vertebrae. It had a small head, a number of short ribs, and incomplete paddles. It was mounted in a slightly "wavy" position with reared-up head, a position familiar to Koch from many sea-serpent reports.

Many New Yorkers came and paid good silver pieces to marvel at the fossil wonder and listen to Koch's lectures. Unfortunately for "Dr." Koch, one of his visitors really studied the fossil bones. Professor Wyman happened to be an expert zoologist and anatomist; he soon published an article in the *Proceedings of the Boston Society of Natural History* (November 1845) proving that "these remains never belonged to one and the same individual, and that the anatomical characteristics of the teeth indicate that they are not those of a reptile but of a warm-blooded mammal." Professor Wyman also succeeded in discovering what fossil animal had furnished the bones; it was Zeuglodon, an extinct distant relative of the present-day whales. Koch had stated—truthfully, for once—that he had collected the bones in Alabama, where remains of Zeuglodon have actually been discovered repeatedly. Professor Wyman believed that two individuals of Zeuglodon had been pieced together; this explanation later proved to be an understatement: Koch had strung together as many Zeuglodon vertebrae as he could find.

While Koch's fossil sea serpent, though impressive, was rather short-lived, another earlier sea-serpent hoax had an exceedingly long life. Shortly after the Linnaean Society of Boston had busily collected eyewitness reports of the New England sea serpent of 1817, a Captain Joseph Woodward—he was probably as much a captain as Koch was a doctor—arrived with an exciting sea-serpent yarn. He asserted that in May 1818 his ship, sailing in New England waters, suddenly encountered a huge sea serpent. When it first appeared, it was about 60 feet from the ship and came closer with astonishing speed. They fired a small cannon ball and a number of musket bullets against the monster and heard them strike, but the animal moved on unaffected. "Captain," Woodward ordered the cannon to be loaded again, but before they could be fired his men became badly frightened and ran for shelter. A crash between ship and sea serpent seemed inevitable, but Woodward succeeded in tacking so as to avoid the animal, which afterward continued to pursue them for five hours!

Now, if there ever was a story that had the word "hoax" spread over its entire length, it is this one. But, strange to say, it met with much more success than dozens of simple and sincere reports. After being published in several Boston and New York newspapers, it was reprinted by the *Quarterly Journal of Science, Literature, and the Arts* of the Royal Institute at London (Vol. VI, 1818), then in Lorenz Oken's German journal, *Isis,* and again, thirty years later, in *The Zoologist* (London, 1848), without mention of the source. From there it was translated into German by Froriep for his journal *Notizen,* and it might have continued to haunt newspapers and journals if W. W. Cooper had not taken pains to examine the evidence and to expose it.

Soon afterward the sea-serpent story took on a radically new aspect. In zoological literature the case responsible for this is known as that of "the *Daedalus* serpent." The date is August 6, 1848. Her Majesty's Ship *Daedalus,* under Captain Peter M'Quhae, was returning from a voyage of duty in East Indian waters and had reached a point in the South Atlantic somewhere between the Cape of Good Hope and the island of St. Helena. There, in a fresh breeze and with almost all the canvas up, she must have presented a beautiful picture, but romantic adventure was furthest from the minds of those on board. As for sea serpents, they might be encountered in the arctic twilight off the Norse coast or in the harbors of credulous or exaggerating Yankees, but not by one of Her Majesty's men-of-war on routine duty. For the true Britisher the serious side of the sea-serpent controversy begins on August 6, 1848, and the evidence of it may be found on official British stationery:

SIR,—In reply to your letter of this day's date, requiring information as to the truth of a statement published in *The Times* newspaper, of a sea-serpent of extraordinary dimensions having been seen from Her Majesty's ship *Daedalus,* under my command, on her passage from the East Indies, I have the honour to acquaint you, for the information of my Lords Commissioners of the Admiralty, that at 5 o'clock p.m. on the 6th of August last, in latitude 24° 44' S., and longitude 9° 22' E., the weather dark and cloudy, wind fresh from the N.W., with a long ocean swell from the S.W., the ship on the port tack heading N.E. by N., something very unusual was seen by Mr. Sartoris, midshipman, rapidly approaching the ship from before the beam. The circumstance was immediately reported by him to the officer of the watch, Lieut. Edgar Drummond, with whom and Mr. William Barrett, the Master, I was at the time walking the quarter-deck. The ship's company were at supper.

On our attention being called to the object it was discovered to be an enormous serpent, with head and shoulders kept about four feet constantly above the surface of the sea, and as nearly as we could approximate by comparing it with the length of what our main-topsail yard should show in the water, there was at the very least 60 feet of the animal *à fleur d'eau*, no portion of which was, to our perception, used in propelling it through the water, either by vertical or horizontal undulation. It passed rapidly, but so close under our lee quarter, that had it been a man of my acquaintance I should have easily recognized his features with the naked eye; and it did not, either in approaching the ship or after it had passed our wake, deviate in the slightest degree from its course to the S.W., which it held on at the pace of from 12 to 15 miles per hour, apparently on some determined purpose.

The diameter of the serpent was about 15 or 16 inches behind the head, which was, without any doubt, that of a snake, and it was never, during the 20 minutes that it continued in sight of our glasses, once below the surface of the water; its colour a dark brown, with yellowish white about the throat. It had no fins, but something like a mane of a horse, or rather a bunch of seaweed, washed about its back. It was seen by the quartermaster, the boatswain's mate, and the man at the wheel, in addition to myself and officers above mentioned.

This letter was addressed to Admiral Sir W. H. Gage. Everyone at once became profoundly interested, and a number of drawings, made by an artist of the *London Illustrated News* under the personal supervision of Captain Peter M'Quhae, were regarded (by the majority of the readers of this journal) as the first authentic pictures of the unknown monster. Further excitement was added when a few zoologists, who in all probability had fewer hours at sea to their credit than Captain M'Quhae or Admiral Gage had days, felt obliged to criticize. Leader in the fight against the *Daedalus* serpent was the distinguished, but at that time already somewhat elderly and garrulous, Professor Richard Owen. The direct result of the controversy was nil. Captain M'Quhae would not admit that he had failed to see what he had seen, while Professor Owen would not admit that Captain M'Quhae had seen what he had seen. The indirect result, however, was the publication of a number of earlier observations.

One of these was on the *"Lady Combermere* sea serpent," so called

The *Daedalus* sea serpent (from the *Illustrated London News,* October 28, 1848)

from the vessel from which the unknown animal was observed. The case had been put in writing in about 1820 (apparently immediately after the encounter) by Lieutenant George Sandford, commander of the vessel. Lieutenant Sandford kept a private memorandum book in which the story was discovered after his death by a Dr. Scott. The sea serpent had been seen in the North Atlantic, near Barencthy's Rocks in latitude 46° N., longitude 37° W. The animal was "between 70 and 100 feet" long, and when the vessel approached, "it reared head and neck out of the water and after taking a survey it all at once vanished."

Another published report is that of the *Royal Saxon*. In this account the animal was seen in 1829 by the captain of that ship and by Dr. R. Davidson, a surgeon of the Nagpore Subsidiary Force, and by a number of other persons on deck at that time. The serpent, to quote Dr. Davidson's words, "passed within 35 yards of the ship, without altering its course in the least; but as it came right abreast of us, it slowly turned its head towards us." Dr. Davidson later concluded that this must have been the same kind of animal as that seen twenty years afterward by Captain M'Quhae of the *Daedalus,* but a somewhat larger specimen.

Another observation was made on May 15, 1833, by five officers on a fishing trip about twenty miles off Halifax.

At the distance of from 150 to 200 yards on our starboard bow, we saw the head and neck of some denizen of the deep, precisely like those of a common snake, in the act of swimming, the head so far elevated and thrown forward by the curve of the neck as to enable us to see the water under and beyond it. The creature passed, leaving a regular wake. . . . There could be no mistake, no delusion. . . .

These officers were perfectly willing to accept full responsibility, which they indicated by signing the report with name and rank: W. Sullivan, Captain, Rifle Brigade; A. Maclachlan, Lt., Rifle Brigade; G. P. Malcolm, Ensign, Rifle Brigade; B. O'Neal Lyster, Lt., Artillery; and Henry Ince, Ordnance Storekeeper at Halifax.

Very significant, in my opinion, although deplorably lacking in detail, is the story of Captain George Hope of H.M.S. *Fly,* published in 1849 in the British journal *Zoologist.* Captain Hope was the first who saw not only a part of the strange animal, but all of it. He encountered his sea serpent in the Gulf of California. The sea was perfectly calm and transparent, and he saw through the clear water a large animal moving along the bottom. It had the head and general shape of an alligator, but differed in two important features. The neck of the unknown animal was much longer than that of an alligator, and instead of having four legs the creature displayed four large flippers that moved like those of the large marine turtles. Captain Hope saw distinctly that the front flippers were much larger than the hind ones, which was to be expected of an animal that swims by means of flippers.

All these observations antedated the *Daedalus* sea serpent, although they were not published until Captain M'Quhae "broke the ice." But there was no dearth of new encounters after the *Daedalus* adventure. On December 31, 1848, for instance, H.M.S. *Plumper* fell in with such an animal west of Oporto. Again, on March 30, 1856, the captain and a few passengers of the ship *Imogen* observed one in the English Channel for about forty minutes. Captain G. H. Harrington of the ship *Castilian* reported sighting one in the Atlantic Ocean, ten miles northeast of St. Helena, on December 12, 1857. In August 1872 the Reverend Mr. John Macrae and the Reverend Mr. David Twopenny on a sailing trip from Glenelg to Loch Hourn observed a sea serpent from on board their boat in the Sound of Sleat on the west coast of Scotland. The two reverend gentlemen were not the only observers of this animal; for several days many other persons saw it from various points along the shores of Loch Hourn.

A distinguishing feature of the Loch Hourn reports is again the mention of "lumps" or "bunches" or, as one of the observers put it, "half-rounds"—more precisely, "hemi-elliptical protuberances." The Reverend Mr. Macrae wrote:

Sometimes three appeared, sometimes four, five or six, and then sank again. When they rose, the head appeared first, if it had been down, and the lumps rose after it in regular order, beginning always with that next to the head, and rising gently; but when they sank they sank all together rather abruptly, sometimes leaving the head visible. It gave the impression of a creature crooking up its back to sun itself. There was no appearance of undulation; when the lumps sank, other lumps did not rise in the intervals between them. The greatest number we counted was seven, making eight with the head. The parts were separated from each other by intervals of about their own length.

Another point emphasized in this report is that the animal, if it wants to, can "rush through the water at great speed."

Early on the evening of June 2, 1877, Captain H. L. Pearson of the royal yacht *Osborne* and several of his officers saw a very large animal swimming away from their vessel at a distance of about four hundred yards. The head, large shoulders, and two enormous flippers could be seen. An official report was made to the Admiralty. It finally landed on the desk of Professor Richard Owen, who, then seventy-three years old, did not see any reason to revise his opinion that there was no such animal as a sea serpent and who wrote a "criticism" of several pages which might be condensed into the sentence: "The observers have no expert knowledge of zoology; their observation is, therefore, without value."

At this point it is perhaps well to interrupt the reports for a while and to summarize the general shape of the creature as it may be gathered from these observations. Captain Hope presented the first and most precise description: an animal of the "general shape of an alligator," but with a neck "much longer than that of an alligator," and four large flippers instead of legs. None of the other reports, from Egede's down to the latest stories from Loch Ness, contains elements that contradict this description. Sometimes only the neck was seen, sometimes only two of the four flippers or the line of the back and the tail, but none of the other observations adds features that could not be applied to an animal of the general shape of that seen by Captain Hope.

The reports mentioning color all agree that the back was dark (dark brown, dark gray, or black), while the belly and the underside are generally described as light (white or yellowish). This coloration is also what might be expected from a marine animal. The greatest discrepancies concern size. Some reports, especially recent ones, speak of small animals with an over-all length of 15 to 25 feet. The majority of the observations agree on a total length of about 60 to 80 feet, and only a very few mention larger figures. Now the average, 60 to 80 feet, is comparable to the measurements of a whale of the larger varieties and may be believed without too many scruples. In fact, a 60-foot sea serpent, which has a long, slender neck and a very long tail, would actually be a smaller animal than a 60-foot whale, which is very massive. One interpreter put it very nicely in saying that the sea serpent compares to the whale as the giraffe to the elephant.

If we have agreed so far, we may ask ourselves what type of animal might be expected to have this appearance and these dimensions. The sea serpent is most decidedly not a fish and it also is certainly not an amphibian. Amphibians do not live in salt water, and there exists no fossil evidence that they ever did. The choice therefore lies between reptiles and mammals.

The vast majority of those authors and scientists who, to use the words of Professor E. C. Boulenger, Director of the London Zoological Society's aquarium, gave the sea serpent "the benefit of the doubt," decided at one time that the sea serpent was probably a reptile. One could evolve a quite simple and plausible theory, if reptilian nature was assumed. It was only necessary to postulate that a species of plesiosaurs had managed to survive in the oceans since Cretaceous times and after the extinction of their next of kin. The plesiosaurs

"Sea serpent," modern conception by A. C. Oudemans

had a long neck on a roundish body, which means that they must have been able to raise their heads high out of the water, something a true snake could not possibly do. Furthermore the plesiosaurs had four flippers, just as some of the reports said. Naturally we don't know their coloration but it probably was dark above and light below.

There were two arguments against this hypothesis. If a species of plesiosaurs had succeeded in living on, why haven't we found any fossils from the intervening period? The answer to that question is the usual one when it comes to fossils: We haven't found any because we haven't. Such fossils may exist; it just so happens that nobody ever came across one. The second argument was that the modern sea-serpent reports often mention a long tail and the plesiosaurs were rather short-tailed. That met a similar answer: who can say that we know all the species of plesiosaurs that ever lived? There might have been long-tailed forms which never happen to have been found.

Well, of course, nobody can say that a type did *not* survive—a recent example, the fish *Latimeria,* is discussed in Chapter 21—but the fact is that the *known* types of plesiosaurs do not fit perfectly.

How about the possibility that the sea serpent is a mammal?

This was the hypothesis Professor Oudemans advanced after having collected all the reports he could find and after having read all the "explanations" ever thought up. He postulated a marine mammal, "a huge pinniped," in his own words. While the evidence he cited in support of the mammalian nature of the animal is somewhat flimsy and sketchy, it nevertheless seems that he was right. Those observations of sea serpents in icy waters are more credible if a mammalian nature is assumed.

The year after the publication of Professor Oudemans' book another report appeared, which gloriously confirmed his contentions as to the true shape of the sea serpent.

Log of the S.S. *Umfuli* from London towards Natal, Monday, Dec. 4th, 1893.

P.M.

2 Calm & smooth sea

4 Same weather P.L. 43 [3]

5:30 Sighted and passed about 500 yards from ship a Monster Fish of the Serpent shape, about 80 ft. long with slimy skin and short fins at about 20 feet apart on the back and in cir. [circumference] about

[3] P.L. means patent-log, showing a run of 43 miles since noon at the end of the watch.

the same dimension of a full sized whale. I distinctly saw the fish's mouth open & shut with my glasses. The jaw appeared to me about 7 feet long with large teeth. In shape it was just like a Conger Eel.

C. A. W. Powell, Mate.

To the information rendered by this page from the *Umfuli*'s log it may be added that the ship was approximately at latitude 21° 40′ N. (about the latitude of Havana) and longitude 17° 30′ W., off the west coast of Africa. She was steaming southward on her way to the Cape of Good Hope with a speed of ten and one-half knots and carried eighty passengers. The *Umfuli*'s commander, Captain R. J. Cringle, felt obliged to write a report of his encounter with the Great Unknown of the Seas which contains the following paragraphs:

It was rushing through the water at great speed, and was throwing water from its breast as a vessel throws water from her bows. I saw full 15 ft. of its head and neck on three several occasions. The body was all the time visible. . . . The base, or body, from which the neck sprang, was much thicker than the neck itself, and I should not, therefore, call it a serpent. Had it been breezy enough to ruffle the water, or hazy, I should have had some doubt about the creature; but the sea being so perfectly smooth, I had not the slightest doubt in my mind as to its being a sea-monster.

I turned the ship round to get closer to it, and got much nearer than we were at first; but the sun was then setting and the light gone, so that to have run the ship further off her course would have been folly. . . . This thing, whatever it was, was in sight for over half an hour. In fact we did not lose sight of it until darkness came on.

When Captain Cringle's account became known (in 1895) many scientists still maintained the attitude introduced a few decades earlier by the rather difficult Professor Richard Owen. Sea-serpent reports were not for discussion but were something to sneer at, no matter who made them. Small wonder that Captain Cringle complained in a letter to Rupert T. Gould:

I have been so ridiculed about the thing that I have many times wished that anybody else had seen that sea-monster rather than me. I have been told that it was a string of porpoises, that it was an island of seaweed, and I do not know what besides. But if an island of seaweed can travel at the rate of fourteen knots, or if a string of porpoises can stand 15 ft. out of the water, then I give in. . . .

From then on until after the First World War things remained comparatively quiet. Not that there were no observations, but they

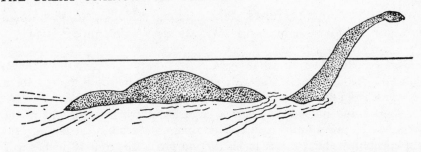

Sketch of the *Umfuli* sea serpent, by Rupert T. Gould from the description by Captain Cringle

did not create much of a stir. Since critics did not say much, Professor Oudemans' book made a deeper impression than was believed at that time.

Also, among the observations reported was one which was especially unpleasant to those who tried by means of ridicule to fend off the realization of having been in error. As long as "only" sea captains and ministers had reported encounters with sea serpents, it had been convenient to say that they were honest men, of course, and sincere in their efforts to describe something they did not know, but, after all, they were not naturalists. Professor Oudemans was a naturalist, yes, but he had not seen the sea serpent. He probably never would see one, because he would recognize the "monster" for what it really was: seaweed or schools of porpoises or whales. He, as a zoologist, would not be handicapped by "excessive imagination," "insufficient scientific knowledge," "lack of training in observation," and whatever else armchair scientists had had to say about Hans Egede, Commandant von Ferry, Captain M'Quhae, and Captain Cringle. But now came a report about which none of these things could be said. The critics all quickly agreed, without even having to ask one another's opinions, that it was best by far to say nothing. This particular chapter in the story of the sea serpent is so intensely disliked by skeptics that, if humanly possible, it is not quoted by them at all.

But there it is, printed in the *Proceedings of the Zoological Society* (London, 1906), pages 719–721, signed by E. G. B. Meade-Waldo and Michael J. Nicoll. Both gentlemen were naturalists by profession, Fellows of the Zoological Society.

They were cruising off Parahiba, Brazil, in the yacht *Valhalla*, owned by the Earl of Crawford, who for reasons of health spent his winters on southern cruises, taking along scientists to give them opportunities for research work. Mr. Meade-Waldo's report states:

On Dec. 7th, 1905, at 10:15 A.M., I was on the poop of the *Valhalla* with Mr. Nicoll, when he drew my attention to an object in the sea about 100 yards from the yacht; he said: "Is that the fin of a great fish?"

I looked and immediately saw a large fin or frill sticking out of the water, dark seaweed-brown in colour, somewhat crinkled at the edge. It was apparently about 6 feet in length and projected from 18 inches to 2 feet from the water.

I got my field-glasses on to it (a powerful pair of Goerz Trieder), and almost as soon as I had them on the frill, a great head and neck rose out of the water in front of the frill; the neck did not touch the frill in the water, but came out of the water in front of it, at a distance of certainly not less than 18 inches, probably more. The neck appeared about the thickness of a slight man's body, and from 7 to 8 feet was out of the water; head and neck were all about the same thickness.

Further details, and the explanation of their failure to follow the creature (the *Valhalla* was, after all, not bound to any schedule) were given by Mr. Meade-Waldo in a letter to Rupert T. Gould:

The color was dark seaweed brown; the frill at the back of the head and along the back crinkled at the edge. About 8 ft. of neck was out of the water, and the under side was dirty white. It made a wave as it went along, and under water behind the neck I could see a good-sized body. As we drew ahead we could see it swing its neck from side to side and it lashed the sea into foam.

The eye and the edge of the neck had a turtle-like appearance to us both. We were so astonished at the time that we could neither of us speak! We then visited (late) Lord Crawford, and he said he would stop the yacht if it was any use; but we decided as we were making about 14 knots it would not be much use.

The creature seen from H.M.S. *Daedalus* . . . might easily be the same.

Mr. Nicoll's report for the *Proceedings* was about the same as Mr. Meade-Waldo's; with only one statement of further importance:

This creature was an example, I consider, of what has been so often reported, for want of a better name, as the "Great Sea-Serpent." I feel sure, however, that it was not a reptile that we saw, but a mammal. It is, of course, impossible to be certain of this, but the general appearance of the creature, especially the soft, almost rubber-like fin, gave one this impression.

The *Valhalla* sea serpent, after the sketch by Mr. Meade-Waldo

This is one of the very few reports that mention a fin. Older reports had spoken of a "mane," but many had specifically denied that they had seen a mane. Professor Oudemans had placed faith in both reports, assuming that the maned individuals were males. Such an assumption is not farfetched; only the male narwhal sports the single long "unicorn horn." Whether a similar assumption can be made about the fin I dare not say, but fin or no fin, two expert zoologists saw a large marine animal they did not know and which they declared to be the same that others had called the sea serpent.

One other report which mentions a dorsal fin is that of Captain F. W. Dean, R.N., of the armed merchant cruiser *Hilary*. Place and date of the encounter: the North Sea, some 70 miles to the southeast of Iceland, May 22, 1917. The *Hilary* was taking part in the North Sea blockade, and the encounter between these two, the mysterious Great Unknown and the armed merchant cruiser, was a dramatic one. Captain Dean's *Hilary* was torpedoed by a German submarine only three days later; but fortunately he escaped with his life and was able to tell the story of his battle with the sea serpent, which took place within sight of Iceland's famous mountain Oraefajökull.

Here is the greater part of the story, as Captain Dean published it in *Herbert Strang's Annual*, 1920 (London):

After a stormy winter we enjoyed some wonderfully fine weather during May 1917. On the morning of, I think, the 22nd the conditions were perfect—brilliant sunshine and not a cat's paw to ruffle the sea. Beyond the horizon to the northward the peaks of Iceland could be seen, the only breaks in our all-round view of sea and sky.

It was about 9 A.M., and I was sitting at the writing-table in my cabin, which was immediately under the bridge, when a report was shouted down to me: "Object on the starboard quarter." In three seconds I was on the bridge asking, "Was it a periscope? Where is it?"

"No, not a periscope," replied the officer of the watch. "It looks more like a living thing, but it is not a whale," and he pointed at an object which at first glance suggested to my mind a tree trunk with only the knobby ends (from which branches and roots had been cut) visible. A careful look through my glasses, however, made it clear that the thing was alive, and that the "knobby ends" were in fact its head and dorsal fin.

We never missed a chance in those days to do a bit of anti-submarine practice, and it at once struck me that here was a good target; so I turned to the 1st lieutenant, Lieutenant-Commander Charles M. Wray, R.N.R., and told him to get our three 6-pounder guns' crews up, so that each one in turn should have a run. Like most of the armed merchant cruisers on that patrol, we had, in addition to our heavier guns, two 6-pounders placed one each side, just abaft the bridge, and part of our defence scheme was to have three guns' crews, one of which was always on watch between these two guns, ready to close up instantly starboard or port, according to which side a submarine might be sighted. . . .

Before taking the liberty of using the stranger as a target, however, I thought it would be a good thing to have a closer look at it, so told Lieutenant Harris, the navigator, to turn the ship round and head towards it. In due course we approached our object end on, and when we were about a cable from it, it quietly moved out of our way, and we passed it about thirty yards off on our starboard side, getting a very good view of it while doing so.

The head was about the shape of, but somewhat larger than that of, a cow, though with no observable protrusions such as horns or ears, and was black, except for the front of the face, which could be clearly seen to have a strip of whitish flesh, very like a cow has, between its nostrils. As we passed, the head raised itself two or three times, apparently to get a good look at the ship. From the back of the head to the dorsal fin no part of the creature showed above water, but the top edge of the neck was just level with the surface, and its snake-like movements could be clearly seen. (It curved to almost a semi-circle as the creature moved its head round as if to follow us with its eyes.)

The dorsal fin appeared like a black triangle, and when the creature was end on, this fin was seen to be very thin and apparently flabby, as the upper part turned over sometimes like the top of a terrier's ear when cocked. The fin was estimated to be about four feet high when in the position highest out of the water.

I was anxious to get as good an estimate as possible of the length of the neck, i.e., the distance from the head to the fin, so asked the 1st lieutenant, the navigator and the officer of the watch each to note, as I did, the length, and we compared with following results:

1st Lieutenant.—"The length of one of our boats."

Navigator.—"Not less than fifteen feet."

Officer of Watch.—"Length of one of our boats."

Myself.—"Twenty feet."

From which it may fairly be assumed that the true length of the neck was probably not less than twenty feet; and, assuming that the dorsal fin would be just behind the junction of neck and body, the total length of the creature would be about 60 feet.

The creature did not seem to be in the least alarmed by the presence of the ship, but continued to bask on the surface, now sinking down till only the tip of its nose and fin were visible, and anon rising again till the whole head and the fin to a height of four feet were above water.

The ship was steaming at twelve knots all the time, so the creature was soon 1000 yards astern, and we then turned around, and I gave the order, when the range was approximately 1200 yards, for the first gun's crew to fire five rounds rapid.

The gunlayer straddled his object (with the third and fourth rounds), but his best shot was some twenty yards off being a hit, and the creature ignored the performance entirely.

The second gun's crew were now closed up, the helm was put over, and the range opened again to about 1200 yards, and the five rounds rapid repeated. This time two shots seemed to fall very close to the object, but still quite failed to disturb its equanimity.

The third gun's crew was now closed up, and on my order, "Five rounds rapid," the first shot fell very close to the creature, the second was a clean hit, and produced at once a furious commotion, which reminded me more than anything else of a bather lying on his back in smooth water and kicking out with all his force to splash the water, only of course the commotion on this occasion was on a vastly greater scale. It continued for perhaps three seconds, and then stopped, and we saw no more of the creature, though we passed close to the spot where it was last seen, so I gave orders for the ship to be put back on her patrol course, and left the bridge, telling the navigator to make a brief notation of the whole circumstance in the log.

Just to confirm the story, it became known later not only that a vessel of the British patrol fell in with a sea serpent but that some of the German blockade-breakers did also. One German submarine reported that while cruising submerged it caught a fleeting glimpse of such an animal. Another German submarine also had a brief view of one, but a *better* view. This was the *U-28,* the commander of which,

Captain Freiherr von Forstner, told the case explicitly when the Loch Ness reports made good copy for the newspapers.

On July 30, 1915, our *U-28* torpedoed in the North Atlantic the British steamer *Iberian* (5223 tons) loaded with valuable goods. The ship, which was about 180 meters long, sank rapidly, stern first, the depth at this point being a few thousand meters. When the steamer had disappeared for about 25 seconds it exploded at a depth which we could not know, but one thousand meters will be a safe guess. Shortly afterwards pieces of wreckage, among them a huge marine animal which made violent movements, were thrown out of the water, flying approximately 20 or 30 meters high.

At this moment we were six men on the bridge, myself, the two officers of the watch, the chief engineer, the navigator and the helmsman. We at once centered our attention upon this marvel of the seas. Unfortunately we had not time to take a photograph because the animal disappeared in the water after 10 or 15 seconds. It was about 20 meters [66 feet] long, looked like a giant crocodile, and had four powerful paddle-like limbs and a long pointed head.

The explanation of this event seems easy to me. The explosion of, or in, the sinking steamer caught the "undersea-crocodile," as we called it, and forced it out of the water.

When his account was attacked Captain von Forstner stood firm and declared that "he would not give up a single meter of the length of his animal."

The sea serpent did not disappear after the First World War; there are at least half a dozen different reports from the period between 1919 and 1933.

Such reports were read by those who were interested and dismissed by those who were not. But in 1933 a story erupted which made headlines first all over the British Isles and then over the rest of the world, with the possible exception of Soviet Russia. I lived in Berlin then and I still remember the headline in an evening paper: "Ancient Saurian Alive in Scottish Mountain Lake?"

The "mountain lake" was Loch Ness and in the English-speaking world the term "Loch Ness monster" quickly became a household word. The facts of the case were simple: so and so many witnesses were ready to swear (and did swear) any oath that they had seen a strange thing swimming in the Loch. It was not an object that floated passively, like a treetrunk; it swam actively, sometimes leaving a wake, sometimes diving and reappearing.

It was in a way unfortunate that this happened in Scotland.

Remarks about cold fog and "wee draps" to dispell the chill came thick and fast; the opportunity to make portmanteau jokes embracing thrifty Scotsmen, sea serpents, and strong drink was just overwhelming. And when finally one witness, Mr. Arthur Grant of Drumnadrochit, declared that he had seen the "monster" on the road at night in the light of his motorcycle lamps, everyone simply roared with laughter.

Mr. Grant, however, defended his story. He drew a sketch of the animal he had seen for a local newspaper. When Professor Oudemans wrote him, asking for confirmation of the newspaper accounts, Mr. Grant made another sketch, which he mailed to the professor. It looked exactly like the first, but was somewhat better drawn, which is not surprising since the first sketch was made at two o'clock in the morning in a garage.

Actually such a statement should be no stranger than, say, a claim that a sea elephant had been seen at some distance from the beach. Large marine mammals can and do move on land, although not very elegantly; if the sea serpent, especially what seems to have been a young specimen, can do the same, it is only additional proof of its mammalian nature. Parliament was urged "to do something" at the time, but nothing happened. Professor Oudemans, in a little pamphlet written in English, urged the British authorities not to be tenderhearted and to kill the animal for the sake of science. He pointed out that observers had often told how quickly the sea serpent can sink. This means, of course, that its body is heavier than water, so that a specimen that died naturally would be lost, which is probably the reason no dead sea serpent has ever been found. But nothing was done, and finally the "monster" disappeared; nobody can tell whether it died or found its way to the open sea.

Arthur Grant's sketch of the Loch Ness "monster"

The case of the Loch Ness "monster" has never been cleared up. Rupert T. Gould made a trip to the Loch to interview all the eye-witnesses he could find and wrote a book about these interviews. It makes tedious reading, somewhat like asking fifty people to describe an elephant and then wading through all fifty descriptions. The photographs which were taken were unfortunately too poor to serve as conclusive evidence. One especially, which *may* show the head and neck, has also been explained as showing the dorsal fin of a killer whale. Since there is no detail in the picture either is possible.

It was said later that the Loch Ness monster was the wreck of a German Zeppelin which was shot down during the First World War and which fell into the Loch. While the drifting hulk of a Zeppelin, with just enough buoyancy left to show at the surface at intervals, would make a fine monster, it does not correspond to the rather specific statements of some of the eyewitnesses.[4]

Before the Loch Ness "unknown" appeared in the newspapers, and caused incidentally the publication of a few older reports such as that by Captain von Forstner, somebody had compiled statistics supposed to show that the number of sea-serpent sightings had declined steadily from a high point around the middle of the nineteenth century. I can't recall just what these statistics were supposed to prove but they obviously were rather incomplete. However, I remember a reply by a sea captain who simply pointed out that the decline in sightings, if drawn as a graph, was the precise mirror image of the increasing use at sea of propellers and noisy machinery. The captain's point was that, whatever the truth behind the sea-serpent story, the decline in sightings could be attributed to noisy ships which frighten marine life away from their vicinity.

Whether this is so is, incidentally, a point of very lively debate among commercial whalers. Some of them stop their engines when whales are near; others insist that it makes no difference and that the whales pay no attention to engine noises.

In any case the decline in sightings is not as great as it may seem. There are persistent reports about a sea monster near San Clemente Island off the shore of California. There are reports from Alaska. I

---

[4] There are two books specifically devoted to the Loch Ness case: *The Loch Ness Monster and Others* by Rupert T. Gould (London: Geoffrey Bles, 1934), and *More Than A Legend* by Constance Whyte (London: Hamish Hamilton, 1957). The latter points out that the Loch Ness story is much older than is generally believed.

have not listed them because they are repetitious and tiring, but such reports exist. Some of them might also be simple mistakes.

But the latter statement can hardly be held to apply to the case of the Grace Line steamer S.S. *Santa Clara* which may serve to close this chapter because it is both recent and definite.

The *Santa Clara* literally ran into a "sea monster" at 11:55 A.M. on December 30, 1947, just when its officers were ready to take the noon sight. The sea was calm and blue, with bright sunshine, the place was 118 miles due east of Cape Lookout. The ship had just crossed the Gulf Stream en route from New York to Cartagena. The master of the vessel, J. Fordan, sent a report which was distributed by the Associated Press. It reads in part:

Suddenly John Axelson (the third mate) saw a snakelike head rear out of the sea about 30 feet off the starboard bow of the vessel. His exclamation of amazement directed the attention of the two other mates to the sea monster and the three watched it unbelievingly as, in a moment's time, it came abeam of the bridge where they stood, and was then left astern.

The creature's head appeared to be about 2½ feet across, 2 feet thick and 5 feet long. The cylindrically shaped body was about 3 feet thick and the neck about 1½ feet in diameter.

As the monster came abeam of the bridge it was observed that the water around the monster, over an area of 30 or 40 feet square, was stained red. The visible part of the body was about 35 feet long.

It was assumed that the color of the water was due to the creature's blood and that the stem of the ship had cut the monster in two, but as there was no observer on the other side of the vessel there was no way of estimating what length of the body may have been left on the other side.

From the time the monster was first sighted until it disappeared in the distance astern, it was thrashing about as though in agony. The monster's skin was dark brown, slick and smooth. There were no fins, hair, or protuberances on the head, neck, or visible parts of the body.

If none of the older reports be considered trustworthy any more, the experience of the *Santa Clara* proves that there is a large unknown animal in the seas. And although we have reason to believe that this great unknown of the seas is a warm-blooded mammal and not a snake, as Norse fishermen once thought, they were right in saying that it brings bad luck. It carries with it the ill luck of lifelong ridicule for any skipper who happened to encounter it and who was honest enough to describe truthfully what he saw.

CHAPTER 13

The Story of the Fish *Anguilla*

Lᴇᴛ ᴜs admit in the very first sentence that the fish *Anguilla chrysypa*
—the common eel—cannot match the sea serpent for glamour. But
when it comes to mystery it can—or rather could—offer considerable
competition.

The comparison, speaking in terms of the year 1900, was simply
this: the sea serpent was suspected to exist but nothing was known
about it. As for the eel, it was certainly known to exist, but nothing
else was known about it. Therefore in the case of the sea serpent you
could, if you wanted to, disbelieve the whole story and be done with
it. But the embarrassing fact that nothing was known about the eel
could not be talked away.

The main thing that was not known about the eel was its method,
time, and place of reproduction, and this was surprising indeed.

Since the earliest times fishermen, when preparing caught fishes
for consumption, have been used to coming across roe or semen in
their fish when the season was right. But with eels there seemed to
be no season. Nobody could truthfully claim to have seen eel roe, and
Aristotle, some two millennia ago, summed up popular experience
when he stated that "the eel has no sex, no eggs, no semen, and origi-
nates from the entrails of the sea."

Pliny the Elder said surprisingly little about eels: his three most
positive statements are that the eel lives eight years, that it can survive
on land for as long as six days, and that it is the only fish which does
not float up to the surface when it dies. The first statement seems to
be about correct, although in isolated cases eels have lived much
longer. The second statement has to refer to very wet grass or moss
to be true; of course, nobody ever measured the time precisely. The
third statement is true too, if you cross out the word "only."

238

It was probably the fact that eels can survive for a very considerable time outside of water, provided only that the surroundings are wet, which gave rise to the story that the eel will leave rivers at night. This belief acquired a definite shape in the book on animals which Albert von Bollstädt (Albertus Magnus) wrote during the second half of the thirteenth century: "The eel is also said to leave the water during the nights and slip onto the fields, where he'll find peas, lentils, or beans growing." The peasants, especially in southwestern Germany, believe this even today and strangely enough they tell it in almost the words used by Albertus. It probably is a piece of folklore which has been passed on through the generations from the late Middle Ages. But when a skeptic dares to doubt its truth he is solemnly assured that so-and-so knew a man who had told him that he had seen it with his own eyes when he was a boy.

The stories were so persistent that scientists repeatedly started inquiries to track down a definite and well-documented case. But they never succeeded. So-and-so did assert that he had found eels in his field on one occasion, but when the time was nailed down it turned out to have been shortly after a small and harmless local flood. Another one had a similar story to report, but investigation showed that there was a poorly fitted sewer running along the edge of the field. One Dr. Emil Walter, a German fisheries expert, who devoted a whole book to the eel (*Der Flussaal,* Neudamm, 1910) came to the conclusion that a number of the reports were simply the result of confusing a common and harmless snake with an eel. This may seem incredible at first glance, but this snake, which grows to a length of 3 to 4 feet, resembles a river eel in size. Moreover—and this fact is well known—this particular snake likes water and swims well and often. Doctor Walter was probably correct in the belief that somebody saw such a snake disappear into the water and assumed that it must have been an eel, especially when this happened at night. If it happened in daylight, the snake was recognized and the incident did not cause a story.

It may be useful to say that the performance would not be completely impossible just because the eel is a fish. Of course, the eel probably would not try to steal green peas or young lentils, since it doesn't eat anything vegetable, but it might go after insects or earthworms. Several varieties of fish do go on land for short periods without hesitation. The story just seems to be erroneous. Italian naturalists, among them the famous Lazzaro Spallanzani, have pointed out that occasionally large numbers of eels have died in Italian waters when they could have reached fresh river water by an overland trip of a few hundred yards. But eels do show up in strange places (that they enter city water supplies and clog the household plumbing is not too strange, considering their shape) and occasionally baffle even naturalists. Dr. Walter reported a case which he had learned from a professional naturalist, even a fisheries expert. This was a Professor Frenzel who ran an experiment station near Berlin. The station was situated close to a fairly large lake, the Müggelsee, but had its own ponds, mostly artificial, several hundred yards from the lakeshore. Near one of those ponds a small dead tree was uprooted. Under its roots was a small eel, 5 inches long and a little less than ¼-inch thick, covered with sand but very much alive otherwise. The scientist first took some measurements to be sure of their facts. The eel was slightly more than a foot below ground level. The place was 12 feet from the rim of the pond and 5 feet above water level. The ground below the 1-foot hole where the tree roots had been was dry and hard.

It was several days before a gardener remembered that they had taken water from that pond in buckets to water the young trees during dry weather. They had stopped when a rainy period set in. The last watering had taken place a full six weeks before the eel was found. This, of course, affords a clue as to how eels might be found in fields. They do not go on land, but they can manage to stay alive on land for a long time if conditions are at all favorable.

But while the idea of the eel's "excursions" did not cause too much discussion because it was simply accepted, the problem of propagation was a different matter. That, everybody agreed, was the real mystery. And because it was such a deep mystery and because the eel is such a common fish, it is not at all surprising that everybody who wrote a book produced his own pet theory. Konrad Gesner, writing in 1558, still tried to be impartial, saying that "those who have written about their origin and procreation" hold three views. One is that eels form in mud and moisture, "as has been written about some other aquatic animals too." Doctor Gesner apparently did not think too highly of the idea. The next opinion he reported was that eels rub their bellies against the ground and that the slime from their bodies causes the mud or soil to form more eels, "wherefore the eels are said not to have a distinction in sex, neither male nor female." The third opinion was that the eels propagate with eggs like other fish, but he added that "our fishermen" say the eels bear living young.

Next after Gesner, another Swiss, Mangolt (in *Fischbuch,* Zürich, 1565), sided with the fishermen without reservations:

> This fish has a special propagation since it has neither milt nor roe but gives birth to live young. At first they are small like a piece of string. They don't give birth at any specific season, but in all seasons. They are best for food in May . . . hate muddy water and are afraid of thunder.

The fishermen thought they spoke the truth. Unfortunately the "tiny eels looking like twine" which were found inside large eels were neither eels, nor fish, nor even vertebrates. They were intestinal parasites, worms (mostly nematodes), which infest all kinds of fish with complete impartiality. But if such worms were found inside a pike or a carp nobody thought anything about it; if they were found inside an eel it was another story. Occasionally somebody also found "proof" that the eel laid eggs like other fish, swearing that he had found fish eggs inside a large eel. That was true, too, even more literally true than the teller of the tale believed. He *had* found fish eggs inside a large eel, eggs of other fish. The eel has the bad luck of combining a large appetite with a small mouth; fish eggs are one of the things it can swallow best.

While the professional fishermen did assume a natural cycle of large eels, small eels growing up, large eels, small eels growing up, others formed weird and wonderful superstitions, which, handed on, took deep root in the course of time. German folklore, put on record in the sixteenth century but probably centuries older, provided a simple recipe for increasing the supply of eels in a given locality: "Take hairs from the tail of a horse, cut them into finger-long pieces and throw them into a clear river; after some time they will swell up, come to life and in due course be transformed into eels."

That folklore and men of learning were in close agreement is shown by a similar recipe, advocated in about 1600 by no less a person than the Flemish physician and chemist Jan Baptista van Helmont: "Cut two pieces of grass sod wet with Maydew and place the grassy sides together, then put it into the rays of the spring sun, and after a few hours you'll find that a large number of small eels have been generated."

If propagation were that simple it posed a major puzzle: why, for example, did the Rhine and all its tributaries swarm with eels while the Danube and its tributaries were void of them? Konrad Gesner had decided that the water of the Danube must be "inimical" to eels and stated that eels thrown into the Danube would die soon. It was an explanation which was probably accepted by his contemporaries; and it is a safe bet that they would have disbelieved the real explanation, had anybody been able to give it.

Zoologists did the logical thing; they dissected eels in the hope of finding, if not milt or roe, at least the organs which might produce them at the proper time. An Italian named Mondini in 1777 found what he believed to be the female organ. It was, as a matter of fact; but Spallanzani did not believe it. Since Spallanzani was the great crusader against the belief that anything living could come into existence without parents, his word was accepted. If the doubts of Mondini's discovery had been expressed by any of the professors who still believed in "spontaneous generation," the vote would probably have gone in favor of Mondini almost automatically. But if Spallanzani doubted it—well, Mondini must have been mistaken. Then, when a German, Otto Friedrich Müller, made the same discovery independently three years after Mondini, he was told that the mistake had already been refuted in Italy. Finally, in 1824, Professor Rathke of the Albertus Universität in Königsberg again discovered the eel's female sex organ, and this time the discovery was accepted.

The male organ was found half a century later, in 1874, by Syrski of Trieste. And in the meantime the seacoast branch of the fishing trade had reported additional and apparently quite simple evidence. Every year in the fall, more or less fully grown eels were seen coming downriver and disappearing into the sea. And in the spring swarms of small 3-inch eels came out of the sea and gradually worked their way upriver. Because of their transparent appearance these young eels were called "glass eels" along the European continental coast. British fishermen referred to them as elvers.

After careful comparing of notes, scientists about a hundred years ago began to consider the question nicely settled. Some well-known fish, like salmon, shad, and others, went upriver for spawning but were not really river fish otherwise. The eel reversed the process; it was a fresh-water fish that went to the sea for spawning. That was true for *Anguilla anguilla,* the European eel, and it was also true for *Anguilla chrysypa,* the American eel. And the Danube river system did not harbor eels because the Danube empties into the Black

Sea where eels probably could not breed. It was already known that the water of the Black Sea is "clean" only in its surface layers; the bottom layers are poisoned by hydrogen sulphide (H_2S). Why this is so has still not been explained to everybody's complete satisfaction, but there is no doubt about the fact, and it is also definitely established that no life above the level of bacteria exists in the Black Sea below the 80-fathom line. That solved the "Danube problem": it was not the water of the river that was "inimical," but the water of the sea beyond the mouth of that river. That water was decidedly "inimical"—it was poisonous.

Beginning in about 1830, that was the way the case was presented. The books of 1850 were still saying the same [1] and so were those of 1880, 1900, and 1905. But meanwhile a quiet revolution had taken place which went unnoticed for several decades.

It had begun in 1856.

During that year a naturalist, our old acquaintance Dr. Kaup, who had named Chirotherium, had caught a very curious small salt-water fish. It was interesting mainly because of its appearance. If some of these fish were in a salt-water aquarium, at first glance the aquarium would appear to be empty. Looking more closely, you would see a few pairs of tiny dark eyes swimming around by themselves. Intent watching would disclose watery shades trailing the eyes. Out of water the fish looked like a laurel leaf, but larger, 3 inches long—a laurel leaf made of flexible glass, thin and fragile and transparent. You could place the fish on the page of a newspaper or a book and read the type through its body without trouble.

Doctor Kaup followed the usual procedure of searching the liter-

---

[1] However, I recently found a book entitled *The Origin of the Silver Eel*, by one David Cairncross, published in London in 1862, which left me breathless with surprise. It was dedicated to "the President, the Vice-President and the Members of the Blairgowrie Angling Club," and the author said about himself that he "had been reared near the mouth of the Tay; [where] education was small in quantity and inferior in quality; little of it came my way." His thesis was that the parents of eels are—*beetles*. He had seen small black beetles go into water and small eels come forth from them; the beetles then died. In one of his cases, "two beetles appeared in the well and gave birth to two eels each." Although he never succeeded in raising young eels from the things that had come out of the beetles, he attributed his failure to the need for flowing water to effect the transformation. Of course, the "eels" were intestinal parasites. I read through half of the small book in anticipation of a joking disclaimer of some kind, but its author was deadly serious.

ature for an earlier description of that fish, and finding none, described it himself. Following scientific custom he also selected a name. It was *Leptocephalus brevirostris*.

Nothing more occurred for some time. But two Italian ichthyologists, Grassi and Calandruccio, read Dr. Kaup's description and decided to investigate Leptocephalus a little further when they got around to it. In retrospect, they said that they would not have waited so long if they had known what they were to discover. But they did not know and there always was other more pressing work; the investigation of Leptocephalus was postponed from year to year. They had learned, meanwhile, that the fish at least was not rare; they could get examples from Messina if they needed them.

The long-postponed investigation began in 1895. At first it was still routine. The fish were caught near Messina, and an aquarium which should please an inhabitant of the waters near Messina was prepared. Several Leptocephali were put into it and Grassi and Calandruccio began their work by trying to find out what Leptocephalus would eat. Many an investigation of living animals has come to an end because of feeding problems. But there was no trouble on that score; the little fish ate about what Grassi and Calandruccio expected them to eat. They fed and swam around and looked—what was visible of them—as if they were in good health.

But they shrank!

The largest of the Leptocephali had been 75 millimeters (3 inches) long when caught. It lost a full 10 millimeters of length while under observation. It also shrank in the other direction, getting narrower and losing that typical leaf shape. And then, with fair suddenness, Leptocephalus became an elver, a "glass eel."

When they had recovered from their surprise Grassi and Calandruccio announced that Dr. Kaup's genus Leptocephalus was invalid. Leptocephalus was merely a kind of larval stage of the elver, which, as everybody knew, was the youthful stage of the eel. The river and lake eel then became the adolescent stage which, upon maturing, returned to the sea, unless prevented from doing so by artificial means or by accident. The mature eel, Grassi and Calandruccio concluded, lays its eggs at the bottom of the sea and presumably dies, since nobody had ever seen large eels returning from the sea and going upriver. The eggs hatch into the larval stage, Dr. Kaup's mistaken Leptocephalus, which stays near the bottom until it is either changed or about to change into the elver stage. The elvers then swim for water of less and less salinity, finally entering the rivers.

Grassi and Calandruccio also had an explanation for the rarity of the Leptocephalus stage. It was rare, they said, because it stays near the sea bottom. They had just been lucky enough to get their eel larvae from the Strait of Messina where currents often swept deepwater forms to the surface. Thus modestly ascribing their own success to their advantageous geographical position, the two Italian scientists concluded their report, which constituted one of the great advances in a zoological field. They even made an additional contribution which was not to become really important until later.

When you make a Leptocephalus reasonably visible by placing it on black paper, you find that its body is built up of a number of segments. The technical term for these segments, which might be compared to the links of a chain, is myomeres. Grassi and Calandruccio suspected that the number of myomeres might correspond to the number of vertebrae in the finished eel. They proved that this was correct: if you have the patience to count the myomeres of a Leptocephalus you can tell the number of vertebrae that will form.

All this was fine, but it was not yet the end of the story. The scene shifted once more, to another year, another sea, and another expert. The year was 1904, the sea the Atlantic Ocean between Iceland and the Faeroes, the expert Danish biologist Dr. Johannes Schmidt, attached to the Royal Ministry of Fisheries and at that time aboard the small Danish steamer *Thor*.

From aboard the *Thor*, Dr. Johannes Schmidt caught, *by means of a surface net*, one of the transparent laurel leaves the two Italian scientists had made so famous. The catch was *Leptocephalus brevirostris* beyond doubt. It was as long as the longest specimens from Messina—75 millimeters. Dr. Schmidt was mildly elated: a case of Leptocephalus having come to the surface for some unknown but probably interesting reason.

Only a few months later a Mr. Farran caught another Leptocephalus from the research steamer *Helga*, based in Ireland. Again a surface net had been used, and again the specimen was some 75 millimeters long. The place was the Atlantic off the Irish coast. It became clear that there was still a lot to be learned. So far all the work had been done in the Mediterranean; now there was a chance to carry the same work through for the area to the west of Europe.

A nautical chart of western Europe shows a line out in the sea where the depth is 3000 feet; sailors refer to it as the 500-fathom line. West of that line there is the deep Atlantic, east of it the shallow sea which is a flooded section of the continental land mass itself. Schmidt found that the 500-fathom line marked, approximately of course, the area of 75-millimeter Leptocephali, and that they stayed that distance from land at the time, in late summer, when they began to undergo the changes described by Grassi and Calandruccio. By the following spring they had become elvers and had reached the mouths of the European rivers.

Schmidt drew up a tentative chart of the eel's spawning grounds. They seemed to have three characteristics: a depth of 500 fathoms or more; a rather high salinity, 35 parts in 1000 parts of water, or higher; and a temperature of 48 degrees Fahrenheit or higher. The last was presumably the difficulty, because in depths greater than 500 fathoms the temperature of the water, while tending to be uniform and unchanging through the seasons, is usually less than 48 degrees Fahrenheit. But a chart could still be drawn up, showing probable spawning places running straight north to south off the Irish coast, then dipping eastward into the Bay of Biscay, following the Spanish and Portuguese coasts at a respectful distance, and going through the Strait of Gibraltar into the Mediterranean for a hundred miles or so.

All this was still based on the assumption which Grassi and Calandruccio had made: that the eggs hatched at the bottom of the sea and that the Leptocephalus stage also grew up near the bottom until it had reached the famous 75-millimeter length, when it came to the surface, ready to change. If you wanted Leptocephalus of a smaller size and of an earlier stage you had to fish in deep water. There existed special nets for this kind of research work, nets which stay closed until a certain depth is reached, open at that depth, and then close up again as soon as the people aboard the research vessel begin hauling them in.

Unfortunately the *Thor* was a small ship, which could not very well cruise for long beyond the 500-fathom line. Doctor Schmidt returned home—and then he got a report from the S.S. *Michael Sars,* a Norwegian survey ship, that a much smaller Leptocephalus had been caught far out in the Atlantic. Not having a ship comparable to the S.S. *Michael Sars,* Dr. Schmidt did the next best thing. He soon got in touch with all the captains of Danish vessels that sailed the Atlantic, asking them to assist in the search. He gave classes to the old salts, telling them what to look for. He promised to furnish special nets. And he begged them, for the sake of science and the Danish fisheries, to make stops in midocean and see what they could catch.

Twenty-three captains promised to cooperate. Among them they made 550 stops en route from and to America and fished for eel larvae. Among them they caught 120, a very small figure indeed, but a significant result if you entered the successful stops on a chart. They showed that Leptocephali seemed to have definite travel routes.

By 1912 Dr. Schmidt knew that his first guess about the spawning grounds near the 500-fathom line had been wrong. Most of the larvae that the Danish sea captains had brought back from their commercial trips had been caught at or near the surface. The original idea of "the deeper the smaller" did not hold true; instead it was clearly a case of "the farther out the smaller." The travel route which showed up faintly on the chart on which the catches had been marked seemed to run with the Gulf Stream; the eel larvae were helped along on their trip to Europe by that warm current. And the place from which they came was in all probability the Sargasso Sea.

The Sargasso Sea, far from being a graveyard of lost ships held immobile in a floating tangle of tough decaying weeds, is actually just an area of the Atlantic Ocean where a specific kind of seaweed grows in the warm waters of southern latitudes. Being of the shape of an egg, the Sargasso Sea, measuring about 1000 miles from north to south and 2000 miles from west to east, slowly turns, receiving a steady push by ocean currents, especially the Gulf Stream. The center of that turning area is a few hundred miles southeast of the Bermudas. The islands themselves are at the fringe of the Sargasso Sea. How close to the fringe depends on the year, for the amount of seaweed varies. In poor years only a few floating bunches can be seen here and there. An old Navy man told me once that as a young man he had sailed through the Sargasso Sea without knowing it. In "good" years it looks from a distance as if the weed formed a solid carpet, but when you approach closely you find that there are yards of water separating the bunches, even in the densest areas. Sampling of the weed enabled oceanographers to make the calculation that the total amounts to about 10 million tons.

Ten million tons of seaweed sounds like a very large amount and in a sense it certainly is a large amount; it is more than doubtful that

any other single plant on earth occurs in such quantities. But if the
10 million tons of weed were distributed evenly over the whole area
of the Sargasso Sea, each acre would contain just 24 ounces.

At the time that Dr. Schmidt learned that his eel investigations led
in the direction of the Sargasso Sea, a good deal was already known
about it. As for the weed itself, *Sargassum bacciferum* (the second
part of the name refers to the "bladders" which keep it afloat), Dr.
Schmidt's compatriot Winge had just proved that it occurred in the
Sargasso Sea only. It had been thought that it grew somewhere on
submarine banks, was torn loose by storm, and then drifted around
for some time in the Sargasso Sea area. Winge (and before him
others) had looked around for such submarine banks, without finding any. The Atlantic Ocean is especially deep just under the Sargasso
Sea, so the weed could not possibly come from the bottom. Its whole
organization is such that it would have to grow in shallow water.
Winge (Danish Oceanographic Expedition of 1908–1909) found
that the strands of weed which drifted around decayed at one end
and grew at the other. He felt justified to conclude that the sargassum
weed had adapted itself to a pelagic life on the high seas, even
though originally it may have grown on the bottom in shallow water
like other seaweeds of its kind.

There was also known to be a numerous and interesting animal
life associated with the sargassum weed. There were two very typical
crabs; one was called "little wanderer," or *Planes minutus,* while the
other has an even more impressive name: *Neptunus pelagicus,* "the
drifting crab of the sea god." Then there is the sea slug *Scyllaea
pelagica,* decorated with folds and flaps of skin which make it look
as if it were a piece of the brownish weed itself. There are little octopi
in large numbers; there are tiny crabs like the *Daphnia* which is used
to feed tropical fish in home aquaria. There is the strange *Halobates,*
a water strider, the only real marine insect. It scurries across the
water by means of six hairy legs and it lays its eggs not on seaweed
which may sink, but on floating bird feathers. As for fishes, there are
sea horses and little zebra-striped yellow jack (*Caranx*) which hide
in tangles of weed. There is the sargassum fish, *Pterophryne,* which
has camouflaging fins and bumps and when taken out of the Sargasso
Sea looks in general as no fish should look, but at home, in the weed,
doesn't look at all, being almost invisible.

Just to inject a little mystery, Pterophryne is always female. Scientists are still puzzling about the whereabouts of the males or won-

dering whether Pterophryne has learned how to do without. As Dr. Schmidt probably knew, fish eggs are often found clinging to the weed, but he doubtless took for granted, as everyone else had since these eggs were found for the first time, that they were eggs of Pterophryne. Much later, in 1925, William Beebe found that they were not; he hatched a string of them under careful observation and from the eggs emerged little flying fish (*Exonautes*). The eggs of Pterophryne do not even resemble those of the flying fish; the sargassum fish produces a long string of gelatinous matter which contains about 2000 eggs. The gelatinous string absorbs water rapidly and thirstily and swells to over ten times its original volume. It then is a lump of quivering jelly which can float without the aid of the air bladders of the sargassum weed.

The expedition which was to track the eel down to its real spawning grounds sailed in 1913 on the small schooner *Margarete*. Johannes Schmidt and his assistants, at first A. Strubberg, later Peter Jaspersen and Åge Vedel Tåning, found that theory began to agree well with practice. The farther they progressed along the Gulf Stream —if it were a river one would say that they sailed "upstream"—the smaller the Leptocephali became. The spawning ground was the area of the Sargasso Sea; the expedition settled that problem definitely. Unfortunately, after only about half a year of service, the *Margarete* ran aground in the West Indies. And then the First World War came.

In 1920 Dr. Schmidt went back to work, on the four-masted engine-powered schooner *Dana*. In the meantime several American ichthyologists had proved what had been suspected all along: that the American eel not only went through a Leptocephalus stage, but that it too went for spawning to the Sargasso Sea.

The expedition could work on both, but it had the problem of distinguishing "American" Leptocephali from the European type. At this point Grassi's and Calandruccio's observations about the number of myomeres proved useful. It is impossible to tell a fully grown European eel from an American one just by looking at it, because eels show a good deal of individual variation, presumably caused by environment and food. And to try to tell an American Leptocephalus from a European one by appearance is even more hopeless. But they could be distinguished by counting vertebrae. Doctor Schmidt got 266 eels from Danish waters and found that they had from 111 to 119 vertebrae. In that batch there was just one with 119 and five with 118. Likewise at the lower end of the range there were only a few: two had 111 vertebrae, nine had 112. The majority had between 113 and 117, and more than half of the total had either 114 or 115. After that he obtained 266 eels from Massachusetts and counted their vertebrae. It turned out that the vertebrae of the American eels ranged from 104 to 111. Again the majority was, as one should expect, in the middle of that range. One of the Americans had 111 vertebrae, seven had 110. There were two with as few as 104, a dozen with 105. The majority had either 106, 107, or 108. The critical figure was obviously 111. If an eel had less, it was an American eel; if it had more, it was European. The occasional specimens with 111 vertebrae were nuisances, but fortunately there were only a very few of them.

The counting of myomeres sounds like tedious work, even if you know that counting only to figures above 100 is involved. But remember that a Leptocephalus is transparent when in water and still almost transparent when in air, and the specimens caught en route to the Sargasso Sea grew progressively smaller; for a while they were 2 inches long, later only 1 inch. The counting had to be done under a strong magnifying glass, and later even under low-power microscopes. And the myomeres of 7000 specimens had to be counted. That this was mostly done on board the *Dana* did not really facilitate matters.

Of those 7000 specimens precisely five had the critical number of 111 segments; nobody can tell whether they would have ended up in the Rhine or in the Hudson, if they had been left alone. All others were clearly either *Anguilla anguilla* (European) or *Anguilla chrysypa* (American).

When Dr. Schmidt had all his facts neatly entered on large charts one could see what happened. The eels that leave their rivers in Europe (Schmidt, of course, was mostly interested in the European variety, for good sound commercial reasons) in the fall seem to travel with steady high speed, arriving in the Sargasso Sea around Christmas and the New Year. Where they lay their eggs is still not quite certain; it is *not* among the drifting weed at the surface, which is weighed down with fish eggs as it is. But it does not seem to be at the bottom of the sea either, because the ocean is so deep under the Sargasso Sea. At any event the smallest larvae, only 7 millimeters or about 1/4 inch long, were caught at the depth of about 1000 feet. During the first summer they grow to a full inch or 25 millimeters;

during the second summer they double that length, and during the third they reach 75 millimeters. Then, after the change, they enter fresh water and go upriver. During the three years before changing, they travel at the rate of about 1000 miles per year, evidently "riding" in the Gulf Stream most of the way.

The American eels lay their eggs under the Sargasso Sea too, but not quite in the same place. The spawning area of the American eels is closer to the American shore and seems to be a little more to the south, in about the latitude of the Florida Keys. The spawning area of the European form is in about the latitude of Florida proper and more to the east. There is an overlap of the areas, but it is no

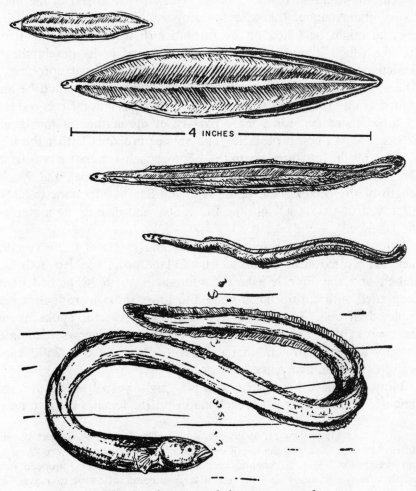

The development of the common eel

"melting pot." It couldn't be, because the rates of growth of the two kinds are entirely different. The American eel also travels at the rate of about 1000 miles per year but it grows to the full Leptocephalus size of 3 inches in one year. It does not need a longer time because it is so much closer to the rivers where it is going to stay for most of its life.

Whether some eel larvae occasionally get "on the wrong track" is an interesting question. Nothing like this has been observed so far and we cannot be sure, of course, whether it happens at all. But if it did one may imagine that an American eel which started to ride the Gulf Stream for Europe by mistake would be killed by the sea water because it would be ready to be a "river eel" when still in the middle of the Atlantic. Likewise a European eel which went west by mistake might be killed off by the brackish water outside of river mouths which it reached at too early a stage in its development. Something similar may be the real solution of the "Danube problem." The strange chemistry of the Black Sea's deeper layers could be accepted as an explanation when it was still thought that the eels wanted to breed there, but for a mere passage at the surface of the Black Sea that would be no obstacle. The answer probably is that the trip is too long; in just three years the Leptocephalus cannot travel from the Sargasso Sea through the Strait of Gibraltar, then the whole length of the Mediterranean, through the Sea of Marmara (against a fairly strong current) into the Black Sea, and then to the mouth of the Danube.[2]

But we can tie up a few loose ends and mention a few specific facts. The discoveries of Grassi and Calandruccio enabled both the Italian and the French fishery commissions to do what had once been tried with cut-up horse hairs and grass sods: to restock water depleted of eels. The French especially kept careful books about their work; they reported that each kilogram of elvers seeded into swamps and small waters off the River Aisne resulted in 2500 kilograms of food in five years.

Pliny may have been right with his "eight years" as the average time which the eel needs to reach maturity: the females seem to need

[2] In *Nature* (February 21, 1959, No. 4660), Dr. Denys W. Tucker of the British Museum advanced the hypothesis that *all* elvers everywhere are "American" eels, stocking both Atlantic shores, and that the adult European eels perish without spawning. It will take a large amount of proof to make this hypothesis palatable.

from eight to twelve years and the males from five to eight. Then
they go on a complete fast. Aquarium specimens have kept this up
for six months and then died, which is the reason for the belief that
the eel spawns only once and dies soon afterward. But some individuals do not mature sexually; they have been found to live more
than twenty years and to reach a length of 6 to 8 feet and a weight
of 30 pounds. I do not know which particular eel established a
weight record or what it was. But the age record for the common
European eel is a celebrated case. An eel known as the Eel of Ross
was caught as an elver in a small Scottish river in 1895 and kept in
an aquarium until it died in 1949, at a total age of 56 years.

The conger eel, which spends all its life in salt water, goes through
the same transformation as the common eel. Its larva is called
Leptocephalus morrisii and can be told from the others when still
quite small.

And now I have one more eel mystery to report.

The ship *Dana* made another expedition after the trip to the
Sargasso Sea. It was an expedition around the world, made in 1928–
1930. The collection of specimens made during this expedition is now
at the Marinbiologisk Laboratorium in Charlottenlund, Denmark,
under the care of Dr. Åge Vedel Tåning, who accompanied Dr.
Schmidt on his later trips. And in this collection is a Leptocephalus
taken, according to a letter from Dr. Tåning, on January 31, 1930,
from a depth of about 1000 feet west of the Agulhas Bank, off the
southernmost point of Africa. Dr. Tåning supplied me with the precise
location: 35 degrees, 42 minutes, south, and 18 degrees, 37 minutes,
east. This Leptocephalus is 184 centimeters long—6 feet and 1/2 inch.

Nobody knows the adult form.

It may be a kind of salt-water eel which grows to its full size as a
Leptocephalus and changes into an adult form which is not ap-
preciably larger. If it grows in the same proportion as the ordinary
eel, the result would be a monster between 60 and 70 feet long. I
don't suggest that this is the "great sea serpent." But, like everybody
else who knows about it, I wonder what it would have grown into.

CHAPTER 14

The Emperor's *Arcanum Magnum*

Rudolf II of Habsburg, emperor of the Holy Roman Empire, king of Hungary and of Bohemia, king of the Germans, duke of this and landgrave of that, was born in Vienna (in 1552) and educated by Jesuit scholars at the Court of Spain. Yet his later relations with Spain were not the best, and his favorite residence—especially later in life—was the old Hradčany castle in Prague. There the head of the Holy Roman Empire would often sit brooding in fits of depression which even his politest biographers had to label as "bordering on insanity." His courtiers, his generals, and his ambassadors might not be able to see the emperor for weeks at a time, but his astrologers and alchemists found access to the Imperial Chambers much more easily. True, other rulers of the time also supported an astrologer or two—one could never know when a horoscope might come in useful for a love affair, a siege, or a battle. They also took what later generations would dub a "calculated risk" on an occasional alchemist. If he did succeed in making gold, all the problems of the royal or ducal treasury would be solved; if not, the loss was small, consisting of a handful of gold and one fraudulent alchemist.

But Rudolf II did not support his astrologers and alchemists for material gain—or if material gain was mentioned it was for the purpose of placating the courtiers and generals. He was interested, intensely and fanatically interested, in their arts and knowledge. A horoscope was not a means of possibly outwitting a probable enemy who had failed to arm himself in like manner. It was a means of understanding the cosmos. Alchemy was not a means of possibly making gold, though the emperor would not have rejected such an achievement. It was the path to higher wisdom; it was to banish sickness and indecision, to prolong and aggrandize life and understand-

254

ing. And the emperor, who had been endowed with the proper up-
bringing of the Most Catholic Court of Spain, also conferred with
the High Rabbi Judah Loew of the Jewish congregation of Prague.
Rabbi Loew was not only celebrated as a man of great scholarship
and wisdom, he was also rumored to be a great magician and was
credited with having made the *golem,* the living clay figure which was
without speech but tireless and of unfailing strength and whose services must never be employed for secular purposes. Rudolf, no doubt,
inquired about magic and about the meanings of the Qabbala.

In less moody moments the emperor would support the fight
against the Protestants, and simultaneously support Tycho Brahe
and Johannes Kepler, two of the brightest stars on the firmament of
the new astronomy which was to come—and both Protestants. And
he would have read to him the reports of countless men, who scoured
all European cities, castles, and mansions for the emperor's collections, for Rudolf was an indefatigable collector. His family finally
decided, in 1606, that he was unfit to rule and declared one of his
younger brothers, Archduke Matthias, head of the family. The decision was indubitably correct and justified, but the collections Rudolf
had brought together, especially the art collections, could have been
the envy of anybody at any time.

There was just one item which Rudolf failed to obtain, even though
his representative was authorized to pay the fantastic sum of 4000
florins for it—a thousand florins more than Tycho Brahe received
per year. The unobtainable item was not a work of art; in fact it was
not man-made at all. It was what was then called a *curiosum naturae,*
a gigantic nut.

Every once in a while the currents of the sea would wash one of
these gigantic nuts ashore, in India or on the coast of Ceylon, or
on the beaches of the Maldive Islands which lie to the southwest of
the Indian triangle. They also occurred—oh, so infrequently—farther to the east; for example, on the coast of Java. All the princes of
the Far East considered them the most valuable possession a prince
could have, and a shipload of merchandise was considered proper
pay for one. A Dutch admiral who had been victorious in a battle
against the Portuguese was presented with one of these nuts by a
native ruler—nothing else would serve to express the gratitude felt
for this victory. The Dutch admiral, Wolfert Hermanszen, who beat
the Portuguese admiral Andrea Fortado de Mendoza in 1602 and
received a specimen of the fabulous nut for his victory, finally re-

turned to Holland, taking his prize along. It was this nut, the only one in Europe, which Rudolf II coveted, but the family would not sell; it was too valuable a possession. The Dutch and the Portuguese and the various natives might have many differences, but they were all agreed that the man who was lucky enough to get hold of a *Coco do Mar,* as the Portuguese called it, or *Maldivische Cocus-noot,* as it was known by the Dutch, would not part with it again.

It must be admitted that even nowadays such a nut is a most impressive specimen. With a circumference of over a yard and a weight approaching 50 pounds, it is now established as the largest seed of any plant. When the outer leathery covering is still in place, the coco-de-mer—the French term is the one which is now most generally used—resembles the much smaller coconut in shape. But when the outer skin has been removed it displays a strange shape, reminiscent of the shape of the "meat" of a walnut. It almost looks as if two nuts had coalesced. Inside this apparent double hull you then find nut meat of similar shape, resembling that of the coconut but much softer in texture. Taste is said to be singularly absent—"a whitish uninviting watery pulp for which I would not trade a single good hazelnut" declared a recent naturalist who actually tasted one.

But the Malays, the Burmese, and the Chinese, and whoever else offered pearls by the bagful and silks by the boatload for these nuts, did not trade for delicacies. They were after the supreme remedy of the ages. The nut meat was first dried and then ground up with ivory, or with deer antlers, or with red coral, in various and strange proportions. Depending on the admixtures this was an effective, nay, infallible, remedy for paralysis or stroke; it cured gall-bladder troubles and hemorrhoids. In addition to that, and most important for many of the princes who sought and bought it, the coco-de-mer destroyed any poison which might be mixed into food or drink, just as the alicorn was supposed to do.

Naturally it has no true medicinal value; its reputation was based solely on the factors of extreme rarity, sheer and impressive size, strange shape, and complete ignorance as to origin. It was not even known then whether this was actually a nut, a seed of a tree; there were some who held that it might be mineral. Presumably this idea originated with an experimenter who had decided that, if it were a nut, it could be planted and would produce a strange tree of some kind which would bear additional nuts, thereby providing a lifetime of luxury for its owner. Whoever tried that must have been

Coco-de-mer, or "Solomon's sea nut," with its outer skin removed to show the deep indentation

disappointed, for the nut probably failed to sprout; we now know that even under the most favorable conditions it takes over a year for the seedling to show signs of life.

Rudolf II probably did not offer 4000 florins to protect his life against disease or to ward off poisoners; unlike most other princes of his time he does not seem to have been unduly afraid of poisoning. Either poisoning was not much practiced in Vienna and in the Hradčany castle, or else he relied on the alicorns which he did possess. But the nut certainly possessed magic properties too. Nobody could say with any certainty just what they were, but to a mystic of that time the shape may have suggested a unification of the male and female principles, which was unique and therefore significant, no matter whether it was vegetable or mineral. And wasn't this very uncertainty another parallel to the alicorn, which also was somehow both animal (in origin, the horn of that rare creature the unicorn) and mineral (in hardness and appearance). And the very best alicorn was dug from the ground, which enhanced its mineral qualities.

The reasoning about King Solomon's Nut—to give it another name then in use—must have been along these lines, and nobody could successfully contradict any of it, unless he could have stated from personal experience and observation that this was an ordinary, though gigantic, tree nut, which had grown on an ordinary, though probably large, tree that could be found in this or that location. But from the day the first coco-de-mer which had drifted ashore somewhere was picked up as a curiosity by somebody, until the middle of the eighteenth century, literally nobody knew where it grew.

One area of the globe was under evident suspicion. The nut had to grow somewhere in the Far East, where expensive spices could be plucked off bushes and trees all year round, where, as some averred in hushed tones, gems were lying around as pebbles on the beaches. There, in the utmost distance of blue seas and steady winds, where the colors of the sunset faded fast to give way to low-hanging stars in the flower-scented night, somewhere in this vast and scarcely known realm the tree with the wonder nuts must grow. There also grew, as some told, strange bushes with leaves which did not fall off but flew away as butterflies when their time came. This was also the area where, as one had heard, the terrible poison tree, the *oepas* of the Dutch, existed, itself alive but inimical to all other life.

In short, the source of the nuts had to be on or near Java. And the priests of the Javanese claimed that they knew where it grew, not on their own island, but some distance to the south of it.

But I am already cribbing from the book which for more than a hundred years from the time of its publication was virtually the only, and in any event the most reliable source about the natural history of that area, the *Herbarium amboinense.* Admiring savants in Europe who read and reread it avidly did not even refer to its author by his name; they called him *Plinius indicus,* the Pliny of the Indies. The author of the *Herbarium* did not know about this appellation, of course, since the work which caused all this admiration had been printed after his death. He had simply stated his name on the title page in its Latinized version of Georgius Everhardus Rumphius, and somebody had added his title, *Oud Koopman en Raadspersoon*—Senior Merchant and Council Member.

Only Dutch readers who read the right-hand columns of the work were even faintly interested in the fact that the author had been an *Oud Koopman* in their East India Company. The others, who read the Latin left-hand columns of the book, paid no attention to the Latin designation of *Mercator Senior.* It was neither title nor affiliation which counted, but the book itself. If anybody wanted to know something about a plant growing in this distant wonderland, whether for sound commercial reasons connected with the spice trade, or because of the dictates of intellectual curiosity, he had to reach for the *Herbarium amboinense*. There he could find information about the strange *Myrmecodia* (discovered by Rumphius). This plant is now called an epiphyte, which means that it grows on the branches of trees but not as a parasite—it does not take anything from the tree except a little space on a branch. The Myrmecodia might be described as looking somewhat like a small pineapple. The bulbous growth, however, is anything but edible; it consists of tough woody fibers, with innumerable tunnels and holes. And the tunnels are inhabited by ants which defend their plant fiercely against any intruder. Or the reader of the *Herbarium* would come across such an astonishingly accurate statement as the one that the cycad trees, though they look like palms, are closer in organization to the tree ferns.

If the problem was not strictly botanical the researcher would reach for the only other printed book of *Plinius indicus,* entitled *D'Amboinsche Rariteitkamer* (*The Amboina Cabinet of Rarities*) which existed both in Dutch and in German. There the reader could find the first picture of a horseshoe crab (eastern version, *Limulus moluccanus*), the first description of the pearly nautilus, the first mention of coconut "pearls" (small stones which occasionally form inside coconuts), and the statement that the butterfly bushes do not actually bear leaves which change into butterflies but that there are butterflies which look like leaves when they fold their wings. The *Rariteitkamer* also contains what is probably the earliest mention of the crab now called *Birgus latro,* or else "robber crab," a big fat crab of the general shape and size of a lobster, but heavier, which eats coconuts only. It comes out of the sea for the coconuts, carefully and slowly tears off the thick cover of fibers, hammers its way with the aid of the large claws through one of the weak spots on top of the nut, and then reaches inside for the meat with the small claws of the legs. It is now accepted as a fact that *Birgus latro* even climbs trees and patiently saws through the stem of a nut if no ripe nuts are lying around on the ground.

I know that "interrupting the narrative" is something which magazine editors and literary critics, even in their most lenient moods, consider old-fashioned if nothing worse. But, having already strayed to some extent, I feel that it would border on injustice if I did not say something about the man who wrote these books. I consider this all the more necessary since standard reference works, like the Encyclopaedia Britannica, do not even mention him.

Georg Eberhard Rumpf, then, was born in 1627, day unknown. We know the year of his birth only because he himself mentioned it in a letter to his superiors in the Dutch East India Company, and we can infer from the words *van Hanau* which follow the signature of this letter that Hanau in Germany was his birthplace. Actually linguistic usage was not so clear-cut as to permit this deduction; the *van Hanau* in the letter, as well as the words *mijn vaderlijke stad Hanau* ("my fathertown Hanau") in the *Herbarium,* only mean that Rumpf came from that city. He may well have been born elsewhere. His father, Augustus Rumpf, had his son baptized as a Protestant and enrolled him at the Gymnasium (High School) of Hanau, where the emphasis was on classical literature and ancient languages. At the age of nineteen, one year after graduating, young Rumpf went to Holland. Apparently he spoke Dutch, and this, coupled with the fact that Hanau and vicinity were a place of refuge for Dutch Protestants, makes it probable that the family was Dutch.

A number of inadvertent adventures followed. Young Rumpf enlisted as a soldier with troops which were supposed to defend the Republic of Venice. The men were embarked at a Dutch port after having been told that the best and easiest way to reach Venice was by sea, even though it meant a longer trip than the overland route. What the men were not told was that they were to be sent to Brazil to defend Dutch claims against Portuguese encroachment. It did not matter much, for they never got there; their ship was captured by a Portuguese warship and the men were brought to Lisbon as prisoners of war. Released after two years, Rumpf returned to Holland and enlisted again, this time with the armed forces of the Dutch East India Company. After several delays and a long slow trip the future *Plinius indicus* set foot on the beach of the island of Amboina, then the center of Dutch activities in the East. The year was 1653, his age was twenty-six. After three years of service he received his first promotion; he was made *vaandrig,* or cornet. One year later he requested transfer to the civilian branch of the company; the request was granted and Rumpf was made *Onderkoopman,* Junior Merchant.

At that time he started his first literary project, a Malay-Dutch dictionary. By then he spoke Malay fluently. Strangely enough he did not write it with Latin letters but with Arabic script, which he must have thought better adapted to Malay sounds. Promotion followed in 1662, when Rumpf became a full-fledged *Koopman,* or Merchant. By then he had seen so many new and interesting things that he decided to write about them. He wrote to the regional directors, telling them about his plan and requesting permission to buy some books and instruments in Amsterdam. The letter was approved and forwarded to Amsterdam. But there was red tape even then. The regional director ordered that any parcels for Koopman Rumphius be inspected at the warehouse. The company had a monopoly and took it seriously. Koopman Rumphius did not mind having his parcels inspected and happily went to work. His only worry was that his eyesight seemed to be failing. In 1670 it turned out that his worry was justified; cataracts developed in both eyes. One was completely blinded and the other one very nearly so. And in those days nothing could be done about cataracts.

The company did what it could to improve matters. Rumpf was called to the main settlement, Amboina Kasteel, to live. He was promoted to Senior Merchant and simultaneously relieved of all duties. He was appointed to the court of justice so that his salary could be continued. His son, Koopman Paulus Augustus Rumphius, received a new assignment, that of seeing that his father completed his books. A secretary for Oud Koopman Rumphius was selected from among the clerks, and the artist Philips van Eijck was called from Amsterdam to assist with the illustrations.

But all the help that money could furnish could not avert several disasters. On Chinese New Year in 1674 the older Rumpf, his wife, and his youngest daughter attended the Chinese celebration. A fireworks display was scheduled to be put on after dark. Rumpf, unable to see the spectacle, decided that he would rather go for his customary evening walk. While he was away an earthquake struck the area; Rumpf, being in the open, was not even injured, but his wife and daughter both died. More than a decade later, in 1687, a fire broke out at Amboina Kasteel, consuming the greater part of the nearly finished manuscript. A few portions were saved, of a few other portions copies had been made which were elsewhere on the island, and after a few weeks of dejection Rumpf decided to write over again what had been destroyed.

In 1692 the manuscript for the first six books of the *Herbarium amboinense* was put aboard a ship which set sail for Batavia. From there the manuscript was to be shipped to Amsterdam to be printed. In 1701 the rest of the manuscript left for Amsterdam. And one year later, on June 15, 1702, Senior Merchant Rumpf died on Amboina, completely blind, very lonely, and convinced that he had failed in life.

It sounds like a chapter from an overplotted bad novel, but the first shipment of the manuscript was almost lost once more. The ship which sailed from Batavia for Holland with the manuscript aboard was the *Waterland*. The *Waterland* never reached Europe; she was sighted, engaged, and sunk by a French vessel. It was fortunate that the manuscript had not been shipped to Holland directly from Amboina, since it was preserved only because of the stopover in Batavia. The Governor-General, Joannes Camphuys, had been hearing about Rumpf and his work for years. When the ship from Amboina arrived he read the manuscript, or at least portions of it. And being an experienced man who knew all the hazards of long voyages in wooden ships, with enemies and pirates on the high seas, he ordered the whole manuscript copied before he parted with it. The manuscript which had been written on Amboina sank with the *Waterland;* the copy made in Batavia reached Amsterdam a year later.

In volume VI of the work which was twice almost destroyed you can find Rumpf's report on the coco-de-mer. It is chapter VIII of the twelfth book, consisting of eight folio pages of text and one more folio page with a picture of the nut. The picture is inferior to the other illustrations in the *Herbarium* and actually contains a mistake: the two halves of the nut are shown as completely separated. Obviously the artist did not have a specimen to draw but had to go by descriptions. And nobody who saw the picture before it went to the engraver's shop had ever seen a specimen either.

Whatever criticism one may make of the picture, there can be none of the text; it is what Linnaeus said about the whole book: *solidissimus*. As has been mentioned, the Javanese claimed to know where the nut grew. One version of the story which Rumpf heard is reasonably simple: the tree grows deep under water all around the island of Sumatra and especially in a certain bay on the southern shore. Occasionally it can be seen in quiet, clear water from a boat. But if you look for the tree under water or try to get closer to it by diving you'll surely drown.

There was, however, a more elaborate story which Rumpf repeated with the introductory remark that this was "the worse fable." The natives told that the tree which bore the sea nut was unique; there was only one like it in the world. It grew in the open sea beyond Java. The bough of the Pausengi Tree, as they called it, rises above the waves and in it a bird called the Geruda has built its nest. This Geruda is the same as the Griffin and it flies about over the islands, taking elephants, tigers, rhinoceri, "or other large animals" with its claws and bringing them to its nest in the sea for its young to eat. One cannot approach the place where the Pausengi Tree grows—or rather one can approach it only too easily, for all the currents in the ocean converge there. A ship that comes near will drift helplessly to the tree and be unable to return. The sailors who thus have an opportunity of seeing the tree can never tell their tale, for they will die of hunger and thirst, unless they fall victim to the Geruda bird first.

For fear of being pulled to the Pausengi Tree none of the Javanese dared to sail farther than a few miles out to sea; as long as they could see their own island they were able to return to it. But in spite of every precaution, some fishermen had been caught in one of the currents and had drifted out to the tree. They succeeded in approaching the Geruda bird unseen and clung to its feathers when it took to the air. As the bird swooped down on some prey on Java they released their hold and, after making their way back to their villages, told what had happened to them. And that was how the location of the Pausengi Tree and the nest of the Geruda became known.[1]

Now the sea nut from the Pausengi Tree had the strange characteristic of moving against currents, which is how it could reach the shore of Java. But even then it still had some power of locomotion left; if the slope of the beach was gentle the nut would cross it and hide itself in the underbrush, well away from the water. Because of this behavior the nuts were even more rare; they were usually spied by men only because the dogs barked and yelped at the moving nut. At that point Rumpf departed from straight reporting and remarked dryly: "From this fable the reader may conclude why this fruit is so highly esteemed and is so dearly sought."

But this last item of the story, which made Rumpf add what was for him an especially caustic remark, is probably not entirely a fable. It may not have applied to the coco-de-mer, if only because the giant nut is too rare, but it does apply to the ordinary coconut. A watcher endowed with enough patience to sit quietly in the moonlight on a

[1] This is precisely the same story that you probably know from the *Arabian Nights,* and which was also told independently in the medieval German romance *Herzog Ernst von Schwaben.* All the story elements are there: the giant bird which carries elephants and rhinoceri to its young, the escape from danger by riding the bird, the place to which all ships are irresistibly drawn. The only difference is that the Javanese version contains converging currents, while the Western versions utilize the Mountain of Lodestone. It may be added that the location of the Mountain of Lodestone was thought to be in the Sunda Sea.

beach in those islands may actually witness the incredible spectacle of a coconut drifting ashore and, after some time, suddenly ascending the beach and beginning to crawl across the sand, shambling and hesitantly, until it has disappeared in the underbrush. Of course the nut did not suddenly acquire the power of locomotion, however feebly; the "motive force" is something else. Ironically it is provided by something that Rumpf himself knew, the crab he called *Cancer crumenatus,* the *Birgus latro* of our books. The crab does drag coconuts across the beach to a place where the waves cannot interfere with its tedious job of opening and eating them.

Having related all the various stories and items he had heard about the rare sea nut, Rumpf was faced by the necessity of forming an opinion of his own. If you trimmed every story and report down to its bare essentials you had two facts, one negative and one positive. The negative fact was that nobody had ever seen the tree which produced the nut. The positive fact was that every nut ever found was found at the seashore. Combining these two Rumpf concluded that it had to be a product of the sea and he imagined a plant, growing on the sea bottom not too far from the shore where the nuts appeared. Obviously he could not tell how the plant looked, but he tended to think of it as quite simple in shape. As for the location, he believed that the plant grew especially frequently in the area of the Maldive islands, which would account for the Dutch name *Maldivische Cocus-noot.*

At the time Rumpf was writing his *Herbarium,* and in fact even before he was born, the place where the coco-de-mer actually grew was more or less clearly marked on nautical charts. It was the group of islands which is now known as the Seychelles. The Dutch name of the nut had been wrong, one is tempted to say, by just one archipelago. The Seychelles are the first group of islands which a traveler sailing on a southwesterly course from the Maldives would reach. The trip would be fairly long, around 1300 miles as the sea gull flies, but there is only water between the two island groups. To go due west from the Seychelles to the African coast is a trip of almost equal length, and the isolation of this group of islands must have been partly responsible for their late discovery.

The earliest charts showing an entry of islands that fits the Seychelles are of Portuguese origin; they are the charts of Alberto Cantino and Nicolas Caneirio, dated 1502. During the course of the sixteenth century islands occupying the approximate position of the actual Seychelles—it was so hard to measure longitude that an error of 5 to 10 degrees was rather customary—were entered on a total of eighteen charts. But the first recorded visit took place in 1609. None of the earlier sea captains seems to have made an attempt to land, not necessarily because there was other and more pressing business on hand. Sea captains did not always write down everything they knew and it may have been routine knowledge among them that the island or islands one might encounter some 600 miles to the north of Madagascar had no inhabitants. On uninhabited islands there was no possibility of trade of any kind, and one could not even take slaves. Hence there was no reason to land.

It was in January 1609 that an English ship commanded by Captain John Jourdain arrived in the archipelago. A boat was sent ashore for fresh water and the beaching of that boat by the water search party constitutes the first known landing of any vessel on any of the Seychelles Islands. Both Captain Jourdain and his shipmate Revett told interesting things about the big land tortoises their men found (of which more is said in Chapter 19), but they did not quite know what to do with an uninhabited island either. And they missed the one on which grew the trees bearing the coco-de-mer.

That nobody was much interested is probably best shown by the time interval that elapsed between the first and the second recorded visits: it was a hundred and thirty-three years!

The second visitor, in 1742, was the French captain Lazare Picault, who returned to the islands in 1744 for the purpose of annexing them formally to France. He acted as an agent for the governor of Mauritius, Mahé de la Bourdonnais, and being a perceptive scoundrel or else well versed in politics (though he couldn't spell), he named the whole group of islands Les Iles de la Bourdonnais. More than that, he called the largest island Mahé. But he explored only a part of the group and also succeeded in missing the one with the coco-de-mer trees.

It took a little while for the French to begin to think about the new group of islands which they had acquired. When they did so, they first changed the name—it was thought in Paris or in Versailles that having the largest island named Mahé was enough honor for the governor of Mauritius, and in 1756 the group as a whole was named for Moreau de Séchelles, then *contrôleur des finances* under King Louis XV. Simultaneously the Duc de Praslin ordered a more thorough investigation of the islands with emphasis on the question of what use they might be. The first result was that the second largest island received the name of Praslin. The man who explored Praslin Island was an engineer named Barré. Hacking his way through the jungle, he came across enormous palm trees, almost 100 feet tall, with fronds measuring close to 30 feet from their tips to the base of the leaf stalk. And among these enormous, rigid, and fan-shaped fronds there hung clusters of enormous palm nuts. The source of the coco-de-mer had been discovered at last.

Monsieur Barré was a perceptive man too, but not quite perceptive enough. He took a shipload of coco-de-mer to India, no doubt with visions of a life of luxury for himself, his potential mistresses, his children and children's children. But a whole shipload of coco-de-mer was too much; when the prospective customers saw the abundance of treasure the price of the coco-de-mer declined rapidly and permanently. If the French had known what could be found on Praslin Island they might, with rigid export control and careful one-at-a-time trading, have brought prosperity to their national treasury on coco-

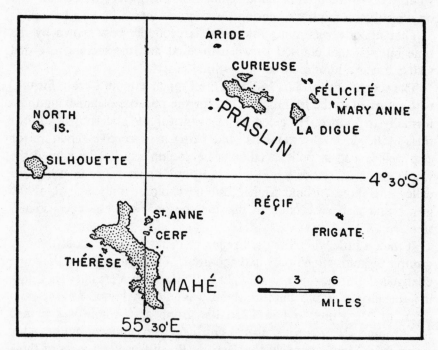

The Seychelles Islands. The island of Praslin is the only remaining natural habitat of *Lodoicea seychellarum*

de-mer alone. Having missed that chance because of Barré's careless action, they began to wonder what else might grow on the islands. The intendant of Ile de France (Mauritius), Monsieur Pierre Poivre, was shrewder and obviously far more experienced than Barré. He realized that the Seychelles were outside the hurricane paths, hence a safe place for plantations. The climate being what it is, spices should grow there; one could compete with the Dutch monopoly on those. Spice plantations—especially for vanilla—were started on various islands and kept strictly secret. The Dutch would not be able to help noticing after a while that spices from other sources were appearing on the market, but nobody was to know where these sources were located. When, in 1778, a ship flying the Union Jack approached, the French felt that their secret might become known and they hurriedly set fire to their spice plantations. After the ship had landed it proved to belong to a French slaver who had run up the British flag because he thought the British might have taken possession of the islands while he was at sea.

His suspicions were not really wrong, merely too early by a few decades. The British did take possession of the islands in 1810 and became the formal owners four years later by the Treaty of Paris of 1814.

As for the islands themselves, Mahé is not only the largest, with an area of 53 square miles, it is also the most centrally located and crowned by the highest and third highest mountains in the archipelago, measuring 2993 and 2390 feet, respectively. Praslin, with an area of 27 square miles, is second in size and the center of a well-defined subgroup of islands. Next in size in this subgroup is La Digue (named after one of the ships which went there in 1744), with 4 square miles; the others in this subgroup are named East and West Silver, Aride, Félicité, Mary Anne, and Curieuse, the last of these names also being taken from one of the ships. A second subgroup consists of only two islands, of which Silhouette is the larger. With an area of 8 square miles, it ranks third among the Seychelles and has the second highest mountain, 2473 feet high, and called Mon Plaisir, although I don't know whose pleasure it happened to be. It was first seen by Captain John Jourdain on January 10, 1609. The other island of that subgroup is North Island.

Naturally, since the Seychelles changed hands, many of the smaller islands no longer bear their original names. The island originally named Ile des Oiseaux is now called Bird Island, which is at least

a straight translation. But the Ile des Vaches Marines ("sea-cow island," so named from the dugongs which were found there) became
plain Denis Island, which sounds like something in some river back of
town.

All the islands are of granite, largely hornblende, indicating great
age. In fact, the Seychelles look like left-overs of a large continent of
the past. A hundred years ago geologists were convinced that there
had once been a continent stretching from Madagascar to the Indian
mainland, and that Madagascar itself, Mauritius, Réunion, the Comores, Aldabra, the Seychelles, and the Maldives are all just remains
of this "Lemuria." But in spite of appearances more modern geological ideas tend to deny that a whole continent can simply disappear under
the sea. However, these same more recent ideas encourage the concept
that the continents are not solidly anchored to the earth but may move.
When such movements take place, the reasoning runs, portions of the
continent may become detached and be left behind, as Madagascar
looks like a piece of Africa that was left behind when the continent
as a whole shifted toward the west. The Seychelles might well be
another such split-off portion which lasted for a while as a large
island a few thousand square miles in extent and then was partly
flooded.

The palm bearing the coco-de-mer would then be a typical "living
fossil" which happened to survive on this split-off area while it became extinct elsewhere. It is true that this palm, though individually
large and powerful and almost indestructible, does not seem to be
able to compete with other tropical plants. After all, it did not even
survive all over the Seychelles islands but only on Praslin. Even the
trees on the neighboring island of Curieuse are said to have been introduced artificially.

Lodoicea seychellarum, to use its scientific name,[2] is remarkable
for many reasons, most of them somehow connected with size. The
tall trunk of the adult tree has been called "as hard as iron and equally
resistant to all outside influences." But it takes a long time for a Lodoicea to become an adult tree.

To begin at the beginning: the nuts need seven to eight years to
ripen. When they are planted at the end of this period it is at least a

[2] The name was given by Jacques Julien Houtou de Labillardière, who was
the naturalist of the expedition sent out to locate the lost expedition of La
Pérouse. The name Lodoicea is a modification of Laodikē, the daughter of
Priam; I don't know what Labillardière had in mind when he chose it.

The palm *Lodoicea seychellarum*. At right, a "young" specimen about 40 years old

year before the seedling appears. The seedling does not necessarily come up in the spot where the nut was planted; it is almost the rule that it grows horizontally underground for several yards before it breaks through the surface. Then it takes thirty-five to forty years before the plant flowers for the first time. Even then it is by no means adult; in fact it isn't old enough to have developed a trunk. Every adult Lodoicea, therefore, must be considerably more than a century old. Some of the larger specimens which are now growing on Praslin may have sprouted at the time Captain Jourdain's men were looking for fresh water on another island. As in the ginkgo, another living fossil, the two sexes are strictly separated; a Lodoicea is either male or female. Since this means that only about half of the adult plants can bear fruit the possible rate of reproduction is slowed down some more.

Professor Carl Chun, the leader of the German oceanographic expedition on S.S. *Valdivia* in 1898–99, who went to Praslin specifically for Lodoicea, did not hesitate to write in his account of the expedition that Lodoicea might well be extinct by now if it had not been for John Horne, the director of the Botanical Garden on Mauritius. In 1875 John Horne convinced the government of Queen Victoria that something irreplaceable would be gone if Lodoicea were permitted to disappear from the islands. In response to his strongly worded request a large valley on Praslin where most of the biggest specimens grew, and the entire island of Curieuse, were declared crown property, and the necessary laws for protecting the plants growing elsewhere on Praslin were made.

John Horne, as well as other British botanists, realized perfectly well that a threatened species can be saved in two ways. One is to protect it where it happens to occur; the other is to extend its range so that a local accident such as a forest fire can have only local effects. Lodoicea nuts were planted in various localities that looked suitable, like Mauritius, and in a botanical garden in Ceylon. They did sprout and take root, but the plant grows so slowly that most visitors were disappointed when they saw them. And although the giant nuts have drifted ashore in Borneo, Java, and Sumatra for many centuries, and not all of them could have been found, there is no known case of a Lodoicea growing on any of these islands.

King Solomon's nut still retains at least one secret—why it failed to spread from its last retreat. And the existence of Lodoicea still hinges on its continued survival on two tiny islands.

PART FOUR

SOME FABULOUS ISLANDS

The Mauritius dodo (drawing
by Adrian van de Venne, 1626)

CHAPTER 15

The Islands of the Moas

THE YEAR WAS A.D. 1642.

The place was the main office of the government of the Dutch East Indies.

The occasion was a conference under the chairmanship of the Governor of the Dutch East Indies, Mijnheer Antoon van Diemen.

And the outcome of the conference was that Captain Abel Janszoon Tasman was ordered to proceed with the good ship *Heemskirk* to the new and poorly known continental coast of Nieuw Holland and to sail south along its coast until such a time as he either could turn east or would be forced west by said coast.

Captain Tasman left from Batavia and sailed as ordered. The coast of Nieuw Holland—what we now call the West Coast of Australia—did not force him to turn west as had been expected. On the contrary, he could turn east after some time, and finally he saw what was unmistakably a southern cape. Tasman thought that it was the southern end of the vaguely known Australian continent and named the area of that southern cape Vandiemensland, in honor of the governor who had ordered this voyage of exploration.

Actually it was not even Australia proper any more; Tasman did not know of the existence of Bass Strait. It was the southern end of the large island now known, in *his* honor, as Tasmania.

But Tasman did not turn around then. His orders were to go on, if possible, and to find open sea to the east of Nieuw Holland, provided that there was an open sea, of course. Expressed in present-day language, these orders were simply to sail around Australia; the problem then was, however, whether that could be done. So Tasman kept the bow of the *Heemskirk* pointing east and went on for another thousand miles. And on December 16, 1642, he saw land again,

273

"great, high, bold land." Although the Netherlands province of Zeeland is neither great, nor high, nor bold, to the view of the traveler approaching it, Tasman named the new land *Nieuw Zeeland*—and it has been New Zealand ever since.

Strangely enough, matters rested there for more than a century.

In November 1769 another vessel approached New Zealand, from the other side. It was the *Endeavour,* commanded by Captain James Cook. Captain Cook did land—Tasman had not attempted a landing; he was interested in the problem of where one could sail, and the land was mostly an obstacle—and made contact with the people living there, the Maori. With the aid of interpreters who seem to have been of doubtful value Captain Cook spoke at length to the Maori chieftain Tawaihura and asked him, among other things, about the animals occurring on the island. Chief Tawaihura told about an enormous man-eating lizard which, as we now know, never existed. And he said nothing about the animals actually native to the islands. One wonders whether he had really understood the request or whether this was another version of that strange form of politeness about which Hans Schomburgk still warned a hundred and fifty years later.

If this interview had not miscarried as badly as it did, Captain Cook's naturalist, Sir Joseph Banks, might have brought some very unusual animals and birds with him when they returned to England. At it was they came back almost empty-handed and New Zealand's strange survivors from past ages drifted into the hands of science piecemeal; we don't even know the dates precisely.

As time went on New Zealand presented naturalists with five different zoological mysteries. Three of them have been solved; two have not.

The first of the strange New Zealanders to come to the attention of science was a bird which is now known to everybody—the kiwi. Captain Barclay of the ship *Providence* sent the first skin to England. The year was about 1814 and nobody knows whether the kiwi was known to anybody—except perhaps the Maori—before that time. Nobody even knows where Captain Barclay's kiwi skin originated, whether it was caught or shot by one of his sailors or whether it was traded from the Maori. The British naturalists who received it knew only that this bird lived on New Zealand.

It was a hen-sized bird, completely wingless and tailless as far as external appearance went, and with hairlike feathers almost belying

Kiwis (*Apteryx australis*)

the old and otherwise so reliable saying that one knows a bird by its feathers. It had enormous four-toed feet and a long snipelike bill with the nostrils placed at the tip. All in all, it looked much more like a taxidermist's concoction than like a bona fide specimen, although there was no doubt as to its genuineness. If these scientists had also been told that this bird lays eggs weighing precisely one quarter of the weight of the adult specimen they would probably have disbelieved it—it *was* disbelieved for decades, and some even went looking for a large bird that could have laid those eggs. The matter was not completely settled until caged kiwis in zoological parks were kind enough to demonstrate that those large eggs were really theirs.

The first examiner of the skin was Professor John Latham, who, after long hesitation, decided to call the bird an "apterous (wingless) penguin," but who cautiously said, at the same time, that this classification was just tentative. "The form of the foot," he wrote, "is not greatly unlike that of the dodo, and in the specimen the toes were not connected by an intervening membrane; yet from certain inequalities on the sides it is possible that there may have been one, and that it had been eaten away by insects."

Why Latham, who examined the skin, did not name the bird is another unanswerable question, but actually the name *Apteryx* (the word just means "wingless") was given by the zoologist Dr. George Shaw.

The next step was to establish the relationship of the kiwi to other birds, and there one Dr. Temminck blundered badly. Influenced by the build of the foot he put *Apteryx,* the kiwi, and *Didus,* the dodo, into the same zoological "order" for which he proposed the name of *Inertes.* This new order he placed next to the order of the penguins to indicate kinship. That way confusion at least was complete!

In reality the penguins are a separate order of birds; their ancestry is not known but it is certain that they are derived from birds which could fly. In fact the penguins still fly, but under water. The kiwi, on the other hand, is a representative of a group of birds which either stopped flying a hundred million years ago or never did fly. As for the dodo, which was lumped with the kiwi by Temminck, it was a relative of the pigeon and had become flightless mostly by growing too heavy.

Most zoologists, though not yet aware of these facts, failed to fall in love with Temminck's cleverness and cast about for something better. In German books the kiwi had meanwhile acquired a German name, *Schnepfenstrauss* or "snipe-ostrich," which at least pointed in the right direction. But for reasons which nobody could explain afterward the snipe-ostrich was then tacked on to the *Galliformes,* or chicken-like birds, where it obdurately remained until the early years of the twentieth century. And this in spite of the fact that the English zoologist William Yarrell had delivered a new scientific description of the kiwi in 1833 and clearly stated which other birds should be considered its relatives. These other birds (Yarrell could not help noticing that all of them lived in the southern hemisphere) were the rhea or nandu of South America, the African ostrich, the emu of Australia, and the cassowary of the Australian region. These birds are not very closely related to each other nowadays, but they all must stem from the same original stock.

As for the living kiwi, one should really use the plural, because there are three species. The most abundant, *Apteryx australis* [1] oc-

---

[1] The word *australis* in this context does not point to Australia. It is just the Latin word for "south"; southern hemisphere is meant.

curs on the North and South Islands of New Zealand as well as on Stewart Island.[2] The species *Apteryx oweni,* called the Little Spotted Kiwi, occurs in the west and south of the South Island, while *Apteryx haasti,* the Great Spotted Kiwi, lives in the north of the South Island. But the three species are so much alike in their habits that they can be treated as one.

To say that the kiwi is a nocturnal forest bird just about exhausts the description of its habits. In daytime the kiwis sleep huddled together and if awakened by force look rather helpless. It is quite likely that sunlight will blind them, since their eyes are adjusted for nocturnal activities which are described by witnesses as "noisy." The kiwis move about restlessly, hunting for earthworms and grubs and insects living on the ground. The guiding sense in these insect and worm hunts seems to be a sense of smell, which is unique among birds. The kiwi is the only living bird in which the sense of smell is developed at all, or, rather, whose ancestors did not lose it millions of years ago. When frightened, the kiwis run in long strides and they can jump well. Whether they can swim is an interesting question but one that cannot be answered. Kiwis sometimes rest in a "three-legged" position, touching the tip of the long bill to the ground. They are also said to sleep in that position.

The kiwi is a kind of keystone in a complex of zoological problems. We have a number of living birds (plus a large number of recently extinct forms) which share a set of unusual features. The one pointed out by Yarrell, that they all live in the southern hemisphere, may be accidental or it may be significant; we don't know yet. But they all lack wings, they all have a breastbone which is not birdlike (it lacks the typical high keel to which the "flying muscles" are normally attached), and in most cases their feathers are stringy and hairlike. Even the feathers are not good for flying, and this statement also goes for the spectacular plumes of the ostrich which are otherwise somewhat exceptional. Zoologists use the term *Ratitae* for these birds and it looks as if they are something apart; it would be useful if there were another word besides "bird" available for them.

Many a zoologist has wondered whether Archaeopteryx actually is ancestral to the Ratitae; the true ancestor of the Ratitae might have been a "pro-avis" which went along on a parallel track with the

[2] *Apteryx australis* is divided into three races, the North Island Kiwi (*Apteryx australis mantelli*), the South Island Kiwi (*Apteryx australis australis*), and the Stewart Island Kiwi (*Apteryx australis lawryi*).

evolution of feathers and so forth but never attempted to fly. Now all the living Ratitae (*and* their recently extinct relatives) are large, except for the kiwi. This is, in itself, reason for expecting the kiwi to represent an old form of the Ratitae. Unfortunately this is about all that can be said because at this point fossils of ancestors of the living Ratitae, and especially fossils of the ancestors of the kiwi, are badly needed, and fossils cannot be produced on order.

If the kiwi can be suspected of being one of the oldest wingless birds, another living fossil from the high, bold land that Captain Tasman saw from a distance is known to be one of the oldest of its kind. This is the "lizard" *Hatteria* or *Sphenodon*.

Like the kiwi, it crept up on science slowly and unnoticed. Nobody knows who discovered it and when. It is true that it does not look too conspicuous to the untrained person. Hatteria has the general shape of a plumpish lizard. When fully grown it is nearly 2 feet long. It has a fairly short but heavy tail, a large head with big eyes, a loose skin of greenish color that looks as if it were too large for the animal inside, and a somewhat tattered crest of spines running along neck, back, and tail.

The Maori called this reptile *tuatera* or *tuatara;* the forms *ruatara* and *tuatete* are also on record. As for its scientific name, you have a case of the United States versus the rest of the planet. In America the name Sphenodon (full designation: *Sphenodon punctatus*) is preferred, while non-English-writing scientists normally use Hatteria (short for *Hatteria punctata*). In the British Commonwealth it is customary, however, to refer to it as tuatara. The French use a Frenchified version of the Maori word (*tuatère* or *touatère*). The Germans say *Brückenechse,* which is a strange combination of an archaism and specialized science, for *Echse* is the old word for "reptile" and the *Brücke* (bridge) refers to a feature of the skeleton which would surprise only an expert anatomist. To spare the reader this international confusion, I shall confine myself to Hatteria.

The sluggish bearer of these many names entered scientific literature in 1831 when Edward Gray published a short paper with the title "Note on a Peculiar Structure in the Head of an Agama." To call Hatteria an agama—a quite modern kind of lizard—was wrong, but the structure was peculiar enough. It was so peculiar that a naturalist named Günther went after it with great thoroughness and in the course of time produced another paper with the title "Contribution

Lizard Hatteria or Sphenodon, from New Zealand

to the Anatomy of *Hatteria"* in which he came out flatly with the statement that this "structure" which had interested Gray was a third eye! On the top of the reptile's head a ring of scales surrounds a larger and transparent central scale. Underneath that transparent scale there is an eye, small in size but well formed and, as far as can be told, able to function.

During the Triassic Period, when reptiles like Hatteria made their first appearance, a third eye was quite stylish among reptiles, as we can see from their fossil skulls. Later they apparently did not find much use for it; at any rate it disappeared. A rudimentary third eye can still be found in the skulls of many living reptiles, and Man himself has such a rudiment in the form of the pineal gland in his skull. But in almost all living reptiles the "pineal eye" is hard to find and the nerve leading to it has atrophied completely. In Hatteria they are both well developed. Runner-up in that respect (and only runner-up) is the large black leguan *Amblyrhynchus* of the Galápagos Islands; the pineal eye and its nerve are not as well preserved as with Hatteria, but almost so, and they are also still functioning.

As distinct from the case of the kiwi, the paleontological history of this living fossil is well known. During the Permian period, a little over 200 million years ago, there existed several orders of primitive reptiles. Some of them became completely extinct; some others evolved into entirely different and new forms. One of these old orders leads to the present "chelonians" (turtles and tortoises) in a straight line, but it happens that none of the living chelonians is a particularly ancient form. Another one of the old orders was that of the rhynchocephalians ("bird-beaks" if you insist on a translation) which flourished especially during the geological period following the Permian, the Triassic period. Hatteria is the surviving representative of these rhynchocephalians.

Remains of rhynchocephalians have been found in many European deposits from the Triassic period and also in southern Africa. During the next geological period, the Jurassic, the rhynchocephalians became less numerous but spread to the North American continent, into Wyoming, to be specific. Among the Jurassic rhynchocephalians there is one, called *Homoeosaurus* (known from Bavaria and from southern England) which, if it were still alive, an observer could not tell from the modern Hatteria, except, possibly, if it happened to have a different coloration.

During this spread in Jurassic times they reached Malaya, New Guinea, and, across a then-existing land bridge from New Guinea via New Caledonia to the North Cape of New Zealand, their present home. It was just a stroke of good luck for everybody concerned that the land bridge disappeared during the Cretaceous period. Not even the marsupials got to New Zealand after that. Both kiwis and Hatteria were safe. A full thousand miles of ocean protected them against invasion, and the only arrivals in recent times, the Maori, fortunately formed superstitious legends about them and left them alone.

Disaster threatened them one hundred and fifty years ago when white settlers came (unaware even of Hatteria's existence) and introduced pigs. The pigs decimated the three-eyed living fossils. At the time of the arrival of these settlers Hatteria lived over both main islands of New Zealand and on a large number of rocky islets off the coast. Now there seem to be none on the two main islands (of course we can't tell about, and may hope for, the more remote sections), but fortunately the rocky islets off the coast were left undisturbed.

The New Zealand government has done what a government can do to protect this unique survivor from the Age of Reptiles. It is absolutely forbidden to kill a Hatteria or even to keep one as a pet, and exceptions from this rule are granted most sparingly. During the last forty years only six specimens were exported—I played with one that had been given to the San Diego Zoo—and the only ones known to be privately kept are at Wellington, where Mr. W. H. I. Dawbin, a zoology instructor at Victoria University College, succeeded in hatching several from eggs and keeping them alive. All other Hatterias are on reservations, those rocky islets offshore which are very hard to land on, nearly impossible to climb, and off limits for everybody except representatives of scientific institutions armed with one of the rare government permits.

From the observations of such scientists we are well acquainted with Hatteria's life habits.

The food consists of small animals of all types—beetles and grass-hoppers, worms and spiders, occasionally a small lizard. They swim well and like the water, and it is possible that they sometimes catch small fish to vary their menu. They can dig holes in the ground, too, but it is interesting to note that they almost never make their own burrows. These are dug by Hatteria's regular roommate, the petrel bird.

If these petrels ever built nests in the open, they long ago gave up doing so in favor of underground shelters. The petrel's nest is a tunnel some 5 inches in diameter and about a yard long, which leads to an underground chamber about 2 feet square and about 6 inches high. It is comfortably lined with dry grass and dead leaves. When the petrels started constructing these underground nests, Hatteria evidently liked the housing project and moved in. The birds do not seem to mind. They have even elaborated upon the structure, so that it is now a firmly established rule that each of the tenants lives in a separate nest, the petrel to the left and the Hatteria to the right of the entrance. Of course the lizards have most of the advantage; it is, in fact, hard to see how the petrels benefit at all from the association. Some zoologists have guessed that Hatteria keeps the house clean by eating the remains of the dead fish brought home by the petrel for its own supper, but there is no certainty about that.

Around the middle of the nineteenth century strange and exciting news began to come from New Zealand, news about big birds. The Maori told white traders, missionaries, and settlers about them, and a single bone furnished proof that these stories were not pure imagination. There might be exaggerations and even some misunderstandings but it could not be doubted that a factual basis existed. Scientists and everybody else interested for any reason whatever used a new word for these birds. It was *moa,* the name which the Maori were said to use for the big birds.

The second half of the nineteenth century, as far as New Zealand affairs were concerned, was ruled by this word moa. Men made the long and at that time arduous trip from Europe to New Zealand with moas uppermost in their minds. The famous English paleontologist and zoologist Dr. Gideon Algernon Mantell sent his son Walter to New Zealand to collect, not just moas, of course, but zoological material in general. Walter Mantell's trip turned out to be an outstanding success, but it led away from the moas for a while.

The Maori often told about another bird, not a moa but a large
bird which they had hunted to eat. This bird, they said, was gone
now but its name lingered on. The Maori of the North Island called
it *moho,* the Maori of the South Island called it *takahe.* Unfortunately, even if there were no linguistic difficulties, the Maori seem
to have been quite unable to give a good description, and nobody
could imagine what this *moho* or *takahe* looked like. Sometime in
1847 Walter Mantell acquired near Waingongoro on the North
Island a bird's skull, breastbone, and some other parts of the skeleton. His first guess was that it was a very large rail. He boxed the
bones with great care and shipped them to his father in London, writing that this might be the unknown *moho* or *takahe.*

Gideon Mantell, the father, handed the shipment which in addition to the remains of the suspected *takahe* contained many moa
bones, to Professor Richard Owen. Owen soon stated that the Maori
had spoken the truth; there had been a rather large bird on the islands which was not a moa. It had been the size of a large goose. It
had been flightless but not wingless; its wings just were not large
enough to support the heavy body in air. As a name Professor Owen
proposed *Notornis,*[3] and in order to honor the collector he suggested
that the full name should be *Notornis mantelli.* The suggestion was
accepted.

Two years later the first big surprise came. It came from the South
Island, more specifically from the extreme southwestern portion
which on maps printed in New Zealand is usually called "West Coast
Sounds." There are a number of fiords which cut deeply into the
land, forming a number of islands. Most of the islands are small, but
some, including Secretary Island and Resolution Island, are quite
large.

In 1849 a group of sealers camped on Resolution Island, hunting
seals. Snow had fallen the previous night and one of the men noticed
the footprints of a large bird in the new snow. Being curious, a
number of them followed the footprints with their dogs and after
some time saw a large bird in the distance. The dogs pursued it at
once. The bird ran away with unusual speed. But the dogs finally
caught it and brought it back to their masters. The bird screamed

[3] *Notornis* translates as "southern bird," from the Greek *ornis* for "bird"
and the Greek *notos* which means the south wind, and by extension "southern
quarter." The more likely name *Australornis* (southern bird) had already been
used up.

loudly when it was taken away from the dogs and fought with bill and claws as best it could.

The sealers were no naturalists, but this bird was something to behold. To begin with it was quite large, with a comparatively short neck, but with long strong legs and strong feet. The heavy sharp bill and the strong legs were bright red, the feathers of head and throat bluish-black—purplish-blue on the back of the neck. The back and most of the rather small wings were dull olive-green, the larger feathers tipped with verditer green, while the breast, the sides of the body, and the flanks were of a very beautiful purplish-blue. The larger wing and tail feathers showed a more metallic blue while the underside of the tail was white. Presumably impressed by the glitter of its plumage, the men did not kill the bird instantly but put it aboard their ship where it was kept alive for three or four days. Then, not quite knowing what else to do with it, the sealers killed the bird, roasted it, and ate it. But they saved the skin and offered it for sale or trade when they landed again.

By an incredible coincidence the skin was secured by the same Walter Mantell who had purchased the remains at Waingongoro on the North Island. He shipped it to his father in London and there excitement ran high. The bird which had been found in "subfossil state" on the North Island was evidently still alive on the South Island. Scientists compared the drawings of the probable appearance of the bird which had been made from those few bones with the shape demonstrated by that skin and felt even more elated. It matched wonderfully; about the only thing the experts had not been able to guess was the coloration.

Specimen number two followed in 1851. It came from almost the same locality, from Secretary Island, where it had been captured by a Maori. The circumstances of this capture do not seem to have been recorded, but apparently the Maori did what the sealers had done: ate the bird and saved the skin. The skin passed through the hands of two generations of the Mantell family and ended up in the British Museum, literally alongside the first.

So far captures of Notornis had been exclusively, if unsatisfactorily, made by New Zealanders, Maori or white. But in the latter years of the 1850s foreign explorers began trying to get into the picture. An Austrian vessel, the *Novara,* in the course of a voyage round the world and to the southern seas, lasting from 1857 till 1859, landed in New Zealand ports. One of the scientists aboard was Professor

Notornis mantelli, the extinct variety of takahe from North Island of
New Zealand (redrawn from an original lithograph made for a book by
Professor Richard Owen, published 1879; when the drawing was made,
only the fossil remains from the North Island and two unskillfully taken
skins from the South Island were known)

Ferdinand von Hochstetter, a geologist by specialization, but also
greatly interested in geographical, zoological, anthropological, and
ethnographical problems. Professor von Hochstetter did what he
could, considering the circumstances and the limited time at his disposal, to obtain a Notornis. He had very little to go on, since up to
that time only the Waingongoro bones and the two skins had been
seen by scientists. Most of the skeleton and all of the intestinal organs
were still missing. Nobody could tell what the bird's habits were,
except that it was obviously either elusive or very rare, or most likely
both. Scientists did guess that the bird ate plants, but could not be
sure even about that. In spite of concentrated efforts Professor von
Hochstetter had no success in finding a takahe, though he did important work in other fields.

Nor did others do much better. Sir James Hector explored the
southwest coast of Otago Province (the second southernmost province of the South Island) in 1863 and succeeded in locating the

Maori who had caught the second specimen. The Maori did not consider the bird rare; he assured Sir James that there were plenty of them at the head of the northwest arm of Lake Te Anau, near a small lake in the valley that leads to Bligh Sound. Sir James did hear some strange noises—"a boom followed by a shrill whistle," and another exploring party confirmed this experience. But neither party found out what produced these sounds.

In 1866 the chronicler of New Zealand birds, Sir Walter Lawry Buller, received a letter from a Dr. Hector, who told him that he had come across "tracks of the takahe near Thompson Sound and the middle arm of Lake Te Anau in 1861–1862." This occurrence had not prompted the doctor's letter, however; what he really wanted to report was the experience of a Mr. Gibson. Mr. Gibson, a botanist, was a newcomer to New Zealand who, in August or September 1866, had seen a large bird near Motupipi. The bird had been only a few feet from Mr. Gibson in the tall swamp grass. The description given by him tallied in every respect with Notornis. Doctor Hector stressed two points. One was that Mr. Gibson did not know about the takahe and had never seen a picture of it. Second, Mr. Gibson *did* know the swamp hen, the *pukeho* of the Maori and *Porphyrio melanotus* of the scientists, which looks somewhat similar.

This swamp hen, which is actually distantly related to the takahe, resembles it in coloration of plumage, but has a smaller bill, somewhat longer and slenderer legs with much longer toes, and a lighter build generally. Moreover, it can fly and it is not rare. Nor is it restricted to New Zealand but occurs in New Guinea, New Caledonia, Australia, Norfolk Islands, Lord Howe Islands, both main islands of New Zealand, and on many of the small islands off New Zealand.

Two years after receiving the letter about Mr. Gibson's sighting of a takahe Sir Walter Lawry Buller had a conversation with Sir George Grey, who had been Governor of New Zealand twice (he had also been Governor of South Australia and Governor of the Cape Colony) and who later rose to be Prime Minister of New Zealand. He had been in the area of the West Coast Sounds and a party of Maori had told him that the takahe was "plentiful" in a certain valley at the head of Preservation Inlet. But Sir George Grey had not gone to that valley himself and could not claim to have seen a takahe. He only repeated what the Maori had told him and he did not doubt that they had spoken the truth.

At this time a book on extinct birds was being prepared in Eng-

land. The authors included *Notornis mantelli*. They felt sure that it
was extinct.

Some years after publication of that book, a rabbit hunter with
his dog camped in the open in the province called Otago on the South
Island, near the Mararoa River and some 9 miles away from the
southern end of Lake Te Anau. One day in December 1879 the dog
brought him a large bird, still alive, still struggling. The rabbit hunter
killed it and hung it up on the ridgepole of his tent. It so happened
that the station manager, a Mr. J. Connor, visited the rabbit hunter's
camp the following day. He was given the dead bird, which he immediately suspected of being a takahe. He took it to the station,
skinned it carefully, and boiled the flesh off the bones, saving every
bone. It was the first complete skeleton of Notornis to arrive in
London.

There follows a financial interlude.

The third takahe was auctioned off in London. A representative of
the British Museum was present and carried instructions in his head
allowing him to bid as much as 100 pounds sterling for it. A representative of the Dresden Museum was present too, with instructions
to go as high as necessary. Following orders, the man from the British
Museum dropped out when the price of 100 pounds was reached; the
man from Dresden bid another 5 pounds and returned home in smug
triumph. In Dresden they went over their loot virtually with a micro-
scope and discovered that there were a number of small but definite
and pronounced differences between the living South Island form
and the North Island specimen from Waingongoro. It was a Notornis,
to be sure, but a different variety. This called for a new name and the
Dresden specimen was called *Notornis hochstetteri* in honor of the
Austrian explorer.

Again year after year passed without a single takahe and again
there were voices prophesying that the specimen that had given rise
to the new and distinct name had been the last one. For a while news
was scarce and what there was, was dismal. In November 1884 a
Mr. R. Henry discovered an incomplete skeleton near the shore of
Lake Te Anau, and eight years later a Mr. A. Hamilton brought in
two almost complete skeletons from the same locality. All three
skeletons were put on exhibit in New Zealand museums and there
was, needless to say, some faint teeth-gnashing that they were only
skeletons. It seemed as if New Zealand would be left without a

stuffed specimen, the few existing ones having been shipped off to Europe before there were any local museums.

At about this point another Austrian enters into the picture, one Andreas Reischek. Reischek was deeply impressed with New Zealand, but in a way which, in view of subsequent developments, appears more than mildly silly. The Maori were a dying race which would not exist much longer. The natural beauty of the islands would soon be ruined, sacrificed to British commercialism. The strange fauna and flora were doomed to extinction. Whatever knowledge could still be gathered in New Zealand had to be gathered at once before it was too late. One has to admit that he actively helped to gather such knowledge; he became one of the most tireless explorers of New Zealand, and wrote a book called *Sterbende Welt* (*Dying World*).

Andreas Reischek spent more than a decade, on and off, hunting for takahe, but never did get to see one, and probably died in the belief that the bird was extinct. We now know why he failed; he stayed too far north. The place where he could have found the elusive bird was precisely the place the natives had pointed out to Sir James Hector, the shores of Lake Te Anau.

I mentioned that the New Zealanders had been made quite unhappy by the fact that all three specimens of their rarest bird had left their country for places of honor in European museums. But they did get a specimen at long last, again by accident. One Mr. Ross was walking along the shore of the Middle Fiord, Lake Te Anau, in the evening hours of August 7, 1898, when his dog suddenly darted off into the bush and returned with a takahe, still feebly struggling. The bird died soon after, but fortunately Mr. Ross recognized it at once. He and his brother rowed the dead bird to the southern end of Lake Te Anau—a trip of some 25 miles—and sent it to Invercargill. This time not only skeleton and skin but even the internal organs could be salvaged, and the bird was bought by the New Zealand government for 250 pounds sterling. The skin was mounted and is on exhibit in the Dunedin Museum. And there the matter rested for another half-century.

Because no other takahe came to light during all the years that followed, most writers began to conclude the Notornis chapter of their books with the statement, "quite rare, possibly extinct," or something similar indicating that the author refrained from saying "extinct" only because that fact was after all not proved. Only the incurable

type of optimist might mutter that the bird had been believed to be
extinct several times before. Rumors about footprints in snow came
in from time to time, but they were not too definite. Such Maori as
claimed to know anything about takahe—very few of them now—
also claimed that the bird lived high up in the mountains and came
down to the lake shore only rarely.

Whether that was correct or not, one could always point out that
Lake Te Anau was no longer remote territory, nothing like, say, the

The takahe of the South Island

interior of Greenland or the Australian Central Desert. I have in
front of me a beautifully illustrated travel booklet, issued by the New
Zealand Government Tourist Department, entitled "Milford Sound."
Milford Sound is the northernmost of the fiords of southwest New
Zealand and the booklet recommends an especially scenic route for
a trip to it. The tourist first goes to Lumsden, either by rail from
Dunedin on the east coast (136 miles) or from Invercargill on the
south shore (50 miles); from there a bus brings him to the Te Anau

Hotel. Then a trip of 40 miles on Lake Te Anau itself—it is stressed that the ship *Tawera* is a modern oil burner which requires about three and one-half hours for the trip—brings you to Glade House, situated at the northernmost point of Lake Te Anau. From there you start out, on foot, along a highly picturesque route called "Milford Track," to the Milford Hotel on Milford Sound.

The booklet indicates that the *Tawera* must keep rather close to the eastern shore of Lake Te Anau. For its whole trip, the place where the takahe is still very much alive, if hiding in the dense underbrush, is theoretically in sight. It probably is below the horizon most of the time, but it is around the western arm of that lake which is really a drowned valley between the mountains.

It was in 1947 that Dr. Geoffrey B. Orbell, a physician of Invercargill, struck out into the dense forest of the west shore of Lake Te Anau. On the east shore the forest had been felled and grazing land created. The west shore is untouched. Doctor Orbell worked his way up the mountains to an altitude of almost 3000 feet. That the many stories he had heard earlier were not completely without foundation became clear on that first trip. There was a small lake about which frontiersmen had told but which was not on any map. Doctor Orbell and his party heard strange bird noises, but also found something more definite: a print of a bird's foot in mud. Whether this was actually a footprint of takahe could not be stated definitely at that time, but later it was found to be.

The discoveries of the uncharted lake and the footprint were enough encouragement for Dr. Orbell; he returned to the scene during the southern spring of 1948, in November. He was well equipped with cameras, even a movie camera with color film, and with nets for catching the birds. A takahe was seen and one of the members of the small expedition threw a net. It caught not one but two takahes. The birds were tied to a stake, photographed, and then released, and Dr. Orbell and his party returned to Invercargill to tell the tale and to show their pictures.

In January 1949 Dr. Orbell went back again, this time setting up camp in what he now knew to be the takahe country. The expedition was a great success. Not only did it establish that the takahe is a complete vegetarian, as had been suspected earlier, but it also found nests. Naturally these nests are situated on the ground since the heavy bird cannot fly. Some thirty nests were examined. It seems that a takahe pair raises only one chick every year—detail still remains to be investigated. The chicks show none of the gaudy coloration of their parents but are simply black. About a dozen adult birds were actually seen by the party and indications were that there are two colonies in two adjacent valleys. The two colonies together are believed to comprise between 50 and 100 birds. Of course there may be more colonies in the area.

When Dr. Orbell's third expedition returned, the New Zealand government took steps. The area actually investigated by Dr. Orbell

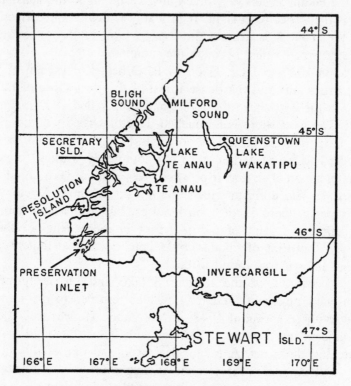

The takahe country

and found to harbor "lost colonies" of takahe is only about 500 acres in extent; the government declared an area totaling 400,000 acres a closed sanctuary for takahe. This area includes all the spots where takahe *may* exist. In addition, a campaign is in progress against predatory animals which may reduce the numbers of the rare bird. The New Zealanders are determined to preserve the bird which was several times thought to be extinct. And judging by what they have done for Hatteria they are likely to succeed.

Walter Mantell, you remember, had gone to New Zealand with the moa uppermost in his mind but had been successful mainly as the discoverer of the takahe. And while pursuing the takahe he ran across another mystery, one that has not been solved. This mystery entered into the annals of science in the most dignified and respectable manner possible. In the evening of November 12, 1850, there was a meeting of the Royal Zoological Society of London. The main paper that had been announced was to be read by Dr. Gideon Algernon Mantell and it concerned Notornis.

The important information was that his son had succeeded in buying the skin of a recently killed Notornis, so that one had to conclude that the bird still existed. But Dr. Mantell had more news to tell:

It may not be irrelevant to add, that in the course of Mr. Walter Mantell's journey from Banks' Peninsula along the coast to Otago, he learnt from the natives that they believed there still existed in that country the only indigenous terrestrial quadruped, except a species of rat, which there are reasonable grounds for concluding New Zealand ever possessed. While encamping at Arowenua in the district of Timaru, the Maoris assured him that about ten miles inland there was a quadruped which they called Kaureke, and that it was formerly abundant, and often kept by their ancestors in a domestic state as a pet animal. It was described as about two feet in length, with coarse grisly hair; and must have more nearly resembled the Otter or Badger than the Beaver or the Ornithorhynchus [platypus], which the first accounts seemed to suggest as the probable type. The offer of a liberal reward induced some of the Maoris to start for the interior of the country where the Kaureke was supposed to be located, but they returned without having obtained the slightest trace of the existence of such an animal; my son, however, expresses his belief in the native accounts, and that if the creature no longer exists, its extermination is of a very recent date.

This is the earliest printed statement in which the mysterious mammal is even mentioned. An earlier writer on New Zealand's natural history, Ernest Dieffenbach, M.D., the naturalist of the New Zealand Company, had stated in his book *Travels in New Zealand* (London, 1843) that "no terrestrial beast has been found wild in these Islands, nor do any appear to be known to the natives." The fact is that the only native mammals of New Zealand are two bats. One of them is closely related to an Australian form; the other is typical for New Zealand only. Locally they are distinguished as the long-tailed and the short-tailed bat, with the explanation that the long-tailed bat has short ears while the short-tailed bat is long-eared.

The Maoris told that when they arrived in Ao-tea-roa ("long white cloud" or else "long shining land"—their name for New Zealand) from Hawa-iki (their original home, most probably the island of Raiatea, about 120 miles to the northwest of Tahiti) in the canoes *Tainui, Takitimu, Te Arawa, Mata-atua, Kurhaupo,* and *Tokomaru,* they brought with them a dog which they kept as livestock. The main wave of the Maori migration to New Zealand must have been around 1350 A.D., but the dog, now extinct, was still mentioned by Captain James Cook as one of the two mammals he saw. The other was a black rat which was rare even then—the Maoris ate it too.

I have to digress from Mantell's unknown "indigenous terrestrial quadruped" for a moment to say a little more about that black rat. No doubt it was there and it even received a scientific name, *Mus maorium,* or Maori rat. The Maori name for it was *kiore.* But one expert claimed in around 1860 that he could not find any difference between the Maori rat and the common Pacific species of rat, *Mus exulans.* And Alfred Russel Wallace points out in his once-famous book *Island Life* (London, 1892) that whenever a man caught a black rat and the Maori jubilantly declared that this was a true kiore (in the meantime other European rats had arrived by ships from England, much against the wishes of everybody) it turned out to be either a European black rat or else an Australian rat which had arrived as a stowaway on ships from Australia.

The story of Mantell's unknown quadruped moved on to include several other names. There was an explorer who is now mentioned in most books as Sir Julius von Haast, but he was born in Bonn on the Rhine (where his father was Burgomaster) as Johann Franz Julius von Haast. And he did not see New Zealand until he was thirty-six, when he arrived in Auckland on December 21, 1858. He became famous as a geologist; he discovered an important pass through the mountains of the South Island which still bears his name; he found coal and gold and founded the Philosophical Institute of Canterbury, New Zealand. But he kept telling friends that because of his beautiful and strong voice, he had wanted to become an opera singer—presumably his dignified father had something to say about that ambition—and that he had played the violin in the symphony orchestra of Düsseldorf under the baton of Felix Mendelssohn.

Sir Julius learned a new name for the unknown mammal. The

Maoris called it *waitoreke,* or *waitoreki,* or *waitoteke.* I haven't been able to find out anywhere whether this name can be translated, but I found in Dieffenbach's book a glossary of Maori words and learned that *waipa* means river, *waikeri* means swamp or a rivulet, *wairere* means waterfall, *waikare* means clear water, and *waitangi* (a place name) means noisy water. *Waitoreke* obviously has something to do with water; maybe it just means "lives in water," or something like that.

When Ferdinand von Hochstetter came to New Zealand he met and made friends with Dr. Julius von Haast. Two years after his return to Austria von Hochstetter started to assemble his notes on New Zealand for a book and asked von Haast whether anything new could be reported. The reply was printed in his book in a footnote.

My friend Haast writes to me about the Waitoreki under the date of the 6th of June 1861 as follows: "3500 feet above sea level I saw at the upper Ashburton River (South Island, Province of Canterbury), in an area where no human foot ever walked before me, its tracks on many occasions. The tracks resemble those of our European otter but are somewhat smaller. The animal itself was seen by two gentlemen who own a sheep ranch at the shore of Lake Heron in the neighborhood of the Ashburton River at an elevation of 2100 feet above sea level. They describe the animal of being of a dark brown color, of the same size as a large rabbit. They hit it with a whip. It emitted a whistling sound and disappeared quickly in the water among the reeds."

That footnote was the sum total that Dr. von Hochstetter (or rather Dr. von Haast) could report. Even at a later date, during the official Inaugural Address at the occasion of the founding of the Philosophical Institute of Canterbury, Sir Julius could not claim ever to have seen the animal. But he repeated that he had seen its tracks many times.

Meanwhile the animal had made its appearance in another footnote. In 1855 a London publishing house printed a book by the Reverend Richard Taylor, entitled *Te Ika A Maui, Or, New Zealand and Its Inhabitants.* The footnote, on page 394, reads in full:

A man named Seymour, of Otaki, stated that he had repeatedly seen an animal in the Middle Island, near Dusky Bay, on the south-west coast, which he called a musk-rat, from the strong smell it emitted. He said, its tail was thick, and resembled the ripe *pirori,* the fruit of the *kie-kie,* which is not unlike in appearance to the tail of a beaver. This account was corroborated by Tamihana te Rauparaha, who spoke of it as being more than double the size of the Norway rat, and as having a large flat tail. A man named Tom Crib, who had been engaged in whaling and sealing in the neighborhood of Dusky Bay for more than twenty-five years, said he had not himself seen the beaver, but had several times met with their habitations, and had been surprised by seeing little streams dammed up, and houses like bee-hives erected on one side, having two entrances, one from above and the other below the dam. One of the Camerons, who lived at Kaiwarawara, when the settlers first came to Wellington, stated that he saw one of these large rats and pursued it, but it took to the water, and dived out of sight.

To clear up possible questions in the reader's mind, the term Norway rat refers to the common brown European rat; the name Middle Island results from the fact that for some time the present Stewart Island was called South Island, which naturally made the present South Island the Middle Island.

As time went on reports about the waitoreke became rarer and rarer (in other words, there weren't any) and books about New Zealand or about natural history followed the style established by Ferdinand von Hochstetter: the waitoreke began to dwell exclusively in footnotes. But naturalists would have given almost anything to find out whether it also lived in New Zealand rivers and lakes. New Zealand had preserved the kiwi and the tuatara; *if* New Zealand also had an indigenous mammal it was bound to be unusual and old, probably a representative of the earliest mammals. It was certainly worth looking for.

The area where it might be found could be reasonably well localized. All the reports, with a single and somewhat doubtful exception, had come from the South Island, more specifically the southern half of the South Island. Walter Mantell heard his story on the east coast to the south of Banks' peninsula. Sir Julius von Haast had seen his tracks in the interior just as far to the south. And Lake Heron—it is a small lake about 1½ miles long, not entered on most maps—can be said to be almost precisely the center of South Island. Dusky Bay, of course, is near the southern end.

Strangely enough, the very first report—if it is one—also came from Dusky Bay. Again I have to quote a footnote, this time from Wallace's *Island Life:*

The animal described by Captain Cook as having been seen at Pickersgill Harbour in Dusky Bay (Cook's 2nd Voyage, Vol. I, p. 98) may have been the same creature. He says: "A four-footed animal was seen by three or four of our people, but as no two gave the same description of it, I cannot say what kind it is. All, however, agreed that it was about the size of a cat, with short legs, and of a mouse color. One of the seamen, and he who had the best view of it, said it had a bushy tail, and was the most like a jackal of any animal he knew." It is suggestive that, so far as the points in which "all agreed"—the size and the dark color—this description would answer well to the animal so recently seen [this is in reference to von Haast's Lake Heron story] while the "short legs" correspond to the otter-like tracks, and the thick tail of an otterlike animal may well have appeared "bushy" when the fur was dry. It has been suggested that it was only one of the native dogs; but as none of those who saw it took it for a dog, and the points on which they all agreed are not dog-like, we can hardly accept this explanation. . . .

Sorry, but this ends the story. The waitoreke has not been found and the most recent remark about it that I could find occurs in *The New Zealand Nature Book* by W. Martin (Auckland, New Zealand, 1930)—for once *not* in a footnote: "Other than the two species of bats New Zealand has no land mammals whatsoever, unless there be more truth than is generally believed in the persistent reports of a native otter."

But now for the moas, the hunt for which led to takahe and via takahe to the mysterious and still unknown mammal. Like the kiwi and Hatteria, the moas came to be known so gradually that it is almost impossible to pin down a definite date. Moreover later writers have, either by design or by carelessness, introduced a number of fables which are still repeated in current books.

There is, for example, that one definite date, the year 1839, when the first moa bone was placed into the hands of a scientist. The scientist was Professor Richard Owen but a legend grew up as to how the bone got to him. The most customary version is that "an illiterate sailor" brought the bone to Owen's house, arriving at a time when the professor happened not to be home. The sailor then left the bone, wrapped in a rag, with the professor's housekeeper. When Owen returned home and found the bone he realized quickly that he had made a great discovery and publicly offered a reward for the sailor who had brought it to him. But the reward was never claimed; the sailor had disappeared.

That may have been the type of story which delighted Victorian England; it has the minor drawback that practically none of it is true. The bone did exist—both ends broken off—but it was brought to England by the surgeon Dr. John Rule, and Dr. Rule did see Professor Owen. In fact, Owen thought, at first glance, that the bone was an

The moa bone brought to Professor Richard Owen by Dr. Rule

ordinary, if old, soup bone. Only at Dr. Rule's insistence did he take it with him to the museum to see what kind of animal might have grown it. When he saw that it most nearly matched the leg bone of an ostrich except for being much larger and more massive, Owen began to hit his stride. His colleagues with whom he discussed the discovery advised him to keep quiet until more proof was available. But Owen felt sure of himself. He had a bone belonging to a bird built like an ostrich, though much larger and heavier, and that bone was not even fossil. Hence there should be at least other remains, if not living birds, on New Zealand. And Owen reasoned that the non-scientists actually in New Zealand would not know what to look for unless a scientist told them. Therefore he ordered five hundred reprints of his announcement, to be sent to New Zealand to shipping agents, traders, and missionaries so that they might supply him with more material. As it happened, the reprints were still on the high seas when Professor Owen did get more material, a large crate full of moa bones.

Even at the time Walter Mantell went to New Zealand to collect for his father and incidentally for Professor Owen there was a nasty discussion going on about the question of who had "discovered" the moas. As a rule such arguments can be fairly easily sorted out in retrospect after enough time has passed, but the rule does not apply too well in this case.

The first report on New Zealand is of course the one by Captain Cook. Several writers later claimed that when Cook's ship dropped anchor offshore a gigantic bird was standing at the shore, which disappeared in the forest when a boat approached. Well, Captain Cook said no such thing. His report contains no mention of anything that might be taken to mean the moas, either directly or indirectly, which is to say neither he nor his ship's company saw a moa or were even told about one. In fact, the absolute silence of Cook's journal on the subject has later been interpreted as proof that the moas no longer existed when Cook arrived in New Zealand.

Beginning about 1800 more people—most of them Englishmen—

began to travel to New Zealand and to write books about their travels. Strangely enough none of the first six books even mentions the moas. The first one to do so (but without using the name) is one published in London in 1838, written by a trader named Joel S. Polack. Trader Polack suffered shipwreck at the North Island in 1831 and spent the next six years on the island. It seems that he had little difficulty in getting along with the Maori and he told in his book that he had been shown very large bones. He then added that the animals the large bones came from were still alive on the South Island. Unfortunately he failed to make clear what made him say so. Did the Maori tell him? Or did he draw this conclusion himself?

Trader Polack's book would be a simple and clear-cut case under ordinary circumstances, but circumstances involving moas never seem to be ordinary. A missionary in New Zealand, the Reverend William Colenso, reached for a goosequill and let it be known that the book must be a hoax. Trader Polack could not have written it because he could not write. Nor could Polack have seen any moa bones because "if so, he surely would have grabbed them." The facts of the case were that he, the Reverend William Colenso, was the first white man to have discovered the existence of the moas.

I don't know what inspired Colenso's dislike for Polack; certainly a book on New Zealand, printed in London in 1838, with Joel S. Polack's name on the title page, exists. The New York Public Library has a copy and I have read it myself. Nor can I imagine that Polack could follow his profession of a trader without being able to write. It is of course possible that he could not or did not write in English and that the original manuscript of the book was in Yiddish or in Russian, but the book itself does not state that it was translated from another language. As for the snide remark that Polack would have "grabbed" the moa bones if he had seen any one can only ask "why?" Polack traded with people who would not consider old bones worth having. His trade goods probably came from China or via China, and the Chinese merchants were not likely to be interested either. I think one can safely assume that Trader Polack knew what could be traded.

The Reverend Mr. Colenso who so loudly stated that he was the first white man to report on the moas heard about them for the first time from Maori, who told him that a lone and old moa had established a reign of terror on and around the mountain Whakapunake. He thought this was just a legend, which is what it probably was. But then he learned about moas from other sources and during the Southern Hemisphere summer of 1841–42 he decided to investigate. He never made the trip because, as he said, he could not find a single native who was brave enough to act as a guide. A few years later the mountain was investigated for a surviving moa without positive result; the search was made by Maori who had become Christians. The man whose teachings had converted them was another one of the early missionaries, the Reverend Mr. William Williams.

As a collector of moa bones Mr. Williams was more successful than anybody else, and the crate which arrived in London while Professor Owen's reports were on their way to assist shipping agents and missionaries had been the result of his efforts. The fate that pursues everything connected with moas caused a British customs official to remember a statute which for some reason prohibited the importation of bones. As a result the customs official tangled with the Royal Society, the Royal Zoological Society, and last but not least Professor Owen himself. The official lost, and the outcome was a magnificent report by Owen on the extinct birds of New Zealand.

The next problem was when the moas had become extinct—and, as a kind of afterthought, whether they were extinct. Just what could the Maori tell about this?

One important tale originated with Governor FitzRoy. In 1844 he met an old Maori chief named Haumatangi. The old man proudly told the governor that in his boyhood he had seen Captain Cook. This referred to Cook's voyage of 1773 and since Haumatangi was about eighty-five he must have been a boy of about fourteen when Cook arrived. This sounded credible enough. Haumatangi then added that the last moa in his province had been seen two years before that. This statement, of course, had to be taken at face value.

Another story which began to circulate a little later had it that another aged Maori chieftain, Kawana Paipai, had actually taken part in a moa hunt as a boy. The date figured out to be 1798 or 1799. Two or three other Maori, questioned around the middle of the nineteenth century, recalled that their grandfathers had told them that they had still hunted moas. They even went into detail, telling that the moas, when attacked, would stand on one leg to kick with the other one, and that the hunting trick consisted of having several men keeping the moa ready to fight while another man sneaked up from behind with a long and heavy pole to hit the leg on which the bird was standing.

In 1858 Ferdinand von Hochstetter got to New Zealand. He listened to all the tales, which were reported to him mostly by Julius von Haast. Of course Hochstetter had read several of the early travel reports on New Zealand and was fully aware of the fact that cannibalism was, or had been, practiced extensively and continually among the Maori. He then evolved a theory which went into all the books for the next seventy years. The Maori had arrived in a mass migration —this event is now referred to by New Zealanders as "The Fleet"— at which time the islands had been full of large moas. The Maori naturally hunted them for food, the moas being the largest animals on the islands. Apparently their rate of reproduction was slow, von Hochstetter reasoned, and the hunting disturbed the balance. The moas became extinct and after they were gone the largest animal on New Zealand was Man. Cannibalism was the logical consequence.

Somebody less well known than von Hochstetter—in fact I have not been able to find out who said it first—advanced the opposing theory that the Maori of The Fleet might have been just in time to see the last of the moas die, if they happened to land at the right spot.

For the rest of the nineteenth century everything written and printed about the moas in New Zealand was written not to establish facts but to defend one or the other of these two schools of thought. Those who said that the moas died out very early had quite a number of ingenious arguments. So and so many Maori (say during the period from 1840 to 1860), when they were shown bones, did not know that the bones had belonged to birds. The word "moa" itself was used to mean "stone" or a raised small piece of land, like a flower bed. There were only a very few proverbs and sayings in which the moas were mentioned, usually figures of speech of the type "gone like the moa." These proverbs all seemed to be especially old proverbs. As regards statements that "my grandfather told me, etc.," it was pointed out that the Maori language made no distinction between the words "grandfather" and "ancestor." As for old Haumatangi, he had probably just embellished on his memories of long ago. And Kawana Paipai could be disposed of in two ways. One was to say that he also had described battles which were obviously invented. The other was to say that he had never made the statement about the moa hunt; this was based on the fact that there were at least three white witnesses present on that occasion and only one of the three repeated it later.

In the meantime places where moas had been slaughtered and cooked were found; there could be absolutely no doubt that humans and moas had lived together at one time. The problem was to say when. Some scientists assumed a different native population, not only pre-Fleet but pre-Maori, which must have been the moa hunters. Other scientists said that the moa hunters did not have to belong to a culture other than Maori; they had been Maori of an earlier cultural level. This idea was contradicted most strongly by the Maori themselves. They refused to believe that their ancestors could ever have changed and imagined the sailors of The Fleet to have been precisely like their grandfathers of about 1800, though of course the Maori, like everybody else, did change considerably through the centuries.

Actually everybody seems to be right, depending on where you look. A number of moa-hunter campsites are indubitably Maori. Some others are almost certainly not Maori of any cultural level; there seem to have been earlier castaways who settled on New Zealand but were not organized immigrants like the Maori of The Fleet.

It is a deplorable fact that the moa hunters failed to draw pictures which would help us to visualize their victims. Our knowledge of the appearance of the moas is therefore based mainly on their bones, which have been found on all three islands. Specifically in the case of birds the skeleton is a rather insufficient guide to probable appearance; imagine what pictures of Archaeopteryx we would draw if we had only found its skeleton without any feathers. It is true that a few moa feathers are known, but to what species they belonged is uncertain. Eggshells, of which a surprisingly large number could be restored, pose the same problem; their size is no indication of the size of the bird that laid them. As has been mentioned, the eggs of the little kiwi are incredibly large. On the other hand, the eggs of the cassowary are much smaller than one would expect.

Footprints are known too, of both the larger and the smaller species. The small ones show a stride of not quite 20 inches, while the large ones show a stride of over 30 inches. The large ones look surprisingly like some dinosaur footprints of a much earlier date. But there is a definite correlation between size of print and length of stride and the size of the bird, and for this reason at least some of the footprints can be tentatively ascribed to a species.

The moas of the past are now subdivided into five different genera, each with several species. It should be said at the outset that some of the species are doubtful, since they are based on only a few remains. It is quite possible that we have in our catalogues a few more species than existed in reality; with other extinct animals male and female have sometimes been classified as two different species if they differed considerably in size.

The following list, by genera, is to be considered tentative:

Dinornis. The moas belonging to this genus were the tallest of the New Zealand moas, their heads towering more than 12 feet above the ground. Largest of the six species was *Dinornis maximus.* All species of the genus Dinornis were rather light-boned.

Euryapteryx. The moas of this genus were squat and heavy but not tall, their heads being between 5 and 6 feet above the ground. They must have been very numerous at certain times. There are five well-defined species, a sixth one is uncertain.

Megalapteryx. Two species from the South Island only. They are large for birds, but small for moas, being only a little more than 3 feet tall. As the name (Greek *megas,* meaning large, plus *apteryx*) indicates, they might also be taken for giant kiwis.

Emeus. Three recognized species, with a fourth one uncertain, standing about 4 feet tall.

Anomalapteryx. Five species, four of them very early (bones are true fossils); about the same size as Megalapteryx. One species grew 7 feet tall; it is the most recent of this genus.

This list of moas must not be misunderstood. At no time could one have found all of them alive on New Zealand; the best one might expect for a specific time would have been, say, ten different species. At a guess this maximum population of moas occurred at the time of the Homeric heroes, say around 1000 B.C.

The decline of the moas is not easy to understand, but all indications are that even if nobody had come to the islands prior to Captain Cook they would be fairly rare by now. They probably bred slowly, their inability to fly must have been a severe handicap in many situations, and they were exceptionally stupid. The brain of a 6-foot moa was the same size as that of a turkey, and turkeys are not noted for intelligence either.

Many moa remains show clearly that the birds drowned in fresh water, presumably mostly in swamps. On the North Island many perished at one time because of forest fires started by volcanic eruptions. There is also some evidence of disease. Specialists of New Zealand's prehistory believe that the main reason for the decline was a rather minor climatic change which diminished the open plains and increased the forest and swamp areas.

In attempting to date the moas, scientists had the advantage of a new technique, known as the carbon-14, or C-14, or radiocarbon method. The whole problem of dating fossils has been made easier in the last thirty years as a result of the discovery that the heavy elements are not stable. Uranium, for example, very slowly "decays" into lead. The rate at which this takes place is known too. In the case of uranium (the common form, the isotope of the atomic weight 238, or uranium-238), half of the atoms present at a given date will have decayed after 4000 million years. Several heavy elements follow the same pattern: uranium-238 becomes lead-206, uranium-235 becomes lead-207, and thorium decays into lead-208. The ratios between the various radioactive isotopes and daughter isotopes permit cross checks which produce reliable figures.

This method, which enables scientists to give accurate figures for the duration of geological periods, is useful only for very long intervals of time; it does not help when the period in question is less than 10,000 years. But after the Second World War Dr. W. F. Libby (then of the University of Chicago) and his associates worked out the carbon-14 method, which is useful for comparatively short intervals.

The isotope of the atomic weight 14 of the element carbon is radioactive and occurs naturally in our atmosphere. All living things, therefore, absorb a certain amount of carbon-14. There is a natural balance; the amount of carbon-14 in the atmosphere stays fairly close to a given level, and so does the amount of carbon-14 in the living bodies of animals and plants. But when the animal dies this amount begins to change. With the moment of death the animal ceases to take in any more carbon-14. The carbon-14 in its body, being radioactive, slowly changes into other atoms which are no longer radioactive. In other words, the amount of carbon-14 in organic matter starts on a downward curve with the moment of death, and to know when the animal, or the tree, died, it is only necessary to establish how much carbon-14 is left.

When this method was under development the researchers first dated materials of known age: wood from tombs which contained statements of when they had been built; beams from houses known to have been constructed in such and such a year. After the amount of radiocarbon left after a certain time was established, the researchers could go on to date materials of unknown age.

There are, however, a few drawbacks to this method. To begin with, only things that were once alive can be dated. If an archaeolologist

Size and probable appear-
ance of a large moa of the
Dinornis type

finds an ancient finger ring of gold or silver he still has to guess, from
the surroundings, from its style, and so forth, when it was probably
made. If he should find a stone-tipped arrow he can date the arrow
shaft, but not the tip. Likewise, in the case of a bone-handled knife,
the handle can be dated, but not the blade.

The drawback of being restricted to things which once were alive
is in the nature of things. Other drawbacks have their roots in the
technique of dating. To begin with, the sample used for dating must
not be too small. At first the minimum weight had to be over 2 ounces,
but now the experts can date smaller samples. Second, and more
important, the sample to be dated is destroyed in the process. This
of course means that nothing rare can be dated; curators like to hang
on to rarities. Finally, there is an upper limit; once a sample has

reached an age at which there is no radiocarbon left at all, one can only say that it must be older than the limit.

This age limit is, of course, tied up with the so-called half-life of carbon-14, the time required for half the atoms to cease being radiocarbon. This half-life was determined by Dr. Libby to be 5568 years, with an uncertainty of 30 years either way. After 5568 years half of the radiocarbon atoms are gone; after about 11,130 years only one quarter of the original number of radiocarbon atoms is left; and so forth. Originally the limit of dating was about 25,000 years; by the end of that time so few radiocarbon atoms are left that the figures derived from the dating attempt became highly uncertain and unreliable. A later refinement of the technique added nearly 15,000 years to that figure, so that radiocarbon dating up to nearly 40,000 years is now possible.

Because the radiocarbon method is only about a decade old and because the number of laboratories equipped to carry out such work is still small, thousands and thousands of samples which scientists would gladly surrender for the sake of learning their ages have not been used yet. However, in the case of the moas, a specimen has been used. One of the drowned moas had a crop full of food (plants) which was fairly intact and could be sacrificed for the purpose. The test showed that the bird was drowned 670 years ago or in about 1300 A.D.

New Zealand archaeologists were not at all pleased with this result; Roger Duff, the director of the Canterbury Museum, stated that he was shocked. The reason for this strange reaction was that the drowned moa was of the Dinornis type, and Duff and his party had always maintained that the Dinornis moas had become extinct very early and that the Maori of The Fleet could only have met the late and heavy-boned Euryapteryx type. Now carbon-14 said that this particular Dinornis drowned just about the time of The Fleet.

If only radiocarbon dating did not destroy the specimen it should be applied to two Maori-made artifacts of moa skin and moa feathers. The moa was a Megalapteryx (South Island), and Roger Duff dates the artifacts as having been made during the seventeenth and eighteenth centuries respectively. This sounds much too old; New Zealand does not have a dry, hot climate that will preserve organic remains for centuries.

These artifacts seem to have come from the southern end of the South Island, the same place from which the last moa hunt is reported. That story occupies one sentence in Volume II of Sir Walter

Lawry Buller's *History of the Birds of New Zealand,* published in London in 1888. The sentence reads: "Sir George Grey tells me that in 1868 he was at Preservation Inlet and saw a party of natives there who gave him a circumstantial account of the recent killing of a small Moa, describing with much spirit its capture out of a drove of six or seven."

Preservation Inlet leads to the takahe country, now strongly protected.

Any Megalapteryx still hiding there too?

CHAPTER 16

The Island of the Upas Tree

SOMETIMES when I find the leisure just to sit and think I wonder what a different course history might have taken if the European winters were not as long as they are—or at least not as dreary. Naturally I am not thinking of the present, with comfortably heated houses, such home entertainment as radio, record players, and television, and means of transportation that can operate in almost any weather.

I have in mind the times when the means of heating a house was an open wood fire which did its job so poorly that heavy robes had to be worn indoors and when the means of transportation consisted of two human feet or the four hoofs of a horse. If the snow was more than a yard deep, and especially if it was freshly fallen, these means of transportation failed to work. As a result one had to stay indoors for days and sometimes weeks on end, and lucky and happy was the man who could read.

And what would he read, if he had a choice? He could take his copy of Pliny and read about the marvels of the East, of India where the trees were big enough to shelter a whole regiment of cavalry. Of the East where the grass grew as tall as a house. While the crows outside were busily fighting he would read of brightly plumaged birds singing in trees which never shed their leaves. While gnawing a piece of heavy bread he would read about fabulous fruit growing on distant islands. While the cold north wind screamed around his house he would read about the scent emanating from the Spice Islands.

I think the winters of northern Europe should receive credit for having preserved Pliny's *Natural History*. Of course, they can also be blamed for having contributed to the enormous distribution of such books as that of Sir John de Mandeville.

As more and more truthful—the term has to be considered as some-

306

what relative—travel reports became available, the reader who had stayed home could do some checking. Generally speaking, the travel tales bore out what the classical authors had said. But they also added new facts and new concepts. There was especially one that had never been so much as hinted at by the ancients: a Tree of Death. The stories about the Tree of Death were necessarily vague, for those who would have known could no longer be alive. Strangely enough, the stories came from both ends of the world, from the Sunda Islands in the extreme East and from the equally tropical islands in the West which still all bore Spanish names.

I have the feeling—though I lack proof so far—that these stories about a tree of death not only produced pleasurable shudders for the ignorant but also delighted the philosophically minded. The Bible, as anyone could read—*if* he could read—in the Book of Genesis spoke of a Tree of Life which grew in the Garden of Eden. In fact, Adam and Eve, after they had eaten from the Tree of Knowledge, were banished from the Garden so that they might not eat from the Tree of Life. But the philosophically minded bookworms knew that everything in Nature had its opposite. Light opposed darkness: material things were either hot or cold, dry or wet. The lion was the king of the beasts, but there also was the awful basilisk which lived underground and could kill with a glance. A Tree of Death, reported to exist in the vast distance, almost seemed a philosophical necessity after the statement in the Bible that the Tree of Life had grown in Paradise and presumably still grew there, even though nobody could tell to which place Paradise had been removed by the Lord.

So nobody doubted the stories of the deathly tree, whether they came from the East or from the West.

The one in the West was called by a variety of names that all had a similar sound—presumably the attempts of different kinds of Europeans to imitate an Indian name. The English versions are *manchineel* or *manzanillo,* the French is *mancenillier,* the German *Manzanilla*. The tree itself was described as beautiful and inviting in appearance, sometimes decorated with fine-looking fruit resembling apples. But the natives knew that it was poisonous and were not deceived by its appearance.

> If rests the traveller his weary head,
> Grim Mancinella haunts the mossy bed,
> Brews the black hebenon, and, stealing near,
> Pours the curst venom in his tortured ear.

These lines are from a long poem called *Loves of the Plants,* written in 1789,[1] by Erasmus Darwin, M.D., grandfather of Charles Darwin. The somewhat fierce and aggressive-looking Dr. Erasmus Darwin did not live long enough to see the boy baby who would later make the family's name known the world over, for Erasmus died in 1802 and Charles was not born until 1809. It is fact, however, that Erasmus Darwin's writing foreshadowed some of the thoughts which were later developed by Charles; grandfather's thoughts may have directly influenced grandson by showing that such ideas could be harbored.

While Dr. Erasmus Darwin liked to tell natural facts in a poetic form he evidently did not think that his contemporaries and potential readers had enough botanical knowledge to understand his references and allusions. Therefore *The Botanic Garden* is equipped, as proclaimed on its title page, "With Philosophical Notes," taking the physical shape of footnotes in prose which take up more space by far than the poem itself. The "philosophical note" to the lines quoted read:

Hippomane.
With the milky juice of this tree the Indians poison their arrows; the dew-drops which fall from it are so caustic as to blister the skin and produce dangerous ulcers; whence many have found their death by sleeping under its shade.

To set the facts straight right here, Dr. Darwin would have been perfectly correct if he had only put a period after the word "skin" and proceeded to the next footnote. The tree now labeled *Hippomane mancenilla,* which grows in the West Indies, does produce a poisonous juice, both in its trunk and in its fruits. The juice does cause blisters on unprotected skin and it was used by the Indians to poison their arrows. Presumably—I lack definite information on this point—it would not be advisable to eat the fruit, for a poison that is dangerous when brought into the bloodstream *and* that blisters the skin is also likely to be "not for internal use." But that a person who went to sleep in its shade did not wake up again because of the "exhalations" of "Grim Mancinella" only happened in books.

And on the opera stage!

Giacomo Meyerbeer, né in Berlin in 1791 as Jakob Liebmann Beer, first studied and performed (as a pianist) in Berlin and Vienna. Then he went to Italy, where he composed operas that sounded a good deal

[1] The *Loves of the Plants* became the second part of a book entitled *The Botanic Garden.* Its first part, *Economy of Vegetation,* was written after the *Loves,* in 1792.

as if they had been written by Rossini, and then he went to Paris, where he settled down for two decades until called back to Berlin to be the musical director of the Royal Opera. This was in 1842. Now the *Herr Generalmusikdirektor* was not only supposed to select, rehearse, and conduct operas and an occasional concert, he was also expected to compose himself. Meyerbeer had been called to Berlin not only because he was a native son, but because he had written operas in Italian and in French. Now he wrote marches and cantatas and an opera to be sung in German. In between he composed another opera for the Paris Opéra, entitled *L'Africaine*. In the last act of that opera the heroine decides to die, which she does in a decorous manner by seeking out a *mancenillier* and reposing in its shade. When the opera was first performed, in 1865, one year after Meyerbeer's death, the assembled Parisians, with a sprinkling of British and German tourists, found this a most touching and very original end. Not one of them thought to inquire whether there was such a tree and whether it grew where the libretto of the opera said it did.

Interestingly enough, the use of the story on the opera stage, with full orchestra for musical background, also marked its end. No later writer could use it without being accused of having swiped from the libretto of *L'Africaine*.

But there was still the other tree of death, the one that grew in the Far East. Upas tree was its name and it was so dreadful that the manchineel seemed a wan shadow by comparison. The upas tree owes its horrible fame mostly to one man, and strangely enough we do not really know who this one man was.

But let's pursue the story in its chronological order.

The first man I know of who mentioned the poisonous tree of Java, though not by name, was quite factual about it. He was Friar Oderich of Portenau. At the age of 32, in 1318, he embarked on a missionary journey to the Far East, from which he returned in 1330. The manuscript about his journey contains the statement: "In this land [Java] there are trees yielding meal, honey, and wine, and the most deadly poison in all the whole world. Against this poison there is but one remedy. . . ."

As I said in Chapter 3, Friar Oderich's manuscript was incorporated *in toto* by John de Mandeville in his own book, so naturally the tale of the poisonous tree appeared there too. But so far the upas tree did not receive any embellishment. John de Mandeville had only that one sentence by Oderich to go by and he acted mainly as a translator.

Oderich's statement took the following form in the Middle-English version of Mandeville:

And there ben other Trees, that beren hony, gode and swete; and other Trees that beren Venym; azenst the whiche there is no Medicyne but on [one]; and that is to taken here propre Leves, and stampe hem [them] and tempere hem with Watre, and than drynke it.

Most restrained indeed, especially if you keep in mind who wrote it. He would have done much better if only he had known about the *Epistolae* and the *Mirabilia* of his contemporary Jordanus Catalani, a French Dominican missionary and explorer. We have no idea when Jordanus Catalani was born, although we know where—in Séverac, in the vicinity of Toulouse. But since he left on his first trip to the East in 1302 he must have been around twenty years old by that time. In 1328 he was made a bishop and nominated to the see of Columbum in 1330. He must have written his book at about that time. In it he spoke of a tree growing in the Spice Islands (the Moluccas) that is virulently poisonous, and especially so when in bloom. At that time one must not approach the tree or one will surely die.

Even though the number of travelers to the Far East increased as time went on, no good description of the poison tree reached Europe. The Europeans were well aware of the fact that the arrows and other weapons of the Javanese and the inhabitants of the other Sunda Islands were often poisoned and that the poison often proved to be very effective. The natives, on the other hand, stated freely that the poison came from a tree, or, more generally, a plant. But they seem to have been silent about which plant or which tree. And if a traveler by chance caught sight of the tree which does produce the poison he did not realize that it was the source. It happens to be a beautiful tall tree with a whitish bark and very "normal"-looking foliage, without any vestige of the threatening appearance the white men indubitably expected. For centuries the reports about the tree were meager, adding various conjectures but no facts.

In the seventeenth century the English, who had meanwhile developed some interest in that area of the globe, decided that it must be possible to find out and they published suggestions that British and other travelers to the Far East pay special attention to the mystery of the poison tree. Any definite information would be gratefully received. One such call for investigation appeared in the *Philosophical Transactions* for 1666 and another in the *Enquiries for East India*.

But the first two reports which did bring some new knowledge—although it was mostly Far Eastern folklore—did not originate with English travelers. In fact, it is doubtful whether the two men who did contribute even knew about the English appeals. One of them was the German physician Engelbert Kämpfer, who lived from 1651 to 1716 and who spent much time in Japan and Siam and also on the Sunda Islands. The other was the Dutch East India Company's Oud Koopman Georgius Everhardus Rumphius (see Chapter 14).

Dr. Engelbert Kämpfer is considered one of the first modern explorers of the Far East and it is somewhat surprising that the Dutch East India Company refused him the employment he sought. Or, for that matter, that the English did not offer him a responsible position, because they were well aware of his value. One of Dr. Kämpfer's two books, the *History of Japan and Siam* was repeatedly printed in England, and in England only. But the first edition, that of 1728, appeared after Dr. Kämpfer's death.

The information about the poison tree can be found in his other book, the only one that saw print during his lifetime, that is, in 1712. A copy of the original edition is now one of the great rarities on the antiquarian book market. Its title was *Amoenitates exoticae,* which is hard to translate, the meaning being, roughly, "amusing exotic things." The chapter which begins on page 573 is devoted to Asiatic poisons of all kinds; the poison tree is just one item. Kämpfer explained that poisons came from various plants, some of them trees, but that the "true poison tree" grows only on Macassar, a name then used for the whole island of Celebes.

This tree can be reached, Kämpfer continued, only under extreme danger of life, "for you have to enter areas of the jungle which abound with wild carnivores." The collector of the poison is usually a criminal who takes with him a piece of well-aged hard bamboo, sharpened at one end. He approaches the tree with the wind, thrusts the bamboo into its bark, and waits until it has filled up with sap "to the next knot." He then pours the sap into an earthen vessel he carries with him for this purpose, leaves the jungle as fast as he can, and brings the vessel to his king, thereby assuring himself an automatic pardon for whatever crime he may have committed. "This," Kämpfer concluded, "is what the natives of Celebes told me, but who can expect unembellished truth from the mouth of an Asiatic? Certain is that the king of Macassar and the other nobles anoint their daggers and weapons with a deadly poison, but it loses in potency with time."

The other reporter, Rumphius, had much more to say, and in a way something far more definite, because he had obtained a twig and a fruit of the poison tree and had pictures of both drawn for his main work, the *Herbarium amboinense*. This book, when it finally appeared in print in Amsterdam in 1741, became a work of seven volumes in largest folio. Its great size is partly due to the fact that it is bilingual, printed in two columns with the left-hand column in Latin and the right-hand column in Dutch. The poison tree has its own chapter (No. 45) in Book III, Volume II. The Latin column is headed *Arbor Toxicaria, Ipo,* the Dutch column *Macassarsche Gift-Boom.*[2]

At no point does Rumphius claim to have seen the tree; all he had seen was that single twig. But he had been told that there were poison trees of different strengths and he assumed that they were male and female trees, the poison of the female being weaker by far. The native method of obtaining the sap is described just as it is in Kämpfer's book (but without involving condemned criminals): the man jabs a sharpened piece of bamboo into the trunk and waits for it to fill up with the sap, which Rumphius calls "bloody."

The poison is so much stronger in the male tree that one cannot approach it without having covered all exposed parts of the body with fabric. And because of the poison nothing grows under the tree, so that the soil is bare. "Under the most powerful kind you are supposed to find another sign, namely dead birds which tried to rest in the boughs of the tree, lost consciousness and dropped to the ground, dead." Rumphius tells in detail how the sap is treated; I am not quite sure whether he is still reporting tales of the natives or whether he actually watched the operation. He concludes the account with a bit of native folklore: when a good quantity of poison has been removed from a tree it is felled, because the natives believe that then all the people who are struck by weapons smeared with this sap will die too. If they left the tree alive the poison would slowly weaken and the weapons would be less deadly. The sentence Rumphius uses to conclude this paragraph is typical of the man: *"Doch ik geloove, datze dit met de weinigste boomen doen, anderzonden die al lang vermindert syn."* ("But I believe that they do that to only a very few trees, otherwise they would have become rare long ago.")

---

[2] This happens to be an especially misleading combination of words for an English-speaking person, since both words look familiar. But in Dutch, as in German, *Gift* means "poison," while the Dutch word *Boom* (in German *Baum*) means "tree."

In the normal course of events later travelers would have visited the trees themselves, observed the process of tapping, and in time produced botanical descriptions of the tree and chemical analysis of the poison. Eventually this happened, but after a fantastic interlude.

Sometime during 1783 the editor of the *London Magazine* received a manuscript on the poison tree. It came to him from a Mr. Heydinger, whom the editor of the magazine identified in print as the former owner of a German bookstore in London. According to Mr. Heydinger, he was not the author of the manuscript, but had merely translated it into English from Dutch; the author was a Dutchman named N. P. Foersch. It was stated in the article itself that Mr. Foersch had been (and presumably still was) in the services of the Dutch East India Company; from 1774 to 1776 he had been stationed at Batavia as a surgeon, and the information contained in the article had been collected at that time.

Since Mr. Heydinger can be traced to some extent—you can't very well run a bookshop and stay anonymous—but Mr. N. P. Foersch remains absolutely untraceable, one might toy with the idea that the manuscript submitted to the editor of the *London Magazine* was not a translation from the Dutch at all and that N. P. Foersch was one of the more successful inventions of Mr. Heydinger. The wording of the short editorial which introduces the article seems to hint ever so gently at this possibility. And it begins with the sentence: "This account, we must allow, appears so *marvellous,* that even the Credulous might be staggered." The editor obviously washed his hands but could not get himself to pass up the opportunity of printing the article. It appeared in the December issue for 1783, beginning on page 511. The main assertions of the piece were that the terrible tree, called Bohun-Upas, grew 27 leagues from Batavia in the interior of Java and that nobody could live within a radius of 12 to 14 miles of it. Naturally under these circumstances Mr. Foersch had not seen the tree himself, but he had spoken to many people who knew all about it and he had even succeeded in obtaining two leaves.

The astonishing report, about which more later, was reprinted as fast as physically possible—translated from the English of the *London Magazine*—in the Dutch *Allgemeene Vaderlandsche Letteroefeningen* in 1784. French and German magazines also published translations, some using the Dutch translation as their raw material. Naturally other publications in England and in Holland reprinted the stuff too, or at least published excerpts. Still, the story might have been forgotten again if Dr. Erasmus Darwin had not used it in his *Loves of the Plants*.

Erasmus Darwin's contribution to the lore of the upas tree ran as follows:

> Where seas of glass with gay reflections smile
> Round the green coasts of Java's palmy isle,
> A spacious plain extends its upland scene,   .
> Rocks rise on rocks, and fountains gush between;
> Soft zephyrs blow, eternal summers reign,
> And showers prolific bless the soil,—in vain!
> —No spicy nutmeg scents the vernal gales,
> Nor towering plantain shades the mid-day vales;
> No grassy mantle hides the sable hills,
> No flowery chaplet crowns the trickling rills;
> Nor tufted moss, nor leathery lichen creeps
> In russet tapestry on the crumbling steeps.
> —No step retreating, on the sand impress'd
> Invites the visit of a second guest;
> No refluent fin the unpeopled stream divides,
> No revolant pinion cleaves the airy tides;
> Nor handed moles, nor beaked worms return
> That mining pass the irremeable bourn.—
> Fierce in dread silence on the blasted heath
> Fell Upas sits, the Hydra-Tree of death.
> Lo, from one root, the envenom'd soil below
> A thousand vegetative serpents grow;
> In shining rays the scaly monster spreads
> O'er ten square leagues his far-diverging heads;
> Or in one trunk entwists his tangled form,
> Looks o'er the clouds, and hisses in the storm
> Steep'd in fell poison, as his sharp teeth part,
> A thousand tongues in quick vibration dart;
> Snatch the proud eagle towering over the heath,
> Or pounce the lion, as he stalks beneath;
> Or strew, as marshall'd hosts contend in vain,
> With human skeletons the whitened plain.

After a little pause to regain his breath the reader no doubt looked for and found the "philosophical note" which justified these lines.

There is a poison-tree in the island of Java, which is said by its effluvia to have depopulated the country for 12 or 14 miles round the place of its growth. It is called, in the Malayan language, Bohun-Upas; with the juice of it the most poisonous arrows are prepared; and, to gain this, the condemned criminals are sent to the tree with proper direction both to get the juice and to secure themselves from the malignant exhalations of the tree; and are pardoned if they bring back a certain quantity of the poison. But by the registers there kept, not one in four are said to return. Not only animals of all kinds, both quadrupeds, fish and birds, but all kinds of vegetables are also destroyed by the effluvia of the noxious tree; so that, in a district of 12 or 14 miles around it, the face of the earth is quite barren and rocky, intermitted only with the skeletons of men and animals, affording a scene of melancholy beyond that what poets have described or painters delineated. Two younger trees of its own species are said to grow near it.

The remaining sentence of this note, following "near it," will strike a modern reader as almost as bad as the story itself. It reads: "See *London Magazine* for 1784 or 1783." Sometime later Dr. Darwin must have found his reference because at the very end of the book the article from the *London Magazine* is reprinted in its entirety, with the exception of one paragraph which is said to be in Malayan. The "philosophical note" summarizes Mr. Foersch's article pretty well, but there are a number of alleged facts which Erasmus Darwin left out. The condemned criminals which are to gather poison from the tree are provided with leather caps with glasses, and leather gloves, and usually assemble in the house of a priest just outside the danger area. They are given a silver or tortoise-shell box which they have to fill. The priest told the Dutch surgeon that he kept book on the criminals, who were often accompanied by their families to his house. In thirty years he saw seven hundred criminals try for their pardon, of which seventy returned. When the man sets out he is instructed "to go to the tree before the wind; to go as fast as possible all the way; and to return against the wind." Mr. Foersch obtained two leaves which had fallen off the tree. He learned that it stood near a rivulet and was only of middling size, with five or six young trees of the same kind growing nearby from a ground covered with dead bodies.

When the priest was asked why God permitted such a monstrous growth, he replied—this is the paragraph which is given both in Malayan and in English in the first publication—that their holy book told them that more than a hundred years earlier the area was inhabited by a tribe strongly addicted to the sins of Sodom and Gomorrah, that Mohammed, after many years of patience, finally applied to God, and God caused the tree to grow which destroyed them all. Later a group of rebels, referred to as the Moo-rebels, fled into the area and started building their huts, knowing that nobody would follow them. Two months later all but two hundred were dead.

Mr. Foersch reasoned that one of the main aspects of the danger caused by the tree was that it grew in an area where there was never a good wind; thus the poison could accumulate. If it were windy there, he reasoned, the poison would be dispersed and only the immediate vicinity of the tree would be dangerous. While he, for obvious reasons, had not seen the tree itself, he had been an eye-witness of something almost as interesting. In 1776 it was found out that thirteen (always an unlucky number) of the Sultan's concubines had been unfaithful and they were sentenced to death. They were undressed to the navel and tied to posts. Then the executioner lanced each of the women between the breasts with a small poisoned knife. Five minutes after the lancing they all showed severe tremors and another eleven minutes later they were all dead. Mr. Foersch himself then secured a poisoned blade and tried it on three or four stray dogs, all of which died within minutes. He remarked further that "on the Macassar coast" there grew a tree called Cajoe-Upas in fair numbers, bearing "poison of the same type, but not half so violent and malignant as that of the tree of Java."

The Dutch, being closest to the scene, were the first to take action. When a copy of the issue of the *Letteroefeningen* containing the translation of Foersch's article finally arrived in Java, a local society, the *Bataviaasch Genootschap,* dispatched an ambassadorial party to the ruler, Sultan Pakoe Boewono III, asking him whether there was such a tree a comparatively short distance from Batavia or anywhere else on the island, and whether he used its poison in the reported manner to dispatch convicted criminals. The Sultan replied that he did not have the pleasure of having such a marvelous tree growing in his domain and, as far as the other question was concerned, he had a sufficient number of effective means. The Dutch were satisfied with that answer and in 1789 the *Letteroefeningen* carried a note that the *Oepas-Boom* [3] was a fable. Of course, it was added, there was a tree which produced a poison juice for arrows, but the poison could be collected easily, and nobody had ever found a dead bird which had died because it had been sitting on such a tree.

[3] In Dutch "oe" is pronounced "oo." The word "upas" (pronounced "oopas") is simply the Malay word for a vegetable poison, while an animal poison (such as that of a snake) is called *bisa* and a mineral poison *ratchoon.*

In Europe they did not quite know what to think. The issue of the Dutch magazine (not of very large circulation) which debunked the story appeared in precisely the same year that Erasmus Darwin wrote his poem. When the poem was published three years later, the appended reprint of the article by Foersch seemed to support the latter. Darwin had even appended another reprint, excerpts from a dissertation by one Johannes Aejmelaeus, prepared under the supervision of the then very famous Swedish botanist Professor Carl Peter Thunberg, a direct pupil of Linnaeus and the successor to his chair at the University of Uppsala. Aejmelaeus apparently took his cues from Rumphius: You can get near the tree if you are completely wrapped up in linen. Even then only the dried sap can be collected; if fresh sap is wanted the tree must be tapped by means of a very long bamboo pole. They try to tap close to the root because the poison is more potent there. Aejmelaeus added, probably paraphrasing Kämpfer, that "the poison loses much of its power in the time of one year and in a few years becomes totally harmless."

In France Monsieur Pierre Joseph Buch'oz, who had written little treatises with titles like *Dissertation sur le café* and *Dissertation sur le cacao* (yes, tea too!), deserted his theme of pleasant drinks for a discussion of the arrow poison of the Ipo tree. And a German, E. W. Martius, used the treatises by Aejmelaeus and Buch'oz to acquaint his compatriots with the marvels of the Sunda Island poison trees.

While *Loves of the Plants* was still selling briskly, the first completely sober and virtually complete description of the tree was being written. Its author was the French naturalist L. T. Leschenault de la Tour, who had traveled in eastern Java in 1804. After his return the *Annales du Muséum d'Histoire Naturelle* printed his story. It was a perfectly simple one. It had been no problem to have the tree identified by the natives; you only had to go where it grew, which was not at the seashore. "*Antiaris* is very large," Leschenault wrote. "I have always found it in fertile places and, owing to such fertility, surrounded by dense vegetation which is in no way harmed by its proximity." He had tapped the tree and had carried "a large quantity" of the poison back to France with him, without poisoning the whole ship or even himself. He had tested the poison on rabbits and chickens and had even made, inadvertently, an experiment with human beings:

The tree which furnished the specimens of the plant itself and the poison which I brought back with me was more than 100 feet tall and the trunk, at its base, was about 18 feet in circumference. A Javanese whom I had hired to get me some branches of the tree while it was in flower climbed up to cut them. He had scarcely climbed 25 feet when he found himself so sick that he had to come down. He was ill for several days with vertigo and nausea and vomited repeatedly. Another Javanese went to the very top of the tree and cut flowering branches for me; he was not affected at all. Later, I had a tree measuring about 4 feet around the trunk felled for me and I walked into the midst of the broken branches, getting face and hands smeared with the gum that oozed from the breaks. True, I took the precaution of washing myself at once. . . . I have seen lizards and insects on its trunk and birds perching on its boughs.

This sober report was followed by a lecture on the effects of the poison by B. C. Brodie, Esq., F.R.S., "read to the Royal Society 21st February 1811" and printed in *Philosophical Transactions,* Part 1 of 1811, stating that the poison acts by paralyzing the heart. In 1814 there followed another perfectly sober and fine report by Thomas Horsfield, entitled *Essay on the Oepas* and published by the *Genootschap* in Batavia.

Did this kill the legend created by Foersch or Heydinger and publicized by Erasmus Darwin?

Well, yes and no. In works of information the story was sharply debunked. But Darwin's poem, with all the appendixes, was still being reprinted. And poets just would not abandon the wonderful idea. In 1820 or thereabouts (the book has no date so one has to judge by its typography) a play with the title *The Law of Java; or, The Poison Tree* was printed in London. In the unlikely case that anyone should come across a copy I hereby issue fair warning.

It was much more important that, as late as 1828, the theme was again adopted by a poet, this time one of the great poets, Alexander Sergeevitch Pushkin. His poem is called *Antchár;* in Russian the name upas, which is used for translations, would sound silly—there is no proper word "upas" in Russian but it suggests an exceedingly ungrammatical way of saying that somebody pastured something, which is obviously not in keeping with the grim theme. And grim the poem is: "On the wan and arid desert, in soil baked red hot, the antchár stands like a grim watcher." It goes on to say that the tree is unique in all the universe—the standard translation has "isolated" instead of the correct "unique," because the translator had to make it rhyme—and "the Nature of the thirsting plain bore it on a day of wrath." The poem is factually wrong on every count but most impressively stated, so impressively that succeeding generations of millions of Russians knew it by heart and presumably believed it.

After Foersch and Pushkin the scientific truth about "dread upas" is necessarily anticlimactic. The only amusement one can get out of the facts is to see how they compare with the wild stories of nearly two centuries ago. The scientific name, given by Leschenault, is *Antiaris toxicaria,* and botanical handbooks say calmly that it is a very tall tree which can easily reach 150 feet; that its wood is white, spongy, and light; that the sap is sticky and thick, white when the tree is young and yellowish when it is old, and hardens quickly, turning brown in the process. "Leaves are short-stemmed, oval-shaped, and sometimes serrated and asymmetrical, upper side shiny and almost smooth with few short hairs, underside with more hairs and rough to the touch. Leaves of young trees tend to be smoother than those of old. Male flowers clustered, female flowers single. Fruit is red, containing one hard-shelled seed, fruit flesh very attractive to birds and edible!" Then the handbooks proclaim with the air of a landscape description that "in the more elevated areas of the Javanese rain forest the poisonous upas trees tower high over the luxuriant underbrush." Pushkin notwithstanding, the upas tree needs lots of moisture to thrive.

Far from being in any way unique, the upas tree has quite a number of relatives. The nearest is *Antiaris innoxia,* which is more numerous and not poisonous at all. Others, some mildly poisonous, some innocuous, are *Antiaris dubia* and *Antiaris rufa.* And a tree originally named *Lepuranda saccadora* should be called by its revised name of *Antiaris saceidora.* All of them are members of the fig family.

Only when it comes to the poison itself is there some slight resemblance between fact and fiction. The sap *is* poisonous and will kill a large animal within minutes, even if it did not strike a vulnerable spot. It has also been found to be true that sap taken from a tap close to the ground is more toxic than that from a tap 10 feet high on the trunk. After a first chemical analysis in 1824 which somehow miscarried, the chemist G. J. Mulder succeeded in 1837 in isolating the poison, which he named antiarin. It forms 6/10 of 1 per cent of the weight of fresh sap and 1.7 per cent of the weight of dried sap. The pure poison is crystalline; the crystals melt at 440 degrees Fahrenheit. The chemical formula was given by Mulder as $C_{27}H_{42}O_{10}$.

So much for detail about the tree which cannot be approached.

If any date can be given at all it would be safe to say that the bo-

The "arrow-poison tree" of Java, *Antiaris toxicaria,* the terrible upas tree
of legend

tanical legend of the terrible tree had been laid to rest by 1837, when
scientific journals had published such detail as has just been quoted.
But in just that year another side avenue in the story of the upas tree
was opened, one which suggests that "Mr. Foersch," though indubitably a liar of the first magnitude, may have been aided by some
rumors he heard in Java—provided he ever actually was there.

In that year the *Journal of the Royal Asiatic Society* published a
lecture by one Lieutenant Colonel W. H. Sykes, F.R.S., with the title
"Remarks on the Origin of the Popular Belief in the Upas or Poison
Tree of Java." Some of the features of the fantastic tale, Lieutenant
Colonel Sykes said, may have been due to a simple misunderstanding.

Java is an island full of active or only very slightly dormant volcanoes. One of the most common by-products of volcanism is carbon dioxide, a gas which, as is well known, is odorless, invisible, and heavier than air. Unless dispersed by wind, carbon dioxide can and will accumulate in depressions very much as water does. While carbon dioxide is certainly not poisonous but completely harmless to animals and people, and even beneficial to vegetation, a high accumulation of carbon dioxide can be dangerous simply because it displaces the oxygen. In such a case death can occur from what might be called "drowning" in carbon dioxide. A famous and long-known example of such a situation is the Grotto del Cane ("dog cave") in Italy, about halfway between Naples and Pozzuoli. A carbon-dioxide well situated inside this cave causes an almost pure layer of the gas to cover the bottom of the cave to a height of, say, 2 feet. There is no danger at all to people, because the air above that layer is perfectly breathable. But a small animal, such as a dog, which enters the cave, cannot reach above the carbon-dioxide layer and dies quickly of suffocation.

The same phenomenon can very easily occur on an island as highly volcanic as Java happens to be. Lieutenant Colonel Sykes stated that there actually was something like the Grotta del Cane on Java, but much larger in extent. He reported that the botanist Horsfield—himself one of the debunkers of the upas tree legend—had heard about a "poisonous valley" from the natives but did not visit it himself since the natives refused to guide him. But Colonel Sykes had received a letter from a Mr. Loudon, a land-owner on Java, who claimed to have seen the "poisonous valley" which the Javanese called Guwo-Upas. It was located some three miles from a place called Batur.[4] After some discussion Mr. Loudon and several other Englishmen residing in the vicinity made up a small party to explore Guwo-Upas. The story of the trip—which took place on July 4, 1830—describes what was very obviously a climb up an extinct volcano and into its crater, although Mr. Loudon did not say so himself. He wrote that the poisonous valley was roughly circular, with a diameter estimated at 300 yards. Vegetation extended downward into the valley almost to the bottom, and the party, somewhat awed by skeletons of animals of various kinds and even of men, which they saw below them, descended as far as they dared. They carried two dogs and several chickens with them. The birds—presumably with their wings tied—were dropped below the vegetation line at a convenient spot. They seemed to be dead

[4] I did not find such a place name on any of the maps I consulted.

a minute and a half later. Then one of the dogs was dropped. It made a few convulsive movements at first and then seemed to settle down to sleep; the observers could see it breathing deeply. The other dog ran down and then behaved very much like the first. The observers estimated that one dog lived for 7 minutes and the other for 18. The figures are estimates because they could not be certain of the moment of death and they did not dare, for obvious reasons, to go lower themselves.

Offhand, this makes a rather attractive explanation. That carbon dioxide will issue from fissures in the floor of a dead volcano is a well-known occurrence. The ringwall of the crater itself, acting as a windbreak, will permit the gas to build up to a high concentration. And animals which somehow get in would surely suffocate, especially since the inner wall of the crater may be difficult to climb. And if such a spectacle is seen by somebody who doesn't even know that carbon dioxide exists and is reported to somebody else who also has no inkling of the true cause, all kinds of stories will originate.

I have not been able to find further mention of this particular poison valley in more recent literature. It may well be that it does not exist any more: if carbon dioxide stopped issuing—in other words, if the steady supply was interrupted—such an open-air valley would clear up rather fast. But I did find a few statements about similar phenomena on Java, on a much smaller scale, to be sure. Since, in any volcanic area, there can be places where animals suddenly collapse and die from no discernible cause, carbon dioxide may well have contributed its share to the story of the Tree of Death which is so poisonous that it cannot even be approached.

CHAPTER 17

The Island of the Man-Eating Tree

Madagascar—228,000 square miles in extent—is one of the world's largest islands, ranking fourth in size after Greenland, New Guinea, and Borneo. Though now separated from Africa by the 250-mile-wide Mozambique Channel, it once obviously was a part of the African continent. Whether the land which once formed the connection is now at the bottom of the Mozambique Channel, or whether the two land masses literally drifted apart, as a smaller ice floe splits off from a bigger one, is still an undecided question. But no matter how the separation took place it must have been accompanied by considerable violence. Ancient volcanoes are numerous on Madagascar, especially in its eastern portion; warm springs still abound; and in the region of the Ankàratra mountains a full 2000 square miles are covered by ancient lava.

Madagascar is also quite unbelievable as regards its native fauna. Through the soft soil of its tropical forests crawl earthworms a full yard long and about an inch in thickness. One of their enemies is the tanrek, a small animal resembling (and related to) the European hedgehog. The tanrek, unassuming as it is in appearance, has relatively the largest mouth of any mammal, maybe because of those enormous earthworms, and absolutely the largest litters of any mammal, twenty young being about the rule—presumably because the tanrek has enemies in turn which like to eat it. Big mouth, large litters, and all, the tanrek's ancestry goes back in a straight and unbroken line to a tribe of ancient mammals which began to inhabit the earth at a time when the last of the dinosaurs were still around. Not quite so ancient but still old enough is another of Madagascar's wonder animals, the fossa or *Kryptoprokta,* a catlike animal of about the size of a fox, with a very long tail and elongated limbs. Harmless to

man—in spite of some wild stories to the contrary—the fossa represents an otherwise extinct group of ancient catlike mammals, one
which evolved in the obvious direction of the modern cats without
quite becoming cats.

But the characteristic animals of Madagascar are the lemurs, which
may be said to bear about the same relationship to the monkeys as
the fossa does to the cats. The vast majority of all the still-living species
of lemurs inhabit the trees of Madagascar, hunting insects and calling
to one another with plaintive wails. Since they are all night prowlers
they are rarely to be seen in zoological gardens, even if the garden
has some theoretically on exhibit. In size they range from that of a
small rat to that of a large cat. Weirdest of them is no doubt the aye-
aye—the name itself is weird enough. It gives the impression of a cat
with many monkey traits, or a catlike monkey; its large protruding
ears are built to catch the faintest sound made by unsuspecting insects, and one of its fingers is more than twice as long as the others,
as skinny as a living limb can be and equipped with a curved hooklike
nail for dragging insects out from under the bark of trees.

Though Madagascar's still-living indigenous animals are quite small
—the only exception being a fairly large crocodile—this is a comparatively recent development. If a shipload of Crusaders—it was at
about the time of the Crusades that Malay sailors reached the island
and began to settle it—had been blown to Madagascar in some manner they would have found some spectacular additions to the present-
day fauna. There were two or three species of hippopotamus, about
two-thirds the size of the well-known African kind; there were a small
zebu, a gigantic land tortoise, and a full dozen species of ostrich-like
flightless birds, the tallest of them, *Aepyornis,* towering high over any
living ostrich. And there was *Megalodapis,* a lemur the size of a man,
which, because of its size and weight, must have lived on the ground
and possibly moved through the night walking on its hind legs only.[1]

The flora of Madagascar is almost as strange as its fauna. The
famous "Traveler's Tree," *Urania speciosa* of the botanists, displays
a flat fan of enormous palm leaves on top of a tall trunk. This 100-
foot-tall palm has its common name because clear water collects in
reservoirs near the trunk and can be tapped without harming the
tree. To the natives it provides much more than water. The trunk is

[1] Our first literary sources about the existence of Madagascar are Arabic in
origin, and I have occasionally wondered whether *Megalodapis* might not be
the "prototype" of the djinns and afrits of the *Arabian Nights.*

timber. The outer covering of the trunk, after a thorough beating with wooden mallets to soften it, serves as a carpet. The fronds thatch the house, and even the individual leaves are used: they are twisted into spoons. Other typical Madagascar flora are the beefwood tree (*Casuarina equisitifolia*), a tall firlike tree, several species of screw pine (*Pandanus*), and the large "Madagascar spice" tree (*Ravintsara madagascariensis*), which bears fragrant fruit and has equally fragrant leaves and bark. There is a relative of the castor-oil plant with seeds which are so oily that they can be strung on a reed like beads and ignited to burn slowly like a candle. Quite obviously, this is called the candle-nut tree. And there is the raphia palm, *Sagus ruffia*, with enormous fronds that have a tough fibrous midrib which can serve as a rope without much treatment and, if treated, provide fibers for weaving. Since the frond of this palm, when dried, looks like an enormous bird feather, it was at least once—but probably more than just once—sent to a curious inquirer as a feather from Sindbad's fabulous roc, which was believed to nest in Madagascar.

One would think that all this should provide enough scientific fame for any island, even one 228,000 square miles in extent. But to many people Madagascar is also known as the home of one more natural marvel: the man-eating tree.

There are, as everyone knows, plants which catch and digest insects, usually plants which grow on poor soil and are able to survive on such soil mostly because they have evolved methods of deriving an extra income from unwary insects. Their methods differ. The sundew *Drosera* has small "tentacles"—more precisely, stalked glands—growing over the upper surfaces of its leaves. If a fly alights on a leaf it will stick to the mucilage drops at the ends of the tentacles it happens to touch. Other tentacles reach over leisurely and the whole leaf slowly closes over the victim. The method of catching insects is actually the flypaper method, *if* flypaper curled itself around the fly after catching it and digested it to make more mucilage. The Venus' fly trap *Dionaea,* on the other hand, actually operates a trap, similar to the steel traps used when wolves put in an unwanted appearance. The two lobes of the leaf can close over an insect, and moreover the edges of the leaf lobes have a number of spikes which interlock. The digestive glands are on the leaf itself, as are three sensitive hairs on each leaf lobe which actuate the mechanism. In cold weather an insect may get away in time; when it is warm the speed of the leaf's movement is fast enough to trap anything that cannot break out by brute strength.

If Dionaea uses a wolf or bear trap, the aquatic bladderwort *Utricularia* evolved a kind of mousetrap—tiny bladders sprouting from submerged shoots which are equipped with a valve that opens inward and in a most ingenious manner even applies a push to the victim. The fourth major method is that of the pitcher plant (*Nepenthes* and others) which has, sprouting from the leaf tips, regular pitchers half filled with weak digestive juice. The half-open lid of the pitcher does not close; it merely has the purpose of keeping rain out.[2]

All these plants are quite small and their victims are tiny, flies and small grasshopper larvae, mosquito larvae in the case of *Utricularia* (using this plant for mosquito control has been suggested), and an occasional tiny freshwater crustacean. A very young tree frog might happen to get into the pitcher of one of the larger varieties of pitcher plants once in a while, but on the whole these plants are what Charles Darwin called them: insectivorous.

But rumor, persistently peddled in Sunday supplements of the more lurid type and in small articles in various odd little magazines, insisted that somewhere, in the interior of distant islands, Nature had applied the principle of the Venus' fly trap on a large scale. It was either on Mindanao in the Philippine Islands or in the interior of Madagascar. In one version the natives shunned the tree which might catch them; in another they appeased it with regular sacrifices, which, of course, had to be kept from the eyes of the white man. (The optimum solution was, of course, to feed the white man to the tree to keep the tale from spreading and the tree satisfied.)

The story of the man-eating tree of Madagascar was alleged to have been started with a letter written from Madagascar in 1878 by an eyewitness of the native ceremony of sacrifice. The name of the eyewitness is given as Carl Liche, the name of the recipient of the letter as Dr. Omelius Fredlowski, a Polish scientist. This letter was printed "in full" in a book called *Madagascar, Land of the Man-Eating Tree,* by Chase Salmon Osborn, LL.D., published in New York in 1924. Since the book had only a small circulation and has been out of print for decades, I'll give the text of the letter here:

The Mkodos, of Madagascar, are a very primitive race, going entirely naked, having only faint vestiges of tribal relations, and no religion be-

[2] The classical work on these plants is Charles Darwin's *Insectivorous Plants* (2d ed., 1875); the most comprehensive is Francis Ernest Lloyd's *The Carnivorous Plants* (Chronica Botanica, 1942), which also lists all the earlier literature.

yond that of the awful reverence which they pay to the sacred tree. They
dwell entirely in caves hollowed out of the limestone rocks in their hills,
and are one of the smallest races, the men seldom exceeding fifty-six
inches in height. At the bottom of a valley (I had no barometer, but
should not think it over four hundred feet above the level of the sea),
and near its eastern extremity, we came to a deep tarn-like lake about a
mile in diameter, the sluggish oily water of which overflowed into a
tortuous reedy canal that went unwillingly into the recesses of a black
forest composed of jungle below and palms above. A path diverging
from its southern side struck boldly for the heart of the forbidding and
seemingly impenetrable forest. Hendrick led the way along this path, I
following closely, and behind me a curious rabble of Mkodos, men,
women and children. Suddenly all the natives began to cry "Tepe! Tepe!"
and Hendrick, stopping short, said, "Look!" The sluggish canal-like stream
here wound slowly by, and in a bare spot in its bend was the most singular
of trees. I have called it "Crinoida," because when its leaves are in action
it bears a striking resemblance to that well-known fossil the crinoid lily-
stone or St. Cuthbert's head. It was now at rest, however, and I will try
to describe it to you. If you can imagine a pineapple eight feet high and
thick in proportion resting upon its base and denuded of leaves, you will
have a good idea of the trunk of the tree, which, however, was not the
color of an anana, but a dark dingy brown, and apparently as hard as
iron. From the apex of this truncated cone (at least two feet in diameter)
eight leaves hung sheer to the ground, like doors swung back on their
hinges. These leaves, which were joined at the top of the tree at regular
intervals, were about eleven or twelve feet long, and shaped very much
like the leaves of the American agave or century plant. They were two
feet through at their thickest point and three feet wide, tapering to a sharp
point that looked like a cow's horn, very convex on the outer (but now
under surface), and on the under (now upper) surface slightly concave.
This concave face was thickly set with strong thorny hooks like those on
the head of the teazle. These leaves hanging thus limp and lifeless, dead
green in color, had in appearance the massive strength of oak fibre. The
apex of the cone was a round white concave figure like a smaller plate set
within a larger one. This was not a flower but a receptacle, and there
exuded into it a clear treacly liquid, honey sweet, and possessed of violent
intoxicating and soporific properties. From underneath the rim (so to
speak) of the undermost plate a series of long hairy green tendrils stretched
out in every direction towards the horizon. These were seven or eight
feet long, and tapered from four inches to a half inch in diameter, yet
they stretched out stiffly as iron rods. Above these (from between the
upper and under cup) six white almost transparent palpi reared themselves towards the sky, twirling and twisting with a marvelous incessant
motion, yet constantly reaching upwards. Thin as reeds and frail as

quills, apparently they were yet five or six feet tall, and were so constantly and vigorously in motion, with such a subtle, sinuous, silent throbbing against the air, that they made me shudder in spite of myself, with their suggestion of serpents flayed, yet dancing upon their tails. The description I am giving you now is partly made up from a subsequent careful inspection of the plant. My observations on this occasion were suddenly interrupted by the natives, who had been shrieking around the tree with their shrill voices, and chanting what Hendrick told me were propitiatory hymns to the great tree devil. With still wilder shrieks and chants they now surrounded one of the women, and urged her with the points of their javelins, until slowly, and with despairing face, she climbed up the stalk of the tree and stood on the summit of the cone, the palpi swirling all about her. "Tsik! Tsik!" ("Drink, drink!") cried the men. Stooping, she drank of the viscid fluid in the cup, rising instantly again, with wild frenzy in her face and convulsive cords in her limbs. But she did not jump down, as she seemed to intend to do. Oh, no! The atrocious cannibal tree that had been so inert and dead came to sudden savage life. The slender delicate palpi, with the fury of starved serpents, quivered a moment over her head, then as if instinct with demoniac intelligence fastened upon her in sudden coils round and round her neck and arms; then while her awful screams and yet more awful laughter rose wildly to be instantly strangled down again into a gurgling moan, the tendrils one after another, like green serpents, with brutal energy and infernal rapidity, rose, retracted themselves, and wrapped her about in fold after fold, ever tightening with cruel swiftness and the savage tenacity of anacondas fastening upon their prey. It was the barbarity of the Laocoön without its beauty—this strange horrible murder. And now the great leaves slowly rose and stiffly, like the arms of a derrick, erected themselves in the air, approached one another and closed about the dead and hampered victim with the silent force of a hydraulic press and the ruthless purpose of a thumb screw. A moment more, and while I could see the bases of these great levers pressing more tightly towards each other, from their interstices there trickled down the stalk of the tree great streams of the viscid honey-like fluid mingled horribly with the blood and oozing viscera of the victim. At sight of this the savage hordes around me, yelling madly, bounded forward, crowded to the tree, clasped it, and with cups, leaves, hands and tongues each one obtained enough of the liquor to send him mad and frantic. Then ensued a grotesque and indescribably hideous orgy, from which even while its convulsive madness was turning rapidly into delirium and insensibility, Hendrick dragged me hurriedly away into the recesses of the forest, hiding me from the dangerous brutes. May I never see such a sight again.

The retracted leaves of the great tree kept their upright position during ten days, then when I came one morning they were prone again, the tendrils stretched, the palpi floating, and nothing but a white skull at the foot of the tree to remind me of the sacrifice that had taken place there. I climbed into a neighboring tree, and saw that all trace of the victim had disappeared and the cup was again supplied with the viscid fluid.

In his book Chase Salmon Osborn, who claims to have spent much time in Madagascar, says that he had not seen the tree himself, that he had never met a missionary who did see it, but that they all asserted that "all the tribes" talk about it. Because he could not obtain a newer description he fell back on the old letter, of which he wrote that it is "the most lurid and dramatic description of the man-eating tree of Madagascar I have seen." That might well be granted, but we now come to the question of whether, in addition to being lurid and dramatic, it is also true.

Offhand, I'd say botanists are apt to shake their heads about the mechanism involved. Not that large leaves rising in the manner described are inherently impossible, but the dancing "palpi" would certainly be unique in the plant kingdom. Besides there is the carefully described fact that the tree does not respond until the victim has climbed to the top of the trunk and presumably touched the "palpi." This arrangement would leave the tree in a badly undernourished condition because it would virtually depend on natives feeding it, with or without ceremony. Its only normal nonhuman victims would be tree-climbing animals, which are all quite small. In tropical countries monkeys are the most numerous tree climbers; in Madagascar these would be lemurs. Both monkeys and lemurs would quickly learn to recognize this type of tree and carefully avoid it. Which leaves an occasional bird as the only possible victim.

But let's approach the story from a different angle.

Sophia Prior, in her *Carnivorous Plants and "The Man-eating Tree"* (Botanical Leaflet No. 23 of the Chicago Museum of Natural History, 1939), stated, as many others had, that Carl Liche's letter was first published in the *Carlsruhe Scientific Journal*. This information is copied from Osborn, who added that the magazine was published by "Graefe and Walther in Karlsruhe." Osborn added further that the letter also was published "in several European scientific publications" and "was first published in America by the *New York World* in 1880."

Copies of newspapers three-quarters of a century old are hard to come by, so I did not check the *World*. But scientific magazines are another story; they are easily accessible in any large library. The first strange fact I turned up was that half a dozen European scientific journals picked at random did not mention the letter. The second strange fact was that the Carlsruhe (or Karlsruhe, which is the more recent spelling) journal was not in any of the libraries I checked. That the files of journals are not complete is, unfortunately, a common occurrence, deplored by both researchers and librarians. That a whole file should be completely missing is rare. But there is always the Library of Congress. No such publication was in its catalogue. Of course, even the Library of Congress doesn't have everything ever printed, but it does have a Union Catalog Division which knows where everything can be found. But whether you spelled Karlsruhe with a "K" or a "C," and whether the English word "journal" had originally been *Zeitschrift,* or *Berichte,* or *Beiträge,* the Union Catalog Division had never heard of it. Nor could they find a publishing firm of "Graefe and Walther"; they asked helpfully whether I meant "Graefe and Unzer," but I didn't, for I knew Graefe and Unzer well, and it was located across the square called King's Garden from the Albertus Universität in Königsberg, East Prussia, and not in Karlsruhe.

Then I started checking—or tried to—on Mr. Liche and Dr. Fredlowski. They might be listed in Webster's Biographical Dictionary, but they weren't. At least one of them should be somewhere in the Encyclopaedia Britannica, but wasn't. Since both were Europeans it seemed likely that they might be mentioned in either one of the two major German encyclopedias, Meyer's or Brockhaus. These two, put together, contain more words than the Britannica. But even when put together they had no word about either Mr. Liche or Dr. Fredlowski.

There was one more avenue to be explored. The date of publication of the letter in the elusive *Carlsruhe Scientific Journal* was given as 1878. The date of the publication of Mr. Osborn's book was 1924. After 1924 you could find references to the Liche-Fredlowski letter in many places. Logically, then, one could assume that books on Madagascar published between 1880 and 1924 should also make some reference to the letter, while books on Madagascar printed prior to 1880 would not, although they might make reference to the story itself, using a different source. This search also did not seem to lead anywhere for quite some time.

One of the classical works on Madagascar is a book published under the title of *Robert Drury's Journal*. Robert Drury was an Englishman, who, according to his own journal, was born in London on July 24, 1687. When he grew up he became a sailor and in 1710 set out on the trip which was to make him famous. He came to Madagascar, was taken captive, and remained on the island for fifteen years as a slave. He saw native life before civilization had wrought any changes; he saw much of the island. He also kept a journal which is our only source for many things; though not a learned man in any respect, he described animals and plants so well that they could be identified later, and even native words and names which he gave can be recognized, although his rendering is anglicized, probably the way he pronounced them himself. But in Drury's *Journal* there isn't a word about such a plant, or any legend about such a plant, or even any reference to a tribe called Mkodos.

Shifting from a classic to a work of painstaking description rendered by modern scientists I next went through *Madagascar au début du XXᵉ siècle,* published in Paris in 1902 under the editorship of Professor of Medicine Raphaël Blanchard. The botanical chapter in this symposium was written by Emmanuel Drake del Castillo, the president of the Société botanique de France; the zoological chapter by Guillaume Grandidier, who was stationed on the island itself. A very edifying book, a nicely printed book, and all that—but no man-eating tree, no legend about man-eating trees, no Mkodos. Instead, a large and beautiful map of the island carefully keyed to show where Traveler's Trees abound and where raphia palms grow.

Since Mr. Osborn had stressed in his book that the natives talked about the man-eating tree and that every missionary was aware of the story, I naturally looked for books by missionaries. There is one by Joseph Mullen, D.D., *Twelve Months in Madagascar,* published in New York in 1875, telling of the author's visit to missionaries in Madagascar. But no tree, no legend, no Mkodos. There is another one by John Alden Houlder, entitled *Among the Malagasy; An unconventional record of missionary experience* (London, 1912). The author went to Madagascar in 1870 and stayed for several decades. Interesting report—but no tree, no legend, no Mkodos.

The next book I searched was a heavy tome by James Sibree with the title *A Naturalist in Madagascar,* published in Philadelphia in 1915, and based on *fifty* years of experience on the spot. Since Mr. Sibree was a missionary too, my hopes ran high. A missionary-naturalist with half a century of what appears to be almost uninterrupted residence should have something to tell. Sure, he had much to tell, but no tree, no legend, no Mkodos. Maybe a naturalist who was not a missionary might be a better source after all. So I picked up Walter D. Marcuse's *Through Western Madagascar in Quest of the Golden Bean*. Mr. Marcuse returned to England in 1912 and his book contains several chapters especially devoted to the fauna and flora of the island. But the final result was the same: no tree, no legend, no Mkodos.

It began to look as if no English-speaking missionary or naturalist had even ever heard of the story, and it seemed certain to me after reading all this that there was no native legend.

Having failed to obtain the *Carlsruhe Scientific Journal* which was supposed to have started it all, I decided that a survey of German books on Madagascar might be fruitful. The Germans at least ought to know their own periodical scientific literature. Well, in 1886 one Robert Hartmann published a book, *Madagaskar und die Inseln Seychellen,* devoted to the natural history of the island rather than its history. It turned out to be somewhat dull and "instructive" but competent and concise. Not a word about a man-eating tree, or about a story about a man-eating tree. Simply nothing. If there had been a publication of the Liche-Fredlowski letter in a German scientific journal only half a dozen years earlier Hartmann would certainly have mentioned it.

Almost the last book on my pile was also in German. Its author was a Swiss naturalist, Dr. Conrad Keller; his book was *Reisebilder aus Ostafrika und Madagaskar (Travel Sketches from East Africa and Madagascar)*, published in Leipzig in 1887. The author had been to the island twice, once in 1881–82, or very soon after the writing of the Liche-Fredlowski letter, and once again in 1886. Most of the book had been published in Swiss newspapers; the chapters had been actual letters which Dr. Keller wrote on his travels.

And one of Dr. Keller's reports contributed a great deal to the solution of the puzzle. He stated that something fantastic had been added to the actually marvelous flora of Madagascar in an alleged letter written "by a traveler Carl Liche whom I don't know" to "a certain Dr. Fredlowski" which was published "in a journal said to appear in Karlsruhe which I could not obtain." Because "the German original" could not be found Dr. Keller translated the letter from the *Antanarivo Annual and Madagascar Magazine for the Year 1881,* which he stated was a small local magazine published and printed by the missionaries. The condensed translation which he then gave shows very clearly that the letter published by Mr. Osborn was taken from that magazine and that the magazine's version is, in all probability, the original.

The facts are pretty clear by now. Of course the man-eating tree does not exist. There is no such tribe. The actual natives of Madagascar do not have such a legend. But at one time somebody made up a hoax, which was put into the only existing local magazine, possibly as a joke of some kind for the amusement of the readers who knew better. But it then got out of hand and the perpetrators thought it best to keep quiet. And if Mr. Chase Salmon Osborn, browsing around on the spot, had not resurrected it, the whole thing would have been forgotten a long time ago.

CHAPTER 18

The Dodo Islands

ONCE upon a time there lived on the island of Mauritius a bird called the dodo, with the scientific name of *Didus ineptus*.

Come to think of it, this is not a good beginning.

The story of the dodo is not a fairy tale but the truth, or as much truth as can still be established. Moreover, this first sentence is a very unscientific oversimplification. Let's try to make it more accurate and also follow the rule drilled into budding newspapermen, that of getting all the facts into the first paragraph. Then it will read something like this:

From a time that cannot be properly dated, but which might be considered roughly equivalent to the beginning of the glacial age in higher latitudes, until about the year 1680 A.D. a large and flightless bird, classified as belonging to a suborder of the *Columbiformes*, or pigeonlike birds, is known to have existed on the island of Mauritius (or Zwaaneiland, also known as Ile de France), which was called dodo, or dodaers, or dronte, but also *dinde sauvage, Walchvogel,* or *gekapte Zwaan* (hooded swan), and several other names, with the scientific designation of either *Didus ineptus* or *Raphus cucullatus,* which are equivalent in scientific usage but with *Raphus cucullatus* holding the chronological priority.

Well, now, that is more accurate.

But I'm afraid it will make most sense to people who know all these facts already and who therefore do not have much reason to read it at all.

I had better start over again, this time with fundamentals. To the east of Madagascar, strung out along the 20th parallel of southern

334

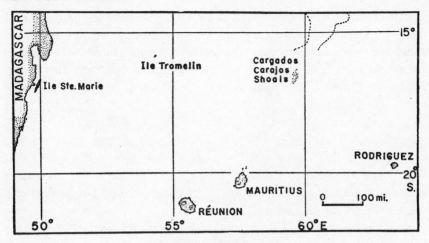

The Mascarene Islands

latitude there are three reasonably large islands. Their current names are Réunion, Mauritius, and Rodriguez. At least that's the way they appear on British Admiralty charts and their American equivalent, but for some unfathomable reason the dependency of Rodrigues, when it makes an official report to the colony of Mauritius, spells its name with an "s" at the end. I am making a point of this difference in spelling for the sole reason that it happens to be the smallest of all the difficulties and discrepancies we are going to encounter. The more serious problems come up later.

It is hard to say just who discovered these islands. At least one old map exists on which the three islands have Arabic names. Arab trading vessels very likely did discover them but without paying any special attention to their discovery since the islands were uninhabited. It is exceedingly difficult to barter on uninhabited islands. In any event the Arabs did not even bother to locate the islands with any degree of care; on the map mentioned they are drawn as forming an equilateral triangle and are placed far too close to Madagascar.

The first European discoverers were Portuguese, but, strange to say, it was the second of the Portuguese discoverers who had his name attached to the islands. The first one was Diogo Fernandes Pereira, who sailed these waters in 1507. On February 9 of that year he found an island some 400 miles to the east of Madagascar which he named Santa Apollonia. It must have been the present Réunion. Soon afterward his ship, the *Cerné,* sighted the present Mauritius. The navigator landed and named the island after his ship, as Ilha do Cerne. This led to two different misunderstandings. Much later, around the middle of the nineteenth century, somebody who apparently did not know the name of Pereira's ship wondered why the navigator should have named the island after the Island of Cerne mentioned by Pliny the Elder. Wherever Pliny's Cerne was located, it could not have been to the east of Madagascar.

The other misunderstanding occurred quite soon after Pereira's voyage. Dutch explorers who came to Mauritius and knew the old name thought that Cerne was a miswriting for *cigne* (swan) and that Pereira had thought the dodos to be swans. The Dutch did not bother with the zoological problem involved but "translated" Diogo Pereira's name into Dutch as Zwaaneiland.

Pereira, who was on his way to India, found Rodriguez later in the same year. It was first called Domingo Friz but also Diego Rodriguez. The Dutch apparently found this hard to pronounce and talked about Diego Ruy's Island, which then was Frenchified into Dygarroys, but the official French name for a time was Ile Marianne.

Six years later came the second Portuguese discoverer, Pedro Mascarenhas, who visited only Mauritius and Réunion. No name change for Mauritius was involved because of this rediscovery, but Santa Apollonia (Réunion) was renamed Mascarenhas or Mascaregne, and to this day the islands are called the Mascarene Islands.

The subsequent history of the islands was just about as complicated as this beginning. Réunion, the largest of the three islands, 970 square miles in extent, was officially annexed to France in 1638 by a Captain Goubert from Dieppe. I don't know why one annexation was not considered sufficient, but the historical fact is that the annexation was repeated in 1643, in the name of Louis XIII, and once more in 1649 by Étienne de Flacourt, who changed the name of Mascarenhas to Ile Bourbon. After the French revolution that name had to go, of course, and that island became Réunion. But then (history can be read quite easily from the various changes), it became Ile Bonaparte. Since 1848 it has been Réunion again.

Considered nonpolitically, Réunion is a volcanic island with three rather tall peaks. The tallest is the Piton des Neiges, which measures 10,069 feet. The other high elevation is simply called Le Volcan by the inhabitants of the island, but Le Volcan has more than one peak. One is called Bory Crater; it is 8612 feet above sea level and extinct. The other, also a crater, is known as Fournaise; it is only 8294 feet tall but is still active. An island in such a location can grow tropical fruit and there are banana plantations and breadfruit trees, not to mention coconut palms. But these plants were introduced later; the original vegetation included a dwarf bamboo, a variety of Casuarina trees and a plant called by the trade name "red tacamahac," botanically *Calophyllum spurium*.

The second island, Mauritius, is somewhat smaller than Réunion (about 720 square miles) and likewise of volcanic origin. But all volcanic activity on Mauritius is a thing of the fairly distant past. The names of its three highest mountains reflect the changing ownership of the island through the centuries. The highest one (2711 feet) is called Black River Mountain. The second one (2685 feet) is Mount Pieter Botte, while the third (2650 feet), is called Pouce. The island is surrounded by coral reefs which a ship's captain has to know well, but it has a fine natural harbor. These two features prompted the Dutch to annex it in 1598 and they gave it its current name in honor of Count Maurits of Nassau. The Dutch abandoned Mauritius in 1710. For slightly more than half a century (1715–1767) it was French and was called Ile de France. In 1810 it was taken by the English, who restored the Dutch name.

Right now Mauritius is a "spice island," where spices, pineapple, mangos, avocados, and bananas are grown, along with sugar cane. But the original vegetation is still represented by ironwood trees, ebony trees, Traveler's Trees, and bamboo. Of course, domesticated animals were introduced on both islands, but Mauritius is somewhat special even in that respect—the deer that can be found there came from Java, not from Europe.

As regards Rodriguez, the story is similar but shorter. Its extent is only 43 square miles. It is volcanic in origin with 1300-foot Mount Limon as its highest peak. There is a fringing coral reef. And the ownership of the island was Dutch, French, and English in succession. In all cases the first inhabitants were either deportees or else people in voluntary exile, some of them mutineers, some others refugees from religious intolerance.

Though all this is necessary to establish the background, none of these facts would have made any of the islands famous. The only one which would enjoy a kind of restricted fame is Mauritius, which is known among stamp collectors because of an early philatelic error that produced some of the rarest stamps in existence. But the Mascarene Islands are famous because they once were the home of the dodo and related birds.

The story of the dodo (let's concentrate on the Mauritius dodo for

the time being) looks rather simple, if somewhat sad, in rough outline. The bird's existence was first reported by Dutch navigators who
were by far less thorough in their descriptions than one would now
wish they had been. But they made up for this to some extent by bringing live specimens back with them to Europe. There these were
painted, mostly by Dutch painters, and again it must be said, not as
well as one would now wish.

But the major blunder was committed in England. In about 1637,
give or take a year, a live Mauritius dodo arrived in England. It lived
there for quite some time and after its death it was "stuffed" (badly,
no doubt) and found a place in Tradescant's Museum in London in
1656. In 1683 (as we now know, two years after the last report of a
live dodo on Mauritius was put on paper by one Mr. Benjamin Harry),
the stuffed dodo was transferred to the Ashmolean Museum at Oxford. In 1755 the curator of the Ashmolean Museum decided that the
moth-eaten old skin was a disgrace to his fine collection and ordered
it to be burned with other trash. At the last moment somebody
wrenched off the head (partly decayed) and one foot (in good condition). They are now about the rarest items on record.

Even this outline story contains one more surprising item. The first
scientist to include the dodo as an exotic bird in a book on natural
history was the French physician Charles de Lécluse (Latinized as
Carolus Clusius), in 1605. Later Linnaeus gave it a scientific name
and quite naturally the dodo entered the zoological works of Buffon
in France and Blumenbach in Germany. But by 1800 nobody had
ever seen a dodo. The available paintings did not seem convincing;
they looked like caricatures to begin with and did not even agree with
one another. Some scientists, bent on a housecleaning in scientific
literature, began to doubt whether there had ever been such a bird.
Maybe it was all a misunderstanding, if not worse, and the descriptions had referred to the cassowary. In any event J. S. Duncan of
Oxford felt obliged, in 1828, to write a paper with the title: "A summary review of the authorities on which naturalists are justified in
believing that the Dodo, *Raphus cucullatus* (*Didus ineptus*), was a
bird existing in the Isle of France, or the neighbouring islands, until
a recent period." Mr. Duncan can be said to have saved the dodo
from secondary extinction in scientific literature.

But now let's go back to the original sources. The first man to
write about the dodo was the Dutch admiral Jacob Corneliszoon van
Neck who went to Mauritius with eight ships. Four of them returned

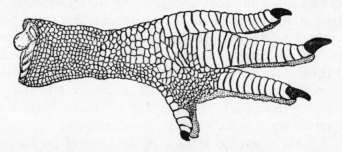

Foot of the dodo which was in Tradescant's Museum, traced from a colored lithograph which had the following caption, written by Nehemiah Grew in about 1700: "The leg here preserved is covered with a reddish yellow scale. Not much above four inches long; yet above five in thickness, or round about the joints: wherein though it be inferior to that of an Ostrich or Cassoary, yet joined with its shortness, may render it of almost equal strength."

to Holland in 1599, the other four in 1601. Admiral van Neck's narrative appeared in Dutch in 1601 and translations into English, French, and Latin were printed during the same year, a German translation one year later.

In spite of all this printed matter there are still a number of questions. The original journal, presumably written on shipboard, was enlarged for publication, whether by the admiral himself or by an editor, we don't know. Moreover, old Carolus Clusius, who did not leave Europe, published a dodo picture which he said was copied from Admiral van Neck's journal. But this picture cannot be found in any known edition of the journal.

The passage in the admiral's journal in which the dodo is first mentioned, reads:

Blue parrots are very numerous there [Mauritius] as well as other birds; among which are a kind, conspicuous for their size, larger than our swans, with huge heads only half covered with skin as if clothed with a hood. These birds lack wings, in the place of which three or four blackish feathers protrude. The tail consists of a few soft incurved feathers which are ash-colored. These we used to call *Walghvogels* for the reason that the more and the longer they were cooked the less soft and more insipid eating they became. Nevertheless their belly and breast were of a pleasant flavor and easily masticated.

The Dutch word *Walghvogels* (also spelled *Walchvogels*) translates literally as "nauseating birds," but it led to one of the many mistakes that crowd the dodo's short life history. About two hundred years later it was asserted in German books that there had been *Waldvogels* (Forest Birds), so named, on Mauritius. There probably were, and still are, forest birds, but the Forest Bird in its German form of *Waldvogel* was only a sloppy translation. Spelling in those days was helter-skelter in any language, so somebody probably thought that *Walgh* was just a poor rendering of *Waldt,* a then frequent spelling of the German word *Wald,* which means forest.

Since this has raised the problem of the name of the bird it might be well to clear up this additional difficulty as nearly as possible. In the most recent specialized professional work on the dodo by the Marquis Masauji Hachisuka [1] not less than seventy-nine different names are listed, but the confusion is not quite as large as this figure seems to indicate, for the names clearly fall into a small number of classes. One set tries to be descriptive; these are mostly French, as for example *autruche encapuchonné* (hooded ostrich), *cygne capuchonné* (hooded swan), and *dinde sauvage* (wild turkey). Another set consists of either translations or mistranslations of Dutch names; the Dutch names themselves are either variations on the *Walghvogel* theme, or else descriptive terms similar to the French ones. Just two words emerge as, so to speak, "exclusive" terms. One is "dodo," with the variations "dodaars" and "dodaerts," and the other is "dronte."

It is reasonably certain that "dodo" is a name coined by the Portuguese, as witness a letter written in 1628 by Emanuel Altham about "very strange fowles called by ye portingals Do Do." The fact that Altham pulled the two syllables apart, thereby changing their pronunciation, is "very suspicious-making" as a French lady I know phrased it. It is so suspicious, or rather indicative, because old Dutch and German writings spell the name as "doedoe" and "dudu," both of which must be pronounced "doodoo." Since the word has no real meaning in any language, it may well be, as has been asserted, an imitation of the bird's call.

The Dutch variation dod-aars or dod-aerts is rather clear to an English-speaker, especially in view of the descriptive remarks: "and has a round rump," as Admiral van Neck put it, or, "round of stern," as Captain Willem van West-Zanen wrote in 1602.

[1] *The Dodo and Kindred Birds,* or, *The Extinct Birds of the Mascarene Islands,* by Masauji Hachisuka, Ph.D., Sc. D. (London: H. F. & G. Witherby Ltd., 1953.)

However, the name dronte, which in Dutch and in German writings was used just about as often as the name dodo, is still unexplained. When the Englishmen H. E. Strickland and A. G. Melville wrote the first major work on the dodo,[2] Strickland, who did the larger share of the writing, accepted the explanation that this term was coined by Danish sailors, using their verb *drunte* which means "to be slow." This is not only farfetched on the face of it, since the Danes, for a change, do not figure in the exploration of these islands, but is probably factually wrong too. We simply don't know whether the dodo was slow and what evidence there is is against this assumption. The Dutch zoologist A. C. Oudemans, the main chronicler of sea-serpent reports, remembered that there was a now obsolete Middle-Dutch verb *dronten*. Its meaning was "bloated" or "swollen." This sounds more reasonable on two counts: it is a Dutch word, and it applies to the bird's usual shape.[3] But Oudemans himself said that he could not prove that this was actually the derivation. Some of the early writings about the dodo seem to be lost.

The records are incomplete also as regards the number of birds taken away alive. If it were not for a chance mention in the journal of Peter Mundy, who served with the East India Company 1628–1634, we would never know that two of them were brought to India. But his statement is definite: "Dodoes, a strange kind of fowle, twice as big as a Goose, that can neither flye nor swimm, being Cloven footed; I saw two of them in Suratt [the first British settlement in India, started 1612] house that were brought from thence [Mauritius]." There is a similar chance mention about one having been sent to Japan, but Japanese scientists have failed, in spite of much effort, to trace its fate from Japanese chronicles and books.

Going by such chance remarks on the one hand and on the other hand by sketches and paintings stated or reported to have been made from life, Dr. Hachisuka listed a total of twelve specimens of the Mauritius dodo as having arrived in Europe: one in Italy, two in England, and nine (five males and four females) in Holland. In other

---

[2] *The Dodo and Its Kindred; or the History, Affinities and Osteology of the Dodo, Solitaire and Other Extinct Birds of the Islands Mauritius, Rodrigues, and Bourbon* (London, 1848). Still a very good book.

[3] Oudemans' work on the dodo is entitled *Dodo-Studien, naar aanleiding van de vondst van een gevelsteen met Dodo-beeld van 1561 te Vere* (Amsterdam: 1917).

books, particularly in works which treat the paintings as paintings instead of as ornithological illustrations, larger figures are usually mentioned. This is partly the result of counting sketches and paintings made from earlier paintings; mostly, however, it is because no distinction is made between the gray Mauritius dodo and similar birds from the other two Mascarene islands.

But no list, whether of specimens or of paintings, can be considered final. In 1914 and 1915 a German scientist, Dr. S. Killermann, made a systematic dodo hunt in museums, libraries, and art galleries and discovered about half a dozen pictures that had simply been overlooked before. Killermann's feat could probably be duplicated by somebody else with the inclination and the necessary time and money. Still among the missing are the original in van Neck's journal from which the Clusius picture was copied; several drawings known to have been made from life by an unnamed artist on board one of the ships of Admiral Wolphart Harmanszoon in Mauritius harbor in 1602; and one of the several oil paintings of dodos by Roelandt Savery. In short, while a dodo investigation is no longer virgin territory, it is still a fertile field with possibilities for a diligent researcher.

One of the earliest and best pictures of a Mauritius dodo drawn from life is the pen-and-ink drawing by Adrian van de Venne. It was made in 1626 and shows a male. This is what we now think of as the normal appearance of the dodo. However, it was Professor Oudemans who first realized that the dodo must have had two "normal appearances," a fat stage and a gaunt stage. This assumption explains many old sketches which look like caricatures, the latter impression being considerably strengthened by the fact that a number of the sketches were made while the birds were molting. Oudemans's idea makes it possible to arrange all these sketches in a logical sequence, pre-molting, at the height of the molt, post-molting, fat, and gaunt. But why a bird on a tropical island, where the food supply should be more or less the same all year round, should acquire a gaunt stage at regular intervals is not yet fully explained.

The Mauritius dodo became extinct between 1681, the last time it is mentioned as living, and 1693, the first time it is missing from a list of the animals and birds of the island made on the spot. By 1750 the people living on the island no longer knew that there had been such a bird.

A hundred years later there lived on Mauritius a man who was an ardent naturalist. His name was George Clark and he not only knew about the dodo but was determined to find dodo remains. They had to be somewhere on the island; nothing becomes extinct without leaving traces. But where?

At first glance the situation did not look too promising. As Clark wrote:

In fact, there is no part of Mauritius where the soil is of such a nature as to render probable the accidental interment of substances thrown upon it. It may be classed under four heads: stiff clay, large masses of stone forming a chaotic surface, strata of melted lava, locally called *pavés*, impervious to everything; and loam, intermixed with fragments of vesicular basalt—the latter too numerous and too thickly scattered to allow anything to sink into the mass by the mere force of gravity. Besides this, the tropical rains, of which the violence is well known, sweep the surface of the earth in many places with a force sufficient to displace stones of several hundred pounds weight.

At this point Clark suddenly had a new idea. If the tropical rains swept everything before them, where did they sweep it? Well, there was a kind of delta formed by three rivers running into the harbor of Mahébourg. If dodo bones had been washed into one of the rivers, this was the place where they were most likely to have come to rest. One part of the delta was a marsh known locally as le Mare aux Songes, where Clark decided to dig as soon as he had the time and some means to pay laborers for the actual work.

In about 1863 he began to dig, finding large numbers of dodo bones at the very bottom of the marsh, to the delight of anatomists, and to the intense astonishment of aged Creoles who were standing around to watch and who were somewhat annoyed at the discovery of something on their own island that they had not known about. As a result, there is at least no doubt about the dodo's skeleton. In fact, it was this material which helped unravel the problems created by the sketches of artists who did not know any anatomy, or at least not bird anatomy.

And while no museum can have an authentic dodo, several museums can at least boast authentic dodo skeletons, like the one at the Smithsonian Institution, which was put together by Norman H. Boss.

The American Museum of Natural History in New York also has such a skeleton. Next to it is a remarkably realistic model, a restoration, made in the taxidermy studios of Rowland Ward in London. The feet and the head are copied from preserved specimens. The feathers are feathers of other birds, chosen for proper coloration and approxi-

The Mauritius dodo as re-
stored from skeleton and con-
temporary pictures at the
American Museum of Natural
History (drawing by Gustav
Wolf)

mately proper size. The restoration portrays the fat stage, the one we
know best from pictures.

The dodo under discussion so far has been the so-called gray dodo,
from Mauritius. But there also was a dodo on Réunion. Since the two
islands are separated by about 130 miles of open water the birds were
not much alike; for simplicity's sake the Réunion bird is usually referred to as the white dodo. It is much less well known than the
Mauritius dodo, partly, no doubt, because for about a century naturalists tried to overlook the difference between the two birds. They just
spoke of "the dodo"; in a few places a white dodo was casually mentioned, but in such a manner that one could assume that there happened to be an albino among the dodos Dutch sailors brought to
Europe.

There are only two original descriptions of the white dodo in its
native habitat. The first one was written by an Englishman named
J. Tatton, who wrote about a voyage he had made with a ship commanded by Captain Castleton. The report dates from 1625, but the
voyage had been made a dozen years earlier. Discussing Réunion,
Tatton wrote:

There is a store of Land-fowl, both small and great, plentie of Doves,
great Parrats, and such like, and a great fowl of the bigness of a Turkie,

The white dodo, as drawn from a live specimen in Holland by Pieter
Holsteyn, early seventeenth century

very fat, and so short-winged that they cannot flie, being white, and in
a manner tame; and so are all other fowles, as having not been troubled
or feared with shot.

The only other witness who saw the Réunion dodo on the island
and wrote about it was the Dutch traveler Willem Ijsbrantszoon
Bontekoe van Hoorn. He spent three weeks there in 1619 and he
not only described what is unmistakably a dodo but even referred to
it as a *Dod-eersen.* Unfortunately he did not say anything about its
color.

But later researchers kept coming across pictures which did not
jibe with the other dodo pictures. Not only was the plumage white,
with yellow wing feathers; there were other differences. The feet were
more slender; the tail was different and so was the bill. Now it is true
that in some sketches of the Mauritius dodo the bill looks different,
because the molting dodo also shed the sheath of the bill. But
these white dodos seemed to have the sheath in place. All the pictures
are by two artists, Pieter Holsteyn (around 1640) and Pieter Withoos
(around 1685). Since it is most unlikely that a full-grown specimen
lived in captivity for forty-five years, this indicates that two different
white dodos reached Europe a few decades apart.

The white dodo was finally introduced to science as a distinct species in 1907 when the Honorable W. Rothschild published his book

Extinct Birds.[4] He proposed for it the scientific name of *Didus bor-bonicus*. Later, in 1937, Dr. Hachisuka proposed to change the name to *Victoriornis imperialis*.

Probably because Réunion is more mountainous than Mauritius, the white dodo survived longer than the gray one. There is a report that Mahé de la Bourdonnais, when he was governor of both islands, sent one to France. As there is no record from the other end, we don't know whether it got to France or not, but Mahé de la Bourdonnais was governor from 1735 to 1746, long after the Mauritius dodo was extinct. The Réunion dodo is omitted from a survey made in 1801; it must have succumbed to dogs, rats, and pigs during the latter half of the eighteenth century.

That Réunion was further involved with this ornithological mystery was not even suspected until recently. This other connection can best be explained by a detour to the third of the Mascarene islands, Rodriguez.

After that island was first reached by Diogo Fernandes Pereira in 1507, settlers did not get there for almost two centuries, and even these went to Rodriguez only as a second choice. They were a group of eleven French Huguenots who were supposed to go to Réunion from Holland. Their chosen leader was François Leguat, a man then in his fifties. A Dutch ship, with the French Protestants aboard, left Holland on September 4, 1690, and arrived at Réunion on April 3 of the following year. Apparently it had been believed in Holland that the French had abandoned the island, and when the ship's captain realized that they had not, he did not land but set course for Rodriguez where the refugees stayed for about two years. Then they built a boat and sailed for Mauritius.

A weird and senseless odyssey was the result of this act. About half a year after they had landed they were discovered by the governor, who, after a few months of deliberation, banished them to a small rocky island off shore. There they were kept prisoners for three years and then shipped, still as prisoners, to Batavia. A year later they were released and sent back to Holland, where they arrived in June 1698. François Leguat then went to England, where he rewrote for pub-

[4] It bore the subtitle: "An attempt to unite in one volume a short account of those birds which have become extinct in historical times, that is, within the last six or seven hundred years. To which are added a few which still exist, but are on the verge of extinction." The "short account" turned into a folio volume with 45 color plates.

lication the journal he had kept. Both the French original and an English translation of the journal appeared in 1708.

Other voyagers before Leguat had said that there were "dodos" on Rodriguez, but Leguat was the first who lived there for any length of time. Moreover, Leguat could draw and provided illustrations for his book; since some of these are rather complicated maps and plans, there can be little doubt that he had made the sketches on the spot. The English edition states:

> Of all the Birds in the Island, the most remarkable is that which goes by the name of *Solitary,* tho' there are abundance of them. The Feathers of the Males are of a brown grey Colour: the Feet and Beak are like a Turkey's, but a little more crooked. They have scarce any Tail, but their Hind-part covered with Feathers is roundish, like the Crupper of a Horse; they are taller than Turkeys. . . . The Bone of their Wing grows greater toward the Extremity, and forms a little round Mass under the Feathers, as big as a Musket Ball. That and its Beak are the chief Defence of this Bird. 'Tis very hard to catch it in the Woods, but easier in open Places, because we run faster than they. . . . Some of the Males weigh forty-five Pounds.

The males, Leguat reported, were brown in color, the females either brown "or fair, the colour of blonde hair"; most likely the brown ones were older females. He also mentioned that the females had a "head-band, like the head-band of Widows, high upon their Beak," and that lighter feathers on their chest formed an outline like the bosom of a women. Evidently Leguat's drawing shows a female, since the males lacked these characteristics.

Leguat's is the only drawing of a solitary, but, as happened with the Mauritius dodo, remains have been excavated, and a few nearly complete skeletons constructed.

The essentially simple story of the Rodriguez solitary—scientific name *Pezophaps solitarius* [5]—later received two amusing addenda. In 1761 one of the so-called "transits" of the planet Venus was to take place. The astronomical term means that Venus, as seen from the earth, is in line of sight with the sun so that it crosses the sun's disk as a round black spot. Such transits are very rare and astronomers do not like to miss a single one of them. But a transit is visible only from a belt which differs for different transits. The island of Rodriguez was in the visibility belt for the 1761 transit, and a French astronomer, the Abbé Pingré, undertook the long trip. He got to Rodriguez in

[5] From Greek *pezós,* "pedestrian" and *phaps,* "pigeon."

time for the transit, and incidentally reported that the solitaries were still around. He is the last man to have seen them alive.

A few years later Pingré's compatriot and colleague Le Monnier decided to honor Pingré, and incidentally the solitary, by combining a few faint stars which he had discovered in the space between the constellations Libra, Scorpio, and Draco to create a new constellation, which he called Solitarius. To get a picture of the solitary, Le Monnier consulted Brisson's great *Ornithologie,* which had been printed in 1760. Looking in the index, he found a *solitaire* listed and faithfully copied the picture. Thus it came about that the heavens bore a new constellation Solitarius to which had been given the imgainary shape of *Turdus solitarius,* the solitary thrush!

The other addendum relates to Geoffroy Atkinson, a professor of Romance literature who wrote several books about "extraordinary voyages" in French literature. In spite of my own interest in science fiction and its forerunners, I failed to be intrigued by these books. They are solid work, but it is obvious that Atkinson's field is literature and nothing else. Besides, if I may say so, his style is dull. But I did not know until I read Hachisuka's work that Atkinson in 1921, going overboard with his interest in extraordinary voyages, declared that Leguat had never traveled! He could, he said, "trace" every item in Leguat's journal to its "sources." The account of the Cape of Good Hope came from one book, the sea turtles from another, the story of his imprisonment from still another, the building of a boat from somebody else's memoirs.

One biologist who read this began to wonder. Leguat had made statements about the anatomy of the solitary which the skeletons had proved correct and which have not been found in any other book. While he was still brooding two French librarians very politely requested that Atkinson answer a few simple questions; to wit: if Leguat had never rounded the Cape of Good Hope, why do the archives of Cape Town tell about the ship, its arrival, departure, and so forth, with the same dates as given by Leguat? If Leguat never saw Rodriguez, why does the earliest map of the island—other than Leguat's own—show places named after him? Why are there official reports from Mauritius telling of the arrival, imprisonment, and deportation of refugees from Rodriguez? And finally, why is there correspondence with the fleet commander about the trip to and the return from Batavia?

Atkinson accomplished one thing, if unintentionally. Before him

Rodriguez solitary, female
(Leguat's *Voyage et Aventures,* 1708)

nobody doubted Leguat's journal. Now we are sure that it cannot be doubted.

We can now return to Réunion. In addition to its neglected white dodo, it too had a solitary, different from the one on Rodriguez, whose existence was ignored for two hundred years. There were sources about it, but they were not recognized until long after the birds had become extinct. One of the best-known references to what we now know to have been the Réunion solitary is the account in Sir Hamon L'Estrange's memoirs:

About 1638, as I walked London streets, I saw the picture of a strange fowle hong out upon a cloth and myselfe with one or two more then in company went in to see it. It was kept in a chamber, and was a great fowle somewhat bigger than the largest Turky Cock, and so legged and footed, but stouter and thicker and of a more erect shape, coloured before like the breast of a young cock fesan, and on the back of dunn or dearc colour. The keeper called it a Dodo, and in the ende of a chymney in the chamber there lay a heape of large pebble stones, whereof hee gave it many in our sight, some as big as nutmegs and the keeper told us that she eats them (conducing to digestion), and though I remember not how far the keeper was questioned therein, yet I am confident that afterwards shee cast them all again.

The keeper no doubt called it a dodo, just as Sir Hamon reports, but this is not the only time that an animal or a bird has been called by the wrong name. The "more erect shape" points to a solitary, and the description of the coloration does not fit the Mauritius dodo and certainly not the white dodo of Réunion. But because the name dodo was used, the bird was for many years accepted as a dodo; it has even been surmised that it was the one that later could be seen stuffed in Tradescant's Museum and was finally thrown away.

Some of the narrators even used the term "solitary" for a bird on Réunion. For example the Frenchman Carré, who was in Réunion in 1668, reported:

I saw a kind of bird in this place which I have not found elsewhere: it is that which the inhabitants call the *Oiseau Solitaire,* for, to be sure, it loves solitude and only frequents the most secluded places; one never

Réunion solitary, female (artist unknown; picture discovered by Dr. Killermann)

sees two or more together; it is always alone. It is not unlike a turkey, if it did not have longer legs.

Another very similar description came from the Sieur Du Bois, who arrived in Réunion in 1669. He listed the birds he saw, and when he came to solitaries he stated:

These birds are so called because they always go alone. They are as big as a large goose and have white plumage with the tips of the wings and tail black. The tail feathers are like those of an ostrich, they have a long neck, and the beak is like that of the Woodcock, but larger; the legs and feet are like those of a turkey.

These statements, especially that of Du Bois, led Strickland to suspect that Réunion might have both birds. Rothschild, after weighing all the evidence, also said that there must have been two different birds on Réunion, either two kinds of dodos which were quite far apart in appearance, or else one dodo and one solitary resembling the Rodriguez type. Oudemans, ten years after Rothschild, took the positon this was all a mistake. The men who made the reports probably were not too observant in regard to the molting stages of the birds. Oudemans's main argument is that nobody described both birds so to speak side by side. This is admittedly true, but from reading what reports there are one gets the impression that the bird called *solitaire* was quite numerous while the white dodo obviously was not. Moreover, Réunion is large enough that the two birds could have had different habitats.

Somewhat ironically, Professor Oudemans himself produced evidence for a solitary, in addition to the one from Rodriguez. In the summer preceding the First World War he was vacationing with his wife on the island of Walcheren, looking at famous old houses and historical sites. At the city of Veere there was an old house known as the Ostrich House. It bore this name because it was adorned with a stone bas-relief of a large and fairly long-legged bird and the inscription:

IN DEN STRUYS, 1561.
(To the Ostrich, 1561)

The house and its bas-relief had been described and pictured many times, but apparently they had never been scrutinized by a professor of zoology. When Dr. Oudemans saw the picture of an ostrich, and such an old one, the expert in him awakened out of his vacation mood. Had the ostrich been known at all in the Netherlands in 1561?

Yes, probably, for Konrad Gesner's long chapter on the ostrich had appeared in 1555. Gesner's book even contained a full-page woodcut of the ostrich, wrong as far as plumage was concerned, but essentially correct in outline. But the picture on the Ostrich House was anything but correct in outline. The neck was too short and so were the legs. The head was wrong and the feet had four toes, whereas ostrichlike birds have three at most.

Had the stonecutter, not having an ostrich or even a picture of an ostrich available, used an ordinary rooster as his model? No, the wings were wrong and so was the neck, and, as Oudemans wrote later, "moreover, no comb adorns the head." All of a sudden he realized that it *might* be a dodo. The first thing he did was to have a photographer take a picture; he sent me a print when we had sea-serpent correspondence in 1936.

Oudemans felt that the sculptor must have seen a dodo in the gaunt stage (there was no written statement of any kind that a dodo had been brought to the Netherlands in that year or earlier), for the bird certaintly could not be a Rodriguez solitary. Leguat had been so specific about that bird's being tail-less with a round, feather-covered rear end. Look at the tail feathers, Oudemans wrote. Almost like those of an African ostrich, or of a dodo.

Well, the answer is that it was not a Rodriguez solitary but a Réunion solitary (now called *Ornithaptera solitaria*). The tail feathers, so prominent on the gable stone, appear just as prominently in the so-called dodo of Florence, one of the pictures discovered by Dr. S. Killermann, which is now taken to portray a male Réunion solitary. Still another picture discovered by Killermann shows a female.

There is one more picture of the same bird which is now at the McGill University in Montreal. It is of Italian origin, being picture no. 29 in the so-called Feather Book made by Dionisio Minaggio in Milan in 1618. This volume consists of 156 large pictures including birds, practically all hunting scenes. The interesting point is that the birds were not painted—the real beaks, feet, and feathers of birds have been used. Unfortunately the picture of the Réunion solitary is "faked"; legs and beak have been painted and the feathers used for the body are those of other birds. But it undoubtedly represents the same bird as the dodo of Florence.

Attempts to ship Réunion solitaries to Europe were reported by Carré who says that two were caught to be sent to the king (of

The gable stone of the Ostrich House, Veere, Neth-
erlands (traced from Oudemans' photograph)

France) but aboard ship they died of "melancholy." But some must
have arrived.

Sir Hamon L'Estrange saw one in London.

The Dutch stonemason must have had a model.

And we do know that a female got to Vienna in 1657.

The story has a postscript called "the dodo of Nazareth," or, more
learnedly, *Didus nazarenus*. This is a case which I thought had been
nicely cleared up by Professor Iosif Kristianovitch Hamel of the
Russian Imperial Academy of Science in St. Petersburg. Professor
Hamel made a careful study of all dodo literature then available and
wrote a report which was published by the Academy in the Bulletin of
its Physico-Mathematical Section in 1848. He called the Nazareth
dodo *den erdichteten Nazarvogel,* "the imaginary Nazareth bird,"
and explained that this had been just a case of linguistic confusion,
starting out with the Dutch term *Walghvogels* or "nauseating birds."

(One source declared firmly that the dodo was for wonder, not for food.) The French had translated *Walghvogels* correctly into *oiseaux de nausée*. But one François Cauche, who spent two weeks on Mauritius in 1638, wrote of the dodos, *Nous les appellions oiseaux de Nazaret*. Cauche probably did not try to taste dodo and did not see why the birds should be nauseating, so he thought that the word *nausée* actually should be *Nazaret*, which sounds somewhat similar. And nautical charts showed a place called Nazareth nearby. They still do, but on modern charts it is labeled a "bank," while on earlier charts there is an island by that name.

Hamel, in explaining the case, used the latest nautical charts then in existence. And his explanation, it must be stated, can easily be correct.

But Oudemans checked old nautical charts too and found several on which the name Nazareth is placed, not next to an island where we now know no island to be, but at the actual, though tiny, island which on modern charts appears as Ile Tromelin.

Nobody knows much about Ile Tromelin. The latest edition of the Admiralty Charts states that its position may be five miles off on the map, and if it were of any importance the location would surely have been ascertained by now. Maybe the mapmakers who produced the old charts seen by Oudemans simply lettered Nazareth next to it because there was supposed to be such a place and this was the only island left in the whole area, the other suspected islands having turned into banks and shoals.

But Oudemans said that *Didus nazarenus* cannot be dismissed completely until Ile Tromelin has been carefully investigated. Not that he expected to find live dodos of any kind; he hoped for subfossil remains like those found on Mauritius and on Rodriguez. In principle he is of course correct; as long as there is an uninvestigated lead left the book should not be closed.

No such investigation has taken place. Until it is made and the facts prove otherwise, I prefer Professor Hamel's explanation.

CHAPTER 19

The Tortoise Islands

THOUGH this chapter also deals with islands and their strange fauna, it will be necessary to begin the exposition on a continent. The continent is Africa, more specifically the southern end of this continent. But it is not the Africa of today that interests us, it is the Africa of about 210 million years ago. At that time, which was during the latter part of the Permian period, there lived a reptile in what is now the Cape Province that later received the name of *Eunotosaurus africanus*.

What is known of Eunotosaurus is not enough to provide a picture of its appearance when it was alive. We know a good portion of the skull bones—the teeth in its jaws were rather small—but we don't know how long its neck was. The tail is missing and of the limbs we have just one major bone of one leg. We do have enough of the pelvis to get a general idea and the same applies to the shoulders. And we do have the rib cage.

It is just this rib cage which makes Eunotosaurus important and, in the proper circles, even famous. There were ten ribs on either side of the spine but only the first and the tenth look reasonably like ribs, while numbers II to IX have a weird shape. They are widened in the middle section to such an extent that they touch each other, while both ends are pointed. There is nothing directly comparable in the animal world; one would have to go to fairly technical concepts to find something that has about the same shape, as, for example, the "gores" of a plastic balloon, or the area enclosed by the 100th and 120th meridian. Or just say the outside of a section of an orange.

This Eunotosaurus was still rather close to the earliest of the reptiles, and it is believed to have been a burrowing form that needed the semi-armor provided by these wide ribs to withstand the pressure

355

of the soil. The important point is that these ribs that are not yet fused but look as if they were on the verge of becoming so put Eunotosaurus in a class all its own. It has been called "the only known archichelonian." Linguistically, the last word is based on the Greek *archaios,* "very old" or "first in time," while *chelonē* is the Greek word for tortoise. Eunotosaurus was ancestral stock for the turtles and tortoises that were still to come.

All turtles and tortoises—zoologists, when they wish to refer to all of them, say "chelonians"—are built on a plan which would be less easy to understand if we did not have this example from the upper Permian of the Cape Province. The chelonians, as everybody knows, are enclosed in a solid box consisting of the "carapace" on top and the "plastron" underneath. This solid bony armor began with widening ribs that finally grew together and, extending both front and back, managed to overlap and enclose the shoulders and the pelvis, so that only head, limbs, and tail stick out, and in most cases these too can be drawn inside. There were no muscles covering the widening ribs on the outside, only skin which has changed into a horny covering. The process was completed very soon after the time of Eunotosaurus. A fossil true chelonian from the Upper Triassic of Germany—logically named *Triassochelys*—shows its ancestry only in rudimentary teeth. All other chelonians, whether fossil or living, are as toothless as birds.

Although this early and, in more ways than one, tightly encased reptilian tribe orginated on dry land—even, as far as we can tell, under desert conditions—it quickly discovered the other extreme, lakes and the open seas. To this day, 200 million years later, we can see that its members tend to extremes of environment. On the one hand, we have the large and clumsy but merrily surviving desert tortoise of our southwestern deserts, while on the other hand we have the gracefully swimming green turtles and hawksbill turtles of the high seas, which touch land only for the serious business of depositing their eggs. Naturally the conquest of the open seas required some changes; the high-domed carapace of the land forms was lowered and smoothed out to reduce water resistance (in a number of fossil forms the solid armor was interrupted by "windows" to reduce weight), and the feet were changed into flippers.

And in all periods of geological history the chelonians have shown a remarkable tendency to produce forms of a size so colossal that it

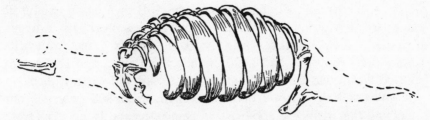

Incomplete skeleton of *Eunotosaurus Africanus,* the only known ancestral form of the later turtles and tortoises (discovered in 1914, in the Pareiasaurus beds, South Africa)

makes one understand the Hindu legends which say that the earth rests on the head of an elephant that, in turn, stands on the back of an enormous turtle. (It is considered bad manners to ask what supports the turtle.) When, during the Upper Cretaceous period, Kansas was flooded by the so-called Niobrara Sea, a gigantic turtle populated the warm waters, along with other marine reptiles, while Pteranodon circled overhead. It was *Archelon ischyros* (this time the "arch" in the name is derived from Greek *archos,* meaning "first in rank" or "ruler") and it measured more than 11 feet in length with a spread of the fore flippers of over 12 feet.

The marine turtles of today cannot quite compete with these titans of the past, but the leatherback turtle, *Dermochelys,* is still a colossal animal. One large specimen measured 9 feet in length and weighed 1500 pounds. The leatherback turtle, which is unfortunately growing rare, is interesting not only because of its record size but because it is a living high-seas form with greatly reduced armor. The original solid carapace and plastron which its ancestors must have had are reduced to ribs which are again free and to a large number of small bony plates imbedded in the tough skin.

The largest land tortoise known is also a fossil, but much younger geologically than Archelon. It lived during the late Tertiary period, not much more than a million years ago, and its habitat, by curious coincidence if you think of the Hindu legends, was India. It was found in the Siwalik beds of northern India and was properly named *Colossochelys atlas* by the British naturalist Dr. Hugh Falconer in 1837, the *atlas* of course referring to that other mythological earth shoulderer. Hugh Falconer had only fragmentary remains at his disposal but he could compute that the carapace must have had a size of 12 feet, measured over the curve. A smaller but far more complete specimen, recovered in India by Dr. Barnum Brown, is on exhibit at the American Museum of Natural History in New York. Its carapace measures 7 feet, 4 inches, over the curve and is 5 feet wide; the tortoise must have weighed 2100 pounds when alive; and Dr. Brown believed that it was between 300 and 400 years old when it died.

A colossal land tortoise of great weight, aged 300 years, is not something that strikes a zoologist as being necessarily an item from the fossil record. Comparatively recent journals and books provide precisely the same picture.

When Captain John Jourdain made his voyage to the Seychelles in January 1609 the customary boat was sent ashore—to North Island—to look for water:

> Butt because our men made noe signe of any water we ankored not. Soe the boate retourned and brought soe many land tortells as they could well carrie. Soe we stoode alonge towards the other islands. The tortelles were good meate, as good as fresh beefe, but after two or three meales our men would not eate them, because they did looke soe uglie before they were boyled; and so greate that eight of them did almost lade our skiffe.

Jourdain's shipmate Revett corroborated this; there were, he wrote, "land turtles of so huge a bidgnes which men will thinke incredible; of which our company had small lust to eate of, beinge such huge defourmed creatures and forted with five clawes lyke a beare."

From another ocean and about another set of islands, almost precisely one century later than Jourdain's account, we have the report of the famous English buccaneer, the very literary pirate William Dampier:

> The Spaniards when they first discover'd these Islands, found Multitudes of Guanoes, and Land-turtle or Tortoise, and named them the Gallapagos Islands. I do believe there is no place in the World that is so plentifully stored with those Animals. . . . The Land-turtle are here so numerous, that 5 or 600 Men might subsist on them alone for several Months, without any other sort of Provision: They are extraordinary large and fat; and so sweet, that no Pullet eats more pleasantly. One of the largest of these Creatures will weigh 150 or 200 weight, and some of them are 2 foot, or 2 foot 6 inches over the Challapee or Belly. I did never see any but at this place, that will weigh above 30 pound weight.[1]

This kind of news kept trickling in during the two centuries from 1600 to 1800. Traveler after traveler reported that they had landed on uninhabited islands where gigantic tortoises abounded. And most

[1] *A New Voyage Around the World,* by William Dampier (London, 1697).

of them reported with relish that they were good to eat—the squeamishness of the men aboard John Jourdain's ship is an almost incredible exception—and thereby advertised to other sailors that fresh meat could be had on those islands.

Any modern reader of such old ships' journals sooner or later begins to wonder about the almost psychotic preoccupation with food on the part of the travelers, and it needs some mental effort to understand their reactions. Man went to sea before he was technologically ready to travel with certainty, not to mention with a reasonable amount of comfort. The wooden ships which discovered the globe lacked anything that would provide power at the will of the captain. They depended on the wind for propulsion, and at almost any moment the wind might increase to unmanageable strength or else might simply die away to a dead calm that might last for weeks if you were unlucky. The food situation was equally unreliable. Since the existence of bacteria was still unknown, the relatively simple process of canning food was still in the future. Refrigeration was an impossibility which nobody had ever even dreamed of, though on land the ice house was in use. Insect-killing poisons were unknown. So the food on board these ships consisted of heavily oversalted meat, sometimes beef, more often horse meat, dished out with the brine in which it floated. The other staple was hardtack, a bread so dry that no mold could get a root-hold (unless the hardtack was swamped by water and could not be dried out fast enough), and limited quantities of dried beans and peas and lentils which were used up quickly before the weevils got into them. To make the bad situation worse, the ships were not undermanned, which would have meant more work per man, but also more food; on the contrary, they were as overmanned as possible, and not because some men might be lost in heavy weather. Every minute of day and night the owners had to think of enemies—somebody usually was at war with somebody else—and of pirates. Ships did carry guns, but the final act of any naval engagement was a hand-to-hand fight with a boarding party, and the more hands there were on board to wield a cutlass, knife, or spike, the better your chances. There was a certain safety in numbers.

The over-all result of these conditions was ships setting out on voyages of unknown durations, overmanned and understocked, so that everybody aboard, with the possible exception of the captain and the first mate, was forever and ever thinking and dreaming of something to eat, something "soft and sweet," something that was food, as contrasted to the subsistence offered by hardtack and salted meat. The interesting and often unique fauna of lonely islands suffered in consequence. And when some of the more foresighted captains, a good number of them buccaneers, put live goats and pigs ashore on islands for the sake of fresh meat at a later date, the island fauna suffered even more; instead of being subjected to the attacks of hungry but transient men, it was constantly exposed to the attacks of hungry pigs.

The men, if offered a choice, preferred meat that could be eaten not only while the ship was at anchor, but that could be taken aboard and kept fresh for some time. But to keep it fresh meant in those days that it had to be kept alive, and very little food was available aboard ship. It was the ability of the large tortoises to stay alive without any food that made them so desirable. But though the ships' crews would return with tales of the big tortoises, they did not bring any specimens. Sometimes an empty carapace was brought home as a curiosity, but even then, more likely than not, the bringer would be unsure or confused about the island on which the tortoise had been taken.

It is significant that two of the earliest books devoted specifically to turtles and tortoises, Walbaum's *Chelonographia* of 1782 and Johann Gottlieb Schneider's *Allgemeine Naturgeschichte der Schild-kröten* (*General Natural History of the Turtles*) of 1783, do not mention the "large tortoises of distant isles" at all. It is of course possible that the authors of these books, living far from any seaport, simply had not heard about them. But it is equally likely that the news which they had received was so much in the rumor category that they decided not to make any mention of it until more was known.[2]

Things remained in a state of insufficient reporting for quite some time. That big tortoises were frequent on a certain group of islands in the Pacific Ocean was certain. That there were, or had been, large tortoises on a number of islands in the Indian Ocean was also known, but on which islands was already doubtful. And to try to classify the few carapaces that had been brought home seemed a hopeless task. Some were undated, the place of origin was not stated, or if it was stated one could be doubtful in many cases that the information was correct, and even if one knew that the label "Madagascar" was wrong

---

[2] Schneider mentioned an older work by one Caldesi, printed in Florence in 1687, which I have not been able to obtain. But if Caldesi had said anything startling I suppose that Schneider would have quoted him.

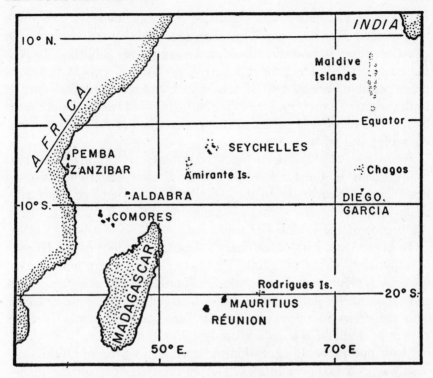

The various island groups north of Madagascar in the Indian Ocean,
between the African coast and the mainland of India (Günther)

one still could not say what the proper label should be. A few islands
in the Indian Ocean came to be mentioned more and more frequently.
They were Mauritius, Réunion, and Rodriguez, the atoll of Aldabra
to the north of Madagascar, and a few tiny islands nearby. And the
Seychelles. The Pacific island group was the Galápagos, but an occasional mention of Juan Fernández, "Robinson Crusoe's Island,"
crept in.

Around 1860 a zoologist decided that where there was a puzzle
there ought to be a solution and that finding the solution should be
merely a matter of tenacious application. He was Albert C. L. G.
Günther, M.D., Ph.D., "Keeper of the Department of Zoology" of
the British Museum.[3] After reading everything that might shed light
on the problem of giant tortoises, and carefully examining what
specimens there were, Dr. Günther published a large work in which

[3] The man who discovered what the "peculiar structure" in the head of Hatteria
really is.

the existing knowledge was organized and systematized. The work was entitled *The Gigantic Land Tortoises (Living and Extinct) in the Collection of the British Museum* and was published by the museum in 1877. The proper cataloguing of the specimens had been made possible because Dr. Günther had found an anatomical clue as to the origin of a preserved tortoise shell. He could tell by the presence or absence of specific plates in the armor whether a label was right or wrong and what it should be.

When you say "tortoise islands" nowadays, everybody quite naturally thinks of the Galápagos. But since the "eastern tortoise islands" were discovered first they should be discussed first, especially since three of the five eastern islands are already familiar to us as the homes of the dodos and solitaries.

To begin again with Mauritius, C. Grant, the author of the *History of Mauritius,* wrote in 1720: "We possess a great abundance of fowl, as well as both Land- and Sea-Turtle, which are not only a great resource for the supply of our ordinary wants, but serve to barter with the crews of ships who put in here for refreshment in their voyage to India." The sailors brought live dodos home with them, but with one probable exception, no specimen of the Mauritius tortoise was ever taken to Europe. During the latter part of the seventeenth century a tortoise reached Paris which Pierre Perrault described as *La tortue des Indes* (the Indian Tortoise) because he had been told that it came from the Coromandel coast. The scientific name given was *Testudo indica* (*testudo* is the Latin word for tortoise) and later, after Perrault's death, *Testudo perraulti.* Since this type of tortoise does not exist on the Coromandel coast, or anywhere else in India, Dr. Günther concluded that the ship may have come from the Coromandel coast but picked up the tortoise on Mauritius on the return trip.

Though there are no other known remains of a Mauritius tortoise taken alive, we have remains of Mauritius tortoises which presumably died of old age before any sailor ever made a landfall on the island. They come from the same Mare aux Songes—some 3 miles from Mahébourg—that yielded the dodo bones now in our museums. Their carapaces measure from 2 to 3 feet in length, and Dr. Günther could establish three species, or subspecies, which he named *Testudo triserrata, T. inepta,* and *T. leptocnemis.* We don't know whether these same species, or one or two of them, also lived on Réunion, because no remains of the Réunion tortoises are known. But there are quite a number of eyewitness accounts of tortoises on Réunion so that we can be sure of the fact itself.

In P. J. Verhuff's *Voyage into the East Indies,* published in Frankfort in 1633, there is a Latin entry about the arrival at "Mascarene" (Réunion) on December 27, 1611. It says that this is an island 80 miles from the island of Mauritius, 16 miles in circumference, uninhabited by people but with many *Testudines* and fish. François Cauche, who started the confusion about the dodo of Nazareth, made a similar report in his *Relation du Voyage à Madagascar* (1638). Writing in the French of his period he stated:

De la, nous tirasmes en l'isle de Mascarhene . . . scituée environ deux degrez delà le Tropique du Capricorne. On y voit grand nombre d'oiseaux, et tortues de terre, et les rivières y sont fort pisqueuses. (From there we proceeded to the isle of Mascarene . . . situated about two degrees from the Tropic of Capricorn. One can see large numbers of birds there, and land tortoises, and the rivers are full of fish.)

Another report told that in 1712 a party of Frenchmen coming from Madagascar landed on Réunion, and that they lived for two years on fish, tortoises, and marine turtles—presumably until they harvested their first crops. One more witness is an abbé who wrote a letter (published in 1724 as *Lettre du Père Jacques*) containing a virtual eulogy of the Réunion tortoise:

Le meilleur de tous les animaux, qu'on y trouve, soit par le goût, soit pour la santé, c'est la Tortue de terre. . . . On assure qu'elle vit un temps prodigieux, qu'il lui faut plusieurs siècles pour parvenir à la grosseur naturelle, et qu'elle peut passer plus de six mois sans manger. (The best of all the animals one finds there, be it for the taste, be it for the health, is the land tortoise. . . . It is assured that it lives a prodigious time, that it needs several centuries to reach its full natural size, and that it can live for more than six months without eating.)

As for Rodriguez, we have the oft-quoted words of François Leguat, written in 1691, that "there are plenty of such land tortoises in this isle that sometimes you see two or three thousand of them in a flock, so that you may walk more than a hundred paces on their backs." Two specimens of this tortoise are in the Paris Museum—I don't know whether they reached Paris alive or not—and some additional bones and carapaces have been found on the island later after the tortoise was gone. The largest carapace measures 4½ feet over the curve and the bones prove that the tortoise was long-legged with a long neck. It obviously differed greatly from those of Mauritius, and Dr. Günther gave it the name *Testudo vosmoeri*.

The sailors' habit of taking the Mascarene tortoises to keep on board as living meat would never have exterminated them; it was the settlement of the islands that spelled their doom. The men caught and cooked the large ones; their pigs and dogs ate the small ones and the eggs. And many small ones perished when the settlers burned off areas of brush to create fields for their crops.

The second group of Indian Ocean tortoises was those of Aldabra, an oval-shaped atoll to the north of Madagascar measuring more than 40 miles in circumference and enclosing a mostly shallow lagoon. Several deep channels split the atoll into four islands, of unequal length but generally of the same width of about 1½ miles. The island was known to, and named by, the Arabs, but the first recorded visit to it was by a Portuguese ship in 1511. Its fauna is typical for a lonely island in an ocean. The only mammals are two kinds of bats, of which one, *Pteropus aldabranus*, is not found anywhere else. Among the birds, one, a rail, is also typical for the island, while an ibis, *Ibis abottii*, is rare. The reptiles are represented by two geckos and one skink, and by *Chelone mydas* (the green turtle) and *Chelone imbricata* (the hawksbill turtle) at the shore. There are no amphibians, probably because they do not survive exposure to salt water. In short, all the rest of the fauna of Aldabra could easily have arrived from the neighboring land, and probably did, but how the Aldabra tortoise got there is a mystery.

Although the tortoise was common it was not mentioned until fairly late. The earliest literary reference to it seems to be an entry made on a map in 1744: "They found a great many land-turtle much larger than those at Rodrige."

When Dr. Günther pieced together the history of the Mascarene tortoises, by then already extinct, he felt that the Aldabra type could still be saved if measures to do so were taken at once. He wrote a long letter to the British Government, signed by the trustees and scientists of the British Museum. The government responded quickly and promised all possible protection for the Aldabra tortoise. But, as has been said with reference to the coco-de-mer, protective measures, to be successful, must go further than just preserving what remnants there are. The remnants must be spread around to increase the area of the habitat, so that a local catastrophe cannot wipe out all the past efforts of the conservationists along with the protected species. For the Aldabra tortoise this was done, and the best new habitat was the home of the coco-de-mer, the Seychelles. Some spreading around had even been done before Dr. Günther wrote his plea.

When, in March 1899, the German oceanographic expedition on S.S. *Valdivia* under Professor Carl Chun visited the Seychelles for

Testudo elephantina from Aldabra (as shown in Günther's *The Gigantic Land Tortoises*)

coco-de-mer, the members received proof of this distribution. "Mr. Harald Baty, the owner of Félicité," Professor Chun wrote,[4] "had sailed in the steam launch accompanied by my navigation's officer to his island and had taken one of the biggest and oldest of the giant tortoises (*Testudo elephantina*) from a small islet to present the expedition with the specimen. It was indeed an almost antediluvian looking monster which had been brought from Aldabra more than a hundred years ago—the grandfather of an aged Negro, a resident of Félicité, had already known this particular tortoise. Since Mr. Baty presented us with two other, though younger, specimens and Dr. Brooks added one as a present to His Majesty the Kaiser a fair number of dim-witted giants crawled around on board the *Valdivia*." Professor Chun added that most of the farms on the Seychelles keep a number of tortoises, of which one may be slaughtered for an especially festive occasion.

[4] In his general account of the expedition, *Aus den Tiefen des Weltmeeres*, (2d ed. Jena, 1905), pp. 473–74.

A later witness is Michael J. Nicoll, one of the two professional naturalists who have gone on record as having seen a "sea serpent." His book, *Three Voyages of a Naturalist* (London, 1908), describes the trips he had made as the guest of the Earl of Crawford on the latter's yacht *Valhalla*. The *Valhalla* anchored at Aldabra but Mr. Nicoll did not see any of the tortoises there. He wrote that they were "once fairly abundant but are now confined to a small area on the northern side. The Hon. Walter Rothschild rents the island of Aldabra from the British Government and protects the tortoises as well as a peculiar species of ibis." The reason Mr. Nicoll could not see the tortoises is that it would have been an exceedingly difficult overland trip, requiring more time than he had. He did get to see numbers of them in the Seychelles, "where they are kept in a semi-domesticated state." Mr. Nicoll reported that the usual means of confining them were low stone enclosures. Some were actually tethered, and all of them had identification numbers painted on their backs with white paint. Of course there were also some that lived in the bush without official owners.

In his work on the giant tortoises Dr. Günther distinguished several species of Aldabra tortoises. The most numerous one, and the one transplanted to the Seychelles, is *Testudo elephantina*. Another one he named *T. ponderosa,* and a third *T. daudinii;* however, it was said later that *T. daudinii* is probably identical with *T. elephantina,* and that the one characteristic which made Dr. Günther think it a separate species was probably an individual characteristic of his specimen.

A specimen whose remains are preserved at the Royal College of Surgeons was named *T. hololissa* by Dr. Günther. While there is no doubt that it is a different species one may have doubts about Günther's insistence that it was from Aldabra. The catalogue of the College contains a rather detailed history of the specimen. It was originally captured by Frenchmen. It was, the catalogue said, "a native of the Seychelle Islands, and was being sent to General de Caën, Governor of the Isle of France, in the French corvette *Gobemouche* which was captured by Captain Corbett of H.M.S. *Nereida,* and the animal was brought to the Cape of Good Hope. It was sent to England by Admiral Bertie, who commanded at the Cape, and remained in a living state at Petworth, the seat of the Earl of Egremont, from August 1809 until April 1810. Its weight was 207 pounds." Dr. Günther brushed the first sentence aside by saying,

"We have no evidence of tortoises on the Seychelles," and declared that *Testudo hololissa* therefore must be a fourth species from Aldabra. Apparently Dr. Günther was not acquainted with Jourdain's journal, which is as clear on this point as is possible. If the French said that they captured the tortoise on the Seychelles they probably did. But what happened to the large numbers seen by Jourdain's men we simply don't know.

There are other minor mysteries, and one major one, left. In 1893 a French naturalist named Sauzier came to Port Louis on Mauritius. Learning that an old tortoise was kept on the drill ground of the artillery barracks, he went and measured it. The carapace, not measured over the curve but straight, was 40 inches long. The tortoise looked about 200 years old to him and upon inquiry he was told that it had been there since 1810 and that it had grown very little, if any, since then. Trying to establish the species according to Dr. Günther's scheme, Sauzier found it had the characteristics of a Galápagos tortoise. Now it was conceivable, though neither proved nor likely, that a ship with a living Galápagos tortoise aboard had restocked its supplies on Mauritius and that the tortoise, presumably still fairly small then, had escaped and established itself in its new home until captured once more. Sauzier found it easier to believe that it was a survivor from the early days and named it *Testudo soumeirei*. Then he dug from the Mare aux Songes four damaged plastrons of tortoises, all with double gular plates which made them either Aldabra or Galápagos. Living Aldabra tortoises on Mauritius would be easy to account for, but subfossil Aldabra tortoises are less easy.

There must be an answer, but it hasn't been found so far.

We now come to the "Western tortoise islands," the Galápagos, situated precisely under the equator some 600 miles west of the west coast of South America. They are a handful of fairly large islands, and another handful of smaller islands, plus a collection of islets, rocks, and cliffs, all of them volcanic. Though heated during the day by the equatorial sun they cool rapidly after sunset, and in general do not have the climate one would expect of islands under the equator, because they are located in the cold Humboldt current. The Humboldt current produces rather confused local currents between the islands, and just as a sailor without previous experience could not predict what the current is going to be like in a given spot he also could not predict what kind of beach he would find on the island to be seen on the horizon. Most likely the beach consists of lava, piled high and dangerous to climb because it is loose, but it could be dense mangrove, and it could even be sandy. But whatever the beach is like, the area near the shore will be arid in virtually every case, with a vegetation of prickly cactus and even more prickly bushes of other kinds. The more fertile places occur farther inland, or, rather, higher up, which on volcanic islands is more or less the same thing.

This amazing collection of islands was discovered by accident in 1535, mostly because Francisco Pizarro misbehaved after the conquest of Peru. To create some kind of order the bishop of Panama, Tomás de Berlanga, was requested to sail to Peru. He did sail on February 23, 1535, but the voyage did not go well. The captain, Diego de Rivadeneira, "navigated" by hugging the shore line—actually avoiding navigation by doing so—and as the ship approached the equator the wind suddenly died. After floating for a number of days the ship began to drift; it had been caught in the still-unknown Humboldt current. The coastline vanished in the east and for weeks nothing was visible but water. On March 10 islands came into sight. The ship landed in the usual quest for water, but there wasn't any.

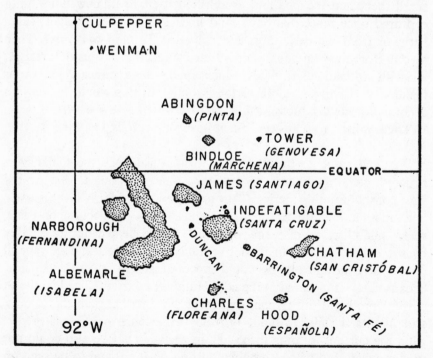

The Galápagos Islands, with customary English and official Spanish names

There were birds of all kinds by the thousands, there were sun-heated lava rocks, there were coldly staring reptilian eyes, and there were spiny plants—from their appearance any botanist could have deduced lack of water at a glance. The men sent ashore to find water for the ship's company and grass for the horses carried aboard found neither the one nor the other. As the bishop later wrote to the king of Spain: "They found nothing but seals and turtles and such big tortoises that each could carry a man on top of itself, and many iguanas that are like serpents."

After saying Mass several days later on another island—for it was Passion Sunday—the bishop's men finally did find some water and they then somehow made their way back to South America, having lost two men and ten horses because of thirst. The bishop, in his report to the king, stressed the aridity of the islands and wrote that he did not think that there was a place on them where one might sow a bushel of grain. In short, he reported the discovery but said the islands were worthless, which impression must have been strong because the expedition had not bothered to take possession of the islands for the king. The bishop did not even name them. And the first name they received is not the name that was later used. About fifteen years after their discovery, Captain Diego de Rivadeneira, who had become hopelessly involved in the fights of the various Spanish factions, looking around for a place where he would be safely out of the way of current events, remembered the bishop's islands. He reached them, but the unknown and fairly strong currents running between the islands did not let him land. Capitán de Rivadeneira decided after a while that it was not his ship which drifted around unpredictably but that he was among shifting islands. They were obviously enchanted. That the bishop had been able to land was only further proof; the enchantment could not stand up against the bishop's cross. So Diego de Rivadeneira called them *Los Encantadas,* the Enchanted Isles.

This name did not take hold, but their permanent name was given them by a European, the mapmaker Abraham Ortelius (né Oertel), who received a report on Berlanga's report. The outstanding thing about the islands was not the aridity—that could be found elsewhere too—but the large tortoises. In Spanish a tortoise is *galápago* and on Ortelius's map of 1587, *Typus Orbis Terrarum,* they appear as *Yslas de los galopegos.* Although Bishop Tomás de Berlanga had clearly said in his letter to the king of Spain that the islands were between ½ degree and 1½ degrees below the equator—correct for most of them—Ortelius placed them quite a distance north of the "line." They appear to the west of Panama and are far too close to the mainland, but there can be no doubt that the real Galápagos are meant—they had just drifted a little, as Rivadeneira had expected.

The captains who sailed the Pacific probably had more accurate charts than the Ortelius map; otherwise its deficiencies might explain why the islands were left alone for a century. The real reason is different, of course, and there is more than one. First, the Spaniards were fully occupied in South America, hunting semi-mythical or fully mythical gold treasures and fighting against Nature, against the Indians, and among themselves. Another reason for the neglect is that the Galápagos are the Galápagos—large heaps of lava almost impossible to walk on, with an unreliable water supply which is meager when not nonexistent, with occasional volcanic eruptions. Moreover, unlike the Mascarenes, stepping stones on the voyage to India, the Galápagos were not even near a trade route; one did not visit them *en passant.*

After this century of neglect, the period of the buccaneers began, also lasting about a century. William Dampier's book of 1697 has already been quoted; his fellow buccaneer Ambrose Cowley had visited the islands in 1684. Cowley produced the first chart of them, and a fairly accurate one. But though buccaneers went there whenever they felt like it—islands *off* a trade route were just what they needed on occasion—and occasionally met, the quality of the buccaneers declined visibly and rapidly. The days of the gentleman pirate who would report on what had been found and seen and thereby enrich geographical knowledge were gone. The second-string pirates who came afterward probably considered themselves clever if they could follow the indications of the mariner's compass and read a chart. But they did know from Cowley's book that the islands "were very plentifully stored with the aforesaid Provisions, as Tortoises, Fowls, Fish and Alguanoes, large and good."

After the century of the buccaneers and the privateers had passed, the period of the whalers began; it did not last quite a century. In 1593 Sir Richard Hawkins had deliberately avoided the Galápagos, not even paying them a curiosity visit;[5] in 1793 Captain James

[5] The sentence: "Some fourscore leagues to the westward of this cape lyeth a heape of Illands the Spaniards call Ilhas de los Galápagos; they are desert and bear no fruite," is the sum total of what Hawkins had to say about them.

Colnett of the Royal Navy was officially sent there. Not only to the Galápagos, of course, but he was instructed to visit them, for Captain Colnett's trip had the purpose of finding out where British whalers might make port in the Pacific for repairs, refitting, and "victualling." The Galápagos were one of the places he recommended (with some reservations), but the whalers had already found the islands for themselves. They had even established a post office, at Post Office Bay on Charles Island. It consisted of a barrel. There was no clerk, no postage, and no formalities. Outward-bound ships left letters for home, or for other ships, in the barrel, and the next homeward-bound ship took them along. By about 1810, although the majority of the whalers were still from Dover, England, there were some from Nantucket and New Bedford.

In 1812 the U.S. frigate *Essex,* fully provisioned for a long cruise and commanded by Captain David Porter (with a midshipman named David Farragut aboard), entered the Pacific with sealed orders. When the orders were opened they said simply that Captain Porter was to drive the British whalers from the Pacific as soon as war was declared. When war was declared, American whalers guided Captain Porter to the Galápagos and to Post Office Bay. The letters in the barrel told better than any intelligence report what English vessels were in the Pacific and where they might be at the moment. Within a week Porter captured eleven ships. When the war was over, most of the whaling ships in the Pacific were from Nantucket and New Bedford. They sailed south along the continental coast, rounded the always difficult Cape Horn, and proceeded northward on the other side of the continent in the Humboldt current, thus making the Galápagos, to the detriment of the giant tortoises.

While the ships rode at anchor, crewmen went "turpining," as the logbooks expressed it. Apparently none of these New England captains, or their first mates, had ever heard the word tortoise, or if they had they did not use it. They sent their men ashore for turpin, tarpain, terapen, turupin, tarphin, or terrepin. They all ate tortoise steak or tortoise stew afterward and assured one another that fried tortoise liver was the best thing a man could possibly eat. And they took a good supply of tortoises along with them, alive, when they hoisted anchor. The logbook entry of the *Sukey* of Nantucket, made June 14, 1812, is typical: "I leave this port [Charles Island] this Day with 250 Turpin."

At the time the whalers were pursuing their trade, hardly any of

Giant tortoises from the Galápagos Islands

them wrote anything longer than a logbook entry, but a few captains wrote reminiscing memoirs after their retirement. The following is an account of "turpining" [6] as it took place in 1858 on Albemarle Island:

After everything was put in shape [aboard ship] about two thirds of the crew went ashore, taking with us boat sails to make tents of and water to drink and cook with, as fresh water cannot be found there. After fitting up our temporary camp we started for the mountains after turpin, which are very numerous, and are not found on any other islands.

Turpin are a specimen of turtle, the shell being in large checks like an alligator's skin, and their flesh is unsurpassed as food for soups and stews: its equal cannot be found. The liver is far superior to any kind of meat I ever ate. It is as large as a beef critter's (from a large one) and is many times superior to it in any way you choose to cook it.

In order to get them we had to go high up in the mountains, as that seems to be their roaming ground. They are black in color and move very slow. We did not disturb the large ones, as we would have had to kill and cut them up and carry the pieces down on our backs, as many

[6] From *Strange but True* by Captain Thomas Crapo, published in New Bedford in 1893. Captain Crapo's ship was the bark *Greyhound*.

of them will weigh, I should think, nearly half of a ton. So we caught the smaller ones, none weighing over five or six hundred.

We went hunting them every day for a week, and as they are so clumsy and move so slow, made it an easy matter to capture them. We built a pen to put them in, and while on shore lived on them mostly and used hard bread from the ship for soups and stews and other ways: the cook dished it out to us. The small ones we caught we carried down to camp on our shoulders, but we had to drag the large ones. They are perfectly harmless and never known to bite. We caught about a hundred during the time. At the close of the week we took them aboard. Their weights would range from about five pounds to five hundred and over. We put them on deck and between decks, and let them crawl around as they chose. It was all of six months before they were all gone. I never knew one to eat or drink a drop while they were on board, and yet they looked as fat as a ball of butter when they were killed.

In order to estimate the number of tortoises that had lived on the Galápagos at the time the whalers made it a regular port of call, Dr. Charles Haskins Townsend of the New York Aquarium examined a total of 79 logbooks of whaling vessels preserved in the libraries of New Bedford, Nantucket, and Salem.[7] The logbooks covered the period 1831–1868, during which time the 79 vessels made 189 visits to the islands. Their combined catch numbered 13,013 tortoises. Since the American whaling fleet at that time numbered around 700 vessels, the 79 logbooks represent only a little more than 10 per cent of the whole. Naturally not all 700 vessels went to the Pacific Ocean; on the other hand, whaling vessels of other nationalities did; the number of tortoises actually taken during these four decades might well be 50,000. The inroads made by the buccaneers before the whalers came can be more or less neglected, even though the figures, if they were available, might look fairly large. Unlike the whalers, the buccaneers did not represent a steady commercial operation.

The islands from which the whalers took tortoises are Albemarle, Chatham, Charles, Hood, James, Abingdon, Duncan, Indefatigable, and Barrington. The island of Jervis is mentioned only once, and the fairly large island of Narborough is not mentioned at all, the reason probably being that there was a major volcanic eruption on Narborough early in the nineteenth century. The buccaneers may have taken tortoises from Narborough in their time; in more recent

[7] See "The Galápagos Tortoises in Their Relation to the Whaling Industry" by Charles H. Townsend, in *Zoologica, Scientific Contributions of the New York Zoological Society,* vol. IV, no. 3, July 29, 1925.

times only a single specimen, an old male, has been recorded there.

The wonder is, of course, that the tortoises lasted as long as they did. That they were numerous before the whalers systematically provisioned themselves with tortoise is easily explained. A tortoise of this type will produce about twenty eggs per year. If there are no natural enemies that eat the eggs, the activity of a single couple of adults will result in two hundred young tortoises after only ten years and soon the first batch of the young ones will start laying more eggs. Because of the longevity of the individual tortoise, the offspring of each female will be numerous, and for the same reason the number of individuals will be enormous, since a score of generations can be alive at the same time. Given a sufficient supply of plant food and the absence of enemies, you get an island virtually paved with tortoises, just as Leguat described it.

The reason the tortoises lived so much longer on the Galápagos than on the Mascarenes is mostly the size and the topography of the islands. Albemarle is 72 miles long and 10 miles wide in the north, 20 miles wide in the south, with elevations up to 5000 feet. Indefatigable is 20 miles across with its highest point 2296 feet above sea level. Chatham measures 24 by 8 miles with a 2500-foot peak, and Narborough is 15 miles across, with a 4300-foot volcano. There were always places on these islands where people could not penetrate. And as long as the supply was really large, the sailors practiced an unconscious conservation program for their own convenience. Small tortoises were spurned because they did not have enough meat, which means that they were left to grow up. And the sailors did not take the very biggest specimens because they were too heavy to move. Captain Crapo's report was already atypical in regard to the size of the tortoises taken. In the days preceding him the rule was to look for specimens weighing between 50 and 75 pounds, which a man could easily carry on his back.

In the middle of whaling activity and "turpining," something else happened: on September 15, 1835, H.M.S. *Beagle* arrived at Chatham Island. The purpose of the voyage was an oceanographic survey around South America. Nobody even asks any more whether H.M.S. *Beagle* accomplished her mission or not, the offshoot of the expedition was so much more important than the expedition itself. For the young man on board H.M.S. *Beagle,* who served as the "naturalist" of the expedition, was named Charles Darwin, and the theory of evolution was born while he was on the Galápagos. But that came later. Darwin, after his return to England, first published his ponderous but very well-written *Journal of Researches* (1839). Now the eyes of science were on the Galápagos and they have stayed on these islands ever since.

Enough had been learned about the past of our planet by the middle of the nineteenth century to cast a special and strange and most intriguing light on these islands. There was this piece of land, somewhat broken up, right under the equator. It teemed with unwieldy tortoises. At the black lava shores there lived something that did not exist anywhere else in the world any more—a sea-going lizard. These large black iguanas, by the tens of thousands, sat motionless in the surf and swam out into the sea to feed on seaweed. Farther up there were thousands of other large iguanas, also vegetarian in their habits, colored sulphur-yellow and red. There were many other smaller lizards and a snake. It looked as if these islands had been bodily left over from the time when the reptiles were the dominant form of life on earth. And just as there had been a few small mammals of insignificant size in the time of the dinosaurs, there was a little mammalian life on the islands: a few bats, which might have been brought there by a storm, and various species of a white-footed rodent, a specimen of which Darwin had caught and which later had been described as *Mus galapagoensis,* the "mouse from the Galápagos." The "white-footed mouse" became a symbol, the only mammal among the dragons on the islands time forgot.

I am sorry to have to say that the Galápagos are not a "Lost World" and that the true explanation is somewhat different, but this romantic, though mistaken, picture provided a powerful stimulus for continued interest.

First the zoological picture was rounded out. There were about sixty kinds of land birds. About two dozen different reptiles. No amphibians. No mammals except for the bats and the "mouse" (really a small rat) in several species. Several hundred insects. The sea life was plentiful: fishes and marine reptiles (turtles), seals, and marine birds. Two of the latter were especially interesting: a smallish penguin which, living under the equator, is the most northerly penguin in existence, and a flightless cormorant.

The big tortoises remained the center of attraction even for the zoologist, who felt that he had still come in time here while the opportunity had been missed on the Mascarenes. Dr. Albert Günther in his work on the gigantic land tortoises provided a separate section for the "Races of the Galápagos Tortoises." He listed six of them, as follows:

Testudo elephantopus	(James Island?)
Testudo nigrita	(?)
Testudo vicina	(Albemarle, South)
Testudo microphyes	(Albemarle, North)
Testudo ephippium	(Charles Island)
Testudo abingdoni	(Abingdon Island)

Nobody could be quite sure at the time Dr. Günther wrote his book which species were rare or how the fate of the giant tortoises as a whole was progressing. Unfortunately it progressed badly. If the islands had been left alone after the whalers stopped going there, the tortoises would probably have recovered; enough specimens were left, either in inaccessible places, or too big or too small for the whalers' purpose, to perpetuate themselves. But Ecuadorians settled on the islands and killed off tortoises for their oil. Even worse, domesticated animals had been released—or had escaped from ships —from time to time. The goats did no harm, but the pigs and the dogs decimated the young tortoises especially.

Zoologists decided that a serious effort ought to be made at least to learn what could still be learned, even if it might be too late for salvage. In 1905 the California Academy of Sciences organized a major expedition to Galápagos and collected 266 specimens. These became the subject of a special study by Dr. John Van Denburgh, who distinguished not less than fifteen species. Sorted by islands, his list looks like this:

Albemarle	{ *T. guntheri, T. vicina, T. microphyes,* *T. becki,* and one unnamed
Narborough	*T. phantastica*
Charles	*T. elephantopus;* extinct
Hood	*T. hoodensis*
Chatham	*T. chathamensis*
Indefatigable	*T. porteri*
Duncan	*T. ephippium*
Jervis	*T. wallacei*
James	*T. darwini*
Abingdon	*T. abingdoni*
Barrington	*T.* sp. (unnamed); extinct

Only on Duncan, Indefatigable, and Albemarle were the tortoises still "numerous" or "fairly abundant"; for everywhere else the labels read "rare," "very rare," or "nearly extinct."

The prediction that the next decade would see the extinction of several more species was the obvious conclusion to be drawn from this list. But in 1917 Professor Samuel Garman of Harvard University went over the anatomy of the Galápagos tortoises once more and came to the conclusion that Dr. Van Denburgh had been somewhat too enthusiastic a systematizer. Professor Garman emphasized that young Galápagos tortoises cannot be distinguished as to species or island of origin. The older they grow the more clearly the various characteristics appear. And the characteristics keep changing with age. What had happened was that too much attention had been paid to anatomy and too little to the living animal. In other words, specimens of different age had been classified as different species. That, of course, should not happen, but it does; it has even happened that the two sexes of a species were classified separately, though not necessarily in the case of the Galápagos tortoises.

The species *Testudo phantastica,* based on the single specimen from Narborough Island, was simply a very old *Testudo elephantopus,* probably changed a little more by recovery from volcanic burns. Van Denburgh's "nearly extinct" *Testudo abingdoni* was also just a very old *T. elephantopus.* Garman threw out a whole raft of other names as mere "synonyms": *T. becki, T. hoodensis,* and *T. ephippium* were all young or middle-aged specimens of *T. elephantopus.* Likewise *T. galapagoensis* and *T. wallacei* were "synonyms" of *Testudo nigra.* More important even than the removal of a lot of superfluous names was the fact that Professor Garman could show that the Galápagos tortoise did not stand as isolated in the system as had been believed and taught for two generations. A tortoise known for a long time—it appeared in literature for the first time in Walbaum's *Chelonographia* way back—was proved to be a relative of the Galápagos tortoise. It occurs in the northern portions of South America but is mainly found in Central America, grows to a length of 2 feet, and is easily and often tamed. Locally it is called "jaboty"; the scientific name is *Testudo tabulata.*

The realization that there was a living relative of the Galápagos tortoise on the mainland changed a lot of thoughts. Up to the time that Garman's work was published, all that naturalists could offer by way of helpful information was that a fossil tortoise resembling the Galápagos tortoise had been found on Cuba. This piece of knowledge had merely deepened the mystery, but with *Testudo tabulata* identified as a related mainland form, it helped to clarify the situation. In some manner the ancestor of the jaboty—possibly indistinguishable from the living form—had reached the Galápagos and changed to the Galápagos tortoise. If this ancestral tortoise had spread westward to Galápagos there was no reason why it could not have spread eastward to Cuba, where it presumably did not survive because of people and other mammals.

The case of the jaboty was new ammunition for a long-smoldering debate. The debate had been started in all innocence by Charles Darwin, who, looking at the islands and finding no land that was not volcanic, concluded that the islands had been built up by a probably long succession of volcanic eruptions from the bottom of the sea. They were islands which had been isolated since the time they originated, never connected to the mainland. Late in the nineteenth century Dr. George Baur declared that Darwin had been wrong in this case. The Galápagos, Dr. Baur was convinced, were "islands of subsidence," which means islands formed by the process of the settling of a land mass so that in the end only the highest peaks still appear above water. Because the fauna seemed to be a little more closely related to Central American than to South American types, a former land bridge from Panama to the Galápagos was assumed, taking in Cocos Island as another point that had been high enough to have survived as an island.

John Van Denburgh applauded this idea enthusiastically, mostly on the grounds that the tortoises cannot swim. He admitted that they float, but they will drift helplessly with the ocean currents. And if they drifted ashore somewhere they would be so battered as to die soon after. This was the reason that each island where tortoises occurred had its own species of tortoise, and only one species, except for large Albemarle Island which had several. "If the transportation of tortoises from one island to another does not occur," he concluded his argument, "there is little reason to believe that tortoises, at some time in the past, have drifted over the vastly greater distance from some continent, and have reached each of the eleven islands on which they have been found. Nor do we know whence they have come. . . ."

William Beebe, who apparently never read Garman's work, accepted all this at face value but had to contradict one point: during his visit to Galápagos he had seen a tortoise swim and swim well.

The tortoise had died a week later and was found to have congested lungs as well as a congested small intestine, and Beebe inclined to the belief that the tortoise, though it could swim, died of the salt water it had swallowed on that occasion. Whether this conclusion is correct or not is relatively unimportant; much of Van Denburgh's argument is based on his own overclassification.

At the present practically everybody is agreed that there is precious little, if any, geological evidence for a former land bridge to Panama. And the viewpoint of the zoologists (with which the botanists agree) has been beautifully expressed by one of them, who asked: "If there was a land bridge, why was it so little used?" Remember: a few mice, some bats, five dozen land birds, two dozen reptiles, no amphibians. The whole fauna is such that it could have arrived by ocean current: the penguins swimming; the finches, the rodents, and the reptiles on drifting trees—all, that is, except the tortoises.

Samuel Garman suspected that they might have been transported by people, prehistoric South Americans. We now know much better than was known in 1917 how far a balsa raft can drift from South America. Such a raft could certainly drift to the Galápagos and the prehistoric South Americans might also have carried tortoises as living food. Since nobody knows how long it took the Galápagos tortoises to differentiate from *Testudo tabulata* or a similar tortoise, there is no way of calculating backward in order to find out whether the prehistoric South Americans built rafts at a sufficiently early date. Nor do we know just when they built rafts first. The thought, therefore, must remain an interesting idea, unproved and unprovable.

In spite of everything the giant tortoise is still with us. An attempt to produce the Aldabra type of semi-domesticated colonies of Galápagos tortoises in California, Arizona, Texas, and Florida unfortunately did not work. But another attempt might be more successful. One other thing that might be done is to check unimportant and therefore neglected islands in the Pacific Ocean. It is just possible that small natural colonies were formed by descendants of Galápagos tortoises which escaped from ships where they were carried as food. At one time a colony of Galápagos tortoises existed on Juan Fernández, but this colony finally served the purpose for which it had been established in the first place: it was eaten. However, there might be others.

We do know, for example, that Captain Porter, when on Madison Island, the principal island of the Marquesas group, gave some tortoises to the chiefs as presents and permitted others to escape. That was in 1813 and to the best of my knowledge the Marquesas have never been checked since. A similar story is connected with the name of Captain Cook; he was said to have given a Galápagos tortoise to the king of Tongatabu of the Tonga Islands in 1777. Visitors to the Tonga Islands are still shown this tortoise—it was named *Tui Malila* —but Dr. James Oliver of the New York Zoological Society stated recently (*Natural History Magazine,* April 1958) that the tortoise being shown is not a Galápagos tortoise at all but a specimen of *Testudo radiata,* the radiated tortoise of Madagascar.

Presumably the Galápagos tortoise brought by Captain Cook died, and this other tortoise was substituted. But how this one got to the Tonga Islands is a mystery in itself.

The main step to save the Galápagos tortoises and the other unique types of Galápagos fauna obviously has to be taken on the islands themselves. This, of course, leaves it all up to the government which exercises sovereignty over the islands, namely the government of Ecuador. A move in the right direction has been made by appointing a governor for the islands—they were previously administered centrally, which makes the enforcing of protective laws difficult, to put it mildly. The Galápagos fauna has been under some kind of protection for a number of years but whatever laws were passed (and enforced, if they were) considered Man the only enemy. The more important enemies, however, are animals which have been introduced, mainly pigs and dogs. Of these two the dogs are the bigger problem, since they are strictly carnivorous. What should be done on at least a number of the islands, if not on all, is to exterminate all nonindigenous animals and then make sure that these islands are left strictly alone. Even though they are not, as was once believed, remains from the Age of Reptiles, they should be restored to the enchantment springing from their uniqueness.

PART FIVE

WITNESSES
OF THE PAST

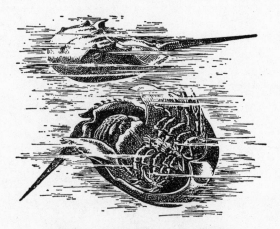

Limulus, the horseshoe crab
(drawing by Gustav Wolf)

CHAPTER 20

"The Attic of the Planet"

It is by no means simple to find, or to construct, a statement that will characterize Australia. Many years ago, when I was in grade school, the one I had to memorize declared that Australia was "the fifth and smallest continent." This sounded simple, but it concealed a lot of assumptions. If you counted North and South America as separate continents (which is logical, though not customary), Australia was the sixth continent. You could make it the fifth only by considering Europe as a mere peninsula of Asia, something no European teacher would permit to be said in a classroom. Of course Antarctica was completely neglected then; if it had not been the existence of this "sixth continent" would have posed another problem. Was Antarctica smaller or larger than Australia? Measured on a globe it was obviously larger, but there was always the danger of counting a lot of ice as land. This question has been answered only recently as one of the results of the International Geophysical Year. If Antarctica is to be called a continent Australia is no longer the smallest. We *did* count a lot of ice as land.

At one time Australia could justly have been called the "unknown continent." In the days when Abel Janszoon Tasman was ordered to sail around "Nieuw Holland" if he could, this land mass was a kind of Ultima Thule of the south, the remotest of the remote. For some time hopes lingered that it might be part of the enormous, beautiful, and wealthy Southern Continent, the *Terra australis incognita* of which sailors and geographers had dreamed for many centuries. But the reports that did come from the few ships which had made landfalls here and there sounded most disappointing. No tropical luxuriance, no riches, not even good-looking and intelligent natives—one can still feel the disappointment of men who, after weeks at sea, had hoped for another Java.

The logical consequence was that Australia, for about two centuries, became the "neglected continent." It is significant, to put it mildly, that the first use to which a tiny piece of Australia was put was as a penal colony. It needed something drastic to cause a change in attitude. Such a drastic thing did happen: around the middle of the nineteenth century gold was found in Australia.

Other things, of less immediate value, were also found, and these finds, scientific in nature, slowly led to another name for Australia. The Australian continent was evidently very old and had been separated from the other land masses of our planet for a very long time. Consequently things lived in Australia that had been discarded and trampled under foot elsewhere. As an antique dealer will sniff around the attic of an old mansion for things discarded and of no particular use but with a special value, so zoologists looked at Australia and wished they could go there. And the comparison with antiques must have been obvious, for zoologists began to refer to Australia with its living ancient animals as "the attic of the planet." If they don't use the term any more it is merely because they now have respected colleagues in Australia whom they do not wish to insult.

The whole business started with one particular animal from Australia which became known to Western science at a surprisingly early date. I might add that Western science for several decades harbored the secret wish that it did not know this animal, because it was so puzzling and confusing.

The animal in question is the platypus.

The name of the man who "discovered" platypus is not on record; possibly the gentleman wished to remain incognito for reasons of his own. But we do know when and where the "first" platypus was caught. The place was the countryside near Hawkesbury in New South Wales. The time was the month of November (summer there) of the year 1797. The man who caught the small animal must have been struck by its curious appearance, as everybody else since his day, and for want of a better name called it a "water-mole."

One may infer from this choice of name that the original discoverer was an Englishman. For while the platypus does make burrows and possesses a fur which may be likened to that of the common black European mole, the resemblance is slight. A Canadian or American who was acquainted with beavers would probably have picked the name "Australian beaver," because a swimming platypus resembles a swimming beaver in its general motions, the habit of burrowing at the water's edge with an entrance hole under water is a beaver habit, and the platypus even has a somewhat flattened tail. Of course there is no real resemblance between the two, and beavers are much larger than platypi. Still, it would have been a more reasonable name.

It is no exaggeration to say that platypus caused a scientific headache (not bothering the common man at all) which lasted just about ninety years. The reasons for this long headache are many and complex, as will be seen, but the cause of the first attack can be stated simply: platypus did not fit into the textbook!

Around the year 1800 zoologists had nice, clean, orderly textbooks. These began with the *Mammalia,* or mammals, and every student had to learn their distinguishing characteristics. This was easy. All mammals were warm-blooded and had a skin characterized by sweat glands and hairs. They all produced live young and suckled them, for which purpose the females had mammary glands. They all had four limbs, while a tail might be present or not. They had a typical jaw construction and usually teeth in those jaws. They usually had external ears . . . and so on, down the list.

The next large group (now called a "class") in the textbook was the *Aves,* or birds. All birds were warm-blooded and their skins grew feathers. All birds were tail-less; they had no external ears, no teeth in their jaws—all this was prior to the discovery of *Archaeopteryx.* They laid eggs and did not suckle their young. The *Reptilia* (for some time thrown together with the *Amphibia*) came next. They were not warm-blooded; they laid eggs, and so forth. Then came the *Pisces,* or fish, which lived in water, were not warm-blooded, laid eggs, etc., etc., etc. And that ended the list of the vertebrate animals.

This was the "system" of Linnaeus and, except for some refinements which had to be made later, there was nothing wrong with it. The trouble really was that it was so clear and easy to learn. What had originally been meant as a device for keeping order in the files quickly began to look like a natural law.

Then the first platypus skin reached England.

Unfortunately nobody wrote down what his impressions were "at first glance"; we don't know whether that first glance saw the head. If it did not the main surprise came up gradually. The skin indicated a mammal of the size, say, of a small cat. The fur was dark umber

Platypus (drawing by Gustav Wolf)

brown on top and on the sides, shading to lighter brown underneath. Quite normal. The feet were webbed—well, that was not too common but also not unusual all by itself. But the head! Taken as a whole it was a normal mammalian head but instead of a mouth there was a bill like that of a bird—to be more specific, a bill like that of a duck. Since the specimen received in London was a dried skin the "bill" looked and felt as hard as a bird's bill. Dr. George Shaw of the British Museum, who had to write the first scientific description, had no way of knowing that in the living animal the bill is soft, flexible, and extremely sensitive.

Shaw's description was published in the tenth volume of *Naturalists' Miscellany* (1799), at that time one of the important scientific journals. Since Dr. Shaw had only the skin, the description was naturally far from complete. But it settled the first question that had arisen: whether the animal existed at all. Certain scientists who had seen the skin had declared it to be a fake, an imposture, a product of art— in short, a Jenny Haniver. Shaw had to assert solemnly that it was real.

Of all the Mammalia yet known, it seems the most extraordinary in its conformation, exhibiting the perfect resemblance of the beak of a Duck engrafted on the head of a quadruped. So accurate is this similitude, that, at first view, it naturally excited the idea of some deceptive preparation by artificial means; the very epidermis, proportion, serratures, manner of opening, and other particulars is the beak of a shoveler, or other broad-billed species of duck, presenting themselves to the view; nor is it without the most minute and rigid examination that we can persuade ourselves of its being the real beak or snout of a quadruped.

In spite of Shaw's description and another description by the German anatomist Blumenbach, which followed in 1801, doubts must have lingered, for in 1823 Robert Knox still felt obliged to defend the real existence of the platypus.

It is well known that the specimens of this very extraordinary animal first brought to Europe were considered by many as impositions. They reached England by vessels which had navigated the Indian seas, a circumstance in itself sufficient to rouse the suspicions of the scientific naturalist, aware of the monstrous impostures which the artful Chinese had so frequently practiced on European adventurers; in short, the scientific felt inclined to class this rare production of nature with eastern mermaids and other works of art.

Naturally Shaw had to invent a scientific name for the new animal, and he had chosen *Platypus anatinus.* The first of these two words simply means "flatfoot" while the second is straight Latin for "pertaining to ducks," in reference to the bill, of course. Then a second scientific description came along, written by Professor J. F. Blumenbach in Göttingen. He provided a new name for the animal, *Ornithorhynchus* ("bird-beak") *paradoxus,* because he knew that his colleague and compatriot Herbst had used up the name "platypus" some six years before for a genus of small beetles. Once a name has been used for one genus of living things it cannot be attached to another one, so Ornithorhynchus is still the scientific name. As a result of Shaw's failure to check on the name, the "platypus" of a scientific catalogue is a small beetle, while the "platypus" of newspapers and magazines is something entirely different.

While the problem of the name was being discussed another platypus (*not* a beetle) arrived from Australia. This was not merely a skin but the body of a female preserved in alcohol. Instead of clearing up doubts the little corpse increased the confusion. Judging by the skin alone, if you could make yourself disregard the beak, platypus was certainly a mammal. The complete body threw the judgment off some more. Here was a female—but it did not have mammary glands! And in a certain intimate region it was built like a reptile or a bird. Female mammals are supposed to have an anus and a vagina, but the female platypus had only one body outlet, technically known as a cloaca. So now there were two birdlike characteristics, a bill in front and a cloaca at the other end. And no mammary glands!

Early in the nineteenth century, nobody seems to know precisely when, platypus was found to have a relative. The settlers in Australia called it the "native porcupine" and sometimes the "spiny ant-eater." Elsewhere the popular name became *echidna*—which is actually the Greek word for a viper—but at least the scientific name makes sense. It is *Tachyglossus* or "swift-tongue." As for echidna, it had spines, a mouth not quite as much like a bird's bill, a cloaca, and no mammary glands—or so it seemed. Its feet were not webbed, but the hind feet were almost turned backward. Why did the Dutch ever discover Australia?

Still, the two animals existed and they had to be fitted into the textbook. The big problem was where? Though they did not really fit among the mammals they fitted even less well among the reptiles and they certainly were not birds. Let's consider them mammals then, and try to find a place. Linnaeus, in his system, had the order of the Primates at the very top and an order he called *Bruta* at the very bottom. Actually that order *Bruta* was such that it might have been called *Miscellanea* with more justification. It contained whatever did not fit elsewhere. But then somebody noticed that all the rather heterogeneous mammals assmbled in this order had at least one thing in common. They were either completely toothless, or very nearly so, when adult. The order was then triumphantly renamed *Edentata,* which means toothless, and no longer looked like the collection of misfits it was. Needless to say, Shaw stuck platypus into the order *Edentata;* if there was one thing that was certain about platypus it was that it did not have a single tooth.

Other naturalists, probably disliking the "order" of the *Edentata* anyway, did not agree with Shaw. The English zoologist Home suggested that platypus and echidna should be an order of their own (as they now are). The Frenchman Etienne Geoffroy Saint-Hilaire (*père*) invented the name this order now bears. It is *Monotremata,* "one-holers," because of the cloaca. But Saint-Hilaire was not sure whether the order of the *Monotremata* should be one of the mammals or of the reptiles; in fact he seems to have felt that a reptile with hair was easier to swallow than a mammal with a cloaca and without mammary glands.

Old Jean Baptiste de Monet, Chevalier de Lamarck, in France made a more radical suggestion. Platypus and echidna were not just

Echidna; *left,* showing pouch

a different "order"; they were a different *class,* like the class of
mammals, the class of birds, and so forth. The name for the new class
should be *Prototheria,* "pre-mammals." About the only reason that
nobody else ever went along with Lamarck was that there were just
two species (actually three, since there are two species of echidna)
and a "class" for just two species did not sound right.

The debate about proper classification was sadly handicapped by
the fact that there was so little known about the animals under
debate. The lack of knowledge was, in part, ameliorated by rumors,
but how far could rumors be trusted? There was one, for example,
which was as persistent as it was unbelievable, namely that at least
platypus laid eggs. Sir John Jamison wrote as early as 1817 that "the
female is oviparous [egg-bearing] and lives in burrows in the ground."
The statement was forthright enough. But was it correct?

Matters became still more complicated in 1824 when Professor
Meckel in Germany discovered that platypus, after all, did have
mammary glands. They had simply been overlooked; we now know
that they are very much reduced during the nonbreeding period.
But, Meckel reported, the mammary glands of the platypus were
different from any others he had ever dissected or even seen, being
"merely composed of a considerable number of ampullae [membra-
nous sacs] with long necks." The necks of the ampullae did not
form teats but covered a small area of the skin like oversized pores.

One would think that this discovery should at least have settled
the argument over classification once and for all: if the platypi had

mammary glands they had to be mammals. But some scientists had already taken a position, as for example the Saint-Hilaires, father and son, in France. They were no longer certain that the monotremes might be furred reptiles, but they were certain that they were not mammals, "in spite of fur, limbs, lungs and a heart with two ventricles." If the monotremes laid eggs—an item not yet settled at the time—they could not be called mammals, especially since they also had a cloaca. "We may today regard it as certain," wrote Saint-Hilaire, *fils,* suddenly siding with Lamarck, "that the vertebrate animals should henceforth be divided into the five following types: mammals, monotremes, birds, reptiles, and fishes." Having taken this position, the father-and-son team had to explain Meckel's discovery away in some manner; these glands had to be scent glands. They could not be milk glands because how could the young suckle milk (with their horny beaks, be it noted) from glands that did not form teats?

The answer is that the beaks actually are not horny, and the young simply lick the milk while the mother is lying on her back. But this surprising fact was then unknown.

The problem of whether Sir John Jamison had been correct with his statement about egg-laying intruded itself on the discussion all the time, as one can imagine. There were three scientific parties, each offering a different opinion about the method of reproduction. Meckel, Cuvier, Oken, and Blainville, all great names in science, argued that platypus was a mammal and therefore held that it must be viviparous, that is to say that it brought forth living young. The Saint-Hilaires and Blumenbach were convinced that it was egg-laying, or oviparous, while Home and Richard Owen believed that it must produce eggs, which, however, hatched within the parent's body, thus making the animal ovoviviparous. "The sad story of the eggs," as the Australian scientist Dr. Harry Burrell, top-ranking expert on the platypus, expressed it, began in 1829. In that year Etienne Geoffroy Saint-Hilaire (*père*) triumphantly published a letter from a Mr. Robert E. Grant who reported the discovery of four Ornithorhynchus eggs. But a great disappointment was in store. The eggs were a bit large and in the drawing that was published they were so well reproduced that experts could classify them as having been laid by *Chelodina longicollis,* the common long-necked Australian tortoise.

The next name to be mentioned in connection with the eggs of platypus is that of Lieutenant Maule. In the years 1831 and 1832 he established the fact that Meckel's glands actually produced milk. He also reported finding eggshells in the nesting burrows, but this was not considered sufficient evidence, for these might not be platypus eggs. The next report that reached Europe came from one Jno. Nicholson, M.D., in a letter sent from Wood's Point, Victoria, Australia, dated September 21, 1864, and addressed to Richard Owen:

Sir,—I have great pleasure in being able to inform you of a very interesting discovery in the anatomy of the *Ornithorhynchus paradoxus,* and one which I have no doubt you will hail with delight. About ten months ago, a female Platypus was captured in the River Goulbourn by some workman who gave it to the Gold-Receiver of his district. He, to prevent its escape, tied a cord to its leg and put it into a gin-case, where it remained during the night. The next morning, when he came to look at it, he found that it had laid two eggs. They were about the size of a crow's egg, and were white, soft and compressible, being without shell or anything approaching to a calcareous covering.

Dr. Nicholson failed to examine the eggs closely, but though the size mentioned in his letter is exaggerated, they certainly were platypus eggs. Owen, belonging to the party that believed the platypus to be ovoviviparous, did not doubt the statement, but he declared that the egg-laying was not normal, and had to be regarded as an "abortion due to fear."

Owen's attitude was not as unreasonable as this statement seems to indicate. The English zoologist Bennett had made a trip to Australia in 1832 for the express purpose of settling this question once and for all. Dozens of nesting burrows had been dug up and young platypi in all stages of development had been found. Bennett once more established that the milk glands were just that, but he had not been able to find a single egg, not even an eggshell. Since platypus does lay eggs Bennett must have arrived just a few days too late.

Even when the egg-laying was established there was still a strange coincidence involved. The fact that platypus lays eggs was observed by Dr. W. H. Caldwell of Australia during the second week of August 1884. On August 25 of the same year Professor Wilhelm Haacke, studying the Australian fauna on the spot, found the egg of echidna. Echidna, during the brooding season, develops a rather large pouch which, like the milk glands, almost disappears for the rest of the year. Professor Haacke caught a female with a pouch and carefully reached inside, feeling around for a young. But he felt an egg; his surprise was so great that he crushed it. After both Caldwell and Haacke, not knowing about each other, had finished their field work they progressed to two different Australian cities and lectured about their discoveries. These two lectures were delivered on the same day! It was fortunate that they had made different discoveries, else a long hassle about priority might have developed.

At the end of the ninety years of uncertainties and doubts the story of the *Monotremata* looked simple by comparison. They are survivors from a much earlier period; if we had a more complete fossil record we could probably trace them in a straight line to the early Triassic period. Their physical characteristics are still very much reptilian: cloaca, egg-laying, and a blood temperature which, while "warm," is several degrees lower than that of other mammals. The "duckbill" which caused so much consternation at first is just a special adaptation to digging worms and shrimps from river mud.

Platypus now lives only in southeastern Australia but could also be found on Tasmania in the past. The range of echidna is much larger than that of platypus; it extends from Tasmania through Australia to southeastern New Guinea. A closely related genus, *Zaglossus,* occurs in Papua. The echidnas are insect-eaters. Besides their dietary habits, they differ from platypus in laying only one egg at a time, which is carried around in the pouch. Platypus lays two eggs and hatches them in a subterranean nest, its pouch being far too small to be of use.

All three monotremes are nocturnal, which makes them very unsatisfactory zoo exhibits.

One still unsolved mystery is the movable spur of the male monotremes, which is located on their hind legs and looks very much like the spur of a rooster. But it is more than just a stabbing weapon. It has a canal, so thin that a horse hair does not pass through it, though a human hair does, and is connected with the duct of a gland. The spur was always reported to inflict poisonous wounds. Sir John Jamison wrote in 1816 that a man, in spite of immediate medical treatment, "exhibited all the symptoms of a person bitten by a venomous snake." The victim "was obliged to keep his bed for several days, and did not recover the perfect use of his hand for nine weeks." Since then many scientists have experienced or seen wounds inflicted by the spurs; the wounds are described as extremely painful, but not fatal. Rabbits injured by the spur did, however, die.

Since the spur is attributed only to the males it can hardly be regarded as a weapon. Burrell believes that the spur serves as a paralyzing weapon in the fights of the males for the possession of the females. Obviously, it is not the aim of these fights to kill, though fatal effects have been observed.

Though platypus held more or less the center of the stage in the attic of the planet, it was by no means alone on stage. Zoologists were enchanted with a continent in which all mammals, with a very few exceptions,[1] were marsupials—pouched mammals, like the American opossum. If it were not for Australia only a very few marsupials would be known. Because of Australia, there are many of them, from the big kangaroo and the tree-climbing koala to the tiny, golden-furred marsupial mole (*Notoryctes*).

There were flying marsupials, fliers of the type of our flying squirrel. There were ground-dwelling forms like the wombat. There were even, which is somewhat hard to imagine, tree-climbing kangaroos, and there were predatory marsupials like the so-called "native cat" (*Dasyurus*). European zoologists embarked jubilantly for "the land of the living fossils" and wrote excited letters (and later books) about the things they saw. To the settlers something lying on the beaches was merely a seashell. To the zoologist this was *Trigonia,*

The clam Trigonia, virtually unchanged from
Jurassic times

abundant in European seas when the ichthyosaurs were swimming about, now living only in the Australian area.

Small Tasmania to the south had additional wonders to offer. There were two predatory marsupials there, which had once lived on the Australian mainland too but had vanished before the explorers came. One was the so-called "Tasmanian tiger" (*Thylacinus*), so named because of its stripes, and the other was the nearly undescribable "Tasmanian devil" (*Sarcophilus*) with its big head on a cat-sized body. The voice of the "devil" has been linked to different sounds by different observers; it must be an unearthly yell of some kind.

[1] They are several bats, the Australian "dingo," a wolflike dog, and, of course, the Australian aborigines, all obviously late arrivals.

The "Tasmanian devil," a carnivorous marsupial

The specialists who went to Tasmania were also enchanted by a fresh-water crustacean, the inch-long orange-colored *Phreatoicus;* which was among crustaceans what the marsupials were among the mammals, an older form. Later (in 1893, to be precise about it) naturalists made an even bigger find along similar lines. A mountain lake in Tasmania harbored *Anaspides tasmaniae.* The settlers knew it well, called it the "mountain shrimp," and complained that it was not edible. The naturalists, once shown the creature, saw several things at once. The brownish 2-inch crustacean does not have fused body segments like other and later crustaceans. Each of its legs has an extra branch. It is also atypical in just laying its eggs on the stems of water plants; most female crustaceans are in the habit of carrying the fertilized eggs around with them until they are about to hatch. The nearest known relatives of Anaspides are fossils from the oceans of the Carboniferous and Permian periods of Europe and North America. They are nearly identical with the living form. If that mountain lake in Tasmania had not preserved the living form we would say that this type became extinct 200 million years ago.

While some scientists went after platypus and echidna and the still-unsolved egg questions, others dug big bones from the ground and sent them to Professor Owen in England. The former owners of these bones had been marsupials too, and usually plant-eaters, as Owen could tell from their teeth. The largest form, with a skull measuring a yard in length, was *Diprotodon australis,* which was as large as a rhinoceros. A form somewhat smaller but similar in build was *Nototherium,* which was contemporaneous with a close relative of the living wombat. But this extinct wombat (*Phascolonus gigas*) was the size of a rather large pig, while the living form is the size of a

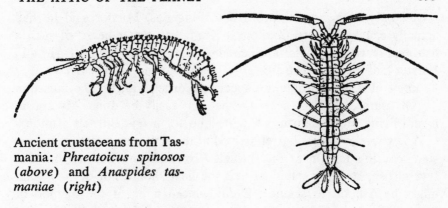

Ancient crustaceans from Tasmania: *Phreatoicus spinosos* (*above*) and *Anaspides tasmaniae* (*right*)

medium-sized dog. There also was a gigantic kangaroo, *Macropus titan.*

Faint hopes of discovering survivors have never been realized. But there was another major discovery waiting. It must be said in advance that this discovery was not made until after the concept of evolution had taken hold among the zoologists. This explains why events moved so fast. As for the history of the discovery, it might begin this way:

An Australian squatter, William Forster by name, who had lived for a number of years on a farm near the Burnett River in Queensland, moved to Sydney in 1869 to settle there. One fine day, looking over the city that was to be his home, he visited the Sydney Museum. There he met the curator of the museum, Gerard Krefft, and they fell into a conversation about Australia's unusual animals. Forster asked quite casually why the museum failed to exhibit a certain big fish from the Burnett River. The curator was not quite certain whether he had properly understood the question.

"Which big fish?" he asked.

"Well, the farmers around there call him the Burnett salmon or something like that," Forster replied, "and the blacks call him *barramundi* or *barramunda.*"

Krefft was not familiar with either of these names, and it is also likely that his ideas about the location of the Burnett River were not too exact. He asked for a more detailed description. Forster did his best to describe the fish: it was about 5 feet long when fully grown, something like a very fat eel, but with large greenish scales and four

—yes, only four, he was positive—strong fins. Forster said he had actually caught it more than once. Krefft had never heard of such a fish, and it was probable that neither had any other scientist. He told Forster that this might be a creature new to science and asked whether he knew of a way to obtain a specimen, or several, for the museum.

"Of course," Forster agreed, "that can easily be done. My cousin is still living on that farm; I'll write him for a few Burnett salmon."

A few weeks later a barrel arrived at the museum direct from Forster's cousin's farm near the Burnett River. It contained not one but several fish, strongly salted so that the heat should not destroy what might be a boon to science. Krefft winced a bit at the method of "preservation" but he examined the contents of the barrel with great curiosity.

It was a big variety of fish, so much was sure. Mr. Forster's description had been as accurate as could be expected. The fish was about 5 feet long, greenish in color on top, whitish underneath, and had unusually large scales. It had four—yes, only four—strong fins, and possessed a very unusual type of tail: not the proverbial forked fishtail nor yet a tail like a shark's, but something that is hard to describe but easy to remember once seen. In scientific parlance it goes under the name of diphyceral tail, and it consists simply of a rim of fin material around the rear end of the body. There was no dorsal fin, and the four fins present looked more like paddles than the fins of any other fish then known.

After having looked at the fins and the tail and the very large scales, Curator Krefft reached into the mouth of the fish. Let's see whether it has teeth. He felt, and then saw, four large teeth in the fish's mouth and told later that he was shocked. He had discovered teeth already known to science.

Large fossil teeth of this type had been found in ancient rock deposits—ancient even in the language of the geologist, who pays little attention to a discrepancy of a million years more or less—and they had caused some perplexity among paleontologists. They were certainly the teeth of a fish, but of what kind could not be said. They looked as if they were a full set of teeth grown together, their general shape having much resemblance to the comb of a rooster. There was nothing similar in any living fish; it must have been a species that had become completely extinct.

For a while it was believed that some extinct shark might have grown them. Then it seemed more probable that they were the dental apparatus of an extinct fish that was perhaps related to the sturgeon, which, unfortunately, has no teeth at all. Louis Agassiz, the great authority on extinct fish, had christened the unknown owner of these teeth *Ceratodus,* meaning "the horn-toothed." How the fish Ceratodus had looked no one dared guess.

Now Gerard Krefft, curator of the Museum of Sydney, saw before him exact replicas of the mysterious fossil teeth that had baffled much better men than himself. And he was most fortunate in having not only the teeth of the fish Ceratodus, but the animal itself. The specimens on his table were dead, but not fossil; they had been killed only a week or so before. Probably there were many more of them in that Burnett River, of which he did not know much more than the name.

As Krefft went through the professional literature in order to write up his report of the discovery he found another incredible item. The teeth of his fish had been known before the fish was known. Its fins—paddles might be better word for them—had not been known. But they had been *prophesied!*

Evolutionary thought required transitional forms. Since the birds could only have evolved from the reptiles there must have been a transitional form—or rather many of them—between the two. Since the amphibians could only have come from the fishes, there must have been transitional forms between these two classes. If you tried to imagine how such a transitional form might have looked a certain picture emerged easily. The general shape was probably more or less like that of a fish. But it had to be a "fish" with a double respiratory system, gills for breathing water and lungs for breathing air. The difficult point was to visualize the limbs.

Anatomists thoughtfully looked at the pectoral fins of all kinds of modern fishes and gravely shook their heads. It was anatomically impossible to derive an amphibian leg—say, the leg of a salamander—from the pectoral fin of a fish. But then the anatomist Karl Gegenbaur proposed a solution. The reason, he said, that we have failed to derive an amphibian leg from the pectorals of a fish is that these pectorals themselves are highly evolved organs, the product of millions of years of adaptation and specialization. First we have to trace the fin back to a primitive form from which both were possible—the salamander's leg in one direction and the fishes' pectoral fin in another. Others looked around as advised by Gegenbaur and could not find such a structure, whereupon Gegenbaur invented it. He drew a skeleton of a very primitive fin with "leg possibilities" and said he hoped it would be found on some fossil one day. This skeleton somewhat resembled a fern leaf, and Gegenbaur's students quickly christened it *Archipterygium gegenbauri* ("Gegenbaur's archaic flipper)."

Well, each of the four strong paddlelike fins of the new fish from the Burnett River was a very special birthday present for Professor Gegenbaur. Here was Gegenbaur's Archipterygium in flesh and cartilage, covered with scales.

Krefft proceeded with the dissection of the fish. Having frantically read everything he could find in a hurry, he now looked for something else. The fish naturally had gills. How about a lung? Did it have a lung too? And, if so, a single one or a pair? It proved to be a single lung, which was an exciting discovery in itself.

I should have mentioned earlier that the fish of the Burnett River was the third lungfish to be discovered. Two others, eel-like in shape (and without such revealing teeth), were already known. The first one had been found by the Austrian collector Johann Natterer in South America, in 1833. The fish was about 2 feet long, and exhibited, besides its gills, a pair of fully functioning lungs. The South American Indios called the creature *caramuru;* Natterer coined the scientific name of *Lepidosiren.* The second lungfish had been found a few years later in the White Nile in Africa. It looked very much like Lepidosiren. The native name was *comtok;* the scientific name became *Protopterus.*

Of course the two lungfishes had produced some annoyance along the lines of that caused by platypus. The classification said that fishes had gills and usually scales; since *Lepidosiren* and *Protopterus* also had lungs they had to be amphibians. But amphibians, the textbook said, had naked skins. It was now necessary to accept the fact that a very few fishes could have lungs.

The lungfishes from the Amazon and from the White Nile were interesting curiosities for other reasons too. Neither of them had real fins, and both displayed that ancient type of unforked tail that had not yet developed to any appreciable size. Their method of locomotion was even more eel-like than their bodies, and their fins (whatever they may have looked like originally) had atrophied from disuse into thin and almost stringlike appendages. During the dry season both types curled up and went to sleep in a round mud cake which dried as hard as stone and could be mailed without disturbing the fishes' slumber. All the addressee had to do when the package arrived was to place the apparent stone in a bathtub of lukewarm water, and after a few minutes the mud cake would dissolve and a very much alive lungfish would emerge from the dirt.

These habits of the lungfish made a very interesting story for natural-history books, but from the point of view of the evolutionists they were not of much importance beyond illustrating the fact that these animals had changed a good deal since they crawled in the swamps of the beginning of the Carboniferous period. The case was similar to that of platypus's bill. This organ, which had caused most of the first astonishment and all the original doubt, was of no significance whatever in the eyes of the evolutionist. It was the platypus's milk glands that were important, and the platypus's eggs. So it was the lungs of these lungfish that were important, not their mud cakes. But the other archaic features that evolutionists were looking for were practically missing.

When Gerard Krefft discovered the single lung of his new fish, he realized that this was the "true" lungfish, the more primitive type—the original, as it were. And since its teeth were so very similar to the fossil teeth for the possessor of which the great Agassiz had already invented the name Ceratodus, Krefft chose for the name of his lungfish *Ceratodus forsteri* Krefft. The common name, however, became Australian lungfish, since the other two types were already called the South American lungfish and the African lungfish. It may seem that the common name is the more descriptive of the two, but it must be borne in mind that the teeth of Ceratodus are its most distinguishing feature. There are three fish known to have lungs, but there is only one fish with archaic teeth like Ceratodus.

The "original"—that is to say, the fossil Ceratodus—had been established from its teeth only, just as Archaeopteryx had originally been established from one feather. And, as in the case of Archaeopteryx, the complete fossil Ceratodus was found, too. In fact, it turned out that fish of the Ceratodus type had been widely distributed once; one of the most recent finds (but fragments only) came from Texas. Nobody was too surprised to see that the fossil Ceratodus was not quite the same as the Ceratodus from the Burnett River. Since the name Ceratodus had been given first to the fish that bore the fossil teeth it was the living form that had to be renamed. That was simple. It was newer than the fossil type. Hence the living form became *Neoceratodus*.

There followed one more rather extended episode.

Neoceratodus forsteri Krefft, the Australian lungfish (drawing by Joseph M. Guerry, courtesy *Natural History Magazine*)

The skeleton of Neoceratodus had been studied. Its internal organs had been dissected, sliced up with microtomes, drawn in four colors, and described in fine detail.

One thing was still lacking: the "ontogenesis."

This was Ernst Haeckel speaking—who, after Charles Darwin's death, had become the central figure in zoology and everything related to it. Haeckel, large and impressive and impossibly erudite, was a much-attacked man, but also a man who had been much honored. In the last decade of the nineteenth century he was no longer just Professor Haeckel. He was His Excellency, Herr Geheimrat Professor Dr. Ernst von Haeckel. His Excellency liked to paint, mainly landscapes, and did it well. His Excellency also had an obsession: ontogenesis.

The technical term for the phenomenon involved is either "biogenetic rule," or "recapitulation theory." During the time that an individual embryo develops from the fertilized egg to the stage at which it is born (or hatched), it races through the forms of all its ancestors. Of course the time available for this recapitulation is short, and there are other limitations too, so the ancestral forms are compressed, abbreviated, and simplified. There are even complete exceptions to this rule, but in general the development of an embryo is useful to know because it permits conclusions as to the ancestry.

Haeckel did not invent this rule, or discover it, though many people thought during his lifetime that he had. But he introduced it into scientific practice and made it so widely popular that for decades every schoolboy in Europe (and I mean that literally) knew by heart Haeckel's formulation: "Ontogenesis recapitulates phylogenesis"— ontogenesis being the individual development and phylogenesis the development of the whole species.

Haeckel wanted to know the ontogenesis of Neoceratodus.

One of his pupils, Professor Richard Semon, was willing to make a special trip to Australia to investigate Ceratodus; and Paul von Ritter, a manufacturer in Basle, Switzerland, who had often donated large sums of money for Haeckel's scientific work, was willing to pay the expenses of the expedition. So Semon set out for Australia to hunt Ceratodus, in order to study its development from the egg.

In August 1891 he arrived in the "attic of the world." What literature there was stated matter-of-factly that the lungfish preferred brackish water, and Semon therefore reasoned that it would most probably be found where the Burnett and Mary rivers flowed into the Pacific Ocean near the city of Maryborough. Consequently he went to Maryborough, hoping for brackish water teeming with Ceratodus. Maryborough was a pleasant, progressive city, complete with Salvation Army and all, but no lungfish. Semon reported to Ernst Haeckel that the available information did not seem to be too trustworthy, since he had learned on the spot that Ceratodus lived in fresh water, not in brackish water. He was going inland in his quest. The next stop was the little village of Gayndah on the Burnett River. This looked promising right from the start; when Semon arrived at Gayndah he found that a specimen of Ceratodus had just been caught. But Semon found that even a small village like Gayndah —or especially a small village like Gayndah where nothing much happens normally—offered too much hospitality for a dedicated researcher. He went still farther inland.

Ten years earlier an Australian, Dr. Caldwell—the man who finally established the egg-laying of platypus—had tried to determine the ontogenesis of Ceratodus. He had not been successful, but he had learned that the fish laid its eggs on the stems of aquatic plants. Semon found this to be correct, but almost everything else that had found its way into print had been wrong. The fish inhabited, not the "region," but only the Burnett and Mary rivers. Contrary to reports it did not eat water plants; it ate small animals of all kinds. It did not go into estivation (summer sleep) in a mudcake. And Semon eventually learned that even the name *barramundi* was wrong: the native word for the fish was *dyelleh*.

While Semon was busy hunting Ceratodus eggs, a visitor arrived: Professor Spencer, biologist from Melbourne, spending his vacation on research. Object: the ontogenesis of Ceratodus! The two scientists shook hands and tried to work together—but without success. There was nothing to work on, no Ceratodus eggs. Eventually Professor Spencer's vacation ended and he had to return to Melbourne. Semon managed without much trouble to conceal his unhappiness over Spencer's departure.

A full month later three eggs were found. Semon at once ordered a thorough investigation of every plant in the river. The first day brought twenty-three eggs. Then for several days new material continued to come in, and the real job began: that of watching the development of the embryos in the eggs and putting them in alcohol at the right time in order to have a series of preserved specimens in all stages of development. But soon the supply of fresh material ceased. Semon quickly discovered the reason for this interruption of his work. Though he had strictly forbidden it, the natives had been catching Ceratodus to eat, and the one female fish that had produced all the eggs had become a victim of native appetite.

This little accident delayed the work for a whole year. One morning Professor Semon found himself alone; the natives had left their jobs without giving notice. They disliked being bawled out in defective English and had their own ideas about "discipline." Then the rainy season began. The time at Semon's disposal was three-quarters gone. He went to Thursday Island, halfway between Australia and New Zealand, where there were a few zoological observations of lesser importance to be made. In the main task he had failed. What was to be done? Go home with very little to show? Or wait for the next opportunity, which would be September of the following year?

Semon decided to wait. Cables from Europe assured him that his vacation would be extended for this purpose. Money followed. In July of the following year, he returned to Gayndah and hired other natives, who to his surprised delight eagerly followed his orders and left Ceratodus alone. Semon offered premiums for the eggs, even thought he knew that the lucky finder would usually be too drunk to report for work for a week after receiving his pay. When it seemed to him that precious time was passing, he frantically raised the premium: twenty-five dollars for the first eggs, *if* you promise not to eat or kill any fish, and keep the promise.

On September 16, 1892, the first eggs were brought in. Luck was good that year: all in all about seven hundred eggs were found. The hatching and breeding presented no difficulties, but after a while it became evident that the growth of the young fish was too slow for the amount of time that was still at Semon's disposal. He had to go home. Friends and colleagues promised to care for the young and to embalm specimens in alcohol at the various stages of development.

Once again specimens of Ceratodus were shipped to a museum in kegs and barrels, but this time the museum was in Jena, and the young specimens were preserved in a scientific way. Semon was able now to work out his observations and notes and studies, and did so with classic German thoroughness. All the important facts on the development of this fish, from the egg to the adult stage, are contained in Semon's work.[2] The most important result of his work was the proof that Ceratodus, while it evolved in the direction of the amphibians, is not directly ancestral to them.

Of course Semon could also report on the life habits of Ceratodus. That it does not go to sleep in a mudcake has been mentioned. Nor is its single lung efficient enough to keep it alive on land, and the four strong fins cannot support the body on land, though they are often used like legs under water. If its gills dry out it dies. But also, if during the Australian summer the rivers shrink to a string of small lakes and puddles, many of the fish collected in them die because the water turns foul. Ceratodus only needs moisture on its gills and pulls through the dry period because of its lung. Even in aquaria where the water is fresh, Ceratodus will come to the surface about every hour to renew the air in its lung, making a peculiar gulping sound while doing it.

The time for zoological discoveries of the magnitude of platypus, echidna, and Ceratodus in Australia has passed. The "attic of the planet" is undergoing transformation into an additional living room.

But at least one lesser discovery is still possible, of an animal which has been seen but never described. The place is the northern-

[2] The evolution of the fossil types was later investigated by Louis Dollo.

most portion of Australia, the York peninsula, and the first known mention of the animal is in the *Proceedings of the Zoological Society* for 1871. Mr. B. G. Sheridan, a police magistrate at Cardwell, told that his son had taken his evening stroll with his terrier when the dog suddenly took up a scent and followed it for about a mile. The encounter was brief and inconclusive and described by the boy with the following words:

It was lying in the long grass, and was as big as a native dog. Its face was round like that of a cat. It had a long tail and its body was striped from the ribs under the belly with yellow and black. My dog flew at it, but could not throw him. The animal ran up a leaning tree. It then got savage and ran down the tree at the dog and me. I got frightened and came home.

Australian naturalists are quite willing to concede the possibility that there is a large unknown catlike mammal (probably a marsupial) hiding in the only sketchily explored forests of the York peninsula which, after all, has roughly twice the area of England. The people living there speak of it matter-of-factly, like the Australian writer Ion Idriess:

Up here in York peninsula we have a tiger-cat that stands as high as a hefty medium-sized dog. His body is lithe and sleek and beautifully striped in black and grey. His pads are armed with lance-like claws of great tearing strength. His ears are sharp and pricked and his head is shaped like that of a tiger. My introduction to this beauty was one day when I heard a series of snarls from the long buffalo grass skirting a swamp. On peering through the grass I saw a full-grown kangaroo, backed up against a tree, the flesh of one leg torn clean from the bone. A streak of black and grey shot towards the kangaroo's throat, then seemed to twist in the air, and the kangaroo slid to earth with the entrails literally torn out. In my surprise I incautiously rustled the grass and the great cat ceased the warm feast that he had promptly started upon, stood perfectly still over his victim and for ten seconds returned me gaze for gaze. Then the skin wrinkled back from the nostrils, white fangs gleamed and a low growl issued from the throat. I went backwards and lost no time getting out of the entangling grass.—The next brute I saw was dead, and beside him was my prized staghound, also dead. . . .

A skillful—or lucky—hunter can gain some fame as a discoverer in Australia even today.

CHAPTER 21

A Fish Also Known as Kombessa

Science, as is often and correctly asserted, is the road to knowledge and understanding. It is also a self-correcting process, and the normal victim in this process of self-correction is the hypothesis. The purpose of a hypothesis is to tie a number of known facts together to see whether they will form a pattern. The natural fate of a hypothesis, however, is to be overwhelmed by other facts and to be replaced by another hypothesis. The road to knowledge consequently is littered with the corpses of defunct hypotheses which at one time seemed to perform a function.

While writing this I am thinking of a series of hypotheses which had three things in common: they were all wrong, they were all rather short-lived, and they were all concerned with the bottom of the ocean.

The first one of these hypotheses does not really deserve that designation; it was more of a belief, either inspired by or else inspiring the term "abyss." We still use the word as a general term when we speak about the ocean beyond the sight of land. But the real and original meaning of the word is "bottomless" and at some time at least some sea captains seem to have used it with its literal meaning.

We know this mostly because a seventeenth-century geographer, Bernard Varenius of Hannover, devoted several pages of print to a refutation of this belief. In the course of this refutation he unearthed an opinion from classical antiquity which said that the symmetry of the world demanded that the greatest depths of the oceans should be equal to the highest elevations of the land. It happens that this is very nearly the fact, although it has nothing to do with artistic or philosophical symmetry. In any event Varenius convinced everybody that the oceans did have bottoms. What these bottoms were like did not interest anybody and how far down they were was also unimportant, provided that there was a comfortable number of fathoms of water between the bottom and the keel of the ship.

With the beginning of the nineteenth century this attitude changed and a few people began to think of exploring the depths of the oceans —the sailor's and the fisherman's interest had been literally superficial. The exploration of the depth began in the easiest way by taking temperature measurements. The results probably produced a surprise. In the cold oceans the water at the surface was near freezing and the temperature stayed nearly the same as far down as the lines would reach. In the warm seas the water at the surface was nice and warm, but only at the surface. Soon it grew cooler and when the thermometer got below a hundred fathoms there didn't seem to be any difference between warm seas and cold seas.

A Frenchman named Péron felt that a conclusion could be drawn from this: at the greatest depths to which the thermometers could be lowered the temperature of the water was just a few degrees above freezing. It was self-evident that at still lower levels the temperature would be still lower and at a still-to-be-determined depth it would reach the freezing point. The bottoms of the oceans, therefore, had to be covered with ice. Naturally there could be no life at the bottom of the ocean, partly because it was too cold, partly because there could not be any food for life forms of any kind.

Just a few years after all this had been elaborated in excellent French, Sir John Ross accidentally caught a marine animal, a brittle star, at a probable depth of 4900 feet. The year was 1818. What made the fact so unpleasant for Péron's hypothesis was that this took place in Baffin Bay where one would logically expect the ice layer to begin at a much lesser depth than in a warm sea. The brittle star received the scientific name of *Gorgonocephalus* (Gorgon's head) but was then not mentioned for a while. Probably, it was thought, the Bay was 4900 feet deep at that spot, as measured by Sir John Ross. But there was no proof that the brittle star lived at that depth; it could have taken hold of the line at any depth.

Péron's hypothesis lasted for another decade or so; to the best of my knowledge it was never specifically refuted by anybody, but just slowly melted away.

In 1843 there followed the Abyssus Theory of the Englishman Edward Forbes. It was fortified with a lot of evidence; Forbes had done a great deal of careful work, first in the North Sea and the

English Channel and later in the Mediterranean. The key factor, as Forbes saw it, was that marine plants needed sunlight to live just as land plants do. Light filtered through the water to a depth of about 45 fathoms and down to that level plant life was abundant. Below that level it began to fail rapidly.[1] Where there was no plant life there could be no animal life either. Any depth below 300 fathoms was not populated, could not be populated. Forbes could point out that he had thoroughly investigated such an "abysmal region" in the Mediterranean.

While Edward Forbes's book was still being recommended to zoology students as a "recent work" on the subject of marine life, a Norwegian zoologist, Pastor Michael Sars, ruined the whole argument. When Michael Sars had been a young man and a theological student he had become interested in marine mollusks and had made a number of brand-new discoveries about their sex life. In the summer of 1850 Pastor Michael Sars, accompanied by his fifteen-year-old son Johan Ernst, fished for life forms at the bottom of the sea near the Lofoten Islands. He not only obtained living things from a depth of 450 fathoms, he even obtained living things which were supposed to be tropical. Or else extinct. What he caught was a crinoid, *Rhizocrinus lofotensis,* a representative of one of the four main groups of the echinoderms.

Everybody knows echinoderms, even if the word itself looks strange. The common starfish is an echinoderm and a representative of one of the four groups. The sea urchin is a representative of the second group, and the sea cucumber of the third. The fourth group, the sea lilies or crinoids, was supposed to be extinct; these were just interesting and sometimes beautiful fossils. This in spite of the fact that, in 1755, a naturalist had received a new specimen which had been dredged from the sea not far from Martinique, depth not stated. It received the name *Pentacrinus caput Medusae* (which I feel like translating as "the five-branched Medusa-headed something"), but for about a quarter of a century nobody knew precisely what it was. Then Johann Friedrich Blumenbach showed that it was an echinoderm. For many years it was thought to be the only surviving species of the crinoids. Even after that was disproved it was still considered incredibly rare; as late as 1890 a naturalist had to part with eleven golden "sovereigns" for a specimen.

[1] Later researchers put the lowest limit of active plant life a great deal deeper, namely at 170 fathoms.

The sea lily *Rhizocrinus lofotensis,* discovered
by Pastor Michael Sars. The little marine animal
is about 4 inches tall

Well, Pastor Sars had caught a second surviving species and the
two facts that it was a living fossil *and* that it came from a depth
which Forbes had "proved" to be lifeless made many people think
and act. A bevy of Scandinavian marine biologists with names like
Asbjörnsen, Lindahl, Lovén, Nordenskjöld, Théel, and Torell went to
work along the shorelines of Norway and Sweden and as far north
as Spitsbergen and Novaya Zemlyá and were unanimous in reporting that a lower limit for marine life simply did not exist. The limit
was the bottom, wherever it might be, and even that was not the whole
truth, for there were life forms *in* the bottom mud.

But as a result of their work, and mainly because of Pastor Sars'
Rhizocrinus a new hypothesis about the bottom of the oceans began
to grow up. At first it had been ice. Then a lifeless region. Now it
became the suspected refuge of survivors from past ages. The only
reason that it was not called a "lost world" was that Sir Arthur Conan
Doyle's novel with that title had not been written.

The hypothesis that the geological past still lived at the bottom
of the oceans reached a climax around 1870. In the meantime
Charles Darwin's *Origin of Species* had been published and Darwin
soon found a number of outstanding disciples: Thomas Huxley and

Alfred Russel Wallace in England and Ernst Haeckel in Germany, to mention only the most outstanding names. Now the concept of evolution demanded that life had started at some time. As to the beginning of life on earth only two possibilities existed. It might have come from space, in the form of life spores. This idea was voiced early but was not elaborated upon until much later. The other choice was that life had started on earth from nonliving matter. The early evolutionists agreed on this as the more probable answer. Ernst Haeckel especially tried to visualize detail.

The simplest animals in existence were single-celled with a nucleus. One could visualize still simpler animals which did not even have a nucleus. Before them there might have been something still simpler, just living matter, not yet broken up into different and independent cells. Of course such matter could have existed only in the water and it probably had looked like thin mucus.

Early in the investigation people had realized that it was important to obtain samples of the sea bottom. A device constructed for the purpose consisted of an iron tube which was weighed down with a massive piece of iron; usually this was an iron cannon ball with a hole drilled through its center. When the tube reached bottom it was forced into the mud by the weight of the cannon ball, but when the cannon ball, a few inches higher up on the tube, touched bottom the tube was released. Simultaneously the tube was closed and the trapped sample of bottom mud was then hauled to the surface. These mud samples had been preserved in glass jars under alcohol.

One day Thomas Huxley, looking at the samples, noticed something strange. There was a thin film of a very tenuous jelly clinging to the mud. Close scrutiny seemed to show a faint veining in the film, somewhat as if it were a spiderweb of soft strands of jelly. Was this the original life, the *Urschleim* Professor Haeckel had been talking about? If there was such noncellular life there was no reason that it should not be of any size. It could extend for acres, for square miles; it could cover the whole ocean bottom. If so, such a bottom-sampling device would naturally cut a section out of it and bring it back to the surface. Moreover there was no reason why it should not still exist; its environment, the bottom of the seas, simply had not changed through the geological periods. The conclusion was inevitable: the bottom of the seas had not only preserved ancient life forms like Pentacrinus and Rhizocrinus, it had even preserved the original life. Thomas Huxley named the stuff *Bathybius haeckeli*.

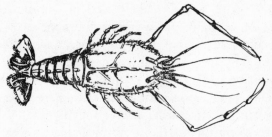

Willemoesia leptodactyla,
one of the eryonid crabs
captured by the *Challenger*
expedition

Haeckel himself was pleased and impressed; his reasoning had been confirmed by discovery.

Not too long after the announcement of the discovery of *Bathybius haeckeli,* the undifferentiated original life which lay like a film on the bottom ooze, an expedition left an English port. The ship was the corvette *Challenger.* The date of sailing was December 21, 1872. The purpose: investigation of the ocean floor and of life in the abyss. The *Challenger* expedition, the first major undertaking of its kind, covered all the oceans with the exception of the Arctic Ocean. When the *Challenger* berthed again in Portsmouth on May 26, 1876, she had spent 719 days at sea, traveled a total of 68,890 nautical miles, measured ocean depths (not counting those depths already entered on nautical charts) at 370 points, and collected 600 crates of specimens. One of the specimens was a bottom-mud sample from a depth of 27,000 feet from the Pacific Ocean near the Philippines.

For those who looked for living fossils at the bottom of the sea the *Challenger* expedition had one piece of good news. It had discovered a crab which had been thought to be extinct. This crab was one of the so-called eryonids, well known from Jurassic sediments which formed about 180 million years ago. The fossil eryonids had lived near the shore; this was definitely established. Then they had apparently become extinct. The catch of the *Challenger* proved that they had migrated into the deep sea instead. The living eryonids— from the deep sea off Africa—have a strange coloration. On top they are a delicate pink, shading to chalk-white on the sides. They look precisely as if pink crabs had crawled through chalk dust which was not deep enough to cover them completely.

The somewhat surprising aspect was that the *Challenger* expedition had only *one* piece of good news in that category. Just one living fossil; otherwise the life of the deep sea, while often strange in shape, was evidently composed of rather recent forms. And the life at the bottom of one ocean appeared to be the same as that at the bottom of another ocean.

Naturally the scientists on board the *Challenger* had also looked for *Bathybius haeckeli.* And they had found it, but what they had found was not at all what had been hoped for. The Bathybius which appeared in a glass jar in the museum would appear in any glass jar if you poured alcohol on bottom mud with ocean water. You could even leave the bottom mud out. It was simply a chemical reaction caused by the alcohol, a precipitate.

Naturally this discovery was progress—a mistake had been eliminated. But Haeckel himself did not take it lightly; a younger friend of his reported that a full thirty years later, he made a humorous remark about Bathybius to Haeckel and the old gentleman grew markedly indignant and changed the subject. Even the fact that he had been called in to work on the specimens of the *Challenger* expedition and had spent ten enthusiastic years doing it had not been able to do more than to dull his disappointment.

The *Challenger* expedition had brought rich results but also posed more questions. The need for more such expeditions was obvious. The next one to follow was the German deep-sea expedition with S. S. *Valdivia,* under Professor Carl Chun. The *Valdivia* left Hamburg on July 31, 1898, sent off in person by the Imperial Secretary of the Interior, Count von Posadowsky, to show that this was a government-sponsored expedition and not just a private venture. She first sailed to Edinburgh, then north around Scotland and Ireland, then took course due south for the Canary Islands and more or less followed the African coastline from then on. From Capetown course was set for SSW for the purpose of finding "lost" Bouvet Island if they could (they did), then east to Enderby Land on the coast of Antarctica, from there north to Sumatra, then across the Indian Ocean to Dar-es-Salaam in East Africa, then north to the Red Sea and through the Mediterranean for home.

The *Valdivia* scientists brought to light some of the most incredible deep-sea fishes—such as coal-black *Melanocetus,* which fails to be frightening mostly because you could hold it in the hollow of your hand. They netted something as incredible as the 7½-inch *Megalopharynx longicaudatus.* The name translates as the "long-tailed big-gullet"; it isn't very sophisticated even though descriptive. The

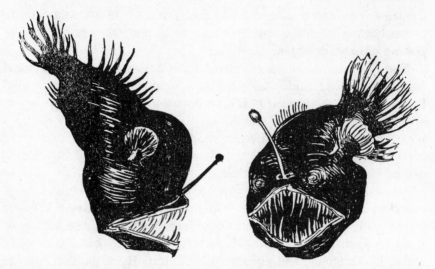

Two deep-sea fishes discovered by the *Valdivia* expedition: (*left*) *Melanocetus johnsoni;* (*right*) *Melanocetus krechi*

Valdivia experts felt that this was probably just the larva of another fish and they were right; we now know that it is the juvenile form of the "pelican eel" (*Eurypharynx pelecanoides*) that can be found in all oceans below the 500-fathom level.

The over-all result of the *Valdivia* expedition was to kill the idea, already mortally wounded by the *Challenger,* that the deep sea was a refuge of ancient life forms, hiding in odd places. It confirmed the *Challenger* finding that deep-sea fauna was recent and rather uniform throughout its whole extent.

This did not mean, of course, that there were no living fossils in the oceans. They did exist, and in odd places too, but most of the time not in the deep sea, as one could realize quickly when taking stock of what was known. Those living crinoids that had started the whole trend of thought could be found in fairly deep water, but that is not where they occur most frequently—and they are by no means as rare as had been thought. The eryonid crabs actually are deep-sea forms now, but in Jurassic times they had been inhabitants of the littoral zone.[2]

[2] It might be practical to explain a few terms here. "Littoral" comes from the Latin word for "shore" and was originally used to describe the area between low and high tide marks. Now it is used somewhat more loosely in the sense of "near the shore." The opposite is "pelagic" which means "of the (open)

Megalopharynx longicaudatus, first discovered by the *Valdivia* expedition. This later proved to be the larva of the pelican eel

For a long time the eryonids were actually the *only* living fossils of the deep sea; only very recently has one other form been added. This was the strange *Neopilina,* which was caught at a depth of 2 miles off the west coast of Mexico in 1952 by the Danish expedition with the ship *Galathea.* It was examined later by Dr. Henning Lemche of the University of Copenhagen, who reported on it to the International Zoological Congress in London in July 1958.

If one tries to give Neopilina an English name this can only be "worm snail," because it exhibits characteristics of both those creatures. The body is essentially that of a mollusk but there is a faint segmentation and some organs, like gills and kidneys, and muscle groups are arranged along the body in a series of pairs. This is no proper arrangement for a mollusk, but it is the proper arrangement for the segmented worms. In short, Neopilina is a connecting link between the worms and the mollusks; the worms, in turn, are linked with all the arthropods (prawns, crabs, spiders, centipedes, and insects). Neopilina is one of those forms in which, if you look backward, entirely different types of animal life seem to come together. The reality is, of course, the other way round. It is one of the forms from which all those different tribes sprang. As a fossil, the "worm snail" has been known for quite some time from early sediments of the Cambrian period which formed 500 million years ago. Naturally it was thought extinct until the *Galathea* expedition's discovery.

---

sea." Pelagic forms are subdivided into "Nekton," the active swimmers (most fishes, porpoises, whales, the large octopi), and "Plankton," the forms, usually tiny, which drift passively with the currents. Finally scientists talk of "Benthos," or "benthic forms," which comprises everything that cannot, or does not, move around; this includes marine plants, corals, barnacles, sea anemones, sponges, crinoids, starfish, sea urchins, and a fair number of marine worms.

More Neopilinas [3] turned up late in 1958, this time from a depth of about 3 miles some 200 miles west of Lima, Peru. They were caught by the American research vessel *Vema*. Like the much later eryonids to which they are generally ancestral, the "worm snails" originally lived in shallow water and migrated to the deep sea later.

The discovery of Neopilina has dislodged the claim of another marine animal to be "the" oldest living fossil. This label was always attached to *Lingula,* which lives in shallow waters in various places, shunning only cold seas. Lingula has also survived without any detectable change for 500 million years; the fossil forms date back to the Cambrian period too. Zoologically speaking, Lingula is a shell-bearing brachiopod. It has a long stalk (called peduncle), while the body itself is enclosed in two shells. These two shells are dorsal and ventral, not right and left as in clams. Nor are the shells of Lingula

Lingula, unchanged for 500 million years. This form is *Lingula pyramidata* from American waters

hinged like those of a clam. They are identical and are held together by muscles. Unlike clam shells they are horny and quite thin and almost flexible, greenish in color. In a sense Lingula can be called more "original" than the "worm snails" of equal age, for the latter have changed their habitat and Lingula has not.

Neither has the next of the living marine fossils, the horseshoe crab. Fossil horseshoe crabs have been beautifully preserved in the Upper Jurassic lithographic slate of Solnhofen (the species is *Limulus walchii*) and have been found from the preceding period, the Triassic. The known age of the horseshoe crab is therefore 200 million years; it might be somewhat older. The horseshoe crabs of today live in two widely separated places: the East Indies, where

[3] Examination disclosed a number of differences between the forms caught by the *Galathea* and those caught by the *Vema;* the latter are a new species and possibly a new subgenus: *Neopilina (Vema) ewingi* (*Science,* April 17, 1959).

Limulus moluccanus was discovered (or at least first described) by Rumphius; and the east coast of the United States. This species is *Limulus polyphemus,* or *Limulus americanus,* and no specific discoverer is known. But every American, at least every American living along the Atlantic shore, knows that they are by no means rare. In fact, their numbers are incredible.

Henry W. Fowler in *The King Crab Fisheries in Delaware Bay* (Washington, D.C., 1907) reported that around the year 1850 a resident of Town Bank, New Jersey, could have collected 100,000 horseshoe crabs within a single week on his beach of a hundred rods. "On a half mile of the strand 750,000 were taken in 1855 and 1,200,000 were taken on about a mile in 1856." A special mill was erected at Goshen for grinding dried horseshoe crabs into a fertilizer which had the trade name "Cancerine" and sold for from $25 to $30 a ton. While the number of horseshoe crabs decreased later it is still large even nowadays. The July 1928 issue of the *National Geographic Magazine* contains a statement that half a million were stacked up to dry near Bowers, Delaware, in 1927.

Limulus, whose picture appears on page 381, is certainly a very numerous living fossil.

It is also of a most distinctive appearance. No other creature has such a domed carapace and such a tail spike. If you lift one by the tail spike and look at the milling legs your first impression is "crab," which accounts for the popular name. (The scientific name is somewhat unfriendly; it means "cross-eyed.") But though the legs look like those of a crab they are really quite different. True crabs have two pairs of antennae or feelers; Limulus has only one pair and that pair also bears claws too, so that it might with equal justification be called a pair of legs.

The legs of Limulus perform a rather large variety of functions. They serve as legs for crawling around on firm sand. They serve as digging tools when it is burrowing in mud hunting for food, which consists of marine worms. They serve as paddles when it swims, which it does in an upside-down position. And finally they serve as jaws. The mouth of the animal is located on the underside between four pairs of strong legs, the upper parts of which are flattened and full of short sharp spines. Working together they form an efficient shredding machine; the mouth has only to swallow what passes through the grinder, which in turn receives pieces of unprocessed food from the so-called feelers.

Limulus does not leave its natural habitat under normal conditions, save for those specimens that may be carried up by the tides. But at mating time—early June, though sometimes May or July— the females come ashore, carrying the smaller males on their backs. At about the high-tide mark the female begins to burrow, usually making the hole deep enough so that even the back of the male on her back sinks below the surface. Then the eggs are laid and fecundated. The number of eggs is large too; the eggs of one female will fill a half-pint jar. Since the greenish-blue, semi-transparent eggs are just about 1/12 inch in diameter the number required to fill such space is around ten thousand.

All this, however, contributes little toward answering the main questions. Just what *is* the horseshoe crab? Where did it come from? It is a living fossil now, and it was a living fossil even back in Jurassic times when little *Limulus walchi* crawled up on a shore where it might have been eyed by an Archaeopteryx.

There is a clue of sorts in the ontogenesis. The eggs laid in our time need about a month to hatch. And Limulus just before hatching shows little resemblance to the adult form. Instead it resembles something else, which has been extinct (we think) for at least 300 million years. That "something else" is the trilobites, of which one can say just two things with certainty. When they still existed they were as numerous as shrimps are now. And like the shrimps they were arthropods, "jointed-footed" animals.

Even the second statement was not an easy one to make. When they were first discovered they were taken to be strangely shaped sea shells and were called *Concha triloba,* three-lobed shell. Even a rather casual look, however, showed that they were segmented, which shells are not.

The question of how the trilobites should be classified happened to come up at the time when the same question had been raised about platypus, and some of the same people were involved. Since some trilobites had fossilized in a curled-up position the Englishman Shaw thought that they might be fossil caterpillars. The Frenchman Latreille declared that he would continue to consider them clams until someone found legs on them and if that came to pass he would consider them centipedes. Well, legs were found, first by cutting open some 3500 curled-up specimens (270 of them clearly showed legs) and later by simply discovering some well-preserved stretched-out specimens. That settled it: trilobites were arthropods, but nobody could go much further.

In the case of Limulus there were, at least, lots of specimens that could be dissected. What was found was the usual mixture of characteristics displayed by living fossils. The final verdict was that Limulus is a primitive arachnid [4] which at a very early time adapted itself to life in the water.

At the time when the trilobites—which must somehow be connected with Limulus—were still numerous the earliest fishes came into

Limulus larva and trilobites: (*center*) Limulus just before hatching; (*left*) *Armonia pelops;* (*right*) *Elrathia kingii*. The latter two are from the Middle and Upper Cambrian, Western Hemisphere. The drawings are not to the same scale; the actual sizes are quite different from one another.

existence. Geologically speaking it was during the latter part of the Silurian period and the earlier part of the Devonian—about 350 million years ago. These early fishes were small, only a few inches long. They had no fins; all swimming was done with the tail. They were quite heavily armored, with scales over the tail section and plates encasing the front part of the body. And they had no jaws. Paleontologists believe that they inhabited rivers.

Some of them managed to become something else, possibly because they left the rivers and swam out into the high seas. They developed jaws and paired fins and lost their armor, relying on speed both for hunting and for protection. None of the early forms is still alive but the type represented by this ancient innovation is well known. They were early sharks, or early selachians, as a zoologist would prefer to call them, since this term also comprises the closely related rays. But the sharks of our time are living fossils only in the sense that their

[4] The arachnids are the spiders and scorpions.

tribe originated early. The forms actually living are of rather recent origin.

Once the fishes had invented jaws and speed they started flourishing. Two main lines, or the ancestors of two main lines, came into existence. One is the line which led to the endless multitudes of the true, or bony, fishes of later geological periods, including the present. The other line was even more successful; it led through an intermediate group to the first amphibians which could go on land. The lungfishes were (and are) an offshoot of the intermediate group; they paralleled the chain which led to the amphibians, but they did not form a link in this chain.

The name of this intermediate group from which both the lungfishes and the "pre-amphibians" sprang is crossopterygians. The customary English substitute for this technical term is "lobe fins"; the Germans translate the Greek word *krossoi* which is imbedded in the name more carefully and call these fishes *Quastenflosser* or "tassel fins." As this term indicates, the ancient crossopterygians had fins like small paddles with a fringe of soft rays. One especially vigorously flourishing tribe of the crossopterygians was the coelacanths (the word means "hollow spine") with large heads, strong, almost limblike fins, and a curious double tail.

They appeared late in the Devonian period and lived through the Carboniferous and Permian periods and through all three periods of the Mesozoic Era—Triassic, Jurassic, and Cretaceous. Some years ago, during excavations for a new building for the Princeton University Library, shale that had formed during the Triassic period was uncovered. It was the remains of an ancient swamp in which coelacanths had flourished 180 million years ago. Many coelacanths had lived there—the shale contained an average of a dozen coelacanth fossils per square foot. Later on, during the Jurassic period, the coelacanth became rarer and near the end of the Cretaceous period they had petered out. The last of the crossopterygians was *Macropoma mantelli*. The first fossil of a crossopterygian ever found happened to be *Macropoma*, and Sir Arthur Smith Woodward reconstructed it with loving care.

He was aware that the crossopterygians had joined the ichthyosaurs which had swum in the same waters and had become extinct at about the same time.

What follows now is a fish story that bears a rather remarkable

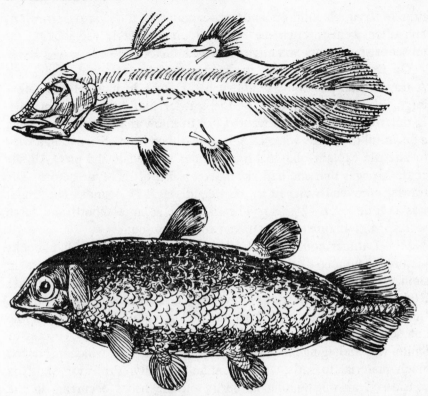

Macropoma mantelli, skeleton (*top*) and restoration

resemblance to the story of the Australian Neoceratodus. On the east coast of Africa, not too far from its southern tip, there is a city called East London. A river called the Chalumna empties into the ocean there, and the shore where the river ends does not drop abruptly into abyssal depths but forms a gradual incline. Then there is a submarine shelf about 10 miles wide, on which the depth of the water is about 40 fathoms at the landward side and 60 fathoms at the outer edge. And then there is a sudden drop to a depth of over 200 fathoms.

East London has a natural history museum of which the curator is Miss M. Courtenay-Latimer. It also has a firm of ship owners, called Irvin & Johnson, operating fishing trawlers in the ocean off shore. Trawler nets, of course, bring to the surface whatever gets in their way, and rarities are sometimes caught inadvertently in that manner. Knowing this, Miss Latimer kept on friendly terms with the firm of Irvin & Johnson and the captains of the various trawlers, and often went through the heaps of unmarketable fish looking for museum specimens. Sometimes she was lucky.

On December 22, 1938, the manager of the company called her. A trawler had just come in and it had caught an unusual and rather large fish. Captain Goosen of the trawler had suggested that Miss Latimer be called and he wanted her to know that the fish had been a beautiful deep blue when caught. It had then been alive and had tried to bite the captain's hand. Miss Latimer hurried to the pier. All she could say was that she had never seen a fish of this type before. The trawler crew had weighed it; the weight was 127 pounds. The length was a little over 4½ feet. The fish had a large mouth and large scales. Miss Latimer had it taken to the museum.

Miss Latimer could not identify the fish; none of her handbooks pictured anything like it. So she did what she had done before in similar cases: she wrote a letter to Professor J(ames) L(eonard) B(rierley) Smith at Rhodes University, Grahamstown, South Africa. But this was just before Christmas and though Christmas is in the hot season in South Africa it is still a major holiday. Professor Smith was indulging in a short vacation at a bay which produced much material to satisfy his scientific curiosity. Professor Smith is considered an outstanding authority on the fishes occurring in the ocean near South Africa. But at that time he was teaching chemistry at the university, and fishes were only an avocation.

The letter did not reach him until weeks later. In the meantime Miss Latimer, convinced that she had something very rare in her custody, had to make a difficult decision. The weather was hot and the fish was getting impossible. Finally she decided to have it mounted—better sacrifice the inner organs than lose the whole specimen.

Farther to the south Professor Smith, who, according to his own account,[5] is a nervous, high-strung, peculiar insomniac whose health is generally poor, and who places an enormous amount of trust in his own forebodings and hunches, finally received Miss Latimer's letter.

It contained a request for help in classification, sketch and description attached. Smith just stared at the sketch at first. Then, he

[5] *Old Fourlegs; The Story of the Coelacanth*, by J. L. B. Smith (London: Longmans, Green & Co., 1956).

says, his "peculiar photographic memory" reproduced for him a page from a work on fossil fishes. The sketch must mean that the fish was a coelacanth. But that was impossible for several reasons. To begin with, every paleontologist knew that the coelacanths had become extinct with the end of the Cretaceous period. And the extinct coelacanths were all quite small; the more common fossils measure 5 inches in length. A few were up to 20 inches long. This fish was stated to meaure 4½ feet.

It probably was a species new to science. But not possibly a coelacanth. Yet the sketch showed a coelacanth. Now it was, of course, not absolutely impossible that a coelacanth had survived; other animals, including fishes, had survived from former geological periods. Still, it could not be a coelacanth because it was too large.[6] The thoughts went round and round in his head; the only thing to do was to go to East London and look at the specimen. He tried to telephone first, but this happened on a weekend and in South Africa telephones are operated by the postal service and the postal service closes up over the weekend.

He finally got to East London. The fish by then had been mounted; the soft inner parts had been thrown into the garbage pail; and, as Professor Smith established to his chagrin, the garbage had been dumped into the sea. Still, he saw that it was a coelacanth. Another spectacular and important living fossil had been discovered. Another scientist wrote later that the emergence of a living Brontosaurus from one of the African lakes might have been more impressive to the public but not as significant to the scientists, if only for the reason that coelacanth is in our own ancestry.

Professor Smith was profoundly impressed, as he had every reason to be. The first thing to be done was to give it a scientific name. Afterward he had to study it as best he could. He reported the find in the journal *The Cape Naturalist* and gave the precise classification, namely: Class: *Pisces;* Subclass: *Crossopterygii;* Order: *Actinistia;* Family: *Coelacanthidae;* Genus: *Latimeria;* Species: *chalumnae.* Then he added that "the genus and the species are new to science."

[6] After the Second World War fossil remains of a 5-foot coelacanth were found in West Germany. Professor Smith himself pointed out later that the better-known fossil forms had been swamp forms where there is not much water. Every fish fancier knows that certain fishes do not grow large if they are kept in a small tank.

This was one of those major understatements that are occasionally
made by people who don't wish to sound enthusiastic. *Latimeria
chalumnae,* as the name was now established, was the biggest discovery in the whole natural-history field since the finding of Neoceratodus.

And it did become a great sensation, with an almost life-sized picture
in the *Illustrated London News,* a full-page article by Professor Smith
in the *Times* of London, and long articles everywhere in the world.

Latimeria, the first specimen

After the first sensation was over, Professor Smith had several jobs
on his hands. The first was a thorough scientific description of the
fish, or rather of what Miss Latimer had been able to save. This was
a large job in itself, by no means ameliorated by the fact that he
insisted on carrying on with his full-time schedule of teaching chemistry at the university. Needless to say, he was also swamped by
correspondence. After that came an even bigger job.

Latimeria had been mutilated; none of the inner organs had been
preserved. The next step was to find a complete specimen. And that
brought up the question of where the fish normally lived. In England
it had been suspected and said that Latimeria probably now lived in
the deep sea, having sought refuge there from the competition of more
modern and more efficient fishes just as the eryonid crabs had done.
One magazine even changed the story of the catch, saying "a trawler,
fishing deeper than usual . . ." even though the first dispatch had
clearly stated that the fish had been caught at 40 fathoms. Professor
Smith bristled over this idea—he is still bristling—and declared that

his Latimeria had enormous blue eyes which it would not need in the deep sea. Moreover, the large and heavy scales overlapped to such an extent that the fish's body was protected by an armor three scales thick; this was much more suggestive of life among sharp rocks.

On the other hand, the fish obviously did not normally live on that submarine shelf 3 miles off shore and 20 miles southwest of East London where the first specimen had been caught. If that were its normal habitat it would have become known many decades earlier. So specimen number one was obviously a stray. But a stray from where? The next thing to finding another specimen would be reports of people who had seen the fish. At least that would point to its normal habitat.

Professor Smith had leaflets printed in the three languages spoken on the African side of the Mozambique Channel. The heading was

**PREMIO £100 REWARD
RÉCOMPENSE**

In the center was a photograph of the mounted specimen. Above the picture the text read *Examine este peixe com cuidado,* the remainder of the Portuguese version promising for the first two specimens a reward of 10,000 dollars local currency. At the bottom the text cajoled in French: *Veuillez remarquer avec attention ce poisson. Il pourra vous apporter bonne chance,* followed by the same promise, with the currency expressed in South African pounds. The English text, in the center, read:

> Look carefully at this fish. It may bring you good fortune. Note the peculiar double tail, and the fins. The only one ever saved for science was 5 ft (160 cm.) long. Others have been seen. If you have the good fortune to catch or find one DO NOT CUT OR CLEAN IT IN ANY WAY but get it whole at once to a cold storage plant or to some responsible official who can care for it, and ask him to notify Professor J. L. B. Smith of Rhodes University, Grahamstown, Union of S.A., immediately by telegraph. For the first 2 specimens £100 (10.000 Esc.) each will be paid, guaranteed by Rhodes University and by the South African Council for Scientific and Industrial Research. If you get more than 2, save them all, as every one is valuable for scientific purposes and you will be well paid.

These leaflets were distributed by the thousands all along the southern half of the East African coast.

As for the statement, "Others have been seen," the facts are that Professor Smith received a good supply of rumors, but as time went on he seems to have grown more skeptical about them. Later he apparently accepted only two reports as true and reliable. In 1948 he met an African in the Bazaruto area of Mozambique who, on seeing the picture, at once declared that he had once caught a fish exactly like it. He caught it in the deep channel south of Bazaruto Island. He had never caught or even seen another one like it. The second report was by a Mr. G. F. Cartwright, who wrote that when he had been skin diving at Malindi in October and November 1952, he had seen a large fish which "looked wholly evil and a thousand years old. It had a large eye and the most outstanding feature was the armour-plate effect of its heavy scales. . . ."

In reality, then, the existence of the coelacanth, at the time the leaflets were distributed, rested entirely on the one specimen caught by Captain Goosen's trawler. Professor Smith leaned toward the belief that the fish lived in the Mozambique Channel between Africa and Madagascar, a belief essentially based on the fact that this area was all but unexplored as far as fishes were concerned.

Then came the Second World War and the hunt for the living fossil had to cease. For thirteen years nothing happened. Then just before Christmas in 1952 Smith received a wire reading:

HAVE SPECIMEN COELACANTH FIVE FEET TREATED FORMALIN STOP HUNT DZAOUDZI COMORES.

To the uninformed reader the most misleading word in this message is "hunt," which was not the noun, but the name of Eric Hunt, a trader who sailed the area between the Comores Islands and the African mainland. To Professor Smith the most puzzling word was "Dzaoudzi," which turned out to be the name of a harbor on Pamanzi, the smallest of the Comores Islands. Then the problem was how to get to the Comores fast. The difficulties were magnified by the fact that this too happened on a weekend in the Christmas holidays.

Professor Smith began trying to telephone high government officials. That he made long-distance calls at all seems to have caused general surprise. That anyone should try to do so on a weekend was unheard of. After everything else had failed, he tried in desperation to reach the Prime Minister, who was not at his official residence and was obviously surrounded by people who would do anything to safeguard his holiday.

Nevertheless Professor Smith somehow succeeded in getting through to the Prime Minister, the late Dr. Daniel P. Malan. By a stroke of incredible luck Mrs. Malan had packed a copy of Smith's book on the fishes of South Africa with other books which the Prime Minister might like to read over the holidays, so Malan knew the name of the caller. He did supply a governmental airplane, an aged DC-3, and Smith was off for the Comores, flown there by a crew which could

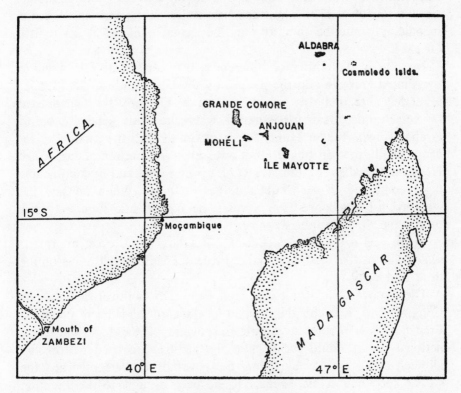

The Comores islands

not imagine why any fish could be important enough to warrant such a mission, during the holidays too.

The story of the capture of the second coelacanth was comparatively simple. Specimen no. 2 had been caught by Ahmed Hussein in late December 1952 some 200 yards off shore on the east coast of the island of Anjuan in 65 feet of water. The fish had struggled so that Ahmed Hussein had to bash its head in. This did not surprise him; he, like all the other natives of the Comores Islands, knew the fish. They had a name for it, which was *Kombessa.* To be sure they preferred other fish to *Kombessa,* but *Kombessa,* though it always cooked to jelly, was edible. Fortunately, before he either ate or sold the fish, the lucky fisherman met another native, a teacher. The teacher had seen the coelacanth leaflet. He also knew that Trader Hunt, who had been handing out the leaflets, was at anchor on the north shore of the island. The teacher and the fisherman decided to carry the fish to the north shore, over about a dozen miles of mountainous territory. If this was the fish which was worth three years' income it would be fine. If not, they could still sell it as a fish. Or eat it.

In spite of a number of differences between the fish brought in by Ahmed Hussein and the picture on the coelacanth leaflet, Trader Hunt felt sure that this was a coelacanth. He took the fish aboard his vessel and set sail for Pamanzi, where he could send a cable to Grahamstown. Trader Hunt, Professor Smith, and the second coelacanth finally met on board Hunt's vessel in the harbor of Dzaoudzi. High emotional strain and lack of sleep on a long and uncomfortable flight combined to set Smith's nerves on edge. When he saw the wrapped fish on board Hunt's vessel he had to ask somebody else to remove the wrappings.

There was a big blue coelacanth with large blue eyes, enormous scales, and catlike teeth in its jaws. Professor Smith knelt down on the deck and wept.

The discovery was somewhat complicated by political factors. The Comores are French; the second coelacanth had been taken in French waters. Professor Smith was aware of the fact that some national rivalry could easily enter the picture. He tried to forestall all such complications by telling the governor that he regarded the second specimen as his, because it had been brought to the attention of science through his efforts, but promising to give the next specimen to French scientists. The crew of the plane, being well aware of all this, amused themselves by telling Smith on the return flight that they had to stay in the clouds, because they had just intercepted a message from a flight of French fighters which were hunting them to get the fish back. Smith was still in a sufficient state of nerves to believe them for a while.

Specimen no. 2 received a different name. It was not quite the same as no. 1; it had only the second of the two dorsal fins displayed by no. 1, and the small "double" of the double tail was lacking. Smith considered it a separate genus, and he named it, in honor of the anti-evolutionist Prime Minister who had made its recovery possible, *Malania anjouanae*. At the time he thought that there might be still a third species of coelacanth around the Comores Islands, because Hunt had collected information about a "small coelacanth." He concluded later that the so-called small coelacanth was probably the "oil-fish" (*Ruvettus*) but he stuck to his guns as far as Malania was concerned. Most other experts, however, feel that Latimeria and Malania are really the same; the scope for individual variations among living coelacanths seems to be large.

On closer examination Professor Smith found to his dismay that even specimen no. 2 was not complete. Since the fisherman had bashed its head in, the brain was gone. The fish had not been expertly opened to pack it with salt for preservation, but had been hacked apart in the way the natives do it when they prepare fish for market. This had naturally led to further damage. However, most of the intestinal organs were there. The formation of the jaws could be investigated, a scientifically important item. And Professor Smith found to his pleasure that the fish had a so-called "spiral valve" in its intestines, a formation (the term "organ" is a bit too specific and too strong) which occurs only among the older types of the living sharks.

Science did not have to wait another dozen years for the third specimen. It was caught by Houmadi Hassani, also off Anjouan, in 110 fathoms of water on September 24, 1953. It was a much smaller specimen, weighing only 88 pounds, and it was brown with white spots. Mainly because of this coloration Houmadi Hassani's assertion that he had "the" fish was not believed at first, but a few hours after death it turned blue. It was flown in an old Junkers plane to Madagascar, where the French ichthyologist Professor James Millot had arrived in the meantime and was waiting for coelacanths to turn up. Millot was the first to state that coelacanths showed so much individual variation that Malania should be considered only as an unusual Latimeria.

Specimen no. 4 was taken near Grande Comore, the main island of the group, on January 29, 1954. On the morning of January 30 specimen no. 5 was brought in, and specimen no. 6 a few hours later. But then there was a wait of ten months for no. 7. Professor Millot and his fellow scientists were overjoyed with the harvest, but they mourned one fact. All the specimens caught—with the possible exception of the very first one, of which too little was left to tell with certainty—had been males.

This could be sheer coincidence, of course. Or it might mean something, though nobody would venture an opinion as to what. In any event half a dozen specimens in reasonable to good condition were enough to learn all about the anatomy of this very remote ancestor. What the scientists wanted next was (1) a female and (2) a live coelacanth, male or female, which could be observed in action. And their desire for coelacanth eggs assumed outrageous proportions. "Ontogenesis" was the battle cry once again.

All this sounds a good deal like the story of Neoceratodus, and the money rewards also followed the same pattern. The French had matched Professor Smith's 100 pounds for a specimen. Now they doubled it, provided the specimen was alive.

The eighth coelacanth fulfilled all hopes. It was brought in by two fishermen, Zema ben Said Mohammed and Madi Bacari, on November 12, 1954. The fish struck a bait at a depth of 140 fathoms, and hauling it in took over half an hour. It was alive *and* it was a female. There was dancing all night in the village. The specimen was put in a swamped boat resting on the bottom in shallow water. A fish net had been stretched over the boat so that the catch would not escape. The color of the live fish turned out to be a very dark gray-blue. And everybody could see that something the natives had told but which nobody had really believed was true: the eyes of the fish glowed strongly with a greenish-yellow light. According to Professor Millot:

Throughout the night the Coelacanth was watched over with admirable care by the *chef de circonscription,* taking turns with his adjutant, Monsieur Solère. It seemed, although quite bewildered at the sequel to its ascent to the surface, to be taking the situation very well, swimming slowly by curious rotating movements of its pectoral fins, while the second dorsal and anal, likewise very mobile, served together with the tail as a rudder.

After daybreak it became apparent that the light, and above all the sun itself, was upsetting the animal very much, so that several tent canvases were put over the boat to serve as some kind of protection. But despite this precaution and the more or less constant renewal of the water, the fish began to show more and more obvious signs of distress, seeking to conceal itself in the darkest corners of the whaler.

At 14.45 hr. it was still swimming feebly; but at 15.30 hr. it had its belly in the air and only the fins and gill covers were making agonized movements.

It was then covered with a sheet and taken immediately to the hospital. There was not a scratch on it, apart from a tiny incision in the centre of the anterior part of the floor of the mouth made by the fisherman when recovering his hook. Altogether it was in remarkably good condition, without any rupture of the viscera or suffusions of blood.

It measured 1.42 m. [about 58 in.] in length and weighed 41 kg. [90 lbs.]. (*Nature,* February 1955.)

Eggs were found in the fish. There was a cluster of eggs of different sizes; three of them seemed to be about fully formed. Professor Smith believes that the eggs, when ready for laying, will probably be encased in some manner, about the way sharks' eggs are. So far nobody seems to have found an egg case of the coelacanth.

The anatomy of Latimeria is now written, though still unpublished, by Professor Millot. But one day there will have to be a sequel to his work. One that deals with the ontogenesis.

There is still a postscript to the story.

In 1949, in or near Tampa, Florida, there was a small shop selling Florida souvenirs to tourists. It was run by a woman who made many of the souvenirs herself, and her raw material quite often consisted of fish scales which she obtained from local fishermen. One day one of these men sold her a gallon can full of fish scales. They were the same size as the scales of a large tarpon—which is to say, about the size of a silver dollar—but they were not tarpon scales. The souvenir maker grew curious and mailed one of these scales to the National Museum in Washington, D.C., where it was routed to Dr. Isaac Ginsburg of the Department of Fishes. Dr. Ginsburg knew several things instantly: one, he had never seen such a scale before; two, no fish with such scales was known to live in the Gulf of Mexico or in American waters generally; three, there had never been even a rumor of a large unknown fish in these waters; and, fourth and finally, the fish which had grown this scale was an ancient type, possibly a crossopterygian.

Dr. Ginsburg wrote to Tampa without delay, requesting particulars. He never received a reply. The other scales were presumably used up for souvenirs and may be gathering dust in some attic, or attics, anywhere in the United States and Canada.

Only one thing is known therefore, namely, that a primitive fish, possibly a coelacanth, must live off the Florida coast, most likely in the Gulf. One day the story of Latimeria may have still another chapter, this time one involving American waters.

CHAPTER 22

African Rhapsody

In the African Southwest, some twenty miles inland from the coast, there is a strip of "badlands" which is locally known as the "Namib." Politically most of it belongs to the Portuguese colony of Angola; geographically it reaches from about Mossamedes in the north to Walfish Bay in the south. In that Namib there lives a relic of bygone days which is one of the proofs for the assertion that the continent of Africa is the most stable land mass on our planet.

This relic is not an animal but a plant. A German traveler, Friedrich Welwitsch, exploring for the king of Portugal, discovered it in 1860 and called it *Tumboa Bainesii*. But later it was decided to change the name and to honor its discoverer by calling it *Welwitschia mirabilis*.

The second part of that name is well justified by the facts. Welwitschia is a tree which when fully grown is about 18 inches tall. But it is not a natural counterpart of those Japanese dwarf trees of perverted horticulture: Welwitschia is merely short—not small. That tree trunk which does not even rise 2 feet above the ground has a diameter of about 4 feet, and a circumference of 13 to 14 feet. As soon as the seedling stage is over, the tree sprouts two leaves; they grow directly from the trunk without any branches or twigs and they are all the leaves that the plant will ever grow during its whole century-long life span. These two leaves will reach a length of 12 feet or more and they are so tough and leathery that even hungry animals leave them alone after some tentative nibbling.

Theoretically the leaves are 4 feet wide when the plant is fully grown, but nobody has ever seen an undamaged Welwitschia leaf. In fact, an undamaged Welwitschia leaf is merely an abstraction—like the square root of minus one, it has no existence in reality. Since the leaf has only parallel veins without cross connections it frays at the tip and is easily ripped lengthwise by a strong wind. The wind is not even necessary, because the leaf is split at the base by uneven growth of the trunk so that a large number of ribbons will form, of about equal length but of arbitrary width.

This strange plant is anchored in the ground by a massive taproot about 5 feet long; the whole looks like a colossal wooden carrot. But it is a fable that the taproot reaches down to the ground water; to do that in the Namib it would have to be 30 or 40 feet long. As regards its water requirements, the plant subsists on the seasonal rains and on the fogs drifting in from the sea; because those fogs do not condense until they are about a score of miles inland, the plant does not occur closer to the coast. The fogs also carry a considerable amount of salt, and Welwitschia depends on it, since, as far as one can tell, it would not be able to grow in unsalted soil. Its inland boundary presumably coincides with the range of the salty fogs.

Among plants Welwitschia occupies about the same place as Hatteria does among the reptiles; in fact it goes back to the same geological period. The ancestors of Hatteria, and other ancient reptiles with mammal-like teeth and mammal-like heads, lived among the direct ancestors of that lone survivor of the Namib desert.

As was stated in Chapter 4 Africa is one of the oldest stable land masses on earth. In that respect it is directly comparable to Australia. But unlike Australia, Africa was never isolated for any length of time. Several times in the course of geological history, it was connected

Welwitschita mirabilis

with land to the north—when there was land to the north—and, at the northeast, with the Asian land mass.

From this fact one should assume the flora and fauna of Africa to be generally quite recent. But because Africa is large and has been stable one should also expect older life forms to have survived here and there. And this is precisely what one finds in Africa. There are the quantities of rather recent mammals, the elephants and the zebras and several kinds of antelopes. But there are also survivors from the past, of which the most extreme example happens to be the plant Welwitschia.

Not all survivors from the past are conspicuous-looking like Welwitschia. Some of them, in fact, look so customary that scientists did not even realize for a long time that there was anything special about them.

The prime example in Africa—possibly the prime example all around—is the coney, or hyrax, which exists in various corners of the African continent, with one species going somewhat outside of Africa and living in Palestine. In appearance the hyrax looks like a foot-long, fat, and pleasantly fuzzy rodent. The external tail is virtually non-existent, all four feet are small and slender, and on its large face it wears an expression of mild disgust and shocked surprise.

The species living in Syria and in Palestine is mentioned in the Bible under the name of *Saphan,* but nobody in Europe knew what the word meant or had ever seen the animal itself. Since the context pointed to something small and furry Martin Luther finally translated *Saphan* as "rabbit." And one early scientific traveler, the surgeon Peter Simon Pallas (1741–1811) actually thought them to be rodents and hence reasonably close relatives of the rabbit. That was a mistake, caused by the fact that the hyrax's dentition looks superficially like that of a rodent (the teeth, taken singly, do not), but the correct classification took a long time. Zoologists are not too sure of it even now, because it still depends to some extent on the point of view.

Cuvier, going by the structure of the cheek teeth, called it *une sorte de rhinocéros en miniature,* and others agreed to the extent that they accepted hyrax as belonging to the ungulates, or hoofed mammals. The reason was that the structure of its feet is like that in the odd-toed ungulates and its stomach resembles that of a horse. In itself it was not too strange that there should be a small form of odd-toed hoofed mammals, but the story of hyrax—which occurs all the way from Palestine to the Boer country in the south and which also has developed a tree-climbing form in Liberia—took an unexpected turn when paleontologists began to dig in the Faiyum of Egypt.

The fossil beds of the Faiyum belong to the Middle and Late Eocene and that is rather annoying, since it is like coming into the theater near the end of the second act. We would much rather have a few large fossil beds in that area from the preceding subperiod, the Paleocene. Things must have been moving then, and moving rapidly, judging by what that later stage presents. There is, to begin with, a tapir-sized mammal that has been called *Moeritherium* after famous Lake Moeris. It foreshadows in many features the coming mastodons and elephants, without being a direct ancestor itself. It is decidedly a sideline. So is a hyrax the size of a small bear. What is really startling is that among all those early hoofed mammals there are also the first sea cows—it is no exaggeration to say that a sea cow is actually more closely related to hyrax than is the rabbit with which it was thrown into one pot later. So are the elephants. Hyrax, in short, is a leftover from the primitive group of original "sub-ungulates" which produced the divergent strains just mentioned.

But hyrax has made me jump ahead a little bit too far; I should have been more systematic. Living mammals fall into three fundamentally different groups. The first and lowest one is that of the egg-laying monotremes, the next one that of the marsupials. All animals above the level of the marsupials are called placentals, for the simple reason that the females develop a placenta when pregnant.

Now which of the placentals occupy the lowest rung on their particular ladder? They would obviously be mammals with a placenta but without a pouch [1] but otherwise not greatly specialized in any one direction. That would be the mammal, or the group of mammals, from which the higher placentals evolved: our whole zoological garden of today, including keepers.

Geologically such primitive "super marsupials" are established in the very early parts of the Tertiary period and, paleontological luck willing, might be dug from late Cretaceous layers.

Zoologically they are still with us, all around and sometimes literally underfoot; only New Zealand and Australia are without them. They are the insectivores or insect-eaters, a term which, like most of such terms, applies to the majority of the members of the group, but not

---

[1] This phrasing is necessary because there are a few marsupials, like the banded anteater of Australia (*Myrmecobius*) which lack a pouch. But no marsupial produces a true placenta.

to all of them. They are actually omnivorous, with a very pronounced preference for live food. That the latter consists mostly of insects, their larvae, and worms, is caused essentially by the small size of the animals themselves. And they all have fabulous appetites.

These insectivores have managed a strange thing. Besides having given rise to all the higher placentals they have managed to survive in forms which look as if most of them were little-changed originals. And in addition they have succeeded in producing a number of specializations which compete with the same specializations of the higher placentals (or would compete if they lived in the same geographical localities) without losing their identity as insectivores. One might almost say that they tried to populate the world twice, once with adaptations of their own tribes, and once by producing the higher groups.

The term "insectivores" may not mean much to many laymen, but everybody knows some of their representatives. The moles that ruin the lawn are insectivores. In this country and in Europe they are as black as the darkness of their subterranean tunnels, but the South African Boer country has its fabulous golden moles—strangely enough, those completely unrelated marsupial moles of Australia have golden pelts too.

The shrews that flit like mice across clearings and ruin the temper and digestion of a cat which catches and eats one by mistake are insectivores too. And so are the hedgehogs of Europe, Asia, and Madagascar.

While these ancient insectivores can still be found on the major continents, Africa has succeeded in producing, or preserving, a few rather spectacular forms. Its moles, as has been mentioned, have golden fur and its shrews are the largest there are. Logically, in a manner of speaking, they are therefore called elephant shrews, but the long nose may have contributed to that name. The elephant shrew (*Macroscelides*—the name means something like "long leg") is also unusual among insectivores by *not* being nocturnal.

The largest and in many respects most unusual insectivore of Africa is *Potamogale velox,* which is also the largest insectivore anywhere, with a body length of over 12 inches and a very strong, muscular, flattened tail 14 to 16 inches long. If the term "insectivore" is used in its literal rather than in its zoological meaning Potamogale is not an insectivore. This, in fact, is the reason for its name: Potamogale means "river weasel." The word is somewhat misleading, the names "otter

African jumping shrew
(one of the *Macrosceli-
dae*)

shrew" (proposed by Richard Lydekker) and "giant water shrew"
(proposed by Ivan T. Sanderson) are more logical and correct. Potamogale's diet consists of fresh-water fish, and for a long time it was believed to consist only of fresh-water fish. But Cuthbert Christy, a British naturalist, reported in his book *Big Game and Pygmies,* that he
came across remains of fresh-water shrimp on a flat stone on which
he had just seen a Potamogale. Since it probably has the same vora-
cious appetite as the better-known insectivores of Europe and America, it will probably accept anything aquatic and alive if no fish are
available.

Potamogale itself is not known in fossil form, so we cannot say just
how old it is. But we know an extinct relative from the very late Cretaceous period, called *Palaeoryctes,* one of the earliest insectivores
known to science. Its cheek teeth are exact duplicates of Potamogale's
cheek teeth (or the other way round) except that those of Potamogale
are four times as large. And the front teeth differ; those of Potamogale
have developed into sharp little spears which will hold a wriggling
fish.

Now about Potamogale we know at least that it is an insectivore.
And we know of hyrax that it is an old and primitive ungulate. But
when it came to *Orycteropus* it looked as if we were condemned to give
up any attempt of establishing relationships. The Greek name which I
have just used means simply and plainly "the digger." The popular
name, due to an accident of Dutch spelling, happens to be the first

word in every index. It is aardvark. Aardvark (plural: aardvarken) means "earth pig" or rather "earth shoat," and has been given to it by the Boers for the culinary reason that its haunches, when smoked, will yield a substitute for ham.

But one should not speak of "the aardvark" as if there were only one kind. There are three different "aardvarken" living in three differ-ent sections of Africa, the smallest of the three being *Orycteropus aethiopicus,* which lives, as indicated by the generic name, in north-eastern Africa. The Cape aardvark, *Orycteropus afer* or *Orycteropus capensis,* is considerably larger, 5 to 6 feet long, and was the first to become known. The most recent addition is *Orycteropus erikssonii,* or Eriksson's aardvark, which is the largest of the three and lives in the dense forest of the Wele, Mubangi, and Ituri regions of Central Africa.

Considering the location and nature of the last one's habitat, it is not surprising that it was discovered as recently as 1950. The other two just crept up on science, the year of discovery not being known.

This is strange in the case of the Ethiopian species. Except for Egypt and the Mediterranean shore of the African continent, no other part of Africa has been known for as long a time as has Ethiopia. But even around the middle of the last century the Ethiopians themselves were mostly doubtful about the aardvark. An Austrian traveler, Theo-dor von Heuglin, was told by natives that in their country there was a flesh-eating beast, with the head of a crocodile, the ears of a donkey and the tail of a monkey.

Since von Heuglin guessed at once that it might be Orycteropus (he was not acquainted with the now common Dutch name), he had

Aardvark,
Orycteropus
capensis

evidently known of the animal before. His guess was based essentially on the donkey ears, and he correctly credited the crocodile's head to a desire to conform with the alleged flesh-eating habits.

The actual year of discovery of the Cape aardvark is not known either, but there is an early report about it which seems to be completely unknown to most zoologists. It can be found in a folio volume published in Germany in 1719. Its title reads, translated, *Description of the Cape of Good Hope,* and its author was a pastor, Peter Kolb. After his return to his native country he acquired the title of *Magister* and also became *Rector* of a school in a small town.

Magister Peter Kolb must have had voluminous notes and the book he wrote must have been rather tedious even for the literary tastes of his contemporaries. An anonymous Frenchman published a set of three volumes of excerpts, translated into French—and badly, if one is to trust the verdict of the original publisher Peter Conrad Monath, who then proceeded to bring out a still heavy volume of excerpts in German, published in 1745.

Because Magister Kolb's report has never been republished or even quoted since its original appearance, it pays to do so now. The book is chiefly concerned with the natives of the area that is now the Union of South Africa. The zoological aspect creeps in via their domesticated animals, which leads to a chapter on "the ferocious and cruel animals" of the area. Finally Part III, Chapter 5 is devoted to such animals as are neither domesticated nor "cruel." It has several subdivisions, one of which is called "On the Pigs" and it says that there are four kinds of pigs in the area. Two of them have been introduced by Man, one from Java and one from Europe. The third kind is the "Spiny Pig" (the porcupine) and then:

The fourth kind is called the Earth Pig. It somewhat resembles the red pigs one meets in some places in Europe. But it has a longer skull and sharper snout, but no teeth [Kolb means tusks] and few bristles. The tail is long, the legs are long and strong. It lives in the ground where it makes a burrow with great speed. As soon as it has its head and fore limbs in the hole, it can hold on so fast that even the strongest man cannot pull it out. Should it be hungry, it will look for an ant-hill. [Kolb means termite hill.] When it has found one, it looks around whether there is any danger . . . then it lies down and extends its tongue as far as it can. The ants crawl upon the tongue. When there are enough, the animal pulls the tongue in and swallows them. This it continues to do until it is fully sated . . . Its flesh has a delicious taste, almost like that of our wild hogs, and is very healthy. The Europeans and the Hottentots often hunt these animals. They are easy to kill by means of hitting them over the head with a stick.

Strangely enough Magister Kolb's simple account was not believed. When the French naturalist Count Buffon assembled the material for his great natural history work, he knew of Kolb's story, presumably via the French translation of excerpts, but decided that the animal was mythical.

This decision could hardly have been prompted by Kolb's account, which is simple and straightforward enough. Buffon must have heard other stories which, though they were probably true, had made him skeptical. However, because of another description by Peter Simon Pallas, published in 1766, Buffon changed his mind and later editions of his work carry an article on *l'oryctérope*.

That an animal of such a size will dig at all is difficult to believe; that it can outdig two strong men with shovels sounds incredible but happens to be true. Digging is the aardvark's favorite method of escape, but it can, if necessary, develop a considerable speed on the ground. One older observer stated that he saw one escape from a lion who gave up the pursuit after a few leaps. Under such extreme circumstances the aardvark is reported to become bipedal for a short while and run on its hind legs only. It would be nice if somebody could take a film of such a performance; judging from the proportions of the body it does not sound at all unlikely. When walking slowly the aardvark sets its feet down in such a way that the spoor of the forefoot is overtrodden by the hindfoot. The result is a "synthetic" spoor which looks as if it had been caused by a gigantic lizard and which is a source of mystery and fright to many people who see it for the first time.

Because of its powerful claws and almost incredible strength the aardvark does not have many enemies—not counting the natives— and among its enemies there is only one which is serious, the python, which can follow into the burrows and eat the young.

Let's now proceed to the crucial question: which animal that is not an aardvark, living or extinct, should be regarded as the nearest relative? Obviously even aardvarken had to have connecting links to some other groups, relatives, in short. But what were they? Fossils did not help much. The best-known fossil type, excavated from the soil of the island of Samos, from the mainland of Greece, and even from Persian soil, is called *Orycteropus gaudryi*. When, in 1888, it was described for the first time, the description stated that "except for its much smaller size, it differs little from the living Cape variety." Later work has shown that there are numerous minor differences, but it is still true that the Samos aardvark, if it were found alive, would simply be a fourth aardvark.

In 1918 W. D. Matthew made the original statement that the aardvarks may be very primitive ungulates. This idea is now generally accepted, and received much support some twenty years after it was first uttered because the San Juan Basin of New Mexico yielded the remains of a large mammal which was called *Ectoconus*. It was a very early mammal, belonging to the ancestral group of the hoofed mammals of our time. Although it had a lighter tail, and although its legs and feet were not adapted to digging, it bore a strong resemblance in general appearance and in bodily proportions to the living aardvarks. In size it ranked with the Ituri Forest giants.

Professor Matthew did not claim that his *Ectoconus* was the ancestor of the African digger. "This general resemblance does not involve any near relationship, but indicates merely that the modern *Orycteropus* has retained with little alteration much of the proportions and structure that were common among primitive placentals of similar size."

And thus the animal doubted by Buffon and later shunted from place to place in zoology books turned out to be a somewhat modified image of a group of very early mammals, completely extinct otherwise. Their hoofed offspring has roamed all over Earth since then, excepting only Antarctica and the Australian region. But the leftover of the original type had to go underground to persist.

For some time zoologists had thought that there might be some kind of relationship between the aardvark and another very ancient African mammal, the pangolin or scaly anteater. Laymen who see a pangolin in a museum are usually at a loss whether they should regard it as a pine cone from some especially gigantic tropical pine tree or as an exceptionally large lizard with unusually large scales.

Actually it is a mammal. There are seven representatives of that tight-knit little zoological family around, right now. Three of them live in Asia as their names (Indian, Chinese, and Malayan pangolin) indicate; the four others, called long-tailed pangolin, white-bellied pangolin, black-bellied pangolin, and giant pangolin, live in Africa south of the Sahara. All four occur in the Ituri Forest, which seems to be as much of a "Lost World" as one can possibly expect. Of these four, the long-tailed and the white-bellied pangolins prefer trees to the ground; the other two are burrowers. All live on termites and other insects. Some fossil remains (highly incomplete) have been found in the Miocene of Europe.

They are not related to the armadillos, as was first assumed because of their scaly covering. They are not related to the giant anteater of South America with which they share some purely functional similarities. They are not related to the aardvark.

They are pangolins—direct offspring of very early placental stock which "fossilized" or "froze" so early in its evolution that it just remained what it was.

To the paleontologist all these survivors from the early age of mammals form a fauna which he calls "Old Africa." Which is by no means the same as the African fauna so well known to the reader of books on Africa and to the visitor to the zoological garden. The animals he has in mind, the African fauna of today, constitute a fauna of late immigrants which arrived at a time when there was a more pronounced land connection between Eastern Europe (the Balkans of today), Asia Minor, and East Africa. The Europe of that time presented a curious mixture of African animals in American forests. The forests of Old Europe consisted of swamp cypresses and palmettos, palm trees, oak trees, and pine trees growing side by side. They sheltered quantities of giraffes, elephants of all descriptions, all kinds of zebra-like horses, lions and other large cats, gnus and antelopes, and hordes of monkeys. The rhinoceros was present and hyenas abounded.

The Ice Age finished this paradise. It eradicated the tropical forests, which could not move south and continue to thrive in a European Georgia or Florida because the Alps were in the way. The fate of the animals was much the same; some adapted themselves, as is proved by the woolly mammoths, the woolly rhinoceroses, and others, but most of them simply died out. Only the Old European animals living south of the Alps, mainly in what is now Greece, did not have to adapt themselves: they could leave for the south. And it is for this reason that the African fauna of today looks so much like the fauna of Greece during the Pliocene subdivision of the Tertiary period, just prior to the Ice Age.

Not very far from famed Marathon there is a small settlement known as Pikermi. In 1835 the British archaeologist George Finlay went to Pikermi to look for promising sites for archaeological excavation. He found none, but discovered a few fossil bones. When he showed them to an ornithologist named Lindermayer, that man of science became enthusiastic and persuaded Finlay to dig for more. Together the two men excavated a small collection of fossils which they took to Athens as a present for the local Natural History Society. At first no one much cared, but three years later a Bavarian soldier literally stumbled upon a deposit of fossil bones in the bed of a small river called Megalorhevna near by. The hollows of these bones were filled with glittering spar crystals, which the soldier believed to be diamonds. Thinking himself rich, he returned to Munich and brought his find to Professor Andreas Wagner to get an evaluation. Wagner saw among the bones something that was then a great novelty, the jaw of a fossil monkey. He published a description of this surprising discovery of a fossil European monkey, and soon afterward intensive and prolonged scientific digging started along the river Megalorhevna.

The river, it was found, had once been much larger, and had dug a fairly deep canyon in the soft soil through which it flowed four million years ago. Large numbers of animals had fallen to death in that canyon, probably in flight from fires. Thus in one big sweep a significant period of the prehistoric animal life of southeastern Europe became known, and it proved so important that scientists began talking about the "Pikermi fauna." Present-day African fauna is to a large extent fauna of the Pikermi type, with additions and omissions, of course. A number of modern African animals did not exist in the Pliocene Pikermi landscape, and among the Pikermi fossils there are many types now extinct.

A typical example of extinct Pikermi fauna was *Helladotherium* ("the Hellas mammal"). It looked fairly much like a giraffe, but with shorter legs and a neck only slightly longer than a horse's. A relative of this animal, also fossil, was discovered later on Samos and was consequently named *Samotherium*. Both were regarded as completely extinct until shortly after the year 1900. Then the okapi was discovered in Africa. Paleontologists suddenly saw before their very eyes a living —or freshly killed—animal which was a close copy of their beloved Greek fossils. Small wonder that they began to talk enthusiastically of the "living Helladotherium." They could also have said—in fact they did—"living Samotherium," but neither term is quite correct. There are a number of small but distinct differences between Helladotherium, Samotherium, and the okapi. The best way to express the relationship is probably to say that the okapi stands midway between the two animals from Greece and the modern giraffe.

The okapi's first appearance in print dates back to about 1890, when Sir Henry Stanley's book *In Darkest Africa* appeared. Reporting on the language of the Wambutti, one of the pygmy tribes of the Congo region, Stanley remarked that a Wambutti he talked to knew a word for "donkey." The word was *atti,* and Stanley's informant stated that the men of his tribe occasionally caught one in pits. Sir Harry Johnston, who is generally regarded as the "discoverer" of the okapi, wondered about this statement. He knew that zebras avoided dense forests.

Okapi (drawing by Gustav Wolf)

If the Wambutti had spoken the truth—and there was no reason why he should have lied—either there existed a variety of zebra which did not shun forests or there was another animal resembling a donkey in that territory. He decided to investigate at the earliest opportunity, which came in 1900.

In a letter dated "Fort Portal, Toru, Uganda, 21st August 1900," and addressed to the Zoological Society of London, he told how the discovery was made:

When I entertained for months the Pygmy band which had been captured by a filibustering German (and the restoration of whom to their homes was one of my motives for going into the Congo Free State), I questioned them on the subject and they were very explicit; they told me that they called the animal *Okhapi*. They described it as being dun-colored or dark gray all over the upper parts of the body, with stripes on the belly and legs. As soon as I reached the Belgian post of Mbeni I began questioning my host, who at once acknowledged the existence of this animal and promised to send me where I could shoot one. . . . The Bambuba natives dwelling alongside the dwarfs called it *Okapi*. The Belgians state that the head is very long *"et très effilée."* One man said that the muzzle was particularly *effilé*—i.e., drawn out. At first they excited me by declaring that there was a skin lying about which I could have; eventually it was found that the skin had been cut up by their native soldiers to be made into waist-belts and bandoliers. Two of these fragments were found and given to me, and I shall send them home to you by first opportunity. Whatever the animal may be to which these pieces belong, it is not any one of the known Zebras or wild Asses; the pieces of skin unfortunately exhibit chiefly the stripes of the belly and legs. . . . We did not succeed in seeing a specimen of this animal in the Forest during our short stay, but one of the Congo Free State officials has promised to send me a complete skin and skull.

The two strips of okapi hide were exhibited at the December 1900 meeting of the Zoological Society and accepted as proof that an unknown variety of zebra actually did exist in the Congo forest. Tentatively (as denoted by the question mark) the animal was named *Equus (?) johnstoni*. In June 1901 a complete skin and two skulls arrived in London. That settled the question of what the new animal was, and Professor E. Ray Lankaster of the Natural History Department of the British Museum proposed the name of *Okapia johnstoni*, which is still in use.

Sir Harry Johnston himself pointed out that Stanley's mention of the *atti* was what had aroused his curiosity, and after talking personally to Stanley, he even concluded that Stanley and his men had once caught sight of okapis west of the Semiliki River, years before he himself had seen the two strips of skin.

After the okapi's true position among living animals had been established, and after several complete skins and skeletons had reached England and Belgium and had been mounted in museums, the directors of zoological parks all over the world began to wonder whether the okapi might not be kept alive. True, it would be difficult to duplicate the conditions of its native forest, known among geographers and zoologists as the Rainy Forest, but other African animals had adapted themselves to a different climate and a new diet and had thrived on it.

Several expeditions were sent into the Belgian Congo, instructed, among other things, to keep an eye out for okapis. A German expedition under Adolf Friedrich, Duke of Mecklenburg, contented itself with shooting a few specimens for a museum group. But the American expedition under Herbert Lang was definitely on the lookout for live okapis for the Bronx Park Zoo. Lang, of course, made other collections for the American Museum of Natural History, ably assisted in this by young Dr. James P. Chapin, whom the natives referred to as "Mtoto na Langi" (Lang's son).

Lang soon found out why it had taken so long for the okapi to be discovered. In an article he wrote later for the *Bulletin* of the New York Zoological Society, he stated:

The okapi, in true hermit fashion, had secured the only retreat that white man would respect, a country that he was forced to acknowledge as the most unhealthy in the world. It inhabits a narrow strip some seven hundred miles long and hardly one hundred and forty miles wide, about seven hundred miles from either coast. . . . Whoever penetrated here was, so to speak, "on the wing," and wings beat doubly fast across these inhospitable regions. The numerous sportsmen who had visited nearly all parts of Africa found no attraction in these forests. Indeed, the many pale, haggard faces that emerged from the western half of equatorial Africa were no incentive for pleasure-seeking people. The immensity of the wilderness is appalling; for over eighteen hundred miles without a break it stretches more than half way across the continent, from the coast of Guinea to the Ruwenzori. In spite of tropical luxuriance, it is one of the most dismal spots on the face of the globe, for the torrid sun burns above miles of leafy expanse, and the unflagging heat of about one hundred degrees day and night renders the moist atmosphere unbearable. Over the whole area storms of tropical violence thunder and rage almost daily. Here natives have become cannibals, and the graves of thousands of white men are merely a remembrance of where youthful energy and adventures came to a sudden end.

Lang's hope of being the first man to send a living okapi to the New World was thwarted by a number of unforeseen and unfortunate circumstances. The first okapi to be captured seems to have been a young animal that lived for a short time at a Belgian government post near the Ituri River. But it did not live long. The second was also a young one, captured in 1909 by Lang's men. To his pleasure he found it tame and friendly and eager for condensed milk. But there was only enough milk to last four days, and before a fresh supply could be brought to the outpost, the little okapi died.

Since then okapis have been successfully brought to various zoological gardens both in the United States and in Europe.

And when the okapi was well established as an existing if rare animal, it turned out that we had had a picture of one all along! There is an okapi on the famous friezes of Persepolis. The Persian bas-reliefs show delegations from many nations bringing presents to the Persian ruler Xerxes the Great, who died in 465 B.C. The section in question shows three unarmed men with Negroid features and hair, led by a Persian usher. The leader of the three-man delegation does not carry anything, the second of the three holds a lidded vessel, while the third carries an elephant tusk and leads an okapi.

The okapi of Persepolis seems to differ somewhat in various respects from the okapi we now know. It is possible that a second species of okapi existed 2500 years ago, but it is just as likely that the differences that can be observed (the head, hindquarters, tail, and genitals do not quite match in shape those features of the present animal) are due to mistakes of the sculptor, who might have seen the animal when it was brought but who then worked from memory, possibly many years later.

To return to the discovery of the okapi, we know that the immediate reaction of zoologists, and specifically of animal dealers, was to think back over all the stories they had heard and wonder what else might still be discovered in Africa.

There were rumors and unverified reports of all kinds; the difficulty was to decide which ones seemed substantial enough to warrant an expedition. Interest began to center on a specific part of Africa, the Republic of Liberia, and an animal known only under the native name of *nigbve*. It was said to be fairly large, black in color, and dangerous. From these characteristics a tentative history of the *nigbve* could be pieced together. The earliest source that seemed to fit was a description of the animals of the "Pepper Coast" written by a Dutch physician named Dapper. The description spoke about three kinds of wild hogs. Two of them were comparatively abundant and well-known; the third, described as much larger than the others, black, and very dangerous because of its sharp teeth, presented a puzzle. Then someone guessed that this third "wild hog" might be the same animal described in 1844 by an American physician, Dr. Samuel G. Morton.

Dr. Morton had acquired a single skull, which, he had been told, belonged to an animal that looked like a large pig. Morton saw at once that it was by no means a pig, but an animal related to the hippopotamus. The relationship did not seem to be very close, so Morton invented a special generic name: *Choeropsis*. The common name unfortunately became "pygmy hippo," which makes it seem as if the *nigbve* of the Negroes was merely a dwarf form—"only" six feet long—of the common hippopotamus. Actually the two are not "brothers" but only distant cousins, as Dr. Morton had deduced from the skull.

In the eighties complete specimens of the animal—killed by native hunters—were seen by the Dutchman Büttikofer and the German Schweizer. Büttikofer did not see the animal alive, and for that reason the skins were mounted very faultily in several museums. For some unknown reason one curator later pasted a label bearing a skull beside the name of the animal. To the visitor this meant that the animal was extinct.

It was evident to experts, however, that the "pygmy hippo" was actually Dapper's "third hog." It was larger than the other two, it was black, and it had a set of very real teeth that seemed to justify even the most exaggerated description of its powers.

Toward the end of 1910 Carl Hagenbeck felt sufficiently certain that the misnamed pygmy hippos were still alive somewhere in the interior of Liberia to assign the best man of his staff of animal collectors, Hans Schomburgk, to find one and to bring it back alive. This was by no means an easy assignment, and Schomburgk at first experienced the fate of all men who try to do something no one else has done before: he was laughed at. All the possible variations were rung on the famous phrase "There ain't no such animal." The Negro officials told him that the animal was extinct, if indeed it had ever lived in the land. The white employees of shipping agencies patronizingly suggested that he go elephant hunting instead; it was safer, and more likely to bring results. A friendly fat Dutchman advised that he stay with him for a few months and then return with the report (which would be true) that the animal did not exist. All in vain; Hans Schomburgk continued with his expedition. It was in the middle of the rainy season, but Schomburgk had disliked the thought of waiting in Hamburg for the rains to cease; besides, since nothing was known of the habits of this "extinct" animal, it was a toss-up which would be the best season to hunt it.

Schomburgk's first discovery during this trip concerned the real hippopotamus. It existed in Liberia, despite all assertions to the contrary in the books. He remembered that a French nobleman had asserted the existence of hippos in Liberian waters as early as 1724, but this had been forgotten along with many other things.

Finally Schomburgk arrived in a district where *nigbve* was not regarded as a superstition. The natives knew it well and delivered a warning speech about it. "Him be big past pig, but him be pig and love water, but him be saucy too much, we all fear him for true. Him teeth be like knife, he fit to bite man in two one time." Schomburgk told them that he wanted some and they nodded: some still remembered Massa Coffelin (Büttikofer—names change curiously in the spoken tradition of another language); he had wanted *nigbve* too. "Yes," explained Schomburgk, "but Massa Coffelin got them dead, I want them alive."

This innocent remark resulted in a parade of the entire tribe, from the oldest man to newborn babes, to Schomburgk's tent. They all looked at him in a most scrutinizing manner. Schomburgk stood it patiently for a while; then he asked the reason for this remarkable procession. He was politely informed that the brave hunters believed him crazy; there was no other explanation for his desire to catch a dangerous *nigbve* alive. And since no one in the village had ever seen a crazy white man, they had all come to have a look.

Schomburgk finally acquired all the help he wanted. And on June 13, 1911, he—the first white man to do so—saw a pygmy hippo alive in its natural surroundings. He was about twenty feet from it, but saw no possibility of catching it. He could easily have shot it but did not dare to. This animal had been regarded as extinct for more than a quarter of a century; it must be very rare; it might even be a Last Mohican. To shoot might do irreparable zoological damage. He had to let it pass.

That was the end of the *nigbve* hunt for that year. The rainy season set in anew; the rivers became dangerous; it was too late. Schomburgk returned to Monrovia, the capital of Liberia, and told about actually seeing a live dwarf hippo. No one believed him; one does not see a mythical, or even an extinct, animal roaming around alive. Fortunately, Schomburgk had had plenty of opportunity to develop armor against such nonbelief. Calm, empty-handed, but with definite knowledge, he returned to Hamburg and to Hagenbeck. On Christmas Eve, 1912, he sailed for Liberia on his second expedition to track down Choeropsis. This time he was successful.

On February 28, 1913, he shot his first pygmy hippo. It was skinned to be mounted in a German museum (it is now at Frankfort on the Main), but first Schomburgk took careful measurements. The animal measured 172 centimeters (about 5 feet 8½ inches) from the tip of its snout to the tip of its tail, but around the body, just in front of the hind legs, it was 173 centimeters!

Schomburgk found that Choeropsis was much less adapted to life in the water than its big cousin. He also found that it had a remarkable set of teeth which made the frightened stories of the natives sound fairly credible. But when he caught his first live Choeropsis the following day, he discovered that it was more intelligent and more tractable than the large variety known since antiquity.

The pygmy hippo is now also quite frequent in zoological gardens, but another discovery, made during the interval between the discovery of the okapi and that of the pygmy hippo, is not.

This one too was called a "black hog," but it really is a hog. Rumors about it had been around for several years and for some time there was doubt whether the dangerous black "hog" from inner Liberia and the much-feared black hog in the Ituri Forest were not one and the same animal. The question was partly settled when in 1904 Captain Meinertzhagen of The King's East African Rifles secured a perfect skull of one specimen and a not so perfect skin of another one. The specimens were examined in the British Museum and were given the scientific name of *Hylochoerus meinertzhageni*. It is the largest wild pig of Africa, now known to exist in four varieties all through the equatorial belt of the African continent. The color is jet black, as the Negroes had stated, and it has an enormous head, exceptionally large even for a wild hog. The tusks are massive and quite long. The black hog from the Ituri Forest is a link between two families of wild pigs, the wart hogs on the one side and the bush pigs on the other.

Strange to relate, while Herbert Lang's expedition was looking for one living fossil, the okapi, it acquired a material clue for the discovery of another one. To make the case sound even more unreal, complete specimens of the other one were actually in a museum, but they were not recognized for what they were. What they needed was, both figuratively and literally speaking, a new and correct label. The man who was finally to write it was "Lang's son," Dr. James P. Chapin— "Chapin of the Congo," as he is called behind the scenes in the American Museum of Natural History, or "Chapin of the Museum," as he is called elsewhere. The two, the man and the specimen, had only to come together, which finally happened after a series of odd coincidences. The specimen waiting to be "discovered" was a large bird—and the scenes of action were New York, Belgium, and the eastern part of the Rainy Forest between Stanleyville and Lake Edward.

During the first okapi expedition Chapin had often been annoyed with the natives because of their beastly habit of pulling the largest and most beautiful feathers from dead birds for use in their headdresses. On the other hand, the headdresses were collectors' items too, and a few of them were secured. When Dr. Chapin returned to America with his collection in 1915, he brought with him a small bundle of loose bird feathers to be classified at leisure at home. Classification in some cases proved difficult, but Chapin was able finally to place all of them except one large feather. This remaining nuisance might have belonged to a bird of the cuckoo family, but it was much too large. Its quill rather suggested a guinea fowl or some related bird, but its color pattern did not correspond to any known guinea fowl. For a short while Chapin thought of an undiscovered bird, but that idea seemed too preposterous. Finally he laid the feather aside.

In July 1936 Dr. Chapin left for Belgium. His destination was the Congo Museum in Tervueren near Brussels. His purpose was the study of the birds preserved there; the results of his study were to be published in the second volume of his great work on the birds of the Belgian Congo. After a friendly conference with Dr. Henri Schouteden, the director of the museum, Dr. Chapin began his work. While nosing about in a little-used corridor he saw two mounted birds on top of a cabinet. The birds looked like pheasants. As Dr. Chapin later wrote in an article in *Natural History Magazine:*

Had I seen these specimens in any other museum, I might have paid little attention. But the Congo Museum contains practically no birds except those from Africa, and never had I seen any like these. They were somewhat larger than domestic fowls; one appeared blackish, the other more rufous. Yet the black-barred wing feathers of the rufous bird awoke a memory. We lifted them down, and found still attached to one of the stands an old cardboard label, reading *"Pavo cristatus, jeune, importé."*

Now the Latin word *pavo* means peacock, and *jeune* is French for young, but Chapin realized at once that the label was wrong. The birds were smaller than peacocks (probably the reason for the *jeune*), but the blackish specimen had large spurs which proved that it was full grown, or at least almost so. Then, of course, peacocks live in

Asia, not in Africa. In fact neither peacocks nor true pheasants had
ever been found in Africa. As Dr. Chapin expressed it:

The pheasant family is well represented in Africa by quails, partridges,
and francolins, but thus far nothing had ever been collected there that
could truly be called a pheasant, with metallic luster on its plumage. The
bird so often called "peacock" in West Africa, or *faisan bleu* in the Congo,
is merely a giant member of the turaco family, related to the cuckoos.

Of course these two specimens might have come from Asia by some
devious means. But they were also not known as Asiatic birds. Moreover, they showed feathers like the mysterious feather Dr. Chapin had
picked up in Africa twenty-two years earlier!

The question of where the two museum specimens had been acquired could be answered at once by Dr. Schouteden. Before the First
World War the Kasai Company, a private concern, had had a trade
monopoly in most of the Southern Congo Free State. It had accumulated a number of mounted birds, and in 1914 the whole company
collection had been turned over to the Congo Museum. There were
about sixty specimens in all, most of them well-known birds from
Africa. Among them were a few domestic fowls and the two "peacocks" that were already labeled the way Dr. Chapin found them.
Since this was not strictly an African collection, there was no definite
proof that these two birds were either wild or African. They could be
anything, and it was not impossible that they were hybrids of Asiatic
peacocks and domesticated fowls. Still, there was that mysterious
feather.

A very few days later Chapin had lunch with an old Congo acquaintance of his, one M. de Mathelin de Papigny, who had been an
engineer in the Kilo gold mines in 1911. While eating, the engineer
began to talk about food and told a story of a strange bird he had had
for dinner in 1930 at his gold mine near Angumu, situated in dense
forest almost under the equator, not far west of Lake Edward. A
native hunter had killed the bird, the first and only one the engineer
had ever seen in twenty years of life in the Congo. He proceeded to
describe the bird—and Chapin, I am sure, did not know just what he
himself was eating at that moment.

For this was the bird that bore those mysterious feathers, the bird
that had come to the Kasai Company as a "young peacock." There was
hardly any doubt left that Africa's Congo forest harbored an unknown
bird of the pheasant family. Its outstanding characteristic, which no

Congo peacocks, *Afropavo congensis*

other bird possessed, was a tuft of stiff white bristles on the crown of the male, just in front of the black crest.

A number of points had to be cleared up to establish the discovery. A feather from the wing of the female specimen was mailed to New York to be compared with the feather collected in 1913. It was found to be the same kind. Then a number of experts had to pass judgment on whether the specimens at the museum might be peacock hybrids. They all decided that they were not. The wing skeleton of the female was uncovered in search of a certain small bony protuberance which distinguishes the pheasants from the guinea fowls. It was there.

Then Dr. Chapin felt sure of his discovery. He named the bird *Afropavo congensis* ("African peacock from the Congo," or Congo peacock, as the name is usually translated). He embodied his findings in a report published in the November 1936 issue of the *Revue de Zoologie et de Botanique Africaines*. The article was reprinted in a magazine with wide circulation in the Congo and, abridged, in a Brussels newspaper.

Several persons wrote in saying that they had seen or shot such a bird. A police officer, M. R. Geldof, wrote that he had had his specimen mounted and given to his sister who lived in Eecloo in Belgium. The specimen was still there; it was a female. Dr. Chapin wanted to complete the story by collecting a few specimens in their natural habitat. But time seemed too short, until a chance meeting with Lincoln Ellsworth in London suggested flying.

After all kinds of preparations and after obtaining a two months' leave of absence from the Museum in New York, Dr. Chapin left Brussels by air on June 19, 1937. Meanwhile, several persons in the Belgian Congo had been instructed to hunt the Congo peacock, and even before Dr. Chapin left the Brussels airport, two specimens had been shot. When he arrived at the Stanleyville airport in the afternoon of June 23, reports of the shooting of six more were waiting for him. The birds were apparently not as rare as had been thought —although, of course, much rarer than other species—and the native hunters were well acquainted with the *itundu,* as the Bakumu call it, or the *ngowé,* as it is known among the Wabali. The latter name is an imitation of the bird's call.

On July 16, 1937, Dr. Chapin saw his first living Congo peacock, a large male that took to the air with "a tremendous beating of wings." A native hunter named Anyasi, who accompanied Dr. Chapin, fired but missed. And while they were looking after the escaping bird, another one took off to the right of them. Two days later Anyasi shot a Congo peacock, the only one killed in Dr. Chapin's presence. Chapin, well satisfied with the results, left Africa from Port Bell, Uganda, on August 27, on an Empire flying boat, taking his specimens with him.

The scientific world was somewhat awed by all this. Africa, which had long lost the adjective "dark" and had come to be regarded as completely explored and almost civilized—what with hydroelectric power plants, agricultural machinery, tourist hotels, bus routes, and airlines—suddenly turned out to be the home of a completely unknown bird—a bird that was noisy at night, that was by no means small, and that had been overlooked even though at least three specimens of it were preserved in Europe.

The passage in zoology books to the effect that "peacocks exist only in southeastern Asia" had to be deleted. There are also peacocks in Central Africa, and it is interesting to learn that the Asiatic peacock and Afropavo bear just about the same relationship to each other as do the giraffe and the okapi. Giraffe and peacock are the more recent, the more spectacular, and the more specialized forms, while the okapi and the Congo peacock (both survivors from the past hiding in the same Rainy Forest) are the older and more primitive types.

And the Congo peacock raised again the old but still open question: what else may be in hiding in the Rainy Forest . . . ?

APPENDIX

Sequence and Duration of Geological Periods

Animals and Climate in Northern Europe
during the Pleistocene Period

INDEX

Sequence and Duration of Geological Periods

The total age of the earth must be more than 3500 million years and is probably nearer 4000 million. Geological history is divided into six "eras," and further subdivided into "periods" and "subperiods." The names of the eras and of some of the other divisions are based on Greek root words, which are given in the table; for other names, the language of origin or geographical source is given. The notes under "Events" chiefly refer to facts mentioned in the text.

ERAS	PERIODS	SUBPERIODS	EVENTS
AZOIC (*azoos* = lifeless) Began 4000 million years ago; duration about 2000 million years	None	None	Gradual accumulation of the planetary mass; later formation of present atmosphere and oceans
ARCHAEOZOIC (*archaios* = first in time + *zoon* = animal) Began 1850 million years ago; duration 650 million years	Lower Pre-Cambrian (Cambria, Latin name for Wales)	Not recognizable	Origin of life; single-celled life in water
PROTEROZOIC (*proteros* = before) Began 1200 million years ago; duration 650 million years	Upper Pre-Cambrian	Not recognizable	Primitive marine life

PALEOZOIC (*palaios* = old) Began 550 million years ago; duration 355 million years	**Cambrian** Duration 70 million years	Primitive invertebrate sea life, slowly increasing in number of species through Cambrian and Ordovician periods
		For all these periods, specialists distinguish subperiods based on local formations, usually labeled with place names
	Ordovician (Latin: *Ordovices*, people of early Britain) Duration 85 million years	
	Silurian (Latin: *Silures*, people of early Wales) Duration 40 million years	**First fishes**
	Devonian (From Devonshire, England) Duration 50 million years	
	Carboniferous (Latin: *carbo* = coal + *fero* = to bear) Duration 85 million years	**More fishes. One descendant of these early types still exists near the Comores Islands**
		Period of maximum coal formation; early insects and amphibians
	Permian (From district of Perm, Russia) Duration 25 million years	**Early reptiles; early mammals;** *Eunotosaurus*

(*Continued on next page*)

ERAS	PERIODS	SUBPERIODS	EVENTS
MESOZOIC (*mesos* = middle) Popular name "Age of Reptiles" Began 195 million years ago; duration 135 million years	Triassic (*trias* = triad) Duration 35 million years	Lower Triassic, or Buntsandstein (German: *Bunt* = colorful + *Sandstein* = sandstone)	Early saurians
		Middle Triassic, or Muschelkalk (German: *Muschel* = clam + *Kalk* = limestone)	Earliest known flying fish
		Upper Triassic, or Keuper (old miners' term)	*Triassochelys;* pseudosuchians
	Jurassic (From Jura Mountains) Duration 35 million years	Lower Jurassic, Black Jurassic, or Lias (French: *liais* = smooth, hard stone)	Marine reptiles; dinosaurs
		Middle Jurassic, Brown Jurassic, or Dogger (Provincial English = round stone)	
		Upper Jurassic, White Jurassic, or Malm (Middle English = sand)	Flying reptiles; *Archaeopteryx*
	Cretaceous (Latin: *creta* = chalk) Duration 65 million years	Lower Cretaceous (Smaller subdivisions usually bear Latinized place names for special formations)	Maximum development of dinosaurs; earliest known flightless (fishing) birds; marsupials like opossum; *Archelon*
		Upper Cretaceous (Smaller subdivisions as in Lower Cretaceous)	

CENOZOIC (kainos = new) Popular name "Age of Mammals" Began 60 million years ago	Tertiary (Latin: tertius = the third; named when there were thought to have been only three geological periods or eras) Duration slightly less than 60 million years	Paleocene (palaios + kainos)	First nonmarsupial mammals, or placentals
		Eocene (eos = dawn)	Amber; rich insect fauna
		Oligocene (oligos = a little)	Steady increase of mammals during Oligocene and Miocene subperiods
		Miocene (meios = less)	
		Pliocene (pleios = more)	"Eoliths"; Colossochelys; only known fossil sea(?) otter
	Pleistocene (pleistos = most + kainos) Popular name "Ice Age"; formerly called Diluvial period. (Latin: diluvium = flood) Duration about 1 million years; ended 10,000 to 15,000 years ago		Several glaciations; mammalian fauna quite like the present; various forms of early man; probable time of formation of Galápagos Islands
	Holocene (holos = entire + kainos) Formerly called Alluvial period, from Latin alluvio, river deposits The geological present		Animals and plants of the geological present; known as "recent"

Animals and Climate in Northern

(Adapted from *Die Jagd der*

SUBDIVISION	PROBABLE DURATION (THOUSANDS OF YEARS)	CLIMATE AND LANDSCAPE
Preglacial	400	Mild climate with seasonal changes; open forest and prairie
Günz glaciation	20	Cold and dry; steppes; tundra near glaciated areas
First interglacial	50	Mild climate, probably slightly warmer than now; mostly forest
Mindel glaciation	35	Cold and dry; steppes; tundra near glaciated areas
Second interglacial	150	Mild climate, probably slightly warmer than now; mostly forest
Riss glaciation	30	Very cold and dry; extensive cold steppes; large tundra areas
Third interglacial	20	Mild climate with large forests
Würm glaciation, first part	20	Very cold and dry (maximum extent of glaciation in Switzerland); cold steppes and tundra
Interval between the two Würm glaciations	25	Fairly mild; forest locally; prairie
Würm glaciation, second part	25	Very cold and dry; extensive cold steppes and tundra
Post-glacial	10–15	Gradually warming; gradual advance of forests into steppes and tundra
Historical time (Pliny and Tacitus)		Extensive forests

Europe during the Pleistocene Period

Vorzeit by W. Soergel, 1922 edition)

CHARACTERISTIC LARGE MAMMALS
(*See following page for scientific names*)

South elephant, Etruscan rhinoceros, zebra, old wisent, old moose, old giant moose, hippopotamus, giant beaver

South elephant, Etruscan rhinoceros, zebra, old wisent, old giant moose

Forest elephant, Etruscan rhinoceros, Merck's rhinoceros, hyena, old horse, old moose, stag, deer, old cave bear, lion, wild hog, panther, old wisent; only known fossil of *Homo heidelbergensis*

Old mammoth, Etruscan rhinoceros, zebra, western horse, old wisent, old moose, musk ox, old giant moose, reindeer, stag, old cave bear, wolverine

Forest elephant, Merck's rhinoceros, old wisent, stag, giant moose, lion, bear —probably cave bear, hippopotamus in western sections; first appearance of *Homo neanderthalensis*

Mammoth, woolly rhinoceros, old wisent, western horse, musk ox, ibex, giant moose, reindeer, cave bear (?)

Forest elephant, Merck's rhinoceros, old horse, old wisent, urus, moose, giant moose, stag, deer, fallow deer, wild hog, beaver, dormouse, bear, cave bear, cave lion, panther, lynx, cat, wolf

Mammoth, woolly rhinoceros, eastern horse, western horse, wild ass, old wisent, musk ox, reindeer, giant moose, lemming, lesser hare, cave bear, northern fox

Mammoth, woolly rhinoceros, Merck's rhinoceros, wild ass, western horse, stag, reindeer, dormouse, bear, cave bear, wolf; small Aurignac race of man

Mammoth, woolly rhinoceros, old wisent, eastern horse, western horse, urus, musk ox, moose, giant moose, reindeer, lesser hare, lemming, cave bear, wolverine

Wisent, urus, eastern horse, moose, stag, deer, snow hare, lesser hare, bear, wolf, fox, northern fox, wolverine; *getting rare:* reindeer, giant moose, cave lion, mammoth *very* rare if present; Cro-Magnon man

Urus, wisent, moose, stag, deer, beaver, bear, wolf, fox, lynx; in north only: reindeer, wolverine; in east only: western horse, possibly eastern horse

Scientific Names of Animals in Preceding Table

Mammoth, *Elephas (Mammuthus) primigenius* (and *Fraasi*)

Forest elephant, *Elephas (Loxodon) antiquitatis*

South elephant, *Elephas (Archidiskodon) meridionalis*

Old mammoth, *Elephas (Mammuthus) trogontherii*

Woolly rhinoceros, *Rhinoceros (Tichorhinus) antiquitatis*

Merck's rhinoceros, *Rhinoceros (Coelodonta) merckii*

Etruscan rhinoceros, *Rhinoceros etruscus*

Bear, *Ursus arctos*

Cave bear, *Ursus spelaeus*

Old cave bear, *Ursus deningeri*

Small bear, *Ursus arvernensis*

Panther, *Felis pardus antiquus*

Lion, *Felis leo fossilis*

Cave lion, *Felis spelaeus*

Lynx, *Felis lynx*

Cat, *Felis cattus ferus*

Wolverine, *Gulo borealis*

Wolf, *Canis lupus*

Fox, *Canis vulpes*

Northern fox, *Canis lagopus*

Hyena, *Hyaena mosbachensis*

Wild hog, *Sus scrofa ferus*

Hippopotamus, *Hippopotamus major*

Wisent, *Bos bison europaeus*

Urus, *Bos primigenius*

Old wisent, *Bison priscus*

Beaver, *Castor fiber*

Giant beaver, *Trogontherium cuvieri*

Musk ox, *Ovibos moschatus*

Moose, *Alces palmatus*

Giant moose, *Cervus eurycerus*

Old moose, *Alces latifrons*

Old giant moose, *Cervus verticornis*

Stag, *Cervus elaphus*

Deer, *Cervus capreolus*

Fallow deer, *Cervus dama*

Eastern deer, *Cervus pygergus*

Reindeer, *Rangifer tarandus*

Ibex, *Capra ibex*

Eastern horse, *Equus przhewalski*

Western horse, *Equus germanicus*

Old horse, *Equus abeli*

Zebra, *Equus suessenbornensis*

Wild ass, *Equus hemionus*

Dormouse, *Miaxus glis*

Snow hare, *Lepus variabilis*

Lesser hare, *Lagomys pusillus*

Lemming, *Myodes torquatus*

INDEX